NABOKOV
IN AMERICA

NABOKOV
IN AMERICA

On the Road to Lolita

ROBERT ROPER

BLOOMSBURY

NEW YORK · LONDON · NEW DELHI · SYDNEY

Bloomsbury USA
An imprint of Bloomsbury Publishing Plc

1385 Broadway	50 Bedford Square
New York	London
NY 10018	WC1B 3DP
USA	UK

www.bloomsbury.com

First published 2015

A portion of chapter 7 of this book appeared in slightly different form in *The American Scholar*, Summer 2015. A portion of chapter 5 appeared in slightly different form in *The Hopkins Review*, volume 8, number 2, 2015.

ISBN: HB: 978-0-8027-4363-3
ePub: 978-1-63286-086-6

LIBRARY OF CONGRESS CATALOGING-IN-PUBLICATION DATA
Roper, Robert, 1946–
Nabokov in America: on the road to Lolita / Robert Roper.
pages cm
ISBN 978-0-8027-4363-3 (hardback) 978-1-63286-086-6 (ebook)
1. Nabokov, Vladimir Vladimirovich, 1899–1977.   2. Nabokov, Vladimir Vladimirovich, 1899–
1977—Homes and haunts—United States.   3. Nabokov, Vladimir Vladimirovich, 1899–1977—
Travel—West (U.S.)   4. West (U.S.)—Description and travel.   5. Authors, Russian—20th
century—Biography.   6. Authors, American—20th century—Biography.
I. Title.   II. Title: On the road to Lolita.
PG3476.N3Z8375 2015
813'.54—dc23
[B]
2014045288
2 4 6 8 10 9 7 5 3 1

Typeset by RefineCatch Limited, Bungay, Suffolk
Printed and bound in the U.S.A. by Thomson-Shore Inc., Dexter, Michigan

For Bill Pearson of Mississippi:
in whom the literature
enduringly dwells

CONTENTS

INTRODUCTION

The slender Russian man is on vacation. He has an arrogantly beautiful face and an oddly tall little boy accompanying him as he stalks
up and down a trout stream in the Wasatch Range, a few miles east
of Salt Lake City, Utah. They deploy butterfly nets. "I walk from 12 to
18 miles per day," he writes in a letter mailed around July 15, 1943,
"wearing only shorts and tennis shoes . . . *always* a cold wind blowing in
this particular cañon. Dmitri has a great time catching butterflies and
gophers and building dams."

The Allies have landed in Sicily. Himmler has ordered the liquidation
of the Polish ghettos. The writer Vladimir Nabokov, meanwhile,
concerns himself with *Lycaeides melissa annetta*, a pretty little shimmery
butterfly. He finds specimens "on both sides of the Little Cottonwood
River, between 8,500–9,000 ft. alt. . . . its habitat . . . characterized by
clumps of Douglas fir, ant-heaps . . . and an abundant growth of *Lupinus
parviflorus* Nuttall," a pale local lupine.

The novelist out chasing insects—the signature image of Nabokov in
America—came to beguile millions. "A man without pants and shirt"
was how a local teenager, John Downey, saw him that summer when he
encountered Nabokov on the Cottonwood Canyon road. He was "dang
near nude," and when Downey asked the stranger what he was up to,
Nabokov refused to explain at first.

He was forty-four. That November he would have his two front teeth
removed, the rest soon following. ("My tongue is like someone who
comes home and finds all his furniture gone.") He was balding and
narrow-chested, a heavy smoker. For twenty years before his arrival, he
had been living on an edge—he was an *artist*, after all, and deprivation

1

went with the territory. His wife, Véra Evseevna, worked odd jobs to help support them, and neither of them had ever been much for cooking or packing on the pounds.

The Nabokovs had been through the historical wringer. They were Zelig-like figures of twentieth-century catastrophe, dispossessed of their native Russia by the Bolsheviks, hair's-breadth escapees of the Nazis in Berlin and Paris, "little" people with a monstrous evil breathing down their necks. Had they been in Russia that summer of '43, they might have been among the thousands starving to death during the Siege of Leningrad, the most murderous blockade in world history; had they been in France, which they'd escaped at *the* last moment, on the last French ship for New York, Véra, who was Jewish, and their young son would likely have been destined for Drancy, the French internment camp that fed Auschwitz-Birkenau.

Instead, *melissa annetta*. Days of hiking in the sun. In Utah there was no cholera, nor was there mass starvation. Although a first impression is of a delicious absurdity—the supercilious Nabokov among the marmots and Mormons—the outdoors had always thrilled him, and America had beckoned to him all his life. He was unlike other desperate European immigrants of the war years, who tended to huddle in anxious enclaves in New York (unless they were artists with connections, in which case they headed straight for Hollywood). Saul Steinberg's 1976 map of the United States, showing the three thousand miles between the Hudson and the Pacific as a tan patch with rocks, surely resembles the mental maps of many émigrés. Out west were the uncultured, the isolationist, the anti-Semitic, the proto-fascist. The stories of American boorishness and proud ignorance, which fed enduring suspicions of American society, were the common inheritance of many educated Europeans. Nabokov knew all that, and he yielded to no man in his savoring of American foolishness. That he, the beneficiary of a superb Old World education, fluent on the most rarefied levels in three languages, the creation, culturally and intellectually, of doting, brilliant parents with advanced ideas and money, should have found himself among the cowboys and religious lunatics was surely a joke of fate.

Invited to teach for a summer at Stanford, he did not hurry cross-country by train but instead took nineteen leisurely days, chauffeured across by an American friend with a Pontiac. The journey was "wondrous," Véra wrote in a letter, and Vladimir told Edmund Wilson, another new American friend, "During our motor-car trip across several states (all of them beauties) I frantically collected butterflies."

In his forties Nabokov was still stubbornly youthful. Despite the dentures and the tubercular look, he was physically vigorous, youthful also in the sense of being deeply enamored of himself, like an eight-year-old who scribbles his name over and over on a schoolbook page. This egoistic vitality, which others often found hard to take, helps explain a strange fact in his résumé. During his twenty years in America, he traveled upward of 200,000 miles by car, much of it in the high-mountain West, on vacations organized around insect collecting. Véra and Dmitri were swept along in this outdoor enthusiasm; they were good sports about it, although Dmitri, as he got older, took care never to be seen in public waving a net. (No photos of him so equipped survive beyond age seven.)

Two hundred thousand miles by car. Divide this total by thirteen, the number of years in which the family took wide-ranging trips, adjust for Véra doing all the driving (until Dmitri was old enough to spell her), factor in Vladimir in the passenger seat checking maps or making the odd note on a four-by-six card, and you arrive at something like a coefficient of deep happiness. The Nabokovs got along, and their days were blessed with a simple purpose: they got *here* from *there*, staying at motor courts that cost a dollar or two a night, in towns so patly, Americanly themselves that a visitor had to smile. Nabokov's descriptions of these trips, in letters to Wilson and others, are glowing but reticent. He talks about getting a tan, about the specimens he's finding, and leaves it at that. Deep happiness does not conduce to writing about itself. Meanwhile, he pursued other matters: the composition of parts of several books, among them the biography *Nikolai Gogol*, the memoir *Conclusive Evidence* (later called *Speak, Memory*), the novels *Lolita*, *Pnin*, and *Pale Fire*, and his multivolume annotated translation of Pushkin's novel-in-verse *Eugene Onegin*. He was a professional, always with projects in the works, and why *not* write while on the road? Writing was another pleasure.

In these postwar years, the nation as a whole was enamored of the West, seeking reflections of itself in tales of cowpokes and pioneers. Western movies had long been popular, but now they were over the moon. The car vacation achieved a sort of consummation in the same period, and the motor court (or, to use the racy new parlance, the *motel*) was becoming ubiquitous. New roads were being built and old ones resurfaced; the Interstate Highway System, begun in '56, at its completion the largest public works project in the history of the world, was but the capstone of a phenomenal outburst of American grading and paving. The cars of the fifties were better, people had money in their pockets, the United States had just won the big war: what better time to drive to Yellowstone?

AMERICAN LITERATURE—a second-rate affair in Nabokov's eyes, although not without interest—reflected all this vagabonding. There is a countercurrent in our homegrown literature, one that runs athwart the mainstream of worthy novels of social complexity—works by Hawthorne, Howells, James, Cather, Dreiser, et al.—and in the period of Nabokov's emergence this countercurrent became reinvigorated. The tradition went back to Walt Whitman, Walt being the Mother Poet of us all, the first American writer to put on slouch hat and sturdy boots and set forth on the open road, in self-conscious impersonation of a vagabond. Henry Miller, a connoisseur not of American locales but of seedy European ones, set forth in the 1930s. The Beats also were wandering and feverishly writing just as Nabokov, fresh off the boat, with his high-modernist bona fides proudly on display, slipped quietly into the American stream.

Yet another part of our home tradition—our rough collection of amusing tall tales, with a few works of unaccountable brilliance glittering among the dross—also gathers in Nabokov. This is that part that begins with Captain John Smith and continues through William Bartram and Hector St. John de Crèvecoeur to Audubon, Emerson, Thoreau, John Muir, John Burroughs, and many modern practitioners, the tradition of itinerant semi-scientific naturalists. Possibly the most revealing resemblance to which Nabokov, who hated to be compared to *anyone*, can be recruited is to Muir, the father of American conservation, whose breakthrough reimagining of how glaciers shape landscapes predicts Nabokov's splendid scientific reordering of the Polyommatini, the tribe of Blue butterflies. Nabokov's prolific tramping of forests and meadows in what he came to call his "native West" finds an answer in Muir's thousands of miles walked hither and thither. Both loved the high-mountain zones best. Both were Darwinists who dissented from orthodoxy, sounding like mystical intelligent-designers at times. Muir was probably the last orthodox Transcendentalist, believing, as Emerson had taught him, that "every natural fact is a symbol of some spiritual fact"; Nabokov, too, was spiritualistic, in part a believer in ghostly forces that infiltrate our fallen mundane world.

But to return to that summer day on the Cottonwood Canyon road. John Downey, the boy who asked him what he was up to, already knew:

Little Cottonwood Canyon, Utah

Downey was a collector himself, and later he would become a distinguished entomologist. In an audio recording he made late in life, he said,

> I continued the one-sided conversation. "I'm a collector too!" This got a millisecond glance, and one raised eyebrow . . . but still no sound from him, nor slowing of his pace as he continued down-canyon. Finally, a nymphalid, as I recall, flitted across the road. "What's that?" he asked. I gave him the scientific name as best I could remember, not having used the terms before with obvious professionals, and fresh out of Holland's *Butterfly Book*. His pace didn't slacken, but an eyebrow stayed higher a little longer this time. Yet another butterfly crossed the road. "What's that?" says he. I gave him a name, a little less sure of myself now. . . . "Hm!" was his only response. A third test specimen crossed his vision. . . . I gave him my best idea and to my surprise he stopped, put out his arm, and said, "Hello! I'm Vladimir Nabokov." And thus we met.

What we see here is the formidable, the often remote and condescending, Nabokov *making a new friend*. Downey was not the first of his many butterfly friends; one of his first stops off the boat from France was at the American Museum of Natural History, on Central Park West at Seventy-ninth Street, where he introduced himself to the staff and immediately charmed them. Nabokov's life for the previous twenty years had been fellow-collector-starved; he had been busy eking out a living, unable to arrange many trips in the field or even to museums. Meanwhile he had read widely in the scientific literature and was eager to visit legendary American sites of collection. People like William P. Comstock, a museum research assistant, were doing work he respected, and just as important, the AMNH staff was a cohort of devotees as eager as he was to get out into the field. They spoke his native language— not Russian, taxonomic Latin—and his boyish pleasure when on the hunt or when looking at butterflies under a microscope made perfect sense to them.

Here we see Nabokov fulfilling another prophecy out of original American writ. It holds that upon these shores will be founded a new relation among men, democratic, frank, noneffete. Though not much of a reader of Whitman, he fulfilled Walt's injunction to befriend ordinary folk, to take rough comrades to one's bosom. Academic entomologists are not New York workmen circa 1855, nor are they the Civil War soldiers whom Whitman nursed, but they *are* real Americans, people imbued with a praxis. They do things in the world, they travel and get dirty. For Nabokov they became devoted friends.

I CAME TO NABOKOV YOUNG, and I have remained a reader for fifty years. The excellence of some of his books moves me—I like especially the ones written while he lived in the United States, in what the biographers call his "American period," 1940 to 1960. During a visit to an archive of historical documents some years ago I found myself seated across the table from an older gentleman who kept chuckling as he read a batch of old letters; when he left for lunch, I peeked and, wouldn't you know it, they were letters of Nabokov. *But that's what* I *want to be reading*, I realized, suddenly disenchanted with my Civil War manuscripts. *Those letters should be on* my *side of the table.*

I traveled several thousand miles in the East and West, looking for his traces, trying to nail down details of where he'd stayed, what he'd seen, who he'd befriended, which mountains he'd climbed. In Afton, Wyoming, I found his favorite motel from the summer of '52, pretty much unchanged, and on the border of Rocky Mountain National Park in Colorado, I found the rustic lodge where Véra and he had rented a cabin—the structure still stands, though now disused. I don't claim to be the first fan to have put hand to forehead and face to dusty window pane and peered inside. There he is, his figment, his ghost—still it walks these cracked floorboards, still it lies down at night on one of those broken cots.

Going where Nabokov had been and seeing what he'd seen did not, in the end, add much to my research. More profitable was to sit in a chair for a couple of years and reread his books, making forays meanwhile into the critical literature that has toadstooled up around the magnificent two-trunked Russian birch that the writer once was. About this literature I have a couple of things to say. One: it is very well written by the standards of the academy, graced with clarity and humor and intellectual honesty—this is the more miraculous considering that the first studies of Nabokov came into being just as critical theory was subduing one university English department after another. Those men and women who chose to write about Nabokov were, in the style of their subject, practitioners of elegant expression, instinctual haters of jargon, and their work, lacking many of the markers of the 1970s *au courant*, remains readable today.

Two: the scholars of Nabokov, being scholars, rejoice in discovering what is recherché, and they bring as much stamina and rigor to their efforts as they can summon. Nabokov sets an affectionate trap for such readers, being of a pedantic turn of mind himself and having left behind a body of work as if designed for picking over. Nuggets of hidden reference are everywhere, if one looks a certain way. There is an ever-narrowing quality to the hunt sometimes, and a common reader such as me feels a quiet dismay: When will the fossicking be finished? Can we not get back to saying simpler, possibly more urgent, things about the great author?

In a small way this book is an attempt to borrow Nabokov back from the scholars. The novelist himself put much effort into teaching ordinary Americans how to catch his devious sense.* Though often

---

* The first book he wrote upon arriving, the exhaustingly insightful, eccentric literary biography *Nikolai Gogol*, is, as many have noticed, at least as much about how to read Nabokov as how to read the nineteenth-century Ukrainian author of *Dead Souls* and *The Government Inspector*. His savage attacks on fellow writers—Hemingway a joke, Faulkner a pompous fraud, etc.—were a related attempt to draw attention to himself and suggest a man in an overgrown field slashing this way and that, willing even to burn it down to clear his path.

condescending, he was not the kind of literary artist to shy away from contact with the common herd, as long as the herd came to him on his own terms. In America he hoped to find a large readership, and unlike many innovative writers of the past century he was willing to think practically about how to go about getting it.

I am deeply indebted, as a reader of this book will soon discover, to the Nabokovs' excellent foundational biographers: Brian Boyd, author of *Vladimir Nabokov: The Russian Years* (1990) and *Vladimir Nabokov: The American Years* (1991), and Stacy Schiff, author of the enchanting *Véra* (1999). Because these writers did such good jobs of re-creating the Nabokovs' lives day to day I did not have to reinvent that wheel—did not, at some points, dare to.

On a number of other matters I came to differ with both of them, however. ("Predictably enough," a reader of second-generation biographies will wryly add.) The sheer flabbergasting *Americanness* of Nabokov's transformation, the way he opened himself to local influences once here—and long before, when he was only dreaming of one day escaping to the United States—impressed itself upon me again and again. In the standard account, Nabokov makes the profound change of writing in English after decades of writing and publishing in Russian, and that's enough—that's intellectual upheaval, profound transformation, enough for anyone. In America, the standard account goes on, he looked around and with his impossibly sharp eye began to render what he saw, *I Am a Camera* fashion. I agree, but there was much more. His wide-ranging and semi-surreptitious immersion in American cultural materials, his assimilating of our literary traditions and bringing them to bear on his own modernist literary enterprise, struck me powerfully. No surprise, if you think of it: he was the kind of classical writer who moves forward by thinking of similarities, ingenious connections, to earlier authors and their works. He had done that when he wrote in Russian, generating his own stories out of a fabulously fertile grasp of older Slavic writers he loved (and some he loved only to make fun of), and he would do the same when he wrote in American English.

Boyd and others are ready to admit that America represented an opening, a refreshing change, but the basic account holds that America was but one phase of an ongoing pageant of greatness. There were twenty years in Berlin and France, where he wrote marvelous books in Russian; then came twenty years in America, where he wrote books in English that were also marvelous; followed by nearly twenty in Switzerland, living in a five-star hotel, writing the incomparable late-career masterworks. To this I say: not quite. There is beauty and magic all over Nabokov's body of work, but the claim to greatness rests most solidly on the American books. This is not just a function of his midcareer fame, of the fact that *Lolita* secured for him the vast readership he had long coveted. *Lolita* may be why millions of people still remember his name (although they tend to mispronounce it*), but his immersion in American life provoked changes far more significant than did, say, his encounters with German life in Berlin or his Swiss encounters in his last decades.

He did not come to love Germany (Russians rarely do), and Switzerland was mostly a place of dignified refuge, a place to work and gather tribute. But he *did* love America—many things about vulgar, far-flung America. His embrace of it and his comfort with the changes it forced on him had something to do with all that joyous butterfly collecting, something also to do with being able to raise a healthy, promising child in America at midcentury. After the murderous nights of Europe, after Russia and Germany in their seizures of totalitarian madness, America was a place in which to breathe more easily, but—and here is the slight twist—he did not become complacent artistically. Instead he began to write with a new audacity, with, I would argue, an American-style effrontery.

NABOKOV'S AMERICAN PERIOD, that neat twenty-year interval, has become mythic. Penniless and without a secure language to write in at first, he became the most famous literary writer in English in the world, author of a sexy smash bestseller and of other works of great distinction. His early Russian novels began to be republished, in translations that he himself controlled, and soon he was declared an immortal, a giant on the order of Proust, Joyce, Kafka. Struggling writers everywhere took note. Even those without much taste for him admired the force of will, the sheer scintillating panache of him. If Nabokov could do it, then maybe they could, too.

Maybe his style, so exacting and sesquipedalian, so larded with puns and learned references, was never really to the taste of the mainstream.

* *Na-BO-kuf* is the right way, although most English speakers, especially those exposed in their impressionable youth to the 1980 hit song "Don't Stand So Close to Me," by the Police (which features the line "Just like the old man in that book by *NAB-a-kof*"), happily persist in *NAB-a-kof*, which somehow comes easier to the English-speaking tongue.

To put it another way: maybe not all of his books are the deathless classics he announces them to be in the arrogant introductions he wrote to those English republications. Maybe *Lolita* continues to work like an Oklahoma tornado—to scandalize and amuse and horrify, while putting a creepy, horny claw on an American obsession with child rape that only he seems to have noticed. But maybe some of us can make it through life without having to reread *Ada*. Maybe *Look at the Harlequins!*, *Transparent Things*, *Bend Sinister*, *Invitation to a Beheading*, *Despair*—even long sections of *The Gift*, the Russian novel of which he was most proud—are less than compelling. He was always a forceful promoter of his own brand, and maybe we have been in some sense sold a bill of goods.

No matter. The myth remains, and the books do, too, ever ready for rediscovery. The story of what he made of adversity is authentically inspiring, and parents of kids who love books should tell it at the hearth and the bedside, pointing out where a refusal to compromise high standards won through in the end (while an ability to politick, to find mentors, to take on new coloring, to borrow shamelessly and exhort tirelessly in one's own behalf came in handy, too).

The flight to America, with the nightmare of war closing upon his wake, was the great stroke of luck—but, as with everything else, it had long been prepared for. The *real* mystery is how he contrived to be taught to read English at age four, before he read Russian; how he managed to have an American-style liberal constitutionalist for a father, who imbued him with Anglophilia and set him to dreaming about Anglophone lands. Wandering the parks of his family's estate he was already imagining himself in a cowboys-and-Indians story, and from early on he was a hunter of wild game (mere butterflies, but wild game nonetheless), just like Hemingway up in Michigan or Faulkner in north-central Mississippi. Is it only in retrospect that he looks fully, if ironically, American? Or did he call a new America into being—a Lolitaesque, Nabokovian new land, layered with perplexities, rippling with edgy laughter—to ratify what he had known he would become?

1.

The American escape began way, way back for Nabokov, but that does not mean it was inevitable; and at a dangerous moment the writer who was also a husband and a father nearly threw it all away. In 1936, while they were living in Berlin, Véra insisted that Vladimir get out of the city, away from the Nazis; the couple had been trying to put together an exit since at least 1930, failing mostly for financial reasons, but now she wanted him out and in the relative safety of France. She would remain behind with their two-year-old son, tying up loose ends.

Véra, if not the family's principal breadwinner, then always essential to their survival, could no longer work. A job as translator for a Jewish-owned company making machinery had ended in spring '35 when the German authorities expropriated the company and fired all its Jewish employees. Nabokov, writing at a great clip at the time—*Glory*, *Camera Obscura*, *Despair*, *Invitation to a Beheading*, and parts of *The Gift* were just some of his 1930s productions—was looking for a job of almost any kind in France or England. Nor was he "afraid of living in the American boondocks," as he wrote to a professor acquaintance at Harvard. Not his Jewish wife but Vladimir himself was the one most under threat, the family believed: a man who meant the blackest of black evil to Nabokov, a Russian exile named Sergei Taboritsky—a fanatical Romanov partisan, Nazi stooge, and one of the two men who had attacked his father, V.D. Nabokov, fatally shooting him at a public meeting in 1922—had been appointed to the agency that monitored Russian exiles in Berlin. Nabokov was not a politician-journalist like his father, but the family name and its liberal associations were enough to put him on a fatal list—so Véra believed.

As he had done the year before, Nabokov arranged to give readings in Brussels and Antwerp. Another event would follow in Paris, in early February, on the rue Las Cases; it would be a smash success, a joyous celebration—he had passionate fans in Paris, many of them women, some of whom delighted in quoting his poetry back to him. Though there were dissenting voices, V. Sirin—his nom de plume in the emigration (he was also known by his own name)—was acknowledged as a brilliant writer and possible heir to the tradition of Pushkin and Lermontov and Tolstoy and Chekhov. Those who dissented from this view included fellow writers, some of them his contemporaries, some his envious elders—for instance, Ivan Bunin, winner of the Nobel Prize for Literature in '33, whose relations with the flash youngster were bantering but brittle, but in any case—to return to Paris early in '37 was to be treated as a kind of hero, as the coming idol.

Between mid-January, when he left his wife, and the third week of May, when he reunited with her, Nabokov wrote her once a day, sometimes twice, without fail. His letters are immensely tender. "My darling, my joy," he addresses her in February, after the Paris reading; and then in April,

> My life, my love, *it is twelve years today* [since our wedding]. And on this very day *Despair* has been published, and *The Gift* appears in *Annales Contemporaines*. . . . The lunch at the villa of Henry Church (. . . an American millionaire with a splendid boil on his nape . . . with a literature-addicted wife of German extraction) turned out remarkably well. . . . I was much "feted" and was in great form. . . . I got on swimmingly with Joyce's publisher Sylvia Beach, who might help considerably with the publication of *Despair* in case Gallimard and Albin Michel *ne marcheront pas*. . . . My darling, I love you. The story about my little one . . . is enchanting. [Dmitri had been trained to recite lines from Pushkin.] *My love, my love*, how long it's been since you've stood before me. . . . I embrace you, my joy, my tired little thing.

The mix of endearments, of droll descriptors ("boil on his nape"), of crowing over literary advances, is very Nabokov. Perhaps needless to say, he was having an affair. Véra could sense it; then some busybody sent her a letter revealing the identity of the home wrecker, one Irina Guadanini, a Russian divorcée who worked as a dog groomer. Guadanini was one of those women who could recite Sirin by the foot or the yard. Nabokov denied all—as the envied new writer, he was the subject of malicious gossip on all sides, he maintained. His daily letters to his wife did not cease, nor did they become any less tender; they were a pack of lies.

A Jewish woman with a two-year-old, near-penniless in Hitler's Berlin: surely Véra's situation was desperate, in the year when the Buchenwald concentration camp opened near Weimar, in the year of the *Entartete Kunst*, the "Degenerate Art" show that featured many Jews, yet Véra did not hasten to join her husband in the South of France, as he urged her to. Instead she concocted a journey in the wrong direction, eastward to Prague, where Nabokov's mother lived on a small pension. Madame Nabokov had never seen her grandson, and this might be her last chance.

In fulfilling this pressing duty to her mother-in-law, Véra tormented her errant husband, who was already half-mad with guilt. He was unwilling to give up the affair, though, to abandon La Guadanini, a witty woman who, to judge by a story she published twenty-five years later, was in the grip of the most transporting love of her life. Vladimir developed psoriasis—it had troubled him before at times of intolerable stress. In the end he took the train to Prague. He saw his mother for the last time; she saw her grandson for the first and last time. The crisis in the marriage did not abate for months. Only in mid-July, when they were in Cannes, temporarily beyond the reach of the Nazis, did Nabokov fully confess his infidelity, thus allowing the catastrophe to proceed toward a climax. (He continued to write to Guadanini, who showed up one day at the beach, begging him to come away with her; he painfully, reluctantly spurned her.)

He had been a lothario before his marriage—this Véra knew. There had been twenty-eight youthful seductions, and in the early years of the marriage he continued to prowl, almost certainly without telling his wife. ("Berlin is very fine right now," he wrote a friend in '34, "thanks to the spring, which is particularly juicy . . . and I, like a dog, am driven wild by all sorts of . . . scents.") Here the rampant philandering stopped, however. The Guadanini affair was too punishing, too savage. His proud and fascinating wife, she whose depths of cleverness and devotion are but suggested by the way she fought back, drawing the frazzled fool of a husband away from liberty in Western Europe, in a geographical direction that flirted with disaster: this was not a wife to abandon, though she might appear wan and worn after ten years on small allowance, after having given birth and having lost a second child (probably) the year before the crisis. Though Véra's biographer, Schiff, says that "the last dalliance was not that with Irina Guadanini in 1937 any more than the last cigarette was that of 1945," when Nabokov gave up smoking four or five packs per day, this was categorically not a marriage that would ever again be about infidelity.

FRANCE WAS NOT GERMANY, luckily. But France in the late thirties was less than hospitable to someone like Nabokov. Despite being treated like an idol and despite his literary connections, he was unable to work legally, nor did he possess a French *carte d'identité* until August '38. They avoided Paris, where people gossiped and where Guadanini resided. He gave a reading in the city in late '38, but for the most part the couple lived in semi-isolation on the Côte d'Azur, in those days a warm alternative to Paris and a place where artists and writers could live on a shoestring. Nabokov wrote and wrote. To say that he escaped the crisis of his marriage and the anguish of putting it back together by diving into work is to overlook his prodigious habit before the crisis; nor did Véra, in the worst passage of her life, fail to complete a translation of *Invitation to a Beheading*, Nabokov's dreamlike novel of oppression and imprisonment, to show an agent in New York.

In '34, a different literary agent, in London, had sold British rights to two other novels, *Camera Obscura* and *Despair*.* The English translation of *Camera* appalled Nabokov; it was "loose, shapeless, sloppy," "full of hackneyed expressions meant to tone down . . . the tricky passages," he wrote the publisher, Hutchinson, but, eager to have a book in the book-stores, he let it stand. Three years later, when American rights to *Camera* were sold by the New York agent Altagracia de Jannelli, Nabokov under-took to retranslate it himself, in the process rewriting much of it and giving it a title he thought would appeal to Americans: *Laughter in the Dark*. He was less than fully confident of his English at this point—his arrangement with Hutchinson required them to examine his work, remove any howlers.

---

* *Camera Obscura* (1933) is a brisk, noir story that plays with cinematic tropes, and *Despair* (1934) is a concoction of other cinematic and Dostoevskian elements, about a double and a lunatic "perfect crime." For a full list of Nabokov's novels and novellas, see pp. 284–285.

French, Swedish, Czech, and German translations also were in the works. Translations for sale in English-speaking countries were most important, considering the size of the market. Sirin's books had no existence inside the Soviet Union; the home of his natural readership of millions, where he might have written in his native idiom and had fewer headaches about translation, while dwelling in splendor as the crown prince of the tradition that meant everything to him, the Pushkinian tradition in Russian verse and prose—that homeland of his literary heart was tragically lost to him. It was lost to everybody else, too, of course. There was no "Russia" anymore in which he might have dwelt in safety and joy, and the boldest writers of his generation who had stayed behind were on their way to hurried procedures conducted in the basements of prisons—writers such as Isaac Babel, author of *Red Cavalry*, arrested in '39 and shot in '40, and Osip Mandelstam, arrested in '38 and dead by that December. Mandelstam's famous poem "Epigram Against Stalin," which compares Stalin's fingers to worms and his mustache to a cockroach, begins with the phrase "We live without feeling the country beneath our feet," and surely one thing the poet meant by that line was the lostness of Russia to a generation.

To be busy translating one's own novels for sale in America was not the worst fate to befall a Russian writer in the thirties. Largely ignorant of American literature, perhaps disdainful of the very concept, Nabokov had a considerable acquaintance with British and Irish literature, Shakespeare and R. L. Stevenson and Joyce being especial favorites. His mother had read him English fairy tales when he was small, and his grip on the language was precocious. As an older boy he was carried away by the books of Mayne Reid, an Irishman who fought in the Mexican-American War and later wrote American Westerns such as *The Scalp Hunters*, *The Rifle Rangers*, *The Death Shot*, and *The Headless Horseman: A Strange Tale of Texas*. Nabokov claimed that Reid, prolific potboiler maker, had given him a vision of the great open range and the vaulting western sky. Here is Reid describing a burned-over prairie in *The Headless Horseman* (1866):

Far as the eye can reach the country is of one uniform colour— black as Erebus. There is nothing green—not a blade of grass—not a reed nor weed!

It is after the summer solstice. The ripened culms of the *gramineae*, and the stalks of the prairie flowers, have alike crumbled into dust under the devastating breath of fire.

In front—on the right and left—to the utmost verge of vision extends the scene of desolation. Over it the cerulean sky is changed to a darker blue; the sun, though clear of clouds, seems to scowl rather than shine—as if reciprocating the frown of the earth.

Ignoring the antique poetic touches, we can, indeed, *see* this—and the rollicking Reid is one of those writers who tell us just what their leveled eyes tell them. On the next page,

The landscape . . . has assumed a change; though not for the better. It is still sable as ever, to the verge of the horizon. But the surface is no longer a plain: it *rolls* . . . not entirely treeless— though nothing that may be termed a tree is in sight. There have been [trees], before the fire—*algarobias, mesquites*, and other of the acacia family—standing solitary, or in copses. Their light pinnate foliage has disappeared like flax before the flame.

In the 1966 edition of *Speak, Memory*, his autobiography, Nabokov says of *The Headless Horseman*, "It has its points." The mix of realistic evidence plain to the eye with scientific-sounding precision—terms such as *culm* and *pinnate* and *algarobia*, all used correctly—gives satisfaction to a certain sort of boy reader, or to any sort of reader, for that matter. A few pages on, a figure appears out of the burned plain:

Poised . . . upon the crest of the ridge, horse and man presented a picture. . . .
    A steed, such as might have been ridden by an Arab sheik— blood-bay in colour . . . with limbs clean as culms [those culms again!] of cane, and hips of elliptical outline, continued into a magnificent tail sweeping rearward . . . on his back a rider . . . of noble form and features; habited in the picturesque costume of a Mexican *ranchero*—spencer jacket of velveteen—*calzoneros* laced along the seams—*calzoncillos* of snow-white lawn . . . around the waist a scarf of scarlet crape; and on his head a hat of black glaze, banded with gold bullion.

This is the novel's dashing hero, Maurice Gerald ("*Sir* Maurice Gerald," Nabokov adds in *Speak, Memory*, "as his thrilled bride was to discover at the end of the book"). Reid's work—seventy-five novels, plus reportage—reveals an enduring concern for matters of costumery. His heroes are rough and ready, yet in their way also *comme il faut*, and dangerously attractive to women:

> Through the curtains of the travelling carriage he was regarded with glances that spoke of a singular sentiment. For the first time in her life, Louise Poindexter looked upon . . . a man of heroic mould. Proud might he have been, could he have guessed the interest which his presence was exciting in the breast of the young Creole.

Nabokov notes that he and an older cousin, Yuri Rausch von Traubenberg, acted out whole scenes from Reid, perfecting the insouciant gestures, and while an effort to find the Nabokovian high style prefigured in this boy's own adventure prose may be going too far—is certainly going too far—there *are* points in common. Fascination with North American geography, with the wide-openness, an invitation to adventure; scientific nomenclature; exotic sensuality; the kind of writerly precision that notes that a cerulean sky looks darker directly overhead. "The edition I had," Nabokov writes, "remains in the stacks of my memory as a puffy book bound in red cloth." It was a British or an American edition; the important thing was that it was the "unabridged original," not the "translated and simplified" Russian version that Yuri and other Russian children had to read because their English wasn't up to the original. The frontispiece of a prairie "has been so long exposed to the blaze of my imagination that it is now completely bleached," Nabokov adds, then observes, "but miraculously replaced by the real thing . . . by the view from a ranch you [Véra] and I rented [in 1953] . . . a cactus-and-yucca waste whence came . . . the plaintive call of a quail—Gambel's Quail, I believe."

NABOKOV'S AMERICAN AGENT WORKED HARD for him—admirably hard. Altagracia de Jannelli's letters show her leaving no door unknocked-upon with Sirin's unconventional early novels, shaped in the smithy-soul of an author then much under the influence of Joyce and Proust. In August '36, she writes,

> Please find enclosed a couple of letters concerning your books. This, of course, always means nothing, because there is the right person somewhere and sometime that will take it:

August 4, 1936

"Houghton Mifflin Company regret to report their decision not to make a publishing offer for the accompanying manuscript."

August 12, 1936

"Thank you for sending us the novel LA COURSE DU FOU [*The Defense*], which is very interesting, but not for us. We would appreciate your calling for it at your earliest convenience."

She forwards another note that December:

We feel that the enormous effort of establishing the name of Nabokoff-Sirin in America would be so great as to militate against the commercial chances of his novel, KONIG DAME BUBE [*King, Queen, Knave*]. It is for this reason that we cannot undertake publication of a book that has many obvious qualities.

The novels, several, existed only in Russian; this complicated the approach to American publishers, who resented the cost of hiring foreign-language readers, but even without that, V. Sirin—or, as he saw no reason not to call himself now, Nabokoff, and soon Nabokov—was a tough sell, someone who wrote purposely against the market trend, it often seemed, offering demented or deluded protagonists who gave a reader scant opportunity for a warm glow of identification. Nabokov, like Joyce before him, was engaged in the high-modernist counterattack against the middlebrow novel, the work of cozy expectations, orderly progression of plot, and moral insight. All his life he would rail against readers who looked for a representation of "social problems" in his books; he was in a real lather about it, as can be seen in this note to Vladislav Khodasevich, a fellow poet:

[Writers should] occupy themselves only with their own meaningless, innocent, intoxicating business and justify only in passing all that in reality does not even need justification: the strangeness of such an existence, the discomfort, the solitude . . . and a certain quiet inner gaiety. For that reason I find unbearable any talk—intelligent or not, it's all the same to me—about "the modern era," "*inquiétude*," "religious renaissance," or any sentence at all with the word "postwar."

Jannelli, who recognized his talent and also a certain commercial promise—but who would be gone, dead at an early age, before the changes of sensibility that allowed him to write books she might have made real money with—submitted one of his novels to more than sixty publishing houses and periodicals. A partial list of outlets contacted, from the collection of rejection notes at the Library of Congress: Houghton Mifflin, Henry Holt, Liveright, Robert M. McBride, Lippincott, Longmans, Green & Co., Chas. Scribner's Sons, Knopf, Random House, Macmillan, Simon and Schuster, MGM, the *New York Times*, the John Day Co., Little, Brown, the Phoenix Press, Frederick A. Stokes Co., *Esquire*, *The Saturday Evening Post*, G. P. Putnam's Sons, Reynal and Hitchcock, Dodd, Mead & Co., Harcourt, Brace & Co., H. C. Kinsey & Co., the *Atlantic Monthly*, D. Appleton-Century Co., Blue Ribbon Books, *Liberty* magazine, Doubleday, Doran & Co., and *Life*.

The sale of *Laughter in the Dark* (1941) to Bobbs-Merrill, the schoolbook publisher, was anomalous. But *Laughter* had benefited from two translations by that point, the second Nabokov's careful own, in which he intuited as best he could American readers' desires, changing German names (Magda to Margot, Anneliese to Elisabeth, etc.) and sharpening the novel's theme of cinematic clichés that are colonizing people's brains. A wealthy businessman becomes obsessed with an usherette in a movie house; the usherette is young and beautiful and cruel. She wants to become a movie star. Cinematic tropes abound, and the businessman loses all—more than all—as he becomes the poodle of the young beauty and her cynical, diabolical boyfriend. German expressionist lighting effects—film noir *avant la lettre*—give the story a black-and-white mood, and the cruelty is played mostly for wincing laughs, always at the expense of the poor besotted businessman:

> As a child [the boyfriend] had poured oil over live mice, set fire to them and watched them dart about for a few seconds like flaming meteors. And it is best not to inquire into the things he did to cats. Then, in riper years . . . he tried in more subtle ways to satiate his curiosity, for it was not anything morbid with a medical name—oh, not at all—just cold, wide-eyed curiosity, just the marginal notes supplied by life to his art. It amused him immensely to see life made to look silly, as it slid helplessly into caricature.

When at last it appeared, *Laughter* sank; Bobbs-Merrill recorded anemic sales, and the house declined to exercise options on other Sirin works. Even so, the book is a triumph, if a minor novel: suspenseful, strange in a fresh way, briskly dismaying. The style of its humor of cruelty was possibly a little ahead of its time; it resembles the black-comedic mode announced to the world in the third section—the Jason section—of *The Sound and the Fury* ("April Sixth, 1928"), a novel that we can be fairly sure Nabokov had not read by the thirties and would possibly never read, Faulkner being one of the American writers he most relentlessly ridiculed. He had hoped to catch the eye of movie producers with *Laughter*, and though no film was made in the thirties, in '69 Tony Richardson's adaptation, starring Nicol Williamson and Anna Karina, appeared, to small acclaim.

Brian Boyd, Nabokov's biographer, presents Altagracia de Jannelli as a figure largely of fun, quoting a letter of Nabokov's in which he describes her as his "literary (or rather, anti-literary) agent—a short, fearsome, bandy-legged woman, her hair dyed an indecent red." The line on Jannelli is that she was a philistine who plied the refined artist with absurd requests for readable books "with attractive heroes and moral landscapes." Yet their exchanges touched on matters of real concern to Nabokov, in his European impoverishment. Just what *was* the tenor of literary life in the United States? What could he realistically expect over there? Jannelli lectured him on matters with a special meaning for her; in '38, before they met and after he had been calling her *Mr.* de Jannelli for years, she wrote,

> No, the "Mr." didn't bother me at all, for the good reason that all people who haven't seen me address me in this way . . . Europeans, not knowing the capacity of our American women, think that any big job must be done by a man. The women here do big things. . . . They are the pal and equal, and they often stand together in a front against men, whom they feel (perhaps like Strindberg) is the enemy.

She boosted America as a place where serious business was to be done; somewhat defensively, she presented herself as immensely well connected, scoffing at the suggestion of Nicolas Nabokov, Vladimir's younger cousin, who had been living in New York since '33, that there was something wrong in the way she had gone about a submission:

> To make you happy, I got in touch with Viking, and found out that your cousin is again wrong in dates, since they tell me that Harold Ginsburg will only be back by middle of September. . . . The editor to whom I spoke is going on his vacation, hence I do not think that I shall send a copy . . . until I can get in touch with

Ginsburg himself. Meantime . . . "Despair" will go to a firm where the heads are very good friends of mine, although, to be sure, they do not buy books for my personality but because they think they can make money on them.

Nabokov had no mentor in matters Americo-literary at this point. He was the refined artist, yes, but why *not* listen as the amusing Jannelli ran down her version of things? He must have been unnerved by the figure of sixty rejections: rejection is the plight of the writer, but Nabokov wasn't used to it. In his Berlin days, his stories and poems had found immediate publication in *Rul'* ("The Rudder"), a newspaper cum literary review cofounded by his father, and other publishers and editors had also hastened to bring out whatever he wrote. *Sixty rejections.* The fear, even for someone as sublimely confident as Nabokov, must have been that the most original things about him as an artist would damn him in America: his formal audacity, his psychological hard edge, his determination "never, never, never [to] write novels solving 'modern problems' or picturing 'the world unrest.' "

BEFORE HE BEGAN TO CALL HER *Mrs.* de Jannelli, Nabokov wrote her in a mode that he almost never employed with mere agents. "Many thanks for your nice long letter of October 12th," he begins.

I quite understand what you have to say about "old-fashioned themes." . . . I am afraid that the "ultra-modernistic" fad is in its turn a little passé in Europe! That sort of thing was much discussed in Russia just before the revolution . . . depicting the kind of "amoral" life on which you comment in such a delightful way. It may be curious, but what charms me personally about American civilisation is exactly that old-world touch, that old-fashioned something which clings to it despite the hard glitter, and hectic nightlife, and up-to-date bathrooms. . . . When I come across "daring" articles in your reviews—there was one about condoms in the last *Mercury*—I seem to hear your brilliant moderns applauding themselves for being such brave naughty boys.

America would not be avant-garde—anyway, he hoped it would not. He himself was not an avant-garde writer; he was an *innovative* writer, something different, with stylistic tricks and formal novelties up his sleeve, and he needed a stolid backdrop sometimes for his tricks to come off. We see him in this note imagining America as an air-conditioned phantasmagoria only thinly built atop an "old-fashioned something," an *Amérique profonde* of conservative or even reactionary temper. Yet America would not be just the lowbrow purlieu depicted in H. L. Mencken and George Jean Nathan's *American Mercury*, especially in the magazine's satirical "Americana" section. "Buster Brown has grown up," Nabokov says to Jannelli, a little hopefully, and though "beautifully young and naïf," it "has a magnificent intellectual future, far beyond its wildest dreams, perhaps."

2.

The Nabokov who was casually researching America—reading American journals, writing friends established over there, exchanging impressions with his agent—was half inclined to move to England instead. There he had gone to university (Cambridge) and had some connections. A nice secure lectureship at his alma mater or at a redbrick university, teaching Slavic literature or something along that line: this had its appeal for him, Nabokov being one of those artists who always found an academic setting congenial. But despite a number of trips to England and stubborn attempts to exploit his contacts, nothing turned up. The years 1937 to '40, which began with the anxious exit from Berlin and the drama of the Guadanini affair, were a time of desperate recourses and temporizing as the Nabokovs worked hard to pay the rent and meanwhile held their tattered banner out in the winds of change, hoping for a response from somewhere.

They lived in Menton, east of Cannes, for almost a year, then in the tiny upland village of Le Moulinet, where he chased butterflies beneath rocky outcrops and, at an elevation of four thousand feet, captured a Blue he had never seen before, one he named, in a paper he later published in America, *Plebejus (Lysandra) cormion* Nabokov. They were poor—as poor as they had ever been. In 1916 Vladimir had inherited, from his maternal uncle Ruka, an estate of two thousand acres plus the equivalent of $6.25 million (worth more than $140 million in 2014); for a year he had been a very wealthy young man, but then came the October Revolution, and, like most of the people he knew, he became an émigré of decidedly modest means. By the late thirties, "modest" probably overstated the case.

From Le Moulinet he moved with his family to Cap d'Antibes, and in October '38 they relocated to Paris, hoping for a change in fortune. In his needful turning this way and that—cadging sums from friends, giving English lessons, and, in one happy instance, receiving twenty-five hundred francs from Sergei Rachmaninoff, who was moved by the plight of the bootless young writer—Nabokov wrote to the Russian Literary Fund, a scholarly organization founded in 1859 and now with an outpost in America. They wired him twenty dollars.

Rachmaninoff, world-bestriding composer-pianist-conductor, was a figure to contemplate. Having lost all in the Revolution, forced to flee to Finland with his wife and daughters in an open sled, Rachmaninoff had overleapt Europe and fled to sleepy but generous-hearted America, where he reckoned a large career might be built. He acquired an excellent booking agent, Charles Ellis, and by 1919 he was touring and on his way to becoming one of the most honored and best-remunerated classical musicians of the twentieth century. Nabokov cared little for music, classical or any other kind, but he knew this story (as did everyone in the emigration) and may be said to have traced a writerly version of Rachmaninoff's trajectory, although his own progress was more halting. Like Nabokov, Rachmaninoff had always had a special feeling for America, which he first visited in 1909, and also like him Rachmaninoff was of a contemplative but adventurous temperament—a gleeful speeder in powerful cars, for instance.

Véra said years later that the move to America became their definite plan at a certain point in time: just before September 3, 1939, when France and England went to war with Germany. Her biographer questions this, arguing that "the family's hold on the planet was so tenuous that a gust could have pushed them in any direction." France was less than promising: work permits were hard to get, and soon it would be overrun with armed Germans. Nabokov's French was rich and flexible, but his English was deeper, more resourceful, and he might have felt that his sensibility belonged naturally among the ranks of English-language authors. England herself could still find no place for him, though—all doors remained closed.

His first cousin, Nicolas, visited them in Menton. Nicolas was now a professor of music at distant Wells College, in exotic Aurora, New York. He was faring remarkably well in the New World: in 1934, the ballet *Union Pacific*, which he scored to a libretto by Archibald MacLeish, had opened in Philadelphia, in a production of the Ballet Russe de Monte Carlo, and this "first American ballet" soon became an international hit, the most successful production of the Ballet Russe in the mid-thirties. Some things worked out in America! Nicolas had composed other works, too—his *La Vie de Polichinelle* also opened in '34, in a Paris Opera production—and he was remarkably well connected for a storm-tossed immigrant, a friend not just of MacLeish and Léonide Massine (choreographer of *Union Pacific*) and Sol Hurok (producer-impresario) but of George Balanchine, Igor Stravinsky, Virgil Thomson, George Gershwin, Henri Cartier-Bresson, and many glittering others.

A charming and handsome tall man, said to be conversant in twelve languages, "emotionally extravagant, physically demonstrative, and always late," Nicolas had befriended Edmund Wilson, by the late thirties the most influential literary journalist in the United States. What the cousins discussed in Menton has gone unrecorded. But the fact of Nicolas's ascent cannot have been uninteresting.*

Vladimir was not salon material, by way of contrast. It was not that he was less charming, and he had no problem accepting favors from influential individuals in his youth—from his well-known publisher father, but also from others. Vladimir was thoroughly an *artist*, however: an artist through and through. He enjoyed rubbing elbows with famous people—with Joyce's sponsor and the first publisher of *Ulysses*, for instance—and in his years in Berlin and Paris he had met everyone illustrious he cared to, including Joyce himself, who showed up at a reading Nabokov gave in February '37, and with whom he attended a dinner party in Paris in February '39. On that evening, the often scintillating, sometimes overwhelmingly mirthful Nabokov failed to shine, and the hostess wondered later if he had been in awe of the great man. When Nabokov read her account, he commented,

> I find it refreshing to be accused of bashfulness (after finding so frequently in the gazettes complaints of my "arrogance"); but is

* Soon Nicolas would leave his Russian wife, Natalia, for an American-born former student. His career as a composer of art music would advance not much farther than this, not necessarily because he had few ideas or a shallow talent: another talent would displace the first, that talent for befriending celebrated people that was already much in evidence, and which would take on an ideological cast during the war, when he became an acolyte of George F. Kennan, Charles E. Bohlen, and Isaiah Berlin, shapers of Cold War policy toward the Soviet Union. He served in uniform during the war and by '51 had become a highly important person himself, general secretary of the Congress for Cultural Freedom, the CIA-funded organization that promoted counter-Soviet cultural initiatives all over the world.

her impression correct? She pictures me as a timid young artist; actually, I was forty, with a sufficiently lucid awareness of what I had already done for Russian letters preventing me from feeling awed in the presence of any living writer.

A writer with sufficiently lucid awareness may spend time in salons, but he does not live there; back in the heatless garret is where he knows himself. The important truth of him, the truth of his gift, is established and ever present in his mind, and the way forward will be through his own agency, unless his talent fails or he loses heart.

Still—and even allowing for a certain condescension toward his younger cousin, who had always been a bit in awe of him—Vladimir could not have been unimpressed. Nicolas had pulled off a great coup, an American-style coup, landing on the rugged far shore and immediately making a big name for himself. An immigrant with nothing but a certain inheritance of cultural capital might take the Americans by storm, it turned out; the "extraordinary openness" of Americans was among Nicolas's first impressions of them, their readiness to "help each other and especially help the newcomer, the immigrant"—and even more especially the immigrant who acted as if he belonged in the game.

VÉRA SAID THAT THEY DECIDED positively on America, and at the hour of their deciding America decided on them. Stanford had invited Mark Aldanov, the popular Russian historical novelist, to teach summer school in 1940 or '41. Aldanov had no plans then to go to the United States (he considered his English subpar), and he suggested getting in touch with V. Sirin, who might be available.

Negotiations took more than a year, finances being the issue; in the end, Professor Henry Lanz, of the Slavic studies group at Stanford, gave over part of his own salary to bring Nabokov to Palo Alto. (He taught two courses—a Russian literature survey, a how-to-write-plays course—for a fee of $750, plus accommodations.)

Between Aldanov's kind tip and the glories of California in summer '41 were many complicated steps, however, not the least of them getting visa approval. Nabokov, still marooned in France, knew what he now had in hand, though: the magical open sesame, grounds for escape. Altagracia de Jannelli had been gathering affidavits on his behalf in New York, in case such an invitation ever came his way, and she pressed the publisher of *Laughter in the Dark* to sign a letter that Nabokov himself composed. He requested recommendations from other notables, too—from Mikhail Karpovich, a historian at Harvard, from Mstislav Dobuzhinsky, a renowned painter, and from Alexandra Tolstoy, daughter of the novelist and president of the Tolstoy Foundation, an aid organization in New York. Nobel laureate Ivan Bunin signed and possibly even composed a letter for Nabokov dated April '39:

> Mr. Vladimir Nabokoff (nom de plume V. Sirine) is a very well known Russian author whose novels . . . enjoy a high reputation among Russian intellectuals abroad. He is the son of the late V.D. Nabokoff, the eminent Russian Liberal Member of the first Russian Parliament and Professor of Criminology. . . . [Sirine] is not only a novelist of quite exceptional talent, but also a profound student of Russian language and literature. . . . All this, together with his mastery of English and great experience in lecturing would make him a teacher of Russian literature and thought of quite exceptional quality. . . . I recommend him warmly.

Letters about his worth as an artist went to the American consul in Paris. But other testaments of worth were required as well. To Dobuzhinsky, his former art tutor, he wrote,

> Please allow me now to direct your concern for me in another direction. The difficulty is such that for two years now I have been unable to piece together a move to America. . . . Since I have no capital, I must present an *affidavit*, to serve as guarantee for the cost of a purchase of tickets. Those friends I have in America have with touching solicitude given proof of my value—but as they are all immigrants themselves they do not command the other sort of value, and rich people I do not know. I thought that you, being already in America, might be able to approach someone with resources . . . to ask for a large favor, to give me an *affidavit*.

It may be that Dobuzhinsky—although unable to provide funds himself—spoke of Nabokov's need to others in New York. Countess Tolstoy was also active on his behalf, lobbying Serge Koussevitsky, conductor of the Boston Symphony Orchestra, who wrote a letter but did not offer to pay for steamship tickets. Should the American visas ever come through—and then there were French exit visas, often requiring bribes—transport for Nabokov and his family would cost around six hundred dollars, an impossible sum for them.*

Fall of '39, with France now in the war, the Nabokovs lived extra-precariously, largely on a loan each month of one thousand francs from the owner of a Paris cinema. Nabokov found a few language students, among them Roman Grynberg, a businessman who would follow him to America and become a close literary friend as well as a source of future loans. The writer Nina Berberova visited them in January '40 and gave the Nabokovs a chicken, which they promptly ate. The year before, Nabokov had written *The Real Life of Sebastian Knight*, his first novel composed in English. *Laughter in the Dark* had sold poorly in translation but had earned an advance about equal to the cost of steam-ship tickets, and this remembered big payday argued for composing all new work in English. But *Sebastian Knight* failed to find a publisher in the short term, in England or America.

Nabokov's father—dead over fifteen years—now proceeded to play a hand. Early in his career as a crusading journalist, in 1903, Vladimir's glamorous, kindly, unflappable, impeccable father had written an editorial protesting a pogrom in Kishinev, a market city seven hundred miles south-west of Moscow. "Nearly fifty dead, nearly one hundred fifty wounded," V. D. had written on the front page of *Pravo*, a liberal journal he helped edit. "Something monstrous and bestial has occurred. . . . In zombie-like disfigurement lay corpses piled atop each other. . . . One mother found her three sons dead. It is self-evident that these killings accompanied bandit-like attacks on property. . . . The size of the tragedies is not measurable, four thousand families ruined."

---

* The difficulty of arranging an exit from Europe, just in its bureaucratic aspect, may be suggested by this account by Stanley M. Rinehart, one of the founders of Holt, Rinehart & Winston, who tried to bring his two English nephews to New York during the London Blitz: "Such was the snarl of combined British and American red tape that [the boys] could have escaped from Sing Sing with less difficulty. I said to my wife . . . while the arrangements were being made, that it would be simpler to have two more children of our own and it would probably take less time. . . . [W]e worked with a battery of lawyers, making up affidavits for the American consular office in England. Four Photostats of your income-tax returns for four years back . . . *and* of the checks that paid them *and* of your bank statements for twelve months *and* of your mortgage payments for two years *and* a list of your stocks and bonds *and* four letters from your bank officials *and* four letters from four prominent American citizens. . . . Finally the affidavits went off by air mail to England. The postage stamps cost fifteen dollars." Stanley M. Rinehart, "The Nefugees," *Good Housekeeping*, January 1943, 28.

Pogroms had gone out of fashion by 1903. The last great ones had been in 1881 and '82, following the assassination of Tsar Alexander II; the next twenty years in Russia had been a time of such savage repression that many anti-Semites had been mollified, as Jews lost their ability to buy or rent land, to seek higher education, to live in the countryside, to enter the legal and medical professions. V. D. Nabokov, thirty-two years old when he wrote "The Kishinev Bloodbath"—he was a lecturer at the Imperial School of Jurisprudence, also a "junior gentleman of the chamber," an eminence of the tsar's court—with this single gesture of disgust self-cashiered, deprived himself of his title at court and of his academic career. His abhorrence of anti-Semitism derived from a critique of state power, partly; officials in Kishinev had facilitated the outrages, and those officials were instruments of the imperial "regime of oppression and lawlessness" that "lives by it"—lived by a murderous hounding of the Jews.

From this day on, he was an opponent of the tsarist regime in absolute terms. He expressed his nonchalance about becoming a nonperson by advertising his court uniform for sale in the daily papers. Other prominent Russians also spoke against the pogrom—Tolstoy, Gorky—but V. D. Nabokov's essay is remarkable for its prescience and its cold fury. Future murderers wishing to bash the skulls of Jewish infants or to cut open the bellies of pregnant Jewish women would understand that "there are no courts for them"—no protections for the Jews, as the system was itself built upon naming them as pariahs, as a people deserving of annihilation. We hear in this a recognition of the century oncoming—a forecast of its most murderous hours.

V. D. wrote against another pogrom, in 1906, and in '13 he reported on the trial of Mendel Beilis, a Jewish brickyard worker accused of ritual murder. He had numerous Jewish friends, and his friendship was notably without condescension.* After his accidental assassination—the killers had been aiming for another speaker on the stage, who escaped unharmed—his Jewish colleague at *Pravo* and *Rul'*, Iosif Hessen, played literary angel to his fatherless son, ushering Sirin's poetry, stories, chess

---

* Not, however, without elements of high-handedness and presumption. "My father," Vladimir wrote years later to a scholar studying him, "felt so infinitely superior to any accusation of antisemitism . . . that out of a kind of self-confidence and contempt for showcase philosemitism he used to make it a point . . . of being as plainspoken about Jew and Gentile as were his Jewish colleagues." About the Bolshevik Moisei Uritski, for instance, he wrote, "I recall now his impudent Jewish face and the repulsive figure. . . ."

problems, and sundry other creations into print, and Hessen's small publishing house, Slovo, brought out the first editions of Sirin's earliest books.

Spring 1940: the *visas de sortie* came through, there were no more legal impediments (only financial ones). The war was now very near. On May 10, Germany invaded the Low Countries and France; three weeks later, just after the Nabokovs got away, British and French forces would escape annihilation at Dunkirk only by what Winston Churchill called a "miracle," in small and large boats. How the Nabokovs caught a very big boat, the great ocean liner SS *Champlain*, that carried them to safety in the New World is a matter of some dispute. Credit has sometimes been assigned to the Hebrew Immigrant Aid Society (HIAS) of New York; the president of HIAS at the time, the lawyer Yakov Frumkin, had personally known V. D. Nabokov and, "like many . . . Russian Jews," as Brian Boyd puts it, he "was glad to be able to repay the dead man for his bold stands against the Kishinyov pogroms and the Beilis trial."

Véra's biographer, Schiff, agrees but also does not agree: her account refrains from mentioning Frumkin or his organization by name. Instead she names the American Committee for Christian Refugees, an agency "committed to assisting non-Jews who had been victims of the Nazis' racial policies." The Committee for Christian Refugees gave Vladimir a small amount of money, as did numerous Sirin fans and personal friends of his; Schiff does not dispute, meanwhile, that the heavy lifting, the crucial financial help, was courtesy of "a Jewish rescue organization headed by a former associate of Vladimir's father," which secured berths for the refugee family on a New York–bound ship. HIAS had chartered the *Champlain*, a French Line vessel of up-to-date art deco appointments, to carry Jewish émigrés to the New World. HIAS also had arranged for the Nabokovs to pay only half fare. Nabokov's own account of the embarkation, in *Speak, Memory*, focuses not on the cost of a cabin or on where the money ultimately came from, but on six-year-old Dmitri walking to the ship between his parents, through a small park above the harbor at Saint-Nazaire, as the "splendid ship's funnel" showed among the roofs of the last line of houses. The parents refrain from pointing out this marvel to the boy—let him notice on his own, let him have that fun.

Once aboard, the Nabokovs occupied a "cabin-class" cabin—the *Champlain*'s version of first class—although they had paid only for third class. Schiff explains that "a benevolent French Lines agent took it upon himself to assign the family to a first-class cabin." Andrew Field, another

SS *Champlain*

biographer, disagrees with this version and explicitly credits Frumkin and HIAS for the pleasant upgrade: Frumkin "not only remembered V.D. Nabokov's passionate defence of Beilis," Field writes in *VN: The Life and Art of Vladimir Nabokov*, as well as "his scathing attack upon Russian anti-Semitism, but . . . remembered it well," i.e., he made sure that V. D. Nabokov's son and family made the crossing in high style. Nabokov endorses this account: "We were given a first-class cabin," he says in Field's book, which he meticulously vetted and whose credit to Frumkin he would surely have cut if he disagreed with it. "I had a lovely bath every morning. It was marvelous."

Proof, at any rate, that Frumkin played the central role can be found in a note Nabokov wrote him in March 1960:

> Your letter and clippings came exactly to the thirty-eighth anniversary of the death of my father. I with great interest read your wonderful article [on Jewish restrictions under the tsars]. In a horrible universe where Bolshevism reigns, we are inclined to forget the disgusting and shameful sides of earlier Russian life, and articles such as yours serve as a useful reminder. . . . PS: I have not forgotten my debt to the organization, which on your initiative helped us move to the United States. Now, finally, I am able to begin to repay this debt. I am attaching for starters $150, which I ask you not to refuse, and to kindly transfer as noted.

By 1960, Nabokov was splendidly able to repay. *Lolita* had been a bestseller for two years, selling, in its first three weeks alone, more than 100,000 copies—the first novel since *Gone with the Wind* to do so. He had sold screen rights as well, to Stanley Kubrick and James B. Harris, who hired him to write a screenplay. On the day he mailed Frumkin the $150, he and Véra were living in a villa off Mandeville Canyon Road, in Brentwood—Kubrick and Harris were putting them up while he wrote the script, and he was enjoying a classic writer's idyll, hobnobbing with Hollywood celebs (Marilyn Monroe, John Wayne, John Huston, David Selznick) and taking the occasional meeting at Universal City. The $150 seems mean given these circumstances. For that matter, why had it taken him twenty years to start to repay?

There may have been earlier, anonymous donations; Nabokov was a generous man who provided stipends to needy relatives in Europe for years, but he was also proud, and Véra and he were at pains to portray their time in Berlin and Paris not as a period of "ghastly destitution," as he himself wrote of one bad patch, but rather as a threadbare adventure, starvation always about to arrive but never quite arriving. They had been young and game; others living in the emigration had also been bad off, many much worse off. Meanwhile, he had written works of genius that would last—he believed this fervently, Véra believing it at least as much—his beloved son had been born, many good things had happened for them. To see their escape as the ordeal of pathetic waifs who would otherwise have gone up in smoke was to get it wrong, importantly wrong.

Véra, if anything more proud, even disputed the chicken that Nina Berberova had added to their pot. The matter of being desperate did not sit well with her; they had wanted to get out, of course, but to say that they had ever been afraid, or that Vladimir had considered leaving her and Dmitri for a while and coming to America on his own—no, that line of argument would never please her, and in her complicated dealings with biographers and journalists in the coming years, she consistently put a less fretful construction on it all.

3.

In Manhattan, they stayed first with Natalia Nabokov, cousin Nicolas's ex-wife, who lived at 32 East Sixty-first Street with her young son, Ivan. Natalia had signed an affidavit promising to shelter them, and she was "delightful, doing all she can for us," Véra would recall; she placed them in a flat just across the landing from her own. Soon the new arrivals moved to a sublet on Madison near Ninety-fourth, then in the fall to a tiny place at 35 West Eighty-seventh, where they stayed until they left for Stanford the following spring.

New York in May 1940: the country was awakening to the war, the inevitable and unavoidable war, although the debate between isolationists and interventionists was not quite finished, and Charles Lindbergh had not been entirely discredited. (Mrs. Roosevelt, responding to a radio address of Lindbergh's about which President Roosevelt remained silent, said she thought "the first part of it excellent . . . the last three paragraphs unfortunate"—paragraphs insinuating that the Jews were tricking the country into war, as the Jews always do.) The arrival of the Nabokovs coincided with the surrender of Belgium, with British and French forces being forced into a dangerous "Flanders pocket." Churchill warned of "heavy tidings," news of the destruction of the Allied army of hundreds of thousands of men sure to come soon.

No one met the Nabokovs at the dock—there had been a mix-up about times—so they took a taxi to the East Side. The morning was cloudy. Some thirty thousand refugees from France were arriving in America in this twelve-month period—arriving, most of them, via New York Harbor, sailing in past the Statue of Liberty, with the lower Manhattan skyline backdropping, then looming, then towering. Claude

Lévi-Strauss, who arrived some months after the Nabokovs, registered the "immense disorder" of the skyline, which he found thrilling, and Fernand Léger, arriving a few years earlier, called the skyline "the most colossal spectacle in the world." To Nabokov the cityscape looked more colorful than he had expected. In his memory, the morning had a lilac tinge. Colors were always meaningful to him: he was a synesthete, someone who transposes sense impressions, the letters of the alphabet, for example, being permanently associated in his mind with distinct colors. ("The long *a* of the English alphabet . . . has . . . the tint of weathered wood, but a French *a* evokes polished ebony. . . . [In] the blue group, there is steely *x*, thundercloud *z*, and huckleberry *k*. . . . In the green . . . alder-leaf *f*, the unripe apple of *p*, and pistachio *t*.") So much talk of color in his first reactions to Manhattan may signal happiness.

Almost before he unpacked his bags, he went looking for butterflies: not in Central Park or some other urban green spot, but at the American Museum of Natural History, whose collections were world-famous. In his Berlin days, he had on occasion approached the heads of state museums: of one, chief of the Entomological Institute at Dahlem, he wrote, "I simply loved that old, fat, red-cheeked scientist . . . with a dead cigar in his teeth as he casually and dexterously picked through the . . . glass boxes. . . . I will go back in a few days for a little more bliss."[*]

At the American Museum he found William P. Comstock, a research associate and expert in the Blue butterflies. They hit it off. Comstock secured him access to the collections, and Comstock's expertise and excitement—he was working on a paper, *Lycaenidae of the Antilles*, the Lycaenidae being the family of the Blues—influenced the direction of all of Nabokov's subsequent research. Comstock was a former construction engineer who, with little employment during the Depression, began spending more and more time on his hobby, lepidopterology. He was about as old as Nabokov's father would have been. From him Vladimir

---

[*] Nabokov's father was himself an enthusiastic chaser of moths and butterflies. In Nabokov's novel *The Gift*, his hero, Fyodor, considers writing a biography of his late father, an eminent field scientist, and his account of his father's adventures in western China has a grand, heartfelt style—the contemplation of a lost father, a daring naturalist, relieves him of his customary irony, is an opening to deep feeling. At the time of Nabokov's arrival, the American Museum was headed by Dr. Roy Chapman Andrews, a naturalist-explorer much in the mold of Fyodor's adventurous father. Andrews as a young man had so desired to work at the AMNH that, upon being denied a scientific job, he went to work as a janitor in the taxidermy department.

learned the fine points of examining the genitalia of different species—this was a method capable of giving definitive answers to questions of speciation, and though professional entomologists knew of it, they often failed to practice it.

Also soon after arrival, Nabokov wrote to Andrey Avinoff, director of the Carnegie Museum of Natural History, in Pittsburgh. Avinoff was an associate of Comstock's and one of the greatest private collectors in modern times. He was an English-speaking Russian, of a semi-noble family connected to the tsar's court, much like V. D. Nabokov; like Rachmaninoff, he had come to America soon after the Revolution, and in 1924 he affiliated with the Carnegie Museum, where he organized the insect holdings. He was also a gifted painter and illustrator. His career closely predicts Nabokov's own shadow career, the years of affiliation with Comstock and other New York scientists, the low-paid but joyous work at Harvard's Museum of Comparative Zoology, where Nabokov labored in the forties, cleaning up Harvard's chaotic collections. Avinoff was another devotee of collecting in high-mountain zones, where groups of butterflies often become separated by geography and where allopatric speciation—whereby populations undergo mutations and evolve into new subspecies—can be dramatically at play.

The writer might have been entirely lost to world literature—might have, if we believe him, gone down the rabbit hole of American entomology—so rich was the fun of collecting on the new continent, and so pressing were his insights into evolutionary biology. With a straight face Nabokov tells us that collecting was his greatest joy ever: "My pleasures are the most intense known to man: writing and butterfly hunting," he said in an interview, and, even more pointedly:

> I have hunted butterflies in various climes and disguises: as a pretty boy in knickerbockers and sailor cap; as a lanky cosmopolitan expatriate in flannel bags and beret; as a fat hatless old man in shorts. . . . Incredibly happy memories, quite comparable, in fact, to those of my Russian boyhood, are associated with my research work at the MCZ. . . . No less happy have been the many collecting trips taken almost every summer, during twenty years, through most of the states of my adopted country.

His collecting and his museum work made the 1940s "the most delightful and thrilling [years] in all my adult life," and this first decade in America also saw a falling off, almost to zero, of his writing of novels.

"Frankly, I never thought of letters as a career," he told an interviewer. "Writing has always been for me a blend of dejection and high spirits. . . . On the other hand, I have often dreamt of a long and exciting career as an obscure curator of Lepidoptera in a great museum."

He *did* return to the novel, of course. We can assume he spoke tongue in cheek. But in the forties he was putting to rest his "natural idiom," his "untrammeled, rich, and infinitely docile Russian tongue," completing the switch to English that had begun with the translations he wrote in the thirties. That transition was painful and saddening. Altagracia de Jannelli forbade his writing anything in Russian, since it could not be sold, and though he sometimes disobeyed her, in the end he submitted to this "private tragedy," to the suppression of his inmost language, his heart's parlance. Lepidoptery was almost as ingrained in him as was Russian, though—*that* they couldn't take away, and he practiced it with relief.

THE REASONS HE LOVED collecting were many. First, the insects themselves: radiant, deceptive, tender beings. Then, "one should not ignore the element of sport . . . of brisk motion and robust achievement . . . an ardent and arduous quest ending in the silky triangle of a folded butterfly . . . on the palm of one's hand." His fascination with the play and adventure of collecting began when he was very young. It was connected with Vyra, the family estate, since the Nabokovs went there in the warmer months, the seasons of good collecting. "The 'English' park that separated our house from the hayfields," he writes in *Speak, Memory*,

> was an extensive and elaborate affair with labyrinthine paths, Turgenevian benches, and imported oaks among the endemic firs and birches. The struggle that had gone on since my grandfather's time to keep the park from reverting to the wild state always fell short of complete success. No gardener could cope with the hillocks of frizzly black earth that the pink hands of moles kept heaping on the tidy sand of the main walk. Weeds and fungi, and ridgelike tree roots crossed and recrossed the sun-flecked trails. Bears had been eliminated in the eighties, but an occasional moose still visited the grounds.

There was a touch of true wildness—especially in the eyes of a seven- or eight-year-old. He had been introduced to collecting by his parents, Victorian and Anglophile in this as in much else. Elena Ivanovna, his mother, brought to the marriage a great dowry but also a collection of books of entomology, some from the seventeenth century. At age eight, Nabokov began to read these texts. He was especially drawn to the newer ones, such as Edward Newman's *An Illustrated Natural History of British Butterflies and Moths* (1871), compendious and authoritative; Ernst Hofmann's *Die Gross-Schmetterlinge Europas* (1894), the German *vade mecum*; and Samuel Hubbard Scudder's systematic and wonderfully illustrated *The Butterflies of the Eastern United States and Canada* (1889).

Other pastimes—botanizing, for example—also come with a rich literature, and young practitioners can read their way into a lifetime hobby. But the physical side of butterfly collecting needs to be emphasized. It took him outdoors, in good if changeable weather—around Vyra, into an intense, short-lived season of up to nineteen hours of sunlight per day, with sudden births and metamorphoses followed by rapid dyings-off. Vyra was less than two hundred miles from the Finnish border. Knut Hamsun, the Norwegian novelist (1859–1952)—he joins Dostoevsky, Turgenev, Leskov, and dozens of other writers of authentic power on Nabokov's list of little or no respect—gave the northland summer one of its classic representations in his novel *Pan* (1894):

> Spring was in full tilt; I found starflowers and yarrow in the fields, and both the chaffinches and the bramblings had arrived. I knew all the birds. Sometimes I would take two quarters from my pocket and chink them together to break the solitude. . . . It was beginning to be no night, the sun barely dipped its disk into the sea before it rose again, red, renewed, as if it had been down to drink. . . . There was a rustling all over the forest. Animals snuffled, birds called one another, their signals filled the air. It was a year when the cockchafers [May bugs] were particularly numerous; their buzzing mingled with that of the moths, it sounded like whisperings through the forest.

Hamsun's hero, Lieutenant Glahn, is a hunter of game; in the course of his ill-considered Rousseauvian return to nature, he experiences intensities of joy and despair that the short Arctic summer exaggerates:

> Sphinx moths . . . come flying soundlessly in through my window, lured by the light of the fireplace and by the smell of my roasted bird. They bump against the ceiling with a dull sound, buzz past my ears

sending cold shivers through me. . . . They sit there . . . silk moths, goat moths. . . . Some of them look to me like flying pansies. . . . I step outside the hut and listen. . . . The air sparkles with flying insects, myriads of buzzing wings. Over by the edge of the forest there are ferns and wolfsbane; the bearberry is in bloom and I love its tiny flowers. I thank you, God, for every ling flower I've ever seen. . . . Large white flowers have . . . unfolded in the forest, their stigmas are open, they are breathing. And furry twilight moths dip down into their petals, setting the whole plant trembling.

The boy Vladimir—roaming at will day after day, in a forest six hundred miles more southerly than Glahn's but equally rich with sudden life—comes to treasure his solitude and also, possibly, to regret it. ("It was many years before I met a fellow sufferer.") Both hunters are profoundly awakened. The living land speaks to them, their contact with it almost too intimate, at the borders of decorum—for Glahn the forest is sexualized and full of ardent women, some of whom set upon him like Maenads, and for nine- or ten-year-old Vladimir, there are sexual overtones if not quite yet sexual feelings. To say that this constitutes a sensual awakening is not to say quite enough:

On the other side of the river, a dense crowd of small, bright blue male butterflies that had been tippling on the rich, trampled mud and cow dung through which I trudged rose all together into the spangled air and settled again as soon as I had passed. . . . I came to the bog. No sooner had my ear caught the hum of diptera around me, the guttural cry of a snipe overhead, the gulping sound of the morass under my foot, than I knew I would find here quite special arctic butterflies. . . . The next moment I was among them. Over the small shrubs of bog bilberry with fruit of a dim, dreamy blue . . . a dusky little Fritillary bearing the name of a Norse goddess passed in low, skimming flight. . . . I pursued rose-margined Sulphurs, gray-margined Satyrs. . . . Through the smells of the bog, I caught the subtle perfume of butterfly wings on my fingers, a perfume which varies with the species—vanilla, or lemon, or musk, or a musty, sweetish odor difficult to define. Still unsated, I pressed forward.

Eleven years old, the boy is undergoing a forest initiation. To invoke the name of another writer Nabokov did not much honor, Faulkner, in

"The Bear" (1931), initiates his protagonist in hunting and the woods beginning at about the same age; that initiation takes place over a few years. The American process is more involved with bloodletting and bonding with doomed father figures, although not much more; young Vladimir is at least as comfortable with killing as is Ike McCaslin ("the soaking, ice-cold absorbent cotton pressed to the insect's lemurian head; the subsiding spasms of its body; the satisfying crackle produced by the pin penetrating the hard crust of its thorax"), and the loss of his father is, as Boyd writes, "a wound he cannot leave alone but can hardly bear to touch."

Nabokov does not hunt "the occasional moose" at Vyra, but he learns absolute competence with the tools of his kind of hunt (net, spreading board, field guide) just as does Ike, and the doomed patches of wilderness that they roam—Faulkner's spread of primeval Mississippi bottom-forest, and Vyra's subarctic bogs and boreal stands—are enough of paradise for a boy or girl never to forget, or a grown man or woman. As Faulkner writes in "The Bear," "Already it was warmer; they could run tomorrow. He felt the old lift of the heart . . . as on the first day; he would never lose it, no matter how old in hunting or pursuit: the best, the best of all breathing."

FOR NABOKOV, BUTTERFLY HUNTING was an intellectual effort, too. His biographers trace the passion over his life's length, showing how he puzzled out the heavy German texts—by age nine, after work with a dictionary, "I had gained absolute control over the European lepidoptera as known to Hofmann," he tells us proudly. From this came more explorations and deeper ones; he was especially fond of English-language studies, which took an evolutionarily more sophisticated approach to butterfly taxonomy. When reading about the captures on which species designations were based, he learned where type specimens (holotypes) had been caught—in what mountain range, at what altitude, near which geographical marker, on what exact date.

The locales of capture—a talus field in the Tian Shan, for instance, the mountain range that divides China from Kyrgyzstan, or a moist Colorado meadow at eleven thousand feet—undergo a transfiguration. As the site of an historic encounter, "a given landscape lives twice," Nabokov explained in an interview, "as a delightful wilderness in its own right and as the haunt of a certain butterfly or moth." When you visit such sites, "things you have gloated over in books, in obscure scientific reviews, on the splendid plates of famous works . . . you now see on the wing . . . among plants and minerals that acquire a mysterious magic through the intimate association."

There was the other kind of intellectual effort in the years to come: thematizing butterflies in literary works of a complicated modernist cast. None of this is the less if we also remember that he was once a boy with suggestive smells on his fingers, tramping through dung, intent on gathering loot—a full game bag, glorious trophies, instances of the marrow of things.

SIX WEEKS AFTER ARRIVING in New York, the Nabokovs left for southern Vermont, where Mikhail Karpovich, the Harvard professor, had a 250-acre property with an old farmhouse on it. In a scene out of a Turgenev novel—maybe *Home of the Gentry*—friends of Karpovich and his wife, Tatiana, lived for months among Russian-inflected berry picking and tea drinking, with kids running around, lots of sunbathing, dips in cool lakes, and comfort taken from the nearness of other Slavs. Here Nabokov first fulfilled his dream of hunting butterflies on a continent not that of his birth. He had consulted Avinoff, at the Pittsburgh museum, and probably he had read American entomological journals for detailed information about species and sites. He found Vermont's skunks and porcupines impressive, and he caught "a number of good moths," as he wrote Edmund Wilson later.*

Cousin Nicolas, now living with his second wife, spent part of 1940 on Cape Cod. Across the sandy road from his house was Edmund Wilson, and they chatted each other up—Wilson, after six years of work, was about to publish *To the Finland Station*, his study of revolutionary ideologies and the Bolshevik Revolution, and things Russian engaged him intensely. Nicolas was drawn to Wilson by the same flawless instinct for cultural importance he displayed elsewhere, and Wilson, as their correspondence shows, took him for a plausible example of a soulful Russian in need of support. Within months Wilson was helping him place magazine articles—he put him in touch, as he would Vladimir,

---

* Wilson was not a sportsman. As a boy he gave away the baseball outfit his mother had bought him in hopes that it would encourage him to be athletic, and by the time Nabokov got to know him he was notably short, stout, and gouty. Nevertheless, Nabokov hoped to recruit him for collecting. "Try, Bunny," he wrote, addressing Wilson by his nickname. Chasing butterflies "is the noblest sport in the world."

with Edward A. Weeks, the *Atlantic Monthly*'s new editor, who readily published both of them. It was Nicolas who made the generous handoff of Vladimir to Wilson; he wrote his cousin at the Karpoviches', and on August 30, 1940, Vladimir wrote Wilson, thus inaugurating one of the great American correspondences:

> My cousin Nicholas has suggested my writing to you. I would be very happy to meet you. I am staying with friends in Vermont (goldenrod and wind, mostly), but I shall be back in New York in the second week of September. My address there will be: 1326, Madison Ave. Tel. At. 97186.

Wilson knew absolutely everyone, and he was tutelary toward other writers. The list of those for whom he acted as de facto agent, editor, employment counselor, life adviser, or *parti pris* reviewer includes F. Scott Fitzgerald, Nathanael West, Randall Jarrell, Elizabeth Bishop, Anaïs Nin, Dawn Powell, Arthur Mizener, Maxwell Geismar, Helen Muchnic, John Dos Passos, Louise Bogan, Mary McCarthy, and Edna St. Vincent Millay, in addition to the two Nabokovs. He got along with Russians; they were his favorite non-Americans. Russian language and literature would be something of a stock in trade for him, the subjects of essays he published in magazines and then republished in books. Nicolas made claims on their new friendship that are hard to credit. After Wilson became *The New Yorker*'s books editor in '43, Nicolas wrote asking for entrée at the magazine. Wilson could not manage it, but he made connections for him at other publications, and Nicolas noted:

> That was awfully sweet of you! Thank you so much. I received a letter from [Paul] Rosenfeld [a music editor] informing me that the piece will be published in the next issue. . . . I also have a little question to ask you then, about the possibility of an essay on the "lives of Conductors" for the New Yorker (which I would have to write under a highly assumed name, to protect my future musical output from being banished from the programs by the -itzki's, -owski's and Co.).

Three years later, Nicolas declined an invitation to visit with Wilson, saying that he was about to leave for California, where he would spend ten days with Stravinsky:

It occurred to me that I might try to write something on Stravinsky of a kind Niccolo Tucci wrote on Einstein. Do you think, if well done, it could suit the New Yorker for the "Reporter at Large" column?—It is my first trip to California. I am going with Balanchine.

Wilson replied, "I have taken your suggestion up with them here . . . and they say they would like to see [a Stravinsky article]. They can't promise anything . . . but I think it would be worthwhile to submit it."

Two years later, when his first book appeared, Nicolas made sure an advance copy got to Wilson:

I hope (so much) that *you* will review it for The New Yorker. . . . It would give me such a pleasure. The fact [is] I not only hope that you *will* review it, but think that you "must" review it (as a teacher "must" review the papers of his students) because you are the godfather of the book insofar as it was you who started me on the "pay the way by writing" career. Will you? Will you *please*?

Whether or not this experience made Wilson cautious about helping other writers named Nabokov, the meeting with Vladimir took place in October 1940, and it proved a success. The men had a Mutt and Jeff radical difference physically, but in other respects they were reflections: literary out to their fingertips; contentious know-it-alls; sons of upper-class families, their fathers distinguished jurists involved in politics; lovers of Proust, Joyce, Pushkin. Both had struggled and would continue struggling to make a living by their pen. Wilson, then at the *New Republic*, offered Nabokov books to review, and the explosive material of dangerous future arguments was immediately before them: reviewing a book called *The Guillotine at Work*, by G. P. Maximoff, about the Soviet Union, Nabokov wrote,

The seven years of Lenin's regime cost Russia from 8 to 10 million lives; it took Stalin ten years to add another 10 million, thus, according to Mr. Maximoff's "very conservative estimate," between 1917 and 1934 there perished about 20 million people, some being tortured and shot, others dying in prisons, others again falling in the Civil War. . . . The appearance of this tragic and terse book is especially welcome because it may help to dispose of the wistful myth that Lenin was any better than his successor.

Wilson, in *To the Finland Station*, argued that Lenin was indeed better, was an indispensable man, in fact, bearer of the torch of history's oppressed. At a dinner at Roman Grynberg's,* Nabokov expressed a lesser estimation of the dictator, which prompted Wilson to send him a copy of his new book "in the hope that this may make [you] think better of Lenin." The attractions of authentic friendship must already have been strong between them, not to mention Nabokov's awareness of the *impolitique* of offending the foremost literary critic in America. Vladimir did not explode, or go off on a contemptuous rant, as at other times he did when encountering American beliefs about Lenin; on the subject of Soviet rulers, he was an absolutist, disinclined to see anything attractive or inspiring in the extermination of millions and the smothering of a liberal alternative in the catastrophe of 1917. Loyalty to his father's memory was part of his anti-Bolshevism (which over the years came to resemble garden-variety American anti-Communism, with, in the fifties, a bemused fondness for Joe McCarthy, and in the sixties outright disgust with long-haired American students protesting the war in Vietnam). Loyalty to his own hopes in America, too, was a factor. Already he was aware that Russians of the emigration—the million-plus people who had been driven out or had fled after the Revolution— were illegitimate as a class, in the eyes of many educated Westerners. If they were anti-Soviet, they must be reactionary, the thinking went; if they condemned the events of 1917, they were standing in the way of history.

Wilson was not a propagandist for Stalin or even Lenin. By the time he finished *Finland Station*, he was in horror of the purge trials and the frenzy of political murders, and he noted in a letter that his writing of *Finland Station* was ending just as Russia was trying to end Finland (in the Russo-Finnish War). Wilson had been shaped by the Depression, which he reported for the *New Republic*. After a professional beginning on the cultural side, he became more interested in social issues, responding to the Crash with a feeling of deep anxiety for his beleaguered country:

* Wilson knew Grynberg independently of Nabokov, who had been his English tutor in France. Grynberg was a book-loving businessman deeply saturated in literature, a publisher of Russian-language journals after his move to the United States. His sister Irina had become a friend of Wilson's while serving as his guide in Moscow in 1935, when Wilson was reporting his book *Travels in Two Democracies* ('36).

> There are today [January 1931] in the United States . . . something
> like nine million men out of work; our cities are scenes of priva-
> tion and misery on a scale which sickens the imagination . . . our
> agricultural life is bankrupt . . . our industry, in shifting to the
> South, has reverted almost to the horrible conditions . . . of
> the England of a hundred years ago.

A "darkness" had descended, Wilson felt, bringing a sense of "a rending
of the earth in preparation for the Day of Judgment." He paid particular
attention to the epidemic of American suicides. This bespoke an
enfeeblement of will, although his feeling toward suicides was entirely
compassionate. He gave up his literary portfolio at the *New Republic* to
travel the country for many months, writing about factory politics and
Henry Ford as an incoherent prophet of capitalism; about starvation
in plain sight; about the trial of the Scottsboro Boys in Chattanooga. In
'32, he assembled his reportage in a book called *The American Jitters: A
Year of the Slump*, a largely nondoctrinaire, upsetting, meticulously
reported account of the deep wound to American prospects. In a chapter
called "The Case of the Author," he offered a bluff self-profile: petit-
bourgeois, conventional, pleasure-seeking, selfish. He reported his
earnings during the twenties, noting that family money had afforded
him leisure time for "reading, liquor, and general irresponsibility."

Part of Wilson's attraction to Soviet Communism came from a
feeling that the American people were being poorly served. With a businessman's president in the White House, there had been a shocking
failure to recognize the near abyss; this same president "kept telling us,"
Wilson wrote, "that the system was perfectly sound," and meanwhile he
sent General Douglas MacArthur "to burn the camp of the unemployed
war veterans who had come to appeal . . . [and] we wondered about the
survival of republican American institutions." The Soviets did not blink
at such profound problems, Wilson felt—they grabbed them by the
throat. "We became more and more impressed by the achievements of
the Soviet Union, which could boast that its industrial and financial
problems were carefully studied by the government, and that it was able
to avert such crises."

By the time of his first meeting with Nabokov, Wilson had wised up
considerably about the Soviets, especially about Stalin. In 1935 he
traveled to Russia on a Guggenheim, and his prolific energy and
capacity for meeting people and getting their story gave him material
for three books. In Russia he was aware of the police state, of the active

Edmund Wilson, early 1940s

fear among intellectuals, many soon to be executed; the crowds on the streets seemed "dingy" and "monotonous," and socialism had not cured an overriding Russian sadness, he felt—quite the contrary. Still, Wilson did not forefront the fear in the books he wrote; instead he looked for elements of the Soviet story that might translate into an American idiom, that signaled competence, a grip on the future. The two lands were comparable, after all: both were vast, both still untamed, all "prairies and wild rivers and forests," and "we never know what we have got in the . . . wastes of these countries; we never know what is going to come out of them."

4.

With Wilson getting him review assignments and making many contacts for him, Nabokov was able to survive his first winter in America without a steady job. There was the Stanford position to look forward to, and cousin Nicolas arranged a lecture for him at upstate Wells College in February. Nabokov had arrived in the United States with "one hundred lectures—about 2,000 pages—on Russian literature" already prepared and ready to be rolled out should opportunities arise. He saw himself as a professor-to-be as well as an artist—saw himself delivering cultural goods, knowledge of an exotic foreign literature, to a deprived audience willing to pay for it. His hopefulness was not misplaced, and his immigrant's adaptive strategy was a good one.

Karpovich of Harvard recommended him to a booking service, and Wellesley College invited him for two weeks of talks in March '41, partly because a copy of his 1922 translation of *Alice in Wonderland* was among the library's Lewis Carroll editions. He proved a seductive, roaringly funny, erudite, and becomingly accented lecturer in English. "My lectures are a purring success," he wrote Wilson. "Incidentally I have slaughtered Maxim Gorky, Mr. Hemingway—and a few others." He liked the Wellesley girls and also the "very charming" women professors, and while in Boston he had lunch with Edward Weeks, who, like Nabokov, had attended Trinity College, Cambridge. Weeks "received my story and me with very touching warmth," he reported—the story, "Cloud, Castle, Lake," was one that Wilson had recommended— and Weeks followed up with such praise ("this is genius") and so unconditional an invitation to further submissions to the *Atlantic* ("this is what we have been looking for") that Nabokov was shocked.

Véra was ill for much of the year, underweight and suffering "from all the migrations and anxieties," as she later described it. She looked for work, found it in January '41—translating for a Free French newspaper—and lost it when laid up for weeks with sciatica. Her troubled back threatened the planned trip to Palo Alto: it seemed unlikely she would be able to travel, but on May 26, a Monday and also the day of a new moon, the family set out for the West, in the car belonging to Dorothy Leuthold, one of Vladimir's language students.

To drive to California in '41 was to go adventuring, in a small way. The system of numbered roads (U.S. 1, Md. Hwy 97) was only about ten years old, and many roads, including major routes, were still poorly surfaced. The world context, meanwhile, was unstable in the extreme. Two weeks before they left, in the heavy American car containing manuscripts and a seven-year-old, 3,600 Jews had been rounded up in Paris by the Gestapo, many of them children.

The Germans had just captured Crete, and their warships were decimating British shipping in the North Atlantic. German intentions vis-à-vis the Soviet Union, its Non-Aggression Pact partner, were showing a new character. To what extent Nabokov or his wife monitored events by newspaper or radio is hard to know, but Vladimir observed in a letter to Wilson after the German attack in the east,

> For almost 25 years Russians in exile have craved for something—anything—to happen that would destroy the Bolsheviks,—for instance a good bloody war. Now comes this tragic farce. My ardent desire that Russia, in spite of everything, may defeat or rather utterly abolish Germany—so that not a German be left in the world, is putting the cart before the horse, but the horse is so disgusting that I prefer doing so.

The Pontiac was a different kind of horse. The travelers called it *Pon'ka,* Russian for "pony." This Lewis and Clark expedition undertaken by the family, with a native guide (Miss Leuthold, who was intent on practicing her Russian), established the template for the summer explorations to come. Each day they drove until evening approached or they felt they had been on the move long enough. A motel or other accommodation hove into view, a vacancy sign displayed. A list that Nabokov compiled of the places where they stayed shows a fondness for motor courts ("Motor Court Lee-Meade," "Wonderland Motor Courts," "El Rey Courts," etc.) and an avoidance of standard hotels, which in 1940 still had dress codes and where employees had to be tipped. The Nabokovs stayed at a single hotel and a single self-described motel: the General Shelby, in Bristol, Tennessee. (Shelby was a Confederate cavalry hero.) They avoided tourist homes; these were boardinghouse-style arrangements with a communal table and bathrooms, and Nabokov wanted his own bath.

At this moment in history, the fate of millions in the balance, American recreational consumerism was following its blithe course, confidently reconfiguring the landscape. The hotel was on the way out; it had been on a downward trend for a while in small cities as Americans traveled less by train. In the past, the railroad had delivered captive passengers to hotels, often located near rail stations. Since about 1910, though, Americans had traveled more and more by car, and at the end of a day's drive, a harried tourist did not wish to have to negotiate the downtown streets of a strange city, looking for an overpriced hotel. The Nabokovs in '41 were joining the parade of change at an advanced point. They were the beneficiaries of a thirty-year evolution whereby American car gypsies at first had carried their own tents and stopped at any pretty spot along the road, or at a public car campground maintained by a municipality; then had begun to favor private campgrounds offering showers, a communal kitchen, and primitive cabins or tent-cabins, basic protection against the weather; then at progressively nicer cabin camps, where freestanding wooden structures with serviceable beds and other furniture could be rented for a small fee; then at cottage camps, a.k.a. cottage courts, the cottage being an evolution of the cabin in the direction of fresher paint, curtains in the window, nicer furniture, a private shower, and a parking space alongside. The motor courts common by the forties, as suggested by Nabokov's list, differed from cottage courts in that the separate units were attached under one roof; often the establishment had a rectangular or oblong plan, creating a central space that might be landscaped, and by the forties the development in the direction of architectural tomfoolery was well under way, with log-cabin, Olde Tudor, Indian-tepee, Colonial-frame-with-flower-box, and even miniature-Alamo-style court units popular.

It took the Nabokovs, with the middle-aged Miss Leuthold driving every mile, three weeks to cross the country. A train would have taken four days. Nabokov collected madly; he later donated his specimens to the AMNH, where they ended up in a stuffy storeroom at the end of a hall, locked up for seventy years with curatorial miscellany. In 2011, two staff scientists, David Grimaldi and Suzanne Rab Green, noticed the

El Rey Court (now El Rey Inn), Santa Fe, New Mexico

name NABOKOV on a label. The specimens were still unpinned, still inside the glassine envelopes on which Nabokov had jotted the place and date of collection. Every day of the trip had produced at least one capture. On May 28, two days out, Vladimir caught specimens he considered worth saving at Luray and Shenandoah, Virginia, locations eighteen miles apart, as Miss Leuthold drove them from Gettysburg, where they stayed their first night, to Luray, where they stayed their second. They made a side trip to Great Cacapon, West Virginia, seventy-five miles west of Gettysburg. Nabokov had three nets in the Pon'ka; this was to be an entomological version of a summer vacation under the regime of someone—a conceivable American dad—who, crazy for golf, say, intended to play every course they passed.

He collected in Great Smoky Mountains National Park, on the Tennessee–North Carolina state line, which had been dedicated only a few months before by President Roosevelt. In Tennessee he also took specimens at Bristol, Crossville, Nashville, and Jackson. His itinerary might have been suggested by road maps handed out at gas stations; also car clubs, such as the American Automobile Association, published guides, and Nabokov became a close reader of these. His penciled comments about establishments frequented ("Motel Shelby—all right,"

"Maple Shade Cottages—no," "Cumberland Motor Court—very nice") recall the ratings of businesses in the guides. The names of places with their connotations of grandeur or leafy ease suggest an embryonic form of the parody of motel names to appear one day in *Lolita*.

They drove southwest along the Blue Ridge, following U.S. Route 11, today's Interstate 81. The traveling was mostly on two-lane blacktop. In Knoxville, they connected with U.S. 40; their stops show Nabokov taking specimens where he also took rooms, which suggests that he found lodgings and then went out the next morning, armed with net. In Little Rock, they left 40 for U.S. 67, which heads southwest. Just outside Little Rock, Miss Leuthold agreed to another detour: it may be she was as eager as the foreigners to see as much of the country as possible, in June's green days, and they traveled to Hot Springs National Park, where Americans had been taking the waters since the early nineteenth century.

How Nabokov responded to the landscape can be inferred, in part, from a letter written after the arrival in Palo Alto: "During our motorcar trip across several states (all of them beauties) I frantically collected." Ten years later, he wrote in a now famous passage in *Lolita* of "the lovely, trustful, dreamy, enormous country" that Humbert Humbert and Lolita see by car. Humbert, whom it is surely perilous to take for Nabokov, nonetheless seems to see with Nabokov's eyes when he records, "Beyond the tilled plain . . . there would be a slow suffusion of inutile loveliness, a low sun in a platinum haze with a warm, peeled-peach tinge pervading the upper edge of a two-dimensional, dove-gray cloud." Humbert has a "fancy prose style," he tells us, but in his reports on the landscape he comes as close as he ever does to addressing the reader plainspokenly. His account of the "average lowland North-American countryside" is fond; as always with him, there is a struggle to go beyond what he brings to an encounter—to escape his own previsions and arch, learned analogies—and have it fresh.

Nabokov might have been thinking as they drove along of William Jacob Holland's *The Butterfly Book*, a popular illustrated guide for the United States and Canada, which was unscientific but full of information. William Comstock or Andrey Avinoff might have told him where to hunt, or he might have gotten hints from articles in the *Journal of the New York Entomological Society*, which he had been reading closely. As the Pontiac crossed into Texas, vistas out of Mayne Reid presented themselves. Still traveling on U.S. 67, the voyagers covered three hundred miles on June 2, from Hot Springs to Dallas, and the signature western landscape change, toward a flat immensity, began to manifest. The sudden openness, with ridges or peaks at the horizons, seems to enlarge the sky, bringing it paradoxically closer; travelers sometimes have a feeling of too much emptiness, too much staring blue.

For Dmitri's sake, the party might have begun to look around for cowboys and Indians. A few months after their return, a babysitter in Wellesley, Massachusetts, on the night of October 31, 1941, would paint Dmitri's face and take him around the neighborhood, on his head an Indian headdress bought in New Mexico. Dmitri was chattering in fluent American by then. His mother and father had not been quick to kit him out à l'Américain; during the summer at Stanford he was seen in lederhosen-like shorts, and before the trip he wore a fur coat in cold weather; his mother, in a portrait of him she wrote, recalled that other children would approach and ask if he was a boy or a girl. "No, I am a boy," he would reply calmly, "and this kind of coat is worn by boys where I come from." He was gentle and friendly and brave, she wrote. From an early age he exhibited a "reserve regarding the deeper emotions"; a loss "hit him the harder the less he spoke of it." About their cross-country drive she said that "he found himself on a motor car trip through many beauty spots . . . and [we] stopped for the nights at motor courts, I remember taking him . . . to a barber's for a hair cut. 'And where is your home, son?' the barber asked. . . . 'I don't have a home,' was the answer. . . . 'Where do you live then?' 'In little houses by the road.' "

The Nabokovs were primed for living in such little houses. Since the year of Dmitri's birth, they had had more than twenty-five addresses, in three countries; Dmitri did not outwardly mourn the places they left, such as the Berlin apartment where he lived his first three years, but in his mother's view he developed an "odd attachment for more passen-gery dwelling places," and "his passionate clinging to every bit of his childish possessions and propensity towards accumulating 'complete' sets of . . . five and ten cent store motor cars and trains [had] its root in that initial loss of home and toys." It represented "a pathetic attempt of a very small and bewildered individual to throw an anchor of his own amidst the incomprehensible."

A series of photos taken in a national park, to judge by the WPA-style stonework, shows Vladimir so intent on his hobby as to seem under a compulsion. His back is turned, or his gaze is on the ground, where the insects are, or his back is turned *and* his gaze is on the ground. His neck is scrawny and bent like a heron's. In a letter he wrote Wilson just before the family left New York, he announced, "I am driving off . . . to-morrow with butterfly-nets, manuscripts, and a new set of teeth." His teeth had been a torment most of his life; at age eleven, he had needed the attentions of "a celebrated American dentist" in Germany, and by the time he got to America he was fighting rearguard actions, having these ones taken out but not those, and then, inevitably, those, too.

Nineteen forty-one was the wettest year in Texas history. The travelers experienced thunderstorms, but the weather was most often baking dry; sun and heat after rain bring out butterflies, and Nabokov took specimens in Mineral Wells and Lubbock as well as Dallas. West of Dallas, they followed Texas 108 and U.S. 84, crossing into New Mexico near Clovis, the town where, in 1929, spearpoints used by Paleolithic hunters had been unearthed. Nabokov caught another desirable insect in Fort Sumner, en route for Santa Fe; Fort Sumner is where Billy the Kid was shot, and his name is in many guidebooks. West of the Pecos and east of the Rio Grande, the party left U.S. 84 for U.S. 66, in '41 already a fabled American route, the romantic favored highway from Chicago to L.A., and in Santa Fe they spent two nights at another motor court ("lovely") and Dmitri was given his Halloweenish headdress.

THE CENTERPIECE OF THE TRIP, collecting-wise, was the Grand Canyon. Here the party stayed at Bright Angel Lodge, on the South Rim, where some of the semi-detached cabins are only yards from the precipice. From U.S. 66 (today's I-40) probably they took U.S. 180 north, continuing as it turned into the park's South Entrance Road. They stayed two days. It rained and snowed; it was so cold on June 9 that Véra and Dmitri huddled in the car while Vladimir and Miss Leuthold walked down the Bright Angel Trail, on that morning but a "slushy mule track." The lodge had recently been renovated, under the supervision of Mary E. J. Colter, an architect working for the Atchison, Topeka, and Santa Fe Railway, which owned the South Rim concessions. Parts of the original lodge, preserved in Colter's renovation, date from 1896. Its progression from primitive inn serving stagecoaches to tent camp for rail tourists to cabin camp to hostelry with whimsical outlying units linked by pergolas (rooms also rented in the lodge itself) replicates much of the history of the motor court, although Colter's mix of local stone and peeled logs and adobe and her care in fitting all the structures to the site lift the lodge far above the level of any motel that the Nabokovs had seen so far.

Now an historic landmark, Bright Angel Lodge typifies the National Park Service rustic style (sometimes known as "parkitecture"), grander examples of it being the Ahwahnee Hotel, in Yosemite, and Paradise Inn, on Washington's Mount Rainier. Colter was one of the inventors. The style's mercurial way with authenticity can be seen in Hopi House, a gift-shop-cum-workshop she designed in 1905. She borrowed freely— obsessively—from the actual Hopi pueblo at Oraibi, Arizona, where, just at the time of her appropriation, traditionalist inhabitants of the pueblo were being forced out by other tribal members more friendly to whites. Hopi House, which is next door to the stately El Tovar hotel, allowed South Rim tourists to sample contemporary Hopi and Navajo craftwork; they could watch real Indians making that work, then buy some.

Nabokov, before setting out on this first journey, asked a friend at the American Museum to write him a note saying that he was an "accredited member" of the institution. That brought him permission to hunt insects in Grand Canyon National Park, and among his captures were males and females of what he joyously took for a new species—he named it *Neonympha dorothea*, in honor of Miss Leuthold, who had chauffeured them safely and had kicked up the specimens he caught on that cold morning on the mule trail. It was a consummation long wished for. Since early boyhood, he had dreamed of finding a new species that would bear his name ("*Neonympha dorothea* Nabokov"). A year or so after the trip he wrote a poem, not about this insect, but about another one that, alas, also turned out not to be of an entirely new species:

> *I found it and I named it, being versed*
> *in taxonomic Latin; thus became*
> *godfather to an insect and its first*
> *describer—and I want no other fame.*
>
> *Wide open on its pin (though fast asleep),*
> *and safe from creeping relatives and rust,*
> *in the secluded stronghold where we keep*
> *type specimens it will transcend its dust.*

The western trip had paid off wonderfully. The group in the Pontiac drove on, Vladimir making further stops and collecting further inter- esting insects at Las Vegas, San Bernardino, Santa Monica, and Ojai.

5.

Architect Mary Colter's appropriation of the design and materials of a nine-hundred-year-old Hopi pueblo to make a gift shop was, for its time, already a familiar gesture. Railroad and hotel promoters of tourism in the Southwest had been stimulating interest in the region for decades, going so far as to build pseudo-pueblos at world's fairs. Colter, whose Hopi House was built by actual Hopi, out of sandstone and juniper, with thatched ceilings and chimneys made from pottery shards, only went further than most.

What Nabokov took from the architectural mélange is hard to say. The built environment he experienced on his first western trip was "not quite fish and not quite fowl," as James Agee, in an article in *Fortune* magazine, said about roadside America in the thirties. For Agee the typical roadside attraction was the cave, a cave that was being exploited as a tourist trap. (The cabin camp ran a close second to the cave.) "The finding of such [an attraction] is, for commercial purposes, merely the first step," Agee wrote:

> Investigate and you will find shafts sunk to reach them (some have elevators). You will find $100,000 "lodges" built over the entrances—to house rest rooms, lunch counters, and, above all, souvenir stands. Uniformed attendants will lead you along . . . concrete paths. . . . All good caves are electrically lighted, often with ingenious indirect effects. Each point of . . . interest is named, the bent being for whimsy and romance.

Such places combine "the art of nature and the art of the entrepreneur," Agee said. "A good cave may gross $150,000 a year. . . . This money-making contraption . . . is more valuable if it twists and turns mysteriously, if it boasts a still pool (always called an 'underground lake') or a running stream (forever the 'River Styx')."

The Nabokovs saw ads for caves on their drive. In Luray, Virginia, they passed a famous cave system, and their route across New Mexico took them north of Carlsbad Caverns, which had been turned into a park under President Hoover. There is mention of caves in *Lolita*; Humbert, seeking distractions for his young sex captive, considers stopping at "a natural cave in Arkansas [or at] a replica of the Grotto of Lourdes in Louisiana." Tacky, hucksterish reconfigurations of the landscape, developed for the purpose of making a buck: America had not invented this game, but it had gone far, far beyond the Old World in the direction of playful shamelessness. Nabokov did not rear back in horror. His letters to friends mostly neglect the man-made sights; he keeps his eye instead on the "slow suffusion of inutile loveliness" in the distance, or on the butterflies at his feet. That he was noticing, and bemused by, Mother Goose–themed motor courts and "tea rooms built like teapots, papier-mâché owls lettered 'I-SCREAM,' [and] laughing swine with Neon teeth," to quote from Agee's litany of marvels, can be assumed from the classic account he later wrote of the roadside.

IN PALO ALTO, THE NABOKOVS lived at 230 Sequoia Avenue, about a block from the Stanford campus. A redwood (*Sequoia sempervirens*) grew out front of the "nice little house," as Vladimir described it, and the backyard had a comfortable deck chair where he sunbathed in a swimsuit. Stanford before the war was not an especially distinguished American university; some noted scholars were on the faculty, several in the sciences, but it was the beauty of the setting and the paradisiacal climate—especially over the course of a summer of predictably perfect days, hot but cooling by night, with ever cloudless cornflower skies and smogless views of the Coast Ranges—that made the strongest impression on many visitors. The fall before the Nabokovs arrived, Jack Kennedy, recently of Harvard, audited classes for a few months, living in a one-bedroom cottage behind a house at 624 Mayfield Avenue, whose owner, Gertrude Gardiner, remembered him as "head and shoulders" above the normal run of student. Kennedy used the lovely valley campus, with its native live oaks and imported palms and eucalyptus, mainly as a place of resort. He drove a cactus-green Buick convertible with red seats bought with earnings from *Why England Slept*, the recent book he had written with the help of two men close to his father, Ambassador to Britain Joseph P. Kennedy. After some relaxing weeks, he wrote a prep-school friend that "the girls are quite attractive—and it's a very good life" on "The Farm," as Stanford called itself.

Dorothy Leuthold returned east. Nabokov was not dozing uselessly in that deck chair: the classes he taught that summer, Modern Russian Literature and The Art of Writing, provoked in him a fury of effort out of all proportion to their enrollment (two in Russian Literature, four in Art of Writing). One of his students remembered that Nabokov lost himself so deeply in his lectures that a froth of spittle would form on his lips, nor would he pause to wipe it away.

The spittle was atypical. Students of his at Wellesley and Cornell in the future never saw such signs of stress—his presentation later would be urbane, singularly self-possessed. In the twenty years of his European exile, he had written distinctive, original work, almost all of which had been published and praised; by this hard labor he had put himself in the forefront of twentieth-century literature, whether or not the Anglophone world knew about it. He had created meanwhile an audience attuned to his sensibility. They were Russian speakers, émigrés like him who had learned not to be put off by his mocking cruelty toward his own characters, or by his wincing way with strong emotion, or by his disdain for shapely stories full of standard meanings. Here in America there would have to be a fresh audience-building effort, though an arduous and uncertain one.

Reclining in his chair, Nabokov applied himself to what would seem a minor task: improving the translations to be read by the students in his Russian Lit class. Translating had always been the nub for him—it mattered more than anything. It mattered because if he could open readers to the full range of music in Pushkin's "A Feast During the Plague," say, or Gogol's "The Overcoat," then much else good would happen. The English-language reader, given something like the flavor of great Russian work, would be on the way to possessing the literature as a whole. He wrote to his former art tutor, Dobuzhinsky, that he had no time for his own writing because "I assign myself a lot of extra work . . . in the sense of translations to English, but what else to do, when existing translations . . . are not chaise-horses of enlightenment but rather wild asses of ignorance. What carelessness, what shamelessness," he lamented.

And if they could be opened to the literature as a whole, to those parts of it that he most valued—Pushkin, Tyutchev, Gogol, Lermontov,

Tolstoy, some others—then the *real* treasure, works by V. Nabokov, would also come within reach.

James Laughlin, the founder-publisher of New Directions, visited Palo Alto early in July. Laughlin had been tipped to Nabokov by Wilson, among others. Laughlin offered him a minuscule advance for the theretofore-much-rejected novel *The Real Life of Sebastian Knight*, and Nabokov accepted: at least it *was* an advance, a guarantee of publication.

He went butterfly hunting in Los Altos, south of Stanford.* To Dobuzhinsky he extolled the "charming, yellowish country" of tawny coastal foothills bordered by dark forest. The California summer—hot in the sun but cold out of it, because the air holds little moisture— reminded him of Pushkin's Parnassian prose, also limpid and a bit cool. Wilson had warned him not to become intoxicated with the Golden State. "I have a fear . . . that you may become bewitched out there and never come back. . . . The weather is fine . . . and the rest of the world [comes to seem] unreal."

Nabokov's lectures developed cachet on campus. Interested faculty and others started sitting in. He was indulgent toward his students, accepting of the flawed work they produced, but ferocious toward famous authors not up to the high standards he propounded. "The prime object of a playwright ought to be not to write a successful play but an immortal one," he declared, as if continuing his heartfelt contention with Altagracia de Jannelli. Despite his missing teeth and sunken chest, despite the hand-me-downs he wore (an ultramarine suit courtesy of Mikhail Karpovich, a tweed jacket from Harry Levin, another Harvard professor), despite shoes without socks, despite the froth at his mouth and an alarming excess of aesthetic intensity—despite or because of all this, he was attractive as a speaker, charismatic, the "real thing."

Henry Lanz had brought him to Stanford, and they became friends. Lanz was a "tall, narrow man with rounded shoulders [and] gently penetrating black eyes," according to a profile of him in the campus newspaper. He was of Finnish descent, son of a naturalized American father, born in Moscow and educated there and in Germany. During

---

* Nabokov did not go to California ignorant of its writers and its literature. A letter to Wilson from Palo Alto acknowledges receipt of Wilson's "delightful book" *The Boys in the Back Room: Notes on California Novelists*, recently published, and Nabokov added that he had read most of the essays when they appeared earlier in the *New Republic*, on such writers as John Steinbeck, Nathanael West, James M. Cain, John O'Hara, and William Saroyan.

World War I, Lanz had found his way to London, where at age thirty he married a fourteen-year-old. In California he taught English to American soldiers of Slavic descent. By the end of the war he was on his way to a professorship at Stanford, in a language department that he created. He was a wonderment of culture on the Farm: fluent in several languages, musical, mystical, amusingly forgetful—an Old World type, rich in charm. He loved chess and played hundreds of games with Nabokov that summer, most of which Nabokov won. Vladimir described Lanz to biographer Andrew Field as *un triste individuel*, a shorthand term for "pedophile" commonly employed in Swiss newspapers. Over the chessboard they exchanged confidences, and Lanz revealed that he was a "fountainist," as well as a seducer of little girls: someone who derives pleasure from watching them urinate.

Lanz must have had *something* to do with the genesis of *Lolita*. This seemed clear to Field, who, when he suggested as much to Nabokov, elicited an outraged denial. The theme of sexual predation of young girls had been present in Nabokov's work much earlier; it went back to a poem of the late 1920s, and the whole of the novel *Lolita* seems to impend in a passage in *The Gift* (1938) in which the hero of that book puts up with his girlfriend's "cocky and corny" stepfather, who one night confesses to him,

> "Ah, if only I had a tick or two, what a novel I'd whip off! . . . Imagine this kind of thing: an old dog—but still in his prime, fiery, thirsting for happiness—gets to know a widow, and she has a daughter, still quite a little girl—you know what I mean—when nothing is formed yet but already she has a way of walking that drives you out of your mind—A slip of a girl, very fair, pale, with blue under the eyes—and of course she doesn't even look at the old goat. What to do? Well, not long thinking, he ups and marries the widow. . . . They settle down the three of them. Here you can go on indefinitely—the temptation, the eternal torment, the itch."

Humbert Humbert, who marries a widow to get at her daughter, realizes all his dreams (and nightmares) when the mother dies. An even more stark prototype exists in the form of *The Enchanter*, a novella that Nabokov wrote in fall '39, about a man who marries an ailing woman who soon dies, leaving him in control of her desirable child. That Nabokov was mulling the *Lolita* plexus for a long while before taking up the subject in America is clear, and he would return to the theme of—possibly to his own private fascination with—the bodies of young girls in other texts, so that, from one perspective, at any rate, his entire body of work can be said to be centrally about this matter.*

What Lanz might have contributed—*seems* to have—was his Old World charmer persona, his handsome, insinuating way. He was an amiable man who got what he wanted sexually. He commanded his young wife to dress as a child in their home, and on weekends, according to what he told Vladimir, he drove out "into the country" to "participate in orgies," presumably with children. Where Lanz was most like Humbert was in his convenient helplessness, his passivity before his obsession. He "suffered from . . . nympholepsy," Nabokov said, according to Field; he was a case study out of "Havelock Ellis," beyond cure. When Lanz died suddenly at fifty-nine—Humbert also dies young—Nabokov was persuaded that he had killed himself, rather than that he had been carried away by "a long infection and peritonitis," as the Stanford alumni magazine reported.

THE ISSUE OF REAL-LIFE MODELS for Nabokov's characters—Lanz as Humbert, or possibly Gaston Godin, another character in *Lolita* who

---

* The English novelist Martin Amis takes the opportunity, in a December 2011 *Times Literary Supplement* review, to express his high regard for Nabokov. Discussing a new essay collection from Brian Boyd, he observes that the biographer "attempts something fairly ambitious: he takes the titanic Nabokov and seeks to revise him *upwards*." But Boyd, he says, is "something of an apologist for the only significant embarrassment in the Nabokov corpus. Of the nineteen fictions, no fewer than six wholly or partly concern themselves with the sexuality of prepubescent girls. . . . To be as clear as one can be: the unignorable infestation of nymphets . . . is not a matter of morality; it is a matter of aesthetics. There are just too many of them."

The pedophilia theme is not only about aesthetics. The repetition suggests a compulsion—a literary equivalent of the persistent impulse of a pedophile. A self-conscious writer in the best sense, Nabokov is unlikely not to have noticed the tendency of his own body of work. In the absence of evidence of actual relations with children—evidence that his biographers, no matter how worshipful, have tried to find—the suspicion arises that he sensed something that he could do, something some writer ought to do, with the theme of a child taken sexually. Mostly ignored or treated covertly before, the subject attracted him for reasons probably not fully clear to him until he rendered it in *Lolita*. The child there is brought to full, suffering life, the bleakness of her captivity shown, along with its suggestive absurdity. There were many children like Lolita at the time, many housed in protective institutions. Nabokov never aimed to "reform," but his affinity for stories of the forbidden, of humiliation and compulsion, played half for laughs, brought him and his readers to a great uncovering.

combines foreignness with libertinism—soon grows complicated. In *The Real Life of Sebastian Knight*, published three months after his return from California, the half brother of a deceased novelist sets out to learn what he can of his brother's existence. Sebastian and V., as the half brother is called, were six years apart in age; they grew up in the same house in St. Petersburg, but Sebastian, in the manner of many older brothers, was aloof and disappearing. V., watching Sebastian paint with watercolors one day, clambers up beside him on a chair, but

> with a shrug of his shoulder he pushes me away, still not turning, still as silent and distant, as always in regard to me. I remember peering over the banisters and seeing him come up the stairs, after school. . . . My lips pursed, I squeeze out a white spittal which falls down and down . . . and this I do, not because I want to annoy him, but merely as a wistful and vain attempt to make him notice my existence.

Sebastian leaves for Cambridge at nineteen. V. and his mother move to France, and contact between the brothers mostly ends. The elements of Nabokov's own biography are everywhere present in the novel, but intriguingly altered; a reader is tempted to say that the novel is a demonstration, with a mild parodic flavor, of the changes that any clever novelist might ring in a story based on his personal material.

Nabokov had two younger brothers. The one nearest him in age, Sergei, died in the Neuengamme concentration camp on January 10, 1945, having been imprisoned by the Nazis for "subversive statements." (He had been imprisoned before for homosexuality and released.) The brothers were not close. Many things about Sergei irritated Vladimir: his jejune aestheticism, his religiosity, his homosexual beau monde friends in Paris, but mostly it was the homosexuality, the homosexuality above all else. To speculate freely—but then, the whole of *Sebastian Knight* invites a reader to speculate about a writer's life and art— Nabokov found his brother to be an embarrassment and a pain but was also aware that he *was* his brother, and that Sergei would have had his own perspective on things. (Kirill Nabokov, the other brother, was twelve years younger than Vladimir; he, too, at times experienced the high hat and the high hand, but their relations were usually sweeter.)

There seems to be something like an attempt to make things right via-à-vis his brothers in *Sebastian Knight*. It is as if, aware of his lack of empathy, Vladimir were granting the possibility that his brothers had all along been honorable, loyal, deeply intelligent men in the mold of V. in the novel, deserving of much better treatment. (So sympathetic is younger brother V. that the novel implies that he himself might have been the writer Sebastian.) In light of Sergei's fate it seems possible, if we grant Nabokov prophetic powers—and why not, since he arrogates all other powers to the artist—that he foresaw the likelihood of Neuengamme or some other horror as an end for him, that already he was mourning him.

Sebastian Knight encourages speculation of this sort, but it disciplines it, too. V. pursues his brother's traces not neglecting to seek clues in his published novels, from which he often quotes, but the detective chase is long and twisty. A bad-biographer figure appears; he is misnamed Goodman, and his ambition is to cash in on Sebastian's fame. Goodman gets everything wrong, is a cad when it comes to the truth. (More prophecy here: Nabokov seems to be addressing Andrew Field, his erroneous first biographer, thirty years before ever meeting him.) V. is not like Goodman, though. He is sensitive and imaginative; he can enter into his brother's secret life, enter but not go too far, because as Nabokov's second, highly scrupulous, biographer, Boyd, puts it, "the mortal quest for another's self" is impossible, that is, we are all unknowable to each other.

The book is equally wonderful and tiresome. Nabokov was the exponent of a zealous modernist approach by the time he wrote it, an approach that owed everything to Proust except what it owed James Joyce. He had emerged as a writer at the hour of the major modernist triumphs, nor did he arrive at his encounters with *À la Recherche du Temps Perdu* and *Ulysses* as a blank slate: already he had swallowed Russian literature whole, along with French and English literatures of several centuries, and as a precocious teen he had thrilled to the poetry of what is sometimes called the Russian Silver Age, which encompasses avant-garde movements like Symbolism and Acmeism. All had washed through him, much staying with him. As he made his way as a young writer, modernism was triumphing among taste-making critics, and his work of a most severe modernist cast dates from just shortly before *Sebastian Knight*.

The novel, about a novel-writing writer, is full of discussions about the writing of novels. There is a breathtaking confidence in the inherent fascination of the creative personality as subject. That this should be *the* focus of literate art is unquestioned, in a novel that submits much else to de-sentimentalized scrutiny. Proust had licensed this sort of thing in his beautiful, exhausting portraits of characters who are stand-ins for an artist-author. Joyce did also. *Sebastian Knight* reads at times like *A Portrait of a Portrait of the Artist as a Young Man*. The question has become how to address the sovereign author-subject, whether, through even the most devoted efforts, he can ever be comprehended in his full magnificence.

Nabokov embeds personal material throughout the book. The near catastrophe of the Guadanini affair belonged to the year just before he began writing *Sebastian*, and it colors everything. Instead of a novelist who nearly wrecks his life by abandoning a loving wife, the novel presents a novelist who *does* wreck his life, who abandons a devoted soul mate for a ravishing mistress, which leads to his ruin. The love letters that Nabokov wrote Guadanini appear in the form of letters that the dying Sebastian bequeaths his half brother, marked "to be destroyed." Brother V., acting unlike any previous biographer known to God or man, burns all of them unread. This consigns the truth about Sebastian Knight to the realm of the undiscoverable. From the point of view of the ordinary reader, the gesture is perverse and unsatisfying, if intellectually rigorous: the author seems to be rapping us on the knuckles, sending us home unfed for our own good.

THE STANFORD SUMMER NOW nearly over, the Nabokovs took a standard California vacation, heading for Yosemite Valley with a couple they knew from Berlin. They had last seen Bertrand and Lisbet Thompson in '37, in the South of France, at the height of the marital crisis. Lisbet, one of Véra's closest friends, might have sensed something amiss at that time, but four years later the family seemed fine, son Dmitri healthy and lively, Vladimir with many new butterfly captures, Véra having much enjoyed her long drive across the continent, her first encounter with America's "beauty spots."

Bertrand, almost old enough to be Vladimir's father, fascinated him. He was a character out of an American novel—something by Saul Bellow from the coming decade, a cross between *The Adventures of Augie March* and *Henderson the Rain King*, perhaps. He was African American. Born in Denver, he had grown up in Los Angeles with a divorced mother and earned a law degree at eighteen. Unable to find work because of his race, he became a Unitarian minister. He went for more study to Harvard, where he wrote *The Churches and the Wage Earners* while earning an advanced degree in economics. His ministry

Yosemite Valley, Yosemite National Park, 1939

took him to storied sites familiar to Hawthorne, among them Salem and Peabody. More transformations were coming. He became secretary of Boston's Chamber of Commerce, encountering there the management theories of Frederick Winslow Taylor, now widely credited with having invented scientific business management. In 1914, he wrote *Scientific Management*, a Taylorist treatise that dissented carefully from the master's orthodoxy.

In 1917, Thompson published *The Theory and Practice of Scientific Management*, still in print and "perhaps the most definitive work ever published on scientific management," according to *Public Administration: Balancing Power and Accountability*, the classic reference on public administration. Wait: even more changes were on the way. Offered a full professorship at Harvard, Thompson instead became a freelance business consultant and introduced Taylorist ideas in France, Germany, and Italy. The French Ministry of Armament hired him to rationalize shell-loading procedures. In the 1920s he became wealthy. He spent a year in the Philippines consulting for the Calami Sugar Cane Plantation and Processing Plant. In '29 he lost much of his wealth. By '37 he was driving an aged Studebaker, suggestive of a slow recovery from the collapse of his finances. By the time of the Yosemite trip, however, he was driving a brand-new '41 Studebaker Commander and pursuing yet another career, studying biochemistry at Berkeley. He researched cell biology throughout his sixties, and by his ninth decade he had become a cancer researcher in Uruguay, where he died, following a trip to Chicago to be honored by a business group, at eighty-seven.

Yosemite was not the oldest or largest American park. It was iconic, though, talismanic: John Muir had labored for decades to secure its preservation, Muir being in some ways the instrument of the original American protector, Abraham Lincoln, who, at the height of the Civil War, had troubled himself to sign a bill giving Yosemite Valley to the state of California for purposes of public recreation, thus establishing the precedent of federal set-asides. By the early forties the park looked much as it does today. Several buildings in the National Park Service rustic style had been built; Herbert Maier, who designed the Yosemite Museum, had been named a regional director of the Civilian Conservation Corps, and his guidebooks on design were followed in construction projects around the country, making the rustic style the default for public park buildings.

Nabokov had an affinity for American parks. Already on his first trip he had visited Great Smoky Mountains National Park, Hot Springs National Park, the Grand Canyon, and possibly Petrified Forest National Monument (close to Holbrook, Arizona, where he recorded having captured a specimen). He also visited several state parks—in Tennessee alone he collected in or near Mount Roosevelt State Forest, Frozen Head State Park, and Cumberland Mountain State Park. While in Yosemite he again used the "accredited member" credential granted him by the AMNH. So intent was he on chasing insects that he stepped on a sleeping bear.* The Nabokov-Thompsons were typical of their era in that they arrived in Yosemite by car.† They might have stayed at the housekeeping tents in the park ($11.50 per week for a family of three; slightly more with linen). Campgrounds where visitors paid no fees at all were also plentiful. They were like the motor camps of the twenties, with water hydrants, picnic tables, and communal restrooms, but on none of their western trips did the Nabokovs live in a tent they themselves carried—sleeping on the ground did not appeal.

When a party arrived from the San Francisco direction, as did the Nabokovs and Thompsons, Sentinel Rock, Cathedral Rocks, El Capitan, and Half Dome came suddenly, wantonly into view—it was one of the most remarked-upon tourist views in North America, an astonishment of granite. Car visitors, who, like the Thompsons and Nabokovs, often stayed for a week, frequently made day trips to Glacier Point, to the Mariposa Grove of sequoias, to Crane Flat, to Hetch Hetchy Valley before its flooding, and to the famous waterfalls.

Ralph Waldo Emerson had come to Yosemite. Presidents including Kennedy, Eisenhower, Roosevelt, Taft, and Grant had come to look and to acknowledge the grandeur. As with all of his western travels, Nabokov began with the desire to capture insects, and though his stepping on a bear suggests the usual obsessive focus, he had other purposes, too. To set Dmitri free in an outdoor setting was one, and to consort with Americans in an American place in an American way was, if not the first item on his agenda, agreeable. In coming years there would be many other trips to parks. In his correspondence with Altagracia de Jannelli, Vladimir had spoken of being charmed by "that old-fashioned something" that clings to America despite the "hard glitter," and the parks,

---

* Black bears were plentiful in the valley in the 1940s. Promotional films of the time show tourists feeding them by hand, and cubs were quick to learn how to stand on their hind legs to take food.

† Yosemite epitomized western tourism. Since the 1870s it had drawn travelers coming west by rail; railroads described its enchantments in the promotional guides they published, which, along with journalism about travel and travelers' memoirs, argued that Yosemite and sites like it justified tourism as much as did the castles and cathedrals of Europe. Travel to Europe had always been out of reach for many Americans; when World War I made Europe temporarily unavailable even to the wealthy, western tourism boomed. Henry Ford introduced the Model T in '08, and roads began to improve in many regions, although slowly. In 1913, a ban on cars in the valley was relaxed. The world's fairs at San Francisco and San Diego in '15 brought thousands of car travelers to California, and many included a Yosemite side trip.

whatever else they do, serve up a benign milieu with a democratic flavor, rustic in style (thus "old-fashioned"), inexpensive, healthful as long as you don't fall off a cliff, and a comfortable distance from what is daring and amoral and ultramodernistic (to cite cultural tendencies that Nabokov said he deplored).*

By September of '41, when the Nabokovs came, the park had made most of its accommodations to the automobile, including paving the roads. The weather in early September is blissful; rain is rare, and days in the valley are warm and cloudless. Nights are good for sleeping at four thousand feet. The Nabokovs were off the peak of the tourist season, although the cars that September before the war were still numerous. On September 9 or 10, the Thompsons drove them back to Palo Alto.

Nabokov might have made a whole life in the West. The lepping was fantastic, and he responded joyfully to the landscapes. Writing to the artist Dobuzhinsky, he remarked on the palette of the Grand Canyon, which he mistakenly located in New Mexico: the uncanny "cleaves and cleavages" of orange earth and blue sky were captivating, he reported. In Russian there are different words for light blue (*goluboy*) and dark blue (*siniy*), and Russian speakers have been shown to be faster at discriminating among blue tones than are English speakers. "How wonderful was the journeying!" he enthused. "I, of course, in the main caught butterflies along the road, but nonetheless by habit investigated the excellent landmarks."

Americans were a restless people. They liked to travel long distances, often for fun, which made them different from many Europeans. The greatest distances in the United States are in the West; westerners are therefore the biggest travelers. Nabokov soon became the kind of traveler who makes a daily record of miles driven and gallons of gas purchased, along with sights seen and motels or other lodgings

---

* It was a milieu that also made a good foil for what *was* daring and amoral and modernistic—for things that went on behind the facade. Thus, in his sexual delirium in fictional 1947–48, when he drives around America with a child captive, Humbert Humbert takes in many national parks and monuments. They visit Rocky Mountain, Mesa Verde, Crater Lake, Yellowstone, and Wind Cave National Parks, and the Bandolier, Gila Cliff Dwellings, Canyon de Chelly, and Death Valley National Monuments. They also stop at the National Elk Refuge, in Wyoming, the Lincoln Home National Historic Site, in Springfield, Illinois, and Mount Rushmore National Memorial.

patronized (including the occasional dude ranch). When away from his vacation haunts, he spoke of plans to return soon to his beloved West, and he mused that it would be ideal to own a cabin out there as well as a New York apartment, a cabin close to "a certain little bit of desert in Arizona which I shall never forget."

6.

From New York, where they arrived by train with colds, the family traveled on to Boston. Vladimir's two-week stint at Wellesley College the previous March had been so successful—so charming, so winning had he proved as a literary visitor—that the college had offered him a writer's residency at a yearly salary of three thousand dollars (an associate professor's pay). By September 18 they were established in an apartment in a house on a dead-end street in Wellesley, twenty miles west of Boston. "We have just rolled back to the East," he immediately wrote Edmund Wilson. "I shall be teaching Comparative Literature here for a year. I want very much to see you."

Anyone who reads of the falling-out that came, two decades later, for the two writers—a savage, ultra-public bloodletting, maybe the last such battle of the pedants ever to be staged in America, although who knows—must marvel at the emotional distance traveled, the tenor of friendship thus sacrificed. "Dear Bunny," Nabokov had written him in the early forties,

> I got that Guggenheim Fellowship. Thanks, dear friend. "You bring good luck" [Russian saying to this effect]. I have noticed that whenever you are involved in any of my affairs they are always successful. . . . I shall pass through N.Y. on Wednesday and Thursday, 14th and 15th of April. I shall ring you up if you tell me your 'phone number.

Wilson had urged Nabokov to apply for the Guggenheim. Then he had written an irresistible letter on his behalf.* In due course the fellowship came through. To say that Nabokov would have been awarded a Guggenheim at age forty-three without Wilson's help is fanciful—no previous grantee had been older than forty.

"Dear Wilson," Nabokov wrote him in '41,

> a big *spaseebo* for "contacting" me with *Decision* and "New Direction." I had a very pleasant talk with Klaus Mann [son of Thomas Mann and editor of *Decision*] who suggested my writing for them an article of 2000 words. I got a letter from James Laughlin and am sending him my English novel.

The English novel was *Sebastian Knight*, and Wilson, besides helping it see print, was at that time "contacting" Nabokov with many influential people, many publishing outlets. In December '40 Wilson had written,

> I am leaving *The New Republic* at the end of this week, but I have arranged with Bruce Bliven [president of the magazine's editorial board] to have you do a periodical article . . . about contemporary Russian literature. I suppose each one ought to be limited to perhaps 1,500 words, unless there is a good deal that is very important.

Earlier he had advised,

> In doing future reviews, please follow exactly *The New Republic* usage giving the title, author, etc., at the top. You will note that the number of pages and the [book] price are included. I am enclosing an example. Another thing: please do refrain from puns,

* Wilson had himself been the beneficiary of Guggenheim largesse, in 1935, when he visited the Soviet Union. From 1930–31, he served on the foundation's literary committee, where he became friends with Henry Allen Moe, Guggenheim head for forty years and, in Wilson's opinion, "the only man connected with a foundation I've ever known who didn't get fat and go to sleep on the job." After serving on the literary committee, Wilson was of the opinion that "the whole thing would be better run if—in the literary department, at any rate—Moe were able to make all the decisions himself." Moe and Wilson remained friends, and Wilson's occasional letters in support of fellow writers carried weight.

to which I see you have a slight propensity. They are pretty much excluded from serious journalism here.

Famously supportive—there is no writer in our literature who so loyally helped so many—Wilson is here pulling out all the stops. Connections to editors ready to pay ("I should think Klaus Mann would . . . pay you more than the [*Partisan Review*]"); advice on submitting clean copy; editorial advice (Nabokov sends him stories, poems, translations, and complete books, and Wilson reads all); strategizing over live editor management ("send it to Nigel Dennis, who is now in charge . . . reminding him that I had arranged . . . with Bliven"): here is the full gamut run. Wilson's helpfulness has been attributed by some Nabokov scholars to self-interest, to his intoxication with all things Russian, to his eagerness to practice the language. While there were benefits to associating with a Russian writer, such explanations fail to account for Wilson's remarkable energy and steadfastness. In '44, he brokered Nabokov's entrée into the *New Yorker* as a prose writer, a crucial maneuver of inestimable value to his career; chapters from what would be *Speak, Memory* soon began to appear, along with short stories, and Katharine White, fiction editor at the magazine, became another important Nabokov rabbi. Alexandra Tolstoy, of the Tolstoy Foundation, had warned him, "All Americans are completely uncultured, credulous fools," and while the verdict is still out on that, Nabokov's experience in his first years in America was that cultured, powerful people were magically available to him.

Without Wilson's stewardship, the road would have been different—there might not have been a road. Boyd, who derogates Wilson, allows that "Nabokov was introduced from the start to the best that American intellectual life had to offer," but the magus of this introduction was surely Wilson. *Sebastian Knight* had had no luck with publishers despite the best efforts of two agents, until Wilson interceded with Laughlin; thereafter, as Nabokov wrote, "My English novel has been accepted by New Directions, and Laughlin came to see me here from Los Angeles. . . . It will appear in Octobre."

Nabokov's prose could attract the attention of the *New Yorker* editors because Wilson had arranged for it to appear earlier in the *Atlantic*; his intimacy with Weeks of the *Atlantic* was such that when Nabokov asked for help getting payment from him, Wilson wrote, "I don't want to mention it to him, because I do a good deal of recommending as to what he ought to print . . . and he might resent it if I tried to tell him when he ought to pay his contributors as well."

Nabokov referred to Wilson as a "magician," intending praise of Wilson's cleverness, but he was speaking also of Wilson's effective sponsorship. Having translated a Pushkin monologue, he turned to Wilson with it: "Could you god-father it—if you find the translation all right?" he asked, meaning find a magazine for it. "And I would be immensely grateful to you for any corrections."*

Though there are arguments from self-interest, if we take Wilson at his word, and Nabokov at his, the grounds for their intense involvement for years were simple: they were good friends. They fell for each other, hard. "Dear Volodya," Wilson wrote him in March '45,

> I get aboard my boat [to Europe] Wednesday. . . . I'll be away four to six months. Good luck in the meantime. By the way, if you really want an academic job, you might write to Lewis Jones, president of Bennington and say that you are the person I mentioned to him. . . . Our conversations have been among the few consolations of my literary life through these last years—when my old friends have been dying, petering out or getting more and more neurotic, and the general state of the world has been so discouraging.

Wilson had lost a close friend, John Peale Bishop, the year before and would soon lose another, Paul Rosenfeld. In the year he met Nabokov, Scott Fitzgerald died, and Nabokov may have received some of the older-brotherly solicitude that Wilson—who had been close to Fitzgerald since college—might have tendered the needful Scott.

Nabokov's signs of affection are everywhere. That he wrote to Wilson personally, rather than having Véra write on his behalf (his later practice even with close friends), is notable, as is the quality of what he wrote: brilliant, fluent passages of radiant prose. In March '43, when Wilson was married to Mary McCarthy, Nabokov wrote, "In the middle of April I shall spend a day in New York . . . and I simply must see you both. I miss you a lot." In another letter, "You are one of the very few people in the world whom I keenly miss when I do not see them."

---

* We see here an innocent early stage in the two writers' involvement with translating Pushkin. Nabokov freely acknowledges Wilson's competence and is happy to offer him a stake in the enterprise. The bloody fight of twenty-five years hence would be premised, from Nabokov's point of view, on Wilson's utter incompetence as a reader and translator of Pushkin.

Nabokov had other male friends. His letters to them, mostly in Russian, are warm and engaging but nothing like the letters to Wilson. Just as in his love letters to Véra, he felt free to report his every literary gambit, his every career win, big or small:

I hope you will enjoy reading my new paper on Lepidoptera, which I am appending. Try reading it *between* the descriptions— though there are some fine bits in them too. I have just finished writing a story for the *Atlantic* (Weeks rang me up 4 times to get another one after "Mlle O" [fifth chapter of the future *Speak, Memory*]—and I got a letter from an Institution called "Better Speech" something, asking me the permission to use a paragraph from "Mlle O" in their manual . . .).

The recitation of triumphs verges on the insufferable. Nabokov blamed Wilson for this: "if I keep talking about my affairs in such detail it is because I feel it is you who have given me the great Push."

Mary McCarthy, trying to account for their devotion, said, "they had an absolute ball together. Edmund was always in a state of *joy* when Vladimir appeared; he *loved* him." There were raucous, bibulous visits back and forth, to Wilson's houses on the Cape and to the residences the Nabokovs rented. Vladimir told biographer Andrew Field that Wilson was "in certain ways my closest" friend; nor did he say, "my closest *American* friend." Their companionability, even in a political sense, needs to be noted, considering their intense disagreements over the Soviet state. Both were extreme individualists and free-speech near fundamentalists. Both were philo-Semitic at a time when prominent English-language authors—Eliot, Pound, Hemingway, Fitzgerald, many others—signaled a sham gentility by disdaining Jews. Nabokov's review of *The Guillotine at Work*, which failed to appear in the *New Republic* despite a preface by Wilson—the magazine wished to take a less hostile stance toward Stalin in the winter of 1942—acknowledged that history needs idealists, which was Wilson's position, too: "without the impetus of such dreams the world would soon cease to turn." Moreover, there were people "to whom the notion of human misery is so utterly revolting that they will plunge into any adventure that holds the faintest chance of improving the world," and this "discloses the kind of unconscious optimism which man, perhaps fortunately, will never forsake."

*   *   *

NABOKOV'S DUTIES AT WELLESLEY were nominal: three classroom appearances in October and three in January, with six community-wide talks given over the course of the year. "I am expected to participate in 'social life,' " he told Wilson, but that was it—light duty and lots of time to write. He continued his report of projects undertaken, of wins: "I have sold another story to Weeks . . . it will appear in the Christmas number. . . . I have been working a good deal lately in my special branch of entomology, two papers of mine have appeared in a scientific journal." He would produce "a rather ambitious work on mimetic phenomena," he promised Wilson, as if Wilson had been waiting to hear this.

Wellesley sustained him for seven years. His employment status was always irregular, following the bumpy course of the war. Shortly after Pearl Harbor, with budget cuts pending and the Soviet Union still in bad repute, college administrators were lukewarm toward Slavic studies, and the stock of Slavic experts declined. With tales of Soviet suffering gaining currency, and news of the Soviets' brilliant, hard-to-be-believed victory over the German Sixth Army at Stalingrad, whereby Hitler's forecast of world conquest became incorrect, a vogue for things Russian set in. Nabokov was not offered employment for fall of '42, after his artist-in-residence year, but by spring of '43 he was at Wellesley teaching on a noncredit basis, and by academic year 1944–45 he was a near professor: the extracurricular instructor in Russian.

His anti-Soviet line, insisting on an equivalence between Communist and fascist tyrannies, made Mildred Helen McAfee, Wellesley's president, uncomfortable. Headed for Washington to become the first director of the WAVES (Women Accepted for Volunteer Emergency Service), McAfee did not see his pox-on-both-your-houses stance as quite correct. She resisted pressure from a wealthy alumna to hire him in spring of '42. It was only after she had left for Washington, and after a year in the vocational wilderness for Nabokov, that conditions favored a return.

His teaching was expert, if eccentric. He was not a wrong-footed foreign lecturer who, straining in a language not his own, professes into a cultural void, into a human unknown; he carefully configured his pedagogy to his audience, and he had a gift for imagining that audience—for imagining any group of other minds. He might have mused upon his own creativity for a year, as a cosseted writer-in-residence, but instead he devised specific talks for specific situations—for students taking Spanish courses, he spoke about Don Quixote's appeal to Russian dissenters, for Italian students he dilated upon Leonardo, and for students taking zoology he spoke on lepidopterological mimicry, a special interest of his. In his community-wide addresses, he chose writers the campus population could be expected to be familiar with: Chekhov, Turgenev, Tyutchev (a mistake there), and Tolstoy; of course Tolstoy.

He esteemed Tolstoy greatly. His father had been acquainted with the author, as a fellow fighter for social reform; as a ten-year-old, Vladimir waited while his father spoke with a "little white-bearded old man" on a street in St. Petersburg, after which his father commented, "That was Tolstoy." Tolstoy was so large, so indisputably the monument of the Russian novel, that Vladimir's relations with him could not but be complex. Sometimes he found the master ludicrous as well as great. "Have you noticed," he wrote Wilson, "when reading *War and Peace* the difficulties Tolstoy experienced in forcing mortally wounded Bolkonsky to come into geographical . . . contact with Natasha? It is painful to watch the way the poor fellow is dragged and pushed and shoved." In one way Tolstoy was unimpeachable, however: it was his ability to match the passage of time within a story to readers' natural feel for time, so that, carried along on the great Volga of narrative, readers felt that everything happened more or less when it ought to, at the pace, seemingly, of "real life." Nabokov's own way with time is also often splendidly right-feeling, if complicated by modernist structural disjuncts—underneath all there is a deft modeling of others' consciousness, others' capacities, generous sympathy with an audience.

JAMES LAUGHLIN, HIS PUBLISHER, visited Boston in May '42. Their first book together had sold little—America had entered a world war just as an obscure Russian was publishing a novel of epistemological doubt—but Laughlin did not turn away from him; he remained eager to publish him, and in defiance of the commercial fate of *Sebastian Knight* and of the tumult of the war, they agreed on two more books to do together, a study of the Ukrainian writer Nikolai Gogol and a volume of translations from Pushkin and Tyutchev.

Laughlin was in his twenties. He had graduated from Harvard only three years before. He was the great-grandson of an Irish immigrant who had founded a steel fortune. His upbringing was privileged; his great-uncle Henry Clay Frick was a coal magnate and chairman of Carnegie Steel, and Laughlins were industrialists of weight and influence. James decided early that "I would not go into the mill," yet his turn away from the family business did not include a turn away from the family; as he wrote when given an award many years later, "none of this [the publishing house he founded and its literary successes] would have been possible without the industry of my ancestors, the canny Irishmen who immigrated in 1824 from County Down [and] built up what became the fourth largest steel company in the country. I bless them with every breath."

He wrote poetry himself. But Ezra Pound, to whom Laughlin made pilgrimage in the mid-thirties, advised him to become a publisher instead, and Pound's recommendations of worthy writers to pursue helped make him *the* independent publisher in the English language in the twentieth century. In May '42, with no academic job in the offing, Nabokov was greatly buoyed to have books to write for him. Gogol could be personally useful, too: to write of Gogol would be another way to introduce himself, to further the planned Russification of the American reader.

Though he worked hard he soon bogged down. The problem was that quotations from Gogol needed for his book had been poorly translated by others. Constance Garnett's translation of Gogol's *The Government Inspector* was "dry shit," he told Laughlin, and his days were taken up with retranslating passages from it and others from *Dead Souls.* Garnett's version of the novel had appeared in '23 and was the standard English translation. But Gogol was too important a writer to be botched; he had brought a bizarre, fantastical mind and a bright new eye to Russian letters, and Nabokov needed to evidence that, to write about it. "Before his and Pushkin's advent,"

> Russian literature was purblind. . . . It did not see color for itself but merely used the hackneyed combinations of blind noun and dog-like adjective that Europe had inherited from the ancients. . . . The sky was blue, the dawn red, the foliage green. . . . It was Gogol (and after him Lermontov and Tolstoy) who first saw yellow and violet at all.

---

* Nabokov does not ridicule Garnett directly in his book, although his chapter on *Dead Souls* begins with this unequivocal assertion: "The old translations of 'Dead Souls' into English are absolutely worthless and should be expelled from all public and university libraries."

A famous passage from *Dead Souls*—made famous by Nabokov, in two books and countless lectures—reads, in the serviceable, certainly not illiterate, Garnett version,

> The big overgrown and neglected old garden which stretched at the back of the house, and coming out behind the village, disappeared into the open country, seemed the one refreshing feature in the great rambling village, and in its picturesque wildness was the only beautiful thing in the place. The interlacing tops of the unpruned trees lay in clouds of greenery and irregular canopies of trembling foliage against the horizon. The colossal white trunk of a birch-tree, of which the crest had been snapped off by a gale or a tempest, rose out of this green maze and stood up like a round shining marble column; the sharp slanting angle, in which it ended instead of in a capital, looked dark against the snowy whiteness of the trunk, like a cap or a blackbird.

Nabokov makes this,

> An extensive old garden which stretched behind the house and beyond the estate to lose itself in the fields, alone seemed, rank and rugged as it was, to lend a certain freshness to these extensive grounds and alone was completely picturesque in its vivid wildness. The united tops of trees that had grown wide in liberty spread above the skyline in masses of green clouds and irregular domes of tremulous leafage. The colossal white trunk of a birchtree deprived of its top, which had been broken off by some gale or thunderbolt, rose out of these dense green masses and disclosed its rotund smoothness in midair, like a well proportioned column of sparkling marble; the oblique, sharply pointed fracture in which, instead of a capital, it terminated above, showed black against its snowy whiteness like some kind of headpiece or a dark bird.

Both versions seem a bit wordy after seventy years. Nabokov cares about that not at all; his standard is not concision but fidelity to Gogol's words and pace (*"udar molnii,"* for example, is rendered as "gale or thunderbolt," not as "a gale or a tempest," which flirts with redundancy, aside from being incorrect). He manages a certain streaming quality in the prose, a subtle onrushingness absent from the Garnett. His first sentence comes to rest on the exciting "vivid wildness"; Garnett concludes instead with the benign, doughy "the only beautiful thing in the place."

This passage of lyric description—somewhat unusual in *Dead Souls*—may have excited Nabokov for reason of its thoroughness, its air of going the whole hog, taking all the time it needs to make its subject live. That subject is a bit of greenery, no more—nature and man's diggings and plantings all run together, higgledy-piggledy, somewhere in Russia. One can walk on, pay it not a moment's thought, or—wait a second—look again. *See* it thoroughly and try afterward to put it in words, using metaphors if necessary, being fanciful and funny and even ominous: "showed black against its snowy whiteness," Nabokov writes, "like some kind of headpiece or a dark bird." (Garnett mistranslates and trivializes, makes cuddly, with "a cap or a blackbird.")

The passage continues,

Strands of hop [a sinuous, twining vine], after strangling the bushes of elder, mountain ash and hazel below, had meandered all over the ridge of the fence whence they ran up at last to twist around that truncate birchtree halfway up its length. Having reached its middle, they hung down from there and were already beginning to catch at the tops of other trees, or had suspended in the air their intertwined loops and thin clinging hooks which were gently oscillated by the air.

This is Nabokov. Garnett does not cut the passage, as other translators had done, but she loses detail, turning the vine's grasping hooks into the vaguer "tendrils faintly stirring in the breeze." Maybe she has begun to tire, to run out of words. (Nabokov *never* runs out of words.) His "truncate birchtree," which reenacts the shattering of a trunk, is for her a simple "broken birch-tree," and his "oblique, sharply slanting fracture," suggesting the violence of the tree-topping but also the shattering of bone—stark white like a birch—is in her milder version a "sharp slanting angle."

A bit of green background, no more. There are millions—billions—of such views to be had in Mother Russia. Someone hoping to write his own books may feel inspired, seeing how much can be done with even the waste places. *Dead Souls* is in a large sense a study of waste places, a bringing to scandalous, teeming life of Russian backwaters and Nowheresvilles, and Nabokov, who first read the novel as a youth, might have felt a sort of invitation from the future. By happy accident this garden, which belonged to the fictional landowner Plyushkin, came to be the focus of a question on Nabokov's honors exams at Cambridge, in 1922; asked to describe the neglected garden, he deliriously ran away with the question, recalling detail after detail.

SUMMER OF '42, NEAR-PENNILESS, the Nabokovs returned to the Karpovich place in Vermont, where they spent an impecunious but sunny July and August. Dmitri, eight years old, had been sick most of the winter and had just had his tonsils out. He was a good-looking, stork-shaped boy whose long limbs and neck were striking—by age ten he had nearly caught up with his tall mother in height, and a few years later he would top out at a full six foot five, a species of young American giant, confident, athletic, car crazy.

In the coming years, the Nabokovs scrimped on everything but his education. Véra sometimes lamented that his natural sweetness had been worn away by contact with rougher American boys. Both parents were anxious that he get the best education affordable, and though Véra feared that American coarsening, both recognized that a process of acculturation was in order. Dmitri would recall his Wellesley days in a memoir published in the 1980s:

> I ride my balloon-tired bicycle to a neighborhood school on my own . . . along a tree-shaded lane. We live in a shingled house on Appleby Road, whose name will remain mnemonically entwined with the green apples that grow in the leafy depths at its dead end, and that serve as missiles for elaborately staged battles. In the spring I shall be initiated into the rites of marbles by the girl next door. Her mysterious femininity at twelve . . . will appear unattainably mature to me at eight, and my crush will remain undeclared.

Often dissatisfied with the schools they find for him—quick to pull him out and put him in others—the Nabokovs are gratified when Americanizing is on the program:

> One wonderful thing will happen here [at a school in Cambridge, Massachusetts]. Mrs. Ruedebush, the music teacher . . . will notice that I, a European child with no grounding in traditional American singing, have trouble carrying the tune of hymns sung during the school assemblies. She will take me under her musical

wing, give me lessons in solfege and piano, and begin training my high soprano. . . . Enthusiasm will replace frustration. I shall go on to sing in choirs and student performances, and eventually reward her early efforts by becoming a professional operatic basso.

True conversion, though, happens on the athletic field:

I sit on the lawny grounds of Dexter School. It is the day of spring sports awards. I entered Dexter three years ago [1944], still quite unequipped for life as an American boy. The school's headmaster, Francis Caswell, has been the second superb pedagogue of my life. He has taught me not only Cicero and Caesar, but also how to bat a ball and throw a block, how to give a firm handshake while looking the other squarely in the eye, how to be a "citizen." . . . I have managed to win maroon Dexter Ds in various sports, but still think of myself as a skinny, imperfectly coordinated outsider. . . . I am in mid-reverie when I hear my name announced as overall winner of the spring sports contest, a cumulative competition comprised of track and field events plus such things as baseball throwing. I look around, thinking I have misheard.

Dmitri and Vladimir in Vermont, Véra traveled to Boston to find them an apartment. The one they could afford, at 8 Craigie Circle, Cambridge, has become a site of pilgrimage for Nabokov fans: here they stayed longer than anywhere else in America, in a third-floor flat (No. 35) in a building of six stories. The redbrick structure, with vertically coursed, bright-white ashlar blocks, has an elegant wood-paneled lobby and a secure feel, with a small courtyard leading to an oaken front door. The flat itself was cramped, and Nabokov once called it "dingy." He had to write "under an old lady with feet of stone and above a young woman with hypersensitive hearing," but during the war he was proud enough of the place to draw his sister Elena a floor plan and to describe watching from an upstairs window as Dmitri, "looking very trim, wearing a gray suit and a reddish jockey cap," set out for school in the morning.

Nabokov would set out an hour later. His daily walk to the Museum of Comparative Zoology, at Harvard, where he had begun to volunteer, took him along level streets beneath mature eastern hardwoods—he seems proud as he informs Elena that Véra and he live "in a suburb . . . in the Harvard area." His walk of fifteen minutes took him past tennis courts gone to weeds during the war. The transformation of Harvard—

8 Craigie Circle, Cambridge, where the Nabokovs lived from 1942 to 1948

its depopulation by ordinary students and its repopulation as a military training facility, with thousands of soldiers, ROTC candidates, and lab workers taking over the grounds—is nowhere reflected in his letters or other writings of the time. As a recent immigrant he can be expected to have been less comprehending of changes than a local; still, his not noticing, or not recording, what he saw suggests his absorption in private matters.

Those were lepidopteral, mainly. Nathan Banks, head of the Department of Entomology at Harvard, welcomed him when Vladimir wandered into the MCZ one day, bearing specimens from the Grand Canyon. Banks knew some of the same people Nabokov knew in New York, and Vladimir's energy and specialist knowledge made him good to have around. Positions at the MCZ would soon go unfilled as men were called away to war. Banks, though a professional entomologist, was somewhat at sea among the lepidoptera—his areas of expertise included wasps, lacewings, fish flies, and mites (he was probably best known for his *Treatise on the Acarina, or Mites*, 1905). To sister Elena Vladimir described his good luck in landing where he had:

> My museum—famous throughout America (and throughout what used to be Europe)—is . . . part of Harvard University. . . . My laboratory occupies half of the fourth floor. Most of it is taken up by rows of cabinets, containing sliding glass cases of butterflies. I am custodian of these absolutely fabulous collections. We have butterflies from all over the world; many are type specimens (i.e., the very same specimens used for the original descriptions, from the 1840s until today). Along the windows extend tables holding my microscopes, test tubes, acids, papers, pins, etc. I have an assistant, whose main task is spreading specimens. . . . My work enraptures but utterly exhausts me.

The collections were in disarray—surprising at such an institution. Sometimes he put in fourteen-hour days at his worktable, which caused Véra to fear that he would be lost to literature. "To know that no one before you has seen" what you are seeing among the specimens, he wrote, "to immerse yourself in the wondrous crystalline world of the microscope, where silence reigns, circumscribed by its own horizon . . . all this is so enticing that I cannot describe it." After a long day of complete fascination, he would stumble home, "already in the blue darkness of winter, the hour of evening newspapers . . . and radio phonographs [that] burst into song in the illumined apartments of large ivy-colored buildings."

Lepidopterology was solace, sanctuary: he needed to be moving on, proceeding with American-style alacrity to make a future as a writer, yet he also needed to absorb, to adjust, to become. He expressed his perplexed state of mind to Wilson, whose own career provided a daunting example of self-furthering: "Funny—to know Russian better than any living person—in America at least—and more English than any Russian in America,—and to experience such difficulty in getting a university job." He was in possession of authentic goods, literary riches, that he knew one day could secure his future. By virtue of the same playful fate that had arranged for him to be born in the last year of the nineteenth century, exactly one hundred years after the birth of his idol, Pushkin, then had arranged for him a ringside seat at the Revolution and the arrival of the Nazis, he found himself in a country badly in need of basic education in matters Russian at that rare moment when America was asking to be taught. Some of his obsessing over issues of translation betrays an anxiety of near possession, a kind of greed. He knew things others did not, had read more deeply and passionately—*he* should be the one delivering the Russian treasure, to claim the new audience.

Meanwhile, he was half out of the living sea of his Russian, half into the dimensionless American air. After complaining that he had bogged down with Gogol because he had to retranslate so much, he stated the problem more honestly: "The book is progressing slowly because I get more and more dissatisfied with my English. When I have finished, I shall take three months' vacation with my ruddy robust Russian muse."

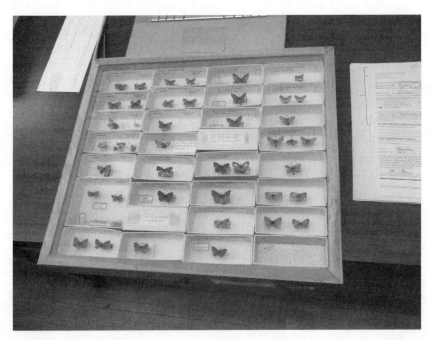

Blue butterflies, collected by Nabokov and others, Museum of Comparative Zoology, Harvard

The truth was that his muse was being left behind.* "I envy so bitterly your intimacy with English words," he wrote Wilson. Whether or not he truly envied Wilson's English, he was effectively tongue-tied: the "urge to write is sometimes terrific, but as I cannot do it in Russian I do not do it at all." He wrote little fiction, only a bit of what would become the dystopian novel *Bend Sinister* (1947). His later descriptions of the ordeal of changing his language have a weary tone, but that does not mean he was not suffering. Isaiah Berlin, who had made the same switch at a younger age, felt loss and regret for the rest of his life, as he expressed to a friend:

> It is our Russian conversations which I adore & look forward to & think about and remember the longest. . . . I can never talk so . . . to anybody in England . . . Russian to me is more imaginative, intimate and poetical than any other [language]—& I feel a curious transformation of personality when I speak it—as if everything becomes easier to express, & the world brighter and more charming.

Tormented by his loss—feeling unreal in English and, incidentally, barely able to pay the rent at Craigie Circle (sixty dollars a month)—he completed a wonderful book, the first manifestly brilliant work of his American years. *Nikolai Gogol* is a work of urgent, amusing directness, the ten-dollar words of his usual style mostly absent. He plunges the reader—his hoped-for American reader—into the bizarre *Slav profonde* material right off: Gogol is dying in Rome. He is forty-two years old and has come under the care of "diabolically energetic" foreign doctors who apply leeches to his long, pointed nose, a nose that he used to touch to his lower lip to impress people. The leeches have been placed inside it, the better to feed from the tender membranes, and a Frenchman, himself a perfect leech, orders that Gogol's hands be restrained when he tries to brush them away.

Nabokov's own face, exhibiting a twisted grin, hovers above the tableau. "The scene is unpleasant and has a human appeal which I deplore," he declares—and here is Point One in "Nabokovian Aesthetics for Americans": the idea that claims on fellow feeling are reprehensible,

---

* He continued to write poetry in Russian well into his seventh decade. Notable examples, collected in his compilation *Poems and Problems* (1970), are "To Prince S.M. Kachurin" and "From the Gray North."

those shameless pluckings of the chords of compassion that literary writers have too long indulged in. The book develops in short form the argument presented at whopping length in *The Gift*: how the dangerous bacillus of social compassion came to infect Russian literature, leading to its near extinction. Angels of reform in the Russian intelligentsia became dictators of taste—if you were not writing against tsarist repression, then you did not deserve to be read—became, inevitably, proto-commissars, precursors of the Soviet beasts who *really* knew how to deal with writers who didn't behave. Nabokov arrived at his hatred of thought policing through experience of the twentieth century, but in the phrase "human appeal which I deplore" there is a glimpse of an arrogant prodigy, a youthful reader of the Russian Futurists and Acmeists, disgusted by old-lady poetry of the heart-tugging sort.

Gogol exhibits a "queer genius," Nabokov goes on, and here is Point Two of his program: great, immortal artists are all *sui generis*. They may appear in suggestive pairings, like Pushkin and Gogol (who both enjoyed fame in the 1830s), but they are not exemplars of "movements" or "developments" in the history of culture. Real writers are inherently "strange; it is only your healthy second-rater who seems to the grateful reader to be a wise old friend, nicely developing the reader's own notions of life." Nabokov is tipping us to something about himself. We will find him daring, he believes; we will also find him a bit cold. The forthright talk of "second-raters" and "geniuses," of "the greatest artist that Russia has yet produced"—this discourse was already old-fashioned in 1942. Writers were discussed more often in terms of schools they could be assimilated to, or were hardly identified as human subjects at all, by critics shy of speculating about their intentions. Nabokov lays claim to the old categories, and by subtle inference to the mantle of genius. Here he is being modernist as well as old-fashioned: Joyce and Eliot, Proust, Pound, Stein, Woolf, Faulkner—these were writers who believed in the old idea, the notion of the towering, unexampled masterwork, the literary product that could stun an entire civilization.* Each suspected that he or she had written such works. The decline from this position to gentle mockery of the whole idea, to recognition of the special privilege enjoyed by certain categories of author or work, to an ironical sense of how any creation is full of shameless gleanings from other cultural

---

* From among this group of writers Nabokov recognized only Proust and Joyce as authentic masters.

artifacts: this was all off in the future, though not too far off. Nabokov might have been the last true, outspoken believer. His assertiveness about geniushood and how you, if you imagine yourself a writer like him, are laughably deluded, betrays unease, an awareness that the ground was shifting beneath his feet. Gogol, in any event, was such a genius. Gogol, with but a wave of his magic wand—maybe of his big nose—had called the Russian novel into being.

STRUGGLING WITH THE LANGUAGES, he consoled himself with science-speak. No one at Harvard had anything like his knowledge of the Blues, the tribe of butterflies that he had decided to make his specialty, following William Comstock's example. But here was more of the same bounty, the plenitude of needful work and glaring niches to fill, that marked his relation to Russian literature in America. To Wilson he wrote, "It is amusing to think that I managed to get into Harvard with a butterfly as my sole backer." The first scientific papers he wrote, using museum specimens for taxonomic context, show him in a process of education like the one with Wilson—hoping to learn the ropes, he relies freely on his American friends, on Comstock and another researcher at the AMNH, Charles Duncan Michener, in particular. "If my paper seems all right to you will you please pass it on," he wrote Comstock after an exhaustive back-and-forth about his first research, "to whatever journal or Proceedings you think would publish it." Later, using the same tone he used with Wilson, he wrote, "I am taking advantage of your kindness but it is your own fault if I have grown accustomed to it."

His science writing was confident—proto-Nabokovian. The first notes he ever made about butterflies, when he was a boy in Russia, had been in English; he admired the British journal *The Entomologist* and learned scientific terms from it, and English was thereafter his language of science. What gave him joy in chasing and writing about bugs is a large question, tantamount to the question of what gave him joy in life, but part of it was surely to have the chance to write to an extreme degree of detail in a style developed over centuries by cognoscenti who, by their command of a style, signaled fellowship with one another. One representative sample of his own science prose, from "Some new or little-known Nearctic *Neonympha* (Lepidoptera: Satyridae)," published in '43 in the Harvard-connected journal *Psyche*:

A broad cinereous border heavily stippled with purplish black transverse striae, merged with the cinereous underside of the fringe and limited inwardly by the arches of the second discal and subterminal lines, occupies the whole outer third (excepting a vineleaf-shaped, as viewed from base, fulvous brown spot between second discal and subterminal lines . . .), thus completely enclosing the ocelli and other markings to be mentioned.

He is here describing a butterfly's secondary wings. Eventually he developed a system for the complete mapping of an insect's wing markings, scale by colored scale. He had been working on his butterfly prose since boyhood, and now he was a near adept, on his way to becoming a master. Imitation or parody had provided him, as with his literary prose, with a basis for launching into matters full of significance for him, in this case, into knotty problems in lepidopteral systematics and evolutionary theory.

7.

Because of Vladimir's hard work as a volunteer, Nathan Banks approved an appointment for him as a research fellow at the MCZ for 1942–43, at the slim salary of one thousand dollars. Véra contributed to the family finances, giving language lessons and working off and on as a Harvard secretary, but she had "married a genius," a friend of hers remembered her thinking, and she saw herself as his support, seeing to it "that he had every opportunity" to write. Their insecure position prompted her to take several wise managerial steps. She made sure he wrote charmingly to two professors at Wellesley who had liked him, to say that he hoped to be invited back again, and she typed up his CV with a list of topics he could speak on, sending that to an organization that put together lecture tours. The agency booked him at a number of colleges in the South and the Midwest, and he set off in October '42 by train, interrupting his work on the Gogol book to do so.

Chichikov's travels in *Dead Souls* found an echo, although without infernal overtones. In Springfield, Illinois, where he was taken on a tour of Lincoln's home and grave, he met a character straight out of the Gogol story "Ivan Fyodorovich Shponka and His Aunt," a man whose passion in life was flagpoles. (The character Shponka dreams of flagpoles.) The Illinois man was "a creepily silent melancholic of somewhat clerical cast," Vladimir wrote Véra, "with a small stock of automatic questions. . . . He livened up and flashed his eyes one single time . . . having noticed that the flagpole by the Lincoln mausoleum had been replaced by a new, taller one." The letters from this second American exploration are intimate but also large. Something about America invites alert vagabonding, along with attempts to embrace the country entire: Audubon's letters and journals, Whitman's reports from the open road (mostly fictional), the five thousand journal pages of Lewis and Clark, Tocqueville's reports on 1830s frontier settlements—these are but a few of the antecedents to the chatty, imaginative letters that Nabokov sent Véra. From Valdosta, Georgia, he wrote on October 14,

> Arrived here, on the Florida border, yesterday around 7 P.M. and leave for Tennessee on Monday. . . . The college has booked a beautiful room for me as well as paid for all my meals, so that . . . I won't be spending anything before I go. They gave me a car as well, but I only look at it, not daring to drive it. The college [Georgia State College for Women], with a charming campus among pines and palms, is a mile out of town. It is very Southern here. I took a walk down the only big street, in the velvet of the twilight and the azure of the neon lamps, and came back, overcome by a big Southern yawn.

Wherever possible he hunted insects. From Hartsville, South Carolina, he wrote,

> After lunch the college biologist drove me in her car to . . . the coppices by the lake, where I took some remarkable hesperids and various kinds of pierids. It is hard to convey the bliss of roaming through this strange bluish grass, between blossoming bushes (one bush here is full of bright berries, as if colored in a cheap Easter purple—an utterly shocking chemical hue . . .) [A]fter "The Tragedy of Tragedy" [one of his talks], I went collecting again. . . . A Presbyterian minister, Smyth, turned up, a passionate butterfly collector and son of the famous lepidopterologist Smyth, about whom I know a lot.

Not only an enormous country: one full of butterfly men. Though anxious about how his talks would be received and recognizing the futility of the venture—profiting little because he was forced to pay for his own travel—and wishing he was home so he could write or go to the MCZ, Vladimir, a still young man with a good digestion, strikes a tone reminiscent of Mark Twain's in *Roughing It*, or Whitman's when he wrote about the fascinations of Manhattan's Broadway. "Couldn't sleep at all," Nabokov tells us early on, since at the numerous stations the wild jolts and thunderings of the train cars' copulations . . . allowed no rest. By day, lovely landscapes skimmed past—huge trees in a profusion of forms—with their somehow oil-painted shade and iridescent greenery reminding me . . . of Caucasian valleys. . . . When I got off in Florence [South Carolina], I was immediately surprised by the heat and the sun, and the gaiety of the shadows—like what one feels upon reaching the Riviera from Paris.

He realized—probably not while he wrote, but again, who knows—that he had the makings of another book. Comical interludes (waiting for a ride to a college, he overhears someone in a hotel lobby wondering why the Russian professor hasn't shown up. "But I am the Russian professor!" Nabokov exclaims); revelatory encounters with Southern racialism ("In the evenings, those who have children rarely go out because . . . they have no one to leave the kids with; Negro servants never sleep over in the whites' homes—it is not allowed—and they cannot have white servants because they cannot work with blacks"); further romps in the sun-shot, weirdly foliaged Southern wilds, chasing insects: the trip aroused and provoked him, led him to think and understand, made him want to write.

The tone resembles that of the letters he wrote in '37. But he is conducting no clandestine affair this time, and the self-pleased tone of the glamorous young writer toasted by *le tout Paris* has been dialed back. He still admires himself a lot and reports evoking extravagant regard in others, but he shows himself as a bumbler, too, as someone who chats up the professors at a college and then reaches into his pocket for his lecture notes and finds nothing. ("It came out very smoothly" anyway.) He meets iconic African Americans, among them W. E. B. Du Bois, and writes from Spelman College that he is at "a black Wellesley" presided over by a formidable woman with a wart beside her nose, someone who requires him to attend chapel with four hundred students in the morning. As he later told interviewers, who hoped to pin down exactly what kind of reactionary or paleo-liberal or reactionary paleo-liberal he was, racial segregation disgusted him. "To the west, cotton plantations," he wrote from South Carolina,

and the prosperity of the numerous Cokers [founders of Coker College], who seem to own half of Hartsville, is founded on this very cotton industry. It is picking time now, and the "darkies" (an expression that jars me, reminding me . . . of the "Zhidok" ["Yid"] of western Russian landowners) pick in the fields, getting a dollar for a hundred "bushels"—I am reporting these interesting facts because they stuck mechanically in my ears.

He is not a Northern liberal shocked to see that things are different in South Carolina, but he goes far, for him, in the direction of recognizing a social evil and showing concern. "My lecture about Pushkin . . . was greeted with almost comical enthusiasm," he tells Véra, after informing his Spelman audience that Pushkin had had an African grandfather. He is pandering, a little, but pandering with a wholesome truth.

These letters later figured in plans for a sequel to *Speak, Memory*, a book he hoped to write someday about his American experience. He would call that book *Speak On, Memory* (or maybe *More Evidence*, or maybe *Speak, America*)—it was to have been about his friendship with Bunny Wilson and his years of exploring the West, with his college lecture tour from the first year of the war as foundation. The bundled letters followed him to Switzerland when he resettled there in the sixties, but the book never quite took form. Rereading his letters was for the older Nabokov intensely moving. "I need not tell you what agony it was," he wrote Edmund Wilson's widow in 1974, two years after Wilson's death, "rereading the exchanges belonging to the early radiant era of our correspondence." He had waited too long to harvest the book, as sometimes happens, even with writers of "genius."

IN MAY '43, NABOKOV told Laughlin that he had finally finished *Nikolai Gogol*, a book that "has cost me more trouble than any other I have composed. . . . I never would have accepted your suggestion to do it had I known how many gallons of brain-blood it would absorb." It had been hard to write because "I had first to create" the writer (that is, translate him) "and then discuss him. . . . The recurrent jerk of switching from one rhythm of work to the other has quite exhausted me. . . . I am very weak, smiling a weak smile, as I lie in my private maternity ward, and expect roses."

Laughlin was puzzled by the manuscript. He had wanted a sturdy introduction, to bring Gogol to the attention of readers who might have barely heard of him, and Nabokov had written an eccentric gloss in the manner of William Carlos Williams's *In the American Grain* or D. H. Lawrence's *Studies in Classic American Literature*. Those works had first appeared in the twenties. Lawrence was another European exile, someone who had struggled to find himself in America, and his study, like Nabokov's, is furiously concerned with the flavor of authorial voice. Hoping to salvage some "classic" American writers—Franklin, Cooper, Crèvecoeur, Poe, Hawthorne, Melville, Dana, Whitman—from their reputation as authors of "children's books," Lawrence argues for their irreducible "art-speech." The "old American art-speech contains an alien quality," he says,

> which belongs to the American continent and to nowhere else. . . . There is a new voice in the old American classics. The world has declined to hear it, and has babbled about children's stories. . . . The world fears a new experience more than it fears anything. . . . The world is a great dodger, and the Americans the greatest.

Lawrence's book cost him much trouble, as did Nabokov's. It grew out of a similar hope: to find in America an audience to replace an audience in Europe with which he felt increasingly out of step. He roughs up his classic Americans in much the way Nabokov does Gogol.* Nevertheless, it seems unlikely that Nabokov had read Lawrence's book. Lawrence was one of the authors he never mentioned without an ostentatious sneer; he had read some Lawrence, he admitted (the novels probably), and Lawrence's daring way with sex and the immense notoriety of *Lady Chatterley's Lover*, the most banned book of the twentieth century, were Lawrentian developments so relevant to Nabokov's future career that his sneer, when he affected it, might have signaled a debt of an uncomfortable size.

In the first chapter of *Studies* Lawrence says,

> There is a new feeling in the old American books, far more than there is in the modern American books, which are pretty empty of any feeling. . . . Art-speech is the only truth. An artist is usually a . . . liar, but his art, if it be art, will tell you the truth of his day. . . . The old American artists were hopeless liars. But they were artists. . . . And you can please yourself, when you read *The Scarlet Letter*, whether you accept what that sugary, blue-eyed little darling of a Hawthorne has to say for himself, false as all darlings are, or whether you read the impeccable truth of his art-speech. . . .

---

* Nabokov's final judgment was that Gogol was a trivializer of his monumental talent.

Like Dostoevsky posing as a sort of Jesus, but most truthfully revealing himself all the while as a little horror.

Lawrence seems to be winking at the future Nabokov here, Dostoevsky being the Russian writer whom Nabokov most scorned. Style is what makes meaning for Lawrence; primitive America makes itself known, becomes real, only in the voices of homegrown artists, whom, however, Lawrence does not exalt as geniuses, whom he regards with a mixture of love and condescension.

March of '43, Nabokov learned he had gotten his Guggenheim: $2,500. Wellesley invited him back to teach again, and the MCZ renewed his research position at $1,200 a year. Immediately he began planning another trip west. On the California trip, he had had fun in New Mexico, collecting "near a place which had some connection with Lawrence," he told Wilson (probably somewhere in Taos County). "You were going to tell me about a place you knew, when something interrupted us. . . . What we want is a modest, but good boarding-house, in hilly surroundings."

Mountains were important, because mountain terrain favored the evolution of new species. Laughlin, who had not yet read the Gogol book, invited the Nabokovs to stay at a ski lodge he co-owned near the village of Sandy, Utah, southeast of Salt Lake City. The place was at an elevation of 8,600 feet, in a long, tumbling canyon full of aspens and granite, under high peaks that reach to 11,000 feet. Utah had been only lightly harvested by lepidopterists. The family traveled west by train.

This was the summer during which Dmitri helped his father bag specimens of *Lycaeides melissa annetta*. In a letter at the end of the war to his sister Elena, who was riding out the war in Prague, Nabokov sketched Dmitri's character. He noted "a propensity for pensiveness and dawdling. . . . He does extremely well at school, but that is thanks to Véra who goes over every bit of homework with him." Dmitri had "an exceptionally gifted nature" but, again, "a dose of indolence," and he could "forget everything in the world" to submerge himself in an "aviation magazine—airplanes, to him, are what butterflies are to me."* His son was "vain, quick-tempered, pugnacious, and flaunts American

---

* An American child under influence of the war, Dmitri was able to "unerringly identify types of aircraft by a distant silhouette . . . or even by a buzz, and loves to assemble and glue together various models."

expressions" that were "pretty crude," although, by the standard of American schoolboys, he was "infinitely gentle and generally very lovable."

Aged eleven, Dmitri was still being sent to school in that "gray suit with a red jockey cap." The waywardness that Nabokov emphasized would be a theme years later, in scolding, loving, anxious letters that Véra wrote her son when he was a student at Harvard and then in Italy, where he was starting an operatic career. While granting Dmitri great freedom, which he used to cultivate excitements of many kinds, the Nabokovs were also shaping him for a kind of work that in the long run would confer honor on him and sustain him morally and financially, in part. They made him a worker in the family cottage industry, whose product was books signed "Nabokov." His Russian, which was his because his parents had made sure to speak it with him, was expressive but "appalling" as a written language; in his first year in college, Vladimir wrote Roman Jakobson, the renowned Harvard structuralist linguist, saying that the boy was "very anxious to take a course with you" and badly needed work on his grammar. This was a step, though by no means the first step, in a long campaign to equip him to translate his father's work.

Alta Lodge, 1945

Alta, Laughlin's lodge, now an iconic American powder-skiing destination, was a kind of mountain fastness. The family took the train to Salt Lake and then caught a ride into the mountains, but then they were more or less stranded, since no one among them drove, and they had no car anyway. Véra was uncomfortable in the weather. She would come to marvel at mountain thunderstorms and hailstorms, but Alta was windy and cold that summer. Relations with Laughlin and his wife were also edgy, verging on chilly. Laughlin had promised "moderate" terms for a room, but in Laughlin the "landlord and the poet are fiercely competing," Nabokov wrote Wilson, "with the first winning by a neck." Like other scions of great fortunes, the publisher was eager not to be taken for a mark, and he drove hard bargains with many of his writers. His argument with Nabokov about the Gogol book was real and inflected what happened over the summer. He wanted plot summaries of Gogol's works, among other additions that Nabokov found laughable. Vladimir grudgingly supplied a chronology and a new final chapter, "Commentaries," which holds the publisher up to ridicule, but which Laughlin had the good form to publish as Nabokov wrote it.

The tone of the chapter—recalling the famous sketch by Hemingway, "One Reader Writes"—reports Laughlin saying such things as " 'Well . . . I like it—but I do think the student ought . . . to be told more about Gogol's books. . . . He would want to know what those books are *about*.' " Vladimir replies that he *said* what they are about, to which Laughlin answers, " 'No. . . . I have gone through it carefully and so has my wife, and we have not found the plots. . . . The student ought to be able to find his way, otherwise he would be puzzled and would not bother to read further.' "

In Hemingway's sketch, published in *Winner Take Nothing* (1933), a woman whose husband has contracted syphilis writes to an advice columnist asking for basic information about the disease. Her prudery invites ridicule and seems intended as an indictment of American women, or maybe just of American wives. Nabokov's sketch is almost entirely dialogue: usually he disdained writing that was heavily dialogue-based, Hemingway's most definitely included in the derogation, but here he uses naturalistic speech to clever effect, showing the thickness of the character identified as "the publisher" with every word out of his mouth. The "I" of the dialogue is patient and sane by contrast and justified in feeling exasperated; he is the victim of someone enamored of his own ideas who also, unfortunately, signs the checks. A technique often said to be an invention of Hemingway's, leaving out passages for a reader to infer, has a near-parodic demonstration in the sixteenth paragraph, when, after the patient author is asked to recite the plot events of *The Inspector General*, and gives a laughably literal summary, the publisher says, "Yes, of course you may use it," in reply to an unvoiced request to put it in the revised manuscript.

Nabokov had an especially keen disregard for Hemingway. Faulkner he dismissed with similarly appalled commentary, but Hemingway bestrode the era of Nabokov's arrival in America as a colossus, his fame and sales evoking in many writers a troubled response. In the year of Nabokov's arrival, 1940, Hemingway was dominatingly present, with the publication in October of *For Whom the Bell Tolls*, his long, sporadically excellent, crowd-pleasing novel of the Spanish Civil War. Nabokov admitted to having read Hemingway. In an interview in the sixties he said, "As to Hemingway, I read him for the first time in the early forties, something about bells, balls, and bulls, and loathed it. Later I read his admirable 'The Killers' and the wonderful fish story." "Bells, balls, and bulls" conflates *For Whom the Bell Tolls* with *The Sun Also Rises*, and "the wonderful fish story" is probably *The Old Man and the Sea*, another crowd-pleaser but definitely minor Hemingway. "The Killers" is an early dialogue-based story, virtually a screenplay. It has influenced American film but gives a decidedly narrow idea of Hemingway's resources as a writer.

Nabokov's attention to the literary goings-on of this period, especially his awareness of his fellow authors, is what can be expected of an ambitious newcomer aiming to play a hand. Just in a single letter of his Utah summer he gives a sense of wide, continuous reading among writers in the American grain. To Wilson on July 15, a month into the Alta stay, he wrote that he had "liked very much Mary [McCarthy]'s criticism of [Thornton] Wilder's play in the *Partisan*." (The play was *The Skin of Our Teeth*, and McCarthy's acid review called it an "anachronistic joke, a joke both provincial and self-assertive.") He had also read, and lustily hated, Max Eastman's long narrative poem *Lot's Wife*, which had just come out as a book. Wilson had mentioned the émigré writer V. S. Yanovsky, and Nabokov, displaying no kindness toward a fellow Slav, one now also writing for the American market, denounced him as "a he-man . . . if you know what I mean." Furthermore, "He cannot write."

Returning to Western subjects, he said,

Twenty years ago this place was a Roaring Gulch with golddiggers plugging each other in saloons, but now the Lodge stands in absolute solitude. I happened to read the other day a remarkably silly but rather charming book about a dentist who murdered his wife—written in the nineties and uncannily like a translation from Maupassant in style. It all ends in the Mohave Desert.

That book was probably *McTeague*, by Frank Norris.

Some of the scene at Alta can be imagined from Nabokov's letters, from passages in the Gogol book, and from Laughlin's accounts of having the Nabokovs as touchy guests. The solitude in the canyon came with marks of desolation; the local silver mines having shut down, Nabokov could see "ancient mine dumps" and derelict equipment when he looked through the plateglass windows. Built four years before by a railroad company, with Laughlin coming on later as investor, the lodge was a modest wooden structure sited on a steep slope of the canyon, with a snow-shedding roof and a deck built on piers on the downhill side. Inside, stone fireplaces and guest rooms catered to skiers in winter. Nabokov relished the views. "A delicate sunset was framed in a golden gap between gaunt mountains," he writes in *Nikolai Gogol*. "The remote rims of the gap were eyelashed with firs and . . . deep in the gap itself, one could distinguish the silhouettes of other, lesser and quite ethereal, mountains."

He went out on the deck nights. According to Laughlin, he "affixed big lights [inside] the plate glass windows . . . and collected moths." (Some of these moths, of the variety known as pugs, he sent to J. H. McDunnough of the AMNH, who named one of the captures *Eupithecia nabokovi*.) Laughlin was astounded by his energy. He "wrote every day and hunted butterflies every good day," Laughlin told *Time* magazine in the sixties. "I never knew what he was writing . . . he was secretive about that, but I could hear the typewriter going." (The typewriter would have been operated by Véra; Vladimir wrote almost exclusively with a pen, whose operation was impeded by the altitude.)

When the weather kept them indoors, the Russians played Chinese checkers. Laughlin and his young wife had a pair of cocker spaniel puppies, and these were often underfoot—they were "a draggle-eared black one with an appealing slant in the bluish whites of his eyes and a little white bitch with a pink-dappled face and belly," Nabokov wrote. They were supposed to stay out on the deck but sneaked in.

Despite the occasional rainstorm, "Never in my life . . . have I had such good collecting as here," Nabokov wrote Wilson. "I climb easily to

An approach to Lone Peak

12000 ft. . . . I walk from 12 to 18 miles a day, wearing only shorts and tennis shoes." The canyon was a wildflower paradise. Feeling strong and animated, possibly, by a resentful urge, Nabokov challenged Laughlin, a fine athlete and tireless hiker, to climb with him to the summit of Lone Peak, a serious ascent that gains over six thousand feet from the valley floor in the space of six miles. Modern-day wilderness hikers consider Lone Peak the most arduous high ascent in the Wasatch Range. Two routes to the summit were known in the forties; neither offered water beyond the trailhead, and well-prepared climbers carried full canteens. There is reason to think the two were not well prepared. Nabokov wore "white shorts and sneakers," Laughlin told the *Time* correspondent, and it was "a very tough mountain and the round trip took . . . nine exhausting hours." The climb requires careful route finding and movement over steep granite. A well-researched modern Web guide speaks of "incredibly steep," "deeply eroded," and "very exposed" passages, with a "sheer wall" below the summit proper that "requires scrambling" to surmount.

The top was all snow, due to heavy precipitation that year. In his report to *Time*, Laughlin recalled that Nabokov on the way down "lost his footing and slid five hundred to six hundred feet," suffering bad friction burns on his buttocks. Slides on summit snowfields of that length are often fatal. Speaking to a different interviewer twenty years further on and recalling events differently, Laughlin emphasized that the outing had been for a scientific purpose—Nabokov had brought his butterfly net, and he collected near the snowy summit. Then, on the way down,

> we [both] lost our footing and began to slide. We were sliding faster and faster . . . toward a terrible bunch of rocks, but Nabokov had his butterfly net [which he] managed somehow to hook . . . onto a piece of rock that was sticking through the snow. I grabbed his foot and held onto him. . . . If it hadn't been for that butterfly net . . .

The climbers were late returning. Véra phoned the county sheriff, who sent a squad car out, and the deputies found the men as they were exiting the forest, exhausted but intact.*

NABOKOV'S UTAH EXPERIENCE, DESPITE some irritations, filled him with joy. He had made excellent captures and had "trudged and climbed some 600 miles in the Wasatch," he told Wilson. To Mark Aldanov, his novelist friend in New York, he wrote in an ecstatic mode, sounding like a nature mystic:

---

* In his communications with Laughlin in future years, Nabokov often took an imperious tone, the tone of someone who has been disrespected. The year after Alta, he wrote, "I want you to do something for me. . . . I have somehow mislaid samples of plants which I brought from Utah . . . There are several species of lupine [and] I need the one growing in the haunts of *annetta* . . . I would also like to have a few [ant] specimens. . . . Kill the ants with alcohol or carbona . . . and put them into a small box with cotton wool. The plants can be mailed in a carton . . . but try to keep them flat." Four years on, writing about a reprint deal involving another publisher, he wrote, "Quite independently of whether or not the deal is a profitable one . . . it is essential for me to keep my records straight, and this I cannot do unless I know the exact text of your contract with the New American Library. . . . [P]lease give it your attention. . . . I am at a loss to understand why you have not done it before." Laughlin had sent along a copy of *The Sheltering Sky*, by Paul Bowles, and Nabokov declared it "an utterly ridiculous performance, devoid of talent. You ought to have had the manuscript checked by a cultured Arab. Thanks all the same for sending me those books. I hope you don't mind this frank expression of my opinion."

We are living in wild eagle country, terribly far from everything, terribly high up. . . . The grey ripple of aspens amid black firs, bears crossing the roads, mint, Saffron crocus, lupin flowering, Uinta ground squirrels (a kind of suslik) [that] stand upright beside their burrows. . . . I know you're no nature lover, but all the same I tell you it's an incomparable pleasure to clamber up a virtual cliff at 12000 feet and there observe, "in the neighborhood" of Pushkin's "God," the life of some wild insect stuck on this summit since the ice ages.

"God" is in quote marks but warrants mention. Nabokov here joins a cavalcade of mountain ascenders who feel themselves in the presence of a "spirit" as they approach a high summit. Americans are not alone in this—the story goes back at least to Moses on Mount Sinai—but Americans have made a practice of it, and John Muir of the Sierra Nevada and Henry Thoreau of Mount Monadnock are only the most famous examples of American mountain pilgrims.

A few years later, when his son was mad for climbing, Nabokov placed him in a program in the Tetons. There Dmitri adventured with the best American mountaineers of his era, some of them charismatic mountain mystics. Nabokov tried to explain to Wilson:

In the meantime [Vladimir and Véra were staying in a rented cabin 100 miles away] Dmitri was camping on Jenny Lake . . . and climbing mountains along their most difficult and dangerous sides. The thing with him is an extraordinarily overwhelming passion. The professional alpinists there are really wonderful people, and the very physical kind of exertion supplied by the mountains somehow is transmuted into a spiritual experience.

Dmitri does not seem to have become mystical. But one of his instructors was probably Willi Unsoeld, the first man to climb the West Ridge of Mount Everest, the most significant ascent by an American in the twentieth century.* Unsoeld was hired at the climbing school the same

---

* In 1963. His climbing partner was Tom Hornbein. Unsoeld had been part of the expedition that put Jim Whittaker atop Everest by the South Col route, which in '63 was already familiar to high-altitude mountaineers because of the British first ascent of the mountain ten years earlier. Unsoeld and Hornbein preferred to climb Everest by a new route, an immensely more challenging one, the outcome of their effort entirely in doubt. That they succeeded in good style enlarged the sport.

summer Dmitri attended. A religious intellectual who wrote a well-regarded doctoral thesis on Henri Bergson, Unsoeld was preternaturally calm in terrifying situations, a world-class athlete and a proponent of insight gained through physical risk. He died in an avalanche on Mount Rainier.

Another legendary climber with whom Dmitri probably trained that summer was Art Gilkey, a geologist who would die in an American attempt on K2 in 1954. Dmitri's initiation into the sport thus was courtesy of spiritually minded outdoorsmen who, while advancing the sport technically, climbed with a dual purpose. Their instruction included the idea that mountaineering was a species of quest—getting to the summit brought on godly thoughts, brought intoxication.

8.

Back in Cambridge, Nabokov underwent a sharp decompression, trading the western sights that thrilled him for trim lawns, fall foliage, boring leps, and tame hills. He again dove into work at the MCZ. His labors were "immense," he told Wilson:

> Part of my scientific work on the Blues . . . in which I correlate the nearctic [New World] and palaearctic [Old World] representatives, is due to appear in a week or two. . . . The number of my index cards exceeds a thousand references . . . I have dissected and drawn the genitalia of 360 specimens and unraveled taxonomic adventures that read like a novel. This has been a wonderful bit of training in the use of our (if I may say so) wise, precise, plastic, beautiful English language.

Somewhat isolated at the MCZ—with no fellow researchers interested in his favorite insect tribe—he reveled in the huge holdings. Nicolas Nabokov had had a similar New World immersion experience ten years before. The composer had agreed to write a ballet, one on "an American subject," for Léonide Massine, and he had gone in search of materials to aid in this assignment, excited to be creating an indigenous American dance. Up to that point he had known America largely from books and movies, he confessed in his memoirs; America was to Nicolas a land of "milk shakes and banana splits," of cars that looked like "funereal monsters," of "noisy, filthy, dilapidated elevated trains": an uncultured, foreboding place. Archibald MacLeish took Nicolas to see Gerald Murphy, the Jazz Age celebrity who, besides being a friend of Hemingway,

Fitzgerald, Picasso, Cocteau, and other icons of the Lost Generation, was a collector of musical artifacts. These treasures included "cylinders with recordings made by Thomas Edison" from the turn of the century, some of them containing "poignantly authentic" bits of American music, the music for " 'bear steps,' 'wolf steps,' 'fox trots,' and . . . pre–Civil War 'cakewalks,' " Nicolas discovered. "Not only their tunes [but] their harmonies, their rhythms, seemed fresh and real, [and] the manner of playing or singing and the choice of instruments" did also.*

Cousin Vladimir, buried beneath insect work, began to stir fictionally. He credited Véra with pulling him back from the brink, from the lepidopteral fascination that was swallowing all of his time:

> Véra has had a serious conversation with me. . . . Having sulkily pulled [the beginning pages of *Bend Sinister*] out from under my butterfly manuscripts I discovered . . . that it was good, and . . . that the [first] twenty pages at least could be typed and submitted. . . . I have [also] lain with my Russian muse after a long period of adultery and am sending you the big poem she bore. . . . I have also almost finished a story in English.

Nikolai Gogol now complete, Nabokov began scheming over how to escape the deal he had with Laughlin, the second part of which required

---

* Nicolas Nabokov's ardent search for the American musical real resembles cousin Vladimir's bewitchment by unique sites and specimens of lepidoptera, but the most systematic and profound seeker of meaning in American materials whose surname happens to be Nabokov is probably Nicolas's second son, Peter, now an emeritus professor of anthropology at UCLA. Peter is the co-author of *Native American Architecture*, an indispensable photographic compendium and scholarly commentary, and author of *A Forest of Time: American Indian Ways of History* and *Where the Lightning Strikes: The Lives of American Indian Sacred Places*, among other titles. A relentless close noticer, P. Nabokov traveled the continent for decades in a style not so different from Vladimir's—both were gripped by lifelong intellectual obsessions that brought them constantly into the outdoors, that made them expert field researchers and led them to significant discoveries. Peter Nabokov's most approachable work is probably *Restoring a Presence: American Indians and Yellowstone National Park* (2004), co-written with Lawrence Loendorf, which briskly overturns the idea that Yellowstone was a natural preserve full of buffalo, bear, and other iconic fauna but devoid of humans. Native peoples were said to have feared the area and to have avoided it; in fact, tribal groups swept through and dwelt within what are now park lands in nonstop migrations over at least eight thousand years.

him to write other books for little pay. Wilson proposed that they use the translations that Nabokov had been making and collaborate on "a book on Russian literature—I contributing [the] essays . . . you contributing translations." Wilson had been writing about Russian authors for *The Atlantic*, and he foresaw a book that "with the mounting interest in Russian, would have a certain sale. There would be nothing like it in English."

This period of their correspondence shows them fully entwined, intimates of the heart and of the page. Wilson sent his *Atlantic* pieces to Nabokov for comment: "You may find them annoying, but they pretend to be nothing more than the first impressions of a foreigner," he wrote. Nabokov replied, "I am returning your proofs. Véra and I liked this and the other article *enormously*." Wilson was trespassing on Nabokov's terrain, the Russian literary mother lode, but Vladimir welcomed it; even Wilson's take on Pushkin, the most revered progenitor, found favor. Wilson needs to not be underestimated. His essay on Pushkin is superb journalism, and its authority and insight may reflect debts he owed Nabokov, which Nabokov was flattered to detect.* But Nabokov knew what a special colleague he had in Wilson. To no other contemporary writer, with the exception of the émigré poet Khodasevich (1886–1939), did he make similar gestures of respect. Hoping to bring *The Gift*, the novel he considered his masterwork, before American readers, he asked Wilson to translate it:

> So I am still looking for somebody who might make a translation of that 500 page book. . . . I know of one man who could do it if I helped him with his Russian. This is a roundabout way of putting it but I am afraid you have other dogs to beat whereas I have no illusions about the sums Laughlin can pay.

Indeed, Wilson had other projects; he wrote back, "If I had the leisure, I'd be glad to translate your book. I'd like to see you translated. . . . But I've got so many things . . . that I couldn't possibly."

---

* Wilson wrote well about Pushkin before he knew Nabokov. Clive James, the Australian-born critic, calls Wilson's 1937 essay "In Honor of Pushkin" the best short introduction to the poet, echoing the judgment of John Bayley, author of the authoritative *Pushkin: A Comparative Commentary*. To round out the back-patting, James calls Bayley's praise of Wilson's short study "a generous tribute, considering that Bayley has written the best long one."

Nabokov now sent nearly everything Wilson's way. Lepidopteral papers, old poems, parts of novels, a play. He sent *Nikolai Gogol* and "the whole book" of what was later *Three Russian Poets*. (It was published by Laughlin: the scheme to co-author a work with Wilson finally came to nothing.) Nabokov resembles an overeager younger brother, perhaps, confident that his every word will find favor. He senses that he goes too far sometimes; in January '44, he wrote, "An obscure paper on some obscure butterflies in an obscure scientific journal is another sample of Nabokoviana which will soon be in your hands," and in March, "I would have sent [the *Gogol* proofs] for a critical examination had I not known how busy you [are] reading books."

The friendship was exciting and inspiring. Uniquely in Nabokov's oeuvre, he acknowledges direct inspiration, the taking of his lead from another:

Are you writing a lot? I liked your school recollections.* I think I shall write about my *Tenishevskoe Oochilishche* [his St. Petersburg high school] soon—you have *declenché* that particular sequence [unleashed that store of memories, such as] the Russian teacher . . . at whom I threw a chair once; the terrific fistfights which I thoroughly enjoyed because, though weaker than the two or three main bullies, I had had private lessons of boxing and *savate* . . . and the soccer in the yard, and the nightmare exams, and the Polish boy who paraded his first clap.

The question of how much to send Wilson, how deeply to presume on his attention, proved important. Nabokov's novel in progress, *Bend Sinister*, went in January '44, then went on to an editor at Doubleday. Wilson, now a regular reviewer for the *New Yorker*, read Nabokov's early pages and liked them "very much," he wrote back; "am eager to see the rest of it." The *New Yorker* was keeping him busy—he produced lengthy reviews on almost a weekly basis. He might have read Nabokov's pages a little hastily. He penciled in some comments, on Nabokov's use of some English verbs, but encouragingly pronounced the thing "excellent."

It did not find favor at Doubleday. That hardly mattered: Nabokov had so powerful a conception of the novel that he confidently told

* Wilson had sent Nabokov his new book *Note-books of Night* (1942), which contained "At Laurelwood," about his New Jersey childhood. *DBDV*, 237n5.

Wilson, "it will contain 315 pages" and that "Towards the end . . . there will be the looming and development of an idea which has *never* been treated before." Most of the book was written two years later, in the winter-spring of 1945–46. A dystopian novel, a political novel, despite Nabokov's disavowal of political novels and message writing, it has affinities with his Kafkaesque novel of the thirties, *Invitation to a Beheading*, but betrays an evolution in the direction of modernist difficulty, of challenging reading. Altagracia de Jannelli, had she still been his career coach, might have declared him headed in exactly the wrong direction. Brian Boyd, whose biography contains readings of all the novels, most of which Boyd judges works of supreme art, speaks of "a programmatic refusal to satisfy the ordinary interests of readers" with *Bend Sinister*. It is "self-conscious" and without the "obvious charms" of some of Nabokov's other works, Boyd says.

The novel's off-putting elements include a modernist mixing of styles: straight narration along with parodies of narration; a witty, tiresome chapter of exegesis of *Hamlet* and other Shakespeare commentary; direct addresses to the reader, to signal that the author is aware of writing a text, as the reader needs to know; fancy words in fussy passages interruptive of the story's flow. Krug, the hero, is a world-famous philosopher and "man of genius" who, early in the book, is easy to take for a stand-in for a self-regarding author. His misfortune consists in being a prominent citizen of a police state, whose dictator, a former schoolmate, wants him to make statements supporting the regime. Nabokov's disgust with Nazism and Stalinism might have influenced his decision to treat the fictional regime with disdain: to show the murderers and torturers to be cretins and clowns. A kind of antic comedy breaks out at intervals, with the punch line darkened by beastliness.

At the beginning, Krug's wife has died. Krug keeps the news from their child:

> There at the [nursery] door he stopped and the thumping of his heart was suddenly interrupted by his little son's special bedroom voice, detached and courteous, employed by David with graceful precision to notify his parents (when they returned, say, from a dinner in town) that he was still awake and ready to receive anybody who would like to wish him a second goodnight.

David will be taken hostage by the state and murdered. The novel, which includes disparagements of some bestselling American novels, proceeds in a conventional way, with deep devotion to family the wellspring of all its action. "The main theme of *Bend Sinister*," Nabokov wrote twenty years later, in a dyspeptic introduction to a new edition, "is the beating of Krug's loving heart, the torture an intense tenderness is subjected to—and it is for the sake of the pages about David and his father that the book was written and should be read." If this is so, then the theme is handled clumsily. The references to David are treacly, and Krug's devotion to his late wife is paraded but remains abstract—a reader hears of it but does not feel it.

A secondary character, Ember, resembles Edmund Wilson in many ways and enjoys an intimate friendship with Krug based on literary affinity. They are deeply simpatico. Some Nabokov scholars argue that Wilson's failure to recognize the elaborate and loving tribute to him was a shock to Nabokov and a disappointment; the Shakespearean exegesis is just the sort of thing that they liked to engage in, and the book is fruitcaked with bits designed for Wilson's taste, including an elaborate play on the title of one of Mary McCarthy's novels. Wilson, when the book appeared, said nothing about the character Ember or about any in-jokes. He disliked the novel. "I was rather disappointed in *Bend Sinister*," begins his letter of January 30, 1947:

> I had had some doubts when I was reading the parts you showed me. . . . Other people may very well think otherwise: I know, for example, that Allen Tate [the editor who acquired the book for Holt] is tremendously excited about it—he told me that he considered it "a great book." But I feel that, though it is crammed with good things . . . it is not one of your greatest successes. First of all, it seems to me that it suffers from the same weakness as that play [*The Waltz Invention*, also about a dictator]. You aren't good at this kind of subject, which involves questions of politics and social change, because you are totally uninterested in these matters and have never taken the trouble to understand them.

This is Wilson's frankest, most detailed critique of a Nabokov novel of which there is written record. There is every reason to think that Nabokov, while irritated or saddened, read it carefully:

> For you, a dictator . . . is simply a vulgar and odious person who bullies serious and superior people like Krug. You have no idea why or how the [dictator in your book] was able to put himself

over, or what his revolution implies. And this makes your picture
of such happenings rather unsatisfactory. Now don't tell me that
the real artist has nothing to do with the issues of politics. An
artist may not take politics seriously, but, if he deals with such
matters at all, he ought to know what it is all about. Nobody could
be more . . . intent on pure art than Walter Pater, whose *Gaston de
Latour* I have just been reading; but I declare that he has a great
deal more insight into [the religious politics] raging in the sixteenth
century than you have into the conflicts of the twentieth.

The book drew few good reviews. As Nabokov would note twenty
years later, it made a "dull thud." Wilson went on:

I think, too, that your invented country has not served you particularly well. Your strength lies so much in precise observation that,
in combining Germanic and Slavic [elements in your setting], you
have produced something that does not seem real. . . . Beside
the actual Nazi Germany and the actual Stalinist Russia, the
adventures of your unfortunate professor have the air of an
unpleasant burlesque. I never believed in him much from the
beginning. . . . As it is, what you are left with . . . is a satire on
events so terrible that they really can't be satirized.

Wilson was bored by the novel. It had "longueurs" unlike anything else
he had read by Nabokov. He understood that his friend was aiming at a
"denser texture of prose" full of learned allusions, but the fatty writing
reminded him of Thomas Mann—one of Nabokov's hated "second-
raters."

The sting of this scolding lasted a long time. In the dyspeptic
introduction already referred to, Nabokov struck back not at Wilson
personally ("A kind friend, Edmund Wilson, read the typescript . . .")
but at obtuse readers who require of an author explanations of his
allusions and imagery. The Nabokov of '63 was among the most successful writers in the world. People could not still doubt his genius, could
they? But still he rode the hobbyhorse of antipolitics, and still he
thundered against the "literature of social comment," like a stern school-
master shaking an errant pupil by the shoulders. The world's conviction
that politics matter offended him—how stupid of the world.

The novel was not entirely unsuccessful. In some of the late chapters,
Nabokov stops scoring points and writes with radiant immediacy, in a

blackly humorous tone that recalls one of his fiercest, most readable earlier novels, *Laughter in the Dark*, and looks forward to his next—to the densely allusive, morally complex, joyously readable *Lolita*. In ways both large and small, *Lolita* looms in the sad action:

> She was standing in the tub, sinuously soaping her back or at least such parts of her narrow, variously dimpled, glistening back which she could reach by throwing her arm across her shoulder. Her hair was up, with a kerchief or something twisted around it. The mirror reflected a brown armpit and a poppling pale nipple. "Ready in a sec," she sang out.

This is Mariette, a diminutive, cruel police spy who comes to work as a governess for Krug. Krug "slammed the door [to the bath] with a great show of disgust," but moments later he imagines Mariette's "adolescent buttocks," and a few days later "he dreamt that he was surreptitiously enjoying Mariette while she sat, wincing a little, in his lap during the rehearsal of a play in which she was supposed to be his daughter."

Humbert-like, Krug attaches to Mariette a sullying categorical term: she is not a nymphet but a *puella*.* Though still a child, she is sexually hungry and sophisticated:

> "Good night," he said. "Don't sit up too late."
> "May I sit in your room while you are writing?"
> "Certainly not."
> He turned to go but she called him back. . . . "When I'm alone," she said, "I sit and do like this, like a cricket. Listen, please."
> "Listen to what?"
> "Don't you hear?"
> She sat with parted lips, slightly moving her tightly crossed thighs, producing a tiny sound, soft, labiate, with an alternate crepitation as if she were rubbing the palms of her hands.

Krug forgives himself in advance. He had "lost his wife in November," and it was "quite natural" for a man to want to rid himself of "tension and discomfort." (Humbert, notoriously, forgives himself in a thousand

---

* From the Latin meaning "little girl," after *puellus*, a contraction of *puerulus*, meaning "young boy, slave."

ways for what he does to the child Lolita.) At the last instant, Krug does not fall, does not take advantage; then there comes a tap at his door:

> He opened. . . . She was standing there in her nightgown. A slow blink concealed and revealed again the queer stare of her dark opaque eyes. She had a pillow under her arm and an alarm clock in her hand. She sighed deeply.
>
> "Please, let me come in," she said, the somewhat lemurian features of her small white face puckering up entreatingly. "I am terrified, I simply can't be alone. I feel something dreadful is about to happen. May I sleep here? Please!"
>
> She crossed the room on tiptoe and with infinite care put the round-faced clock down on the night table. Penetrating her flimsy garment, the light of the lamp brought out her body in peachblow silhouette.

Krug sounds a little like Charlotte Haze, Lolita's mother, in a famous passage from *Lolita*, when he declares,

> "You know too little or too much. . . . If too little, then run along, lock yourself up, never come near me because this is going to be a bestial explosion, and you might get badly hurt. I warn you. I am nearly three times your age and a great big sad hog of a man. And I don't love you."
>
> She looked down at the agony of his senses. Tittered.
>
> "Oh, you don't?"
>
> *Mea puella, puella mea*. My hot, vulgar, heavenly delicate little *puella*.

Among other foretastes of *Lolita* are scenes in which Mariette and others, including Krug's eight-year-old son, speak in American slang. David says, "Uh-uh," and "Gee whizz," and Krug imagines emigrating to a country where "his child could be brought up in security . . . a long long beach dotted with bodies, a sunny honey and her satin Latin— advertisement for some American stuff somewhere seen, somehow remembered." Eventually, a squad of police agents breaks in, beats up Krug, and takes David away to his death, and these thugs sound as if they have been watching too many movies or are intent on restaging parts of "The Killers":

"Sure," said Mac.

"And you won't catch cold because there is a mink coat in the car."

Owing to the door of the nursery suddenly opening . . . David's voice was heard for a moment: oddly enough, the child, instead of whimpering and crying for help, seemed to be trying to reason with his impossible visitors. . . .

Krug moved his fingers—the numbness was gradually passing away. As calmly as possible. As calmly as possible, he again appealed to Mariette.

"Does anybody know what he wants of me?" asked Mariette.

"Look," said Mac to [Krug], "either you do what you're told or you don't. And if you don't, it's going to hurt like hell, see? Get up!"

Mac has a great jaw and a hand "the size of a steak for five." He is a figure out of the funnies, as well as the movies; Bluto in *Popeye* might almost say, as he does, "Aw, for Christ's sake," and "Hold it straight, kiddo," when Mariette fondles his flashlight. These passages offer a brief fantasia on lowbrow American themes. America is where gangsterism found its style, but it is also where, if Krug had pulled off a planned escape, things might have turned out differently for his child:

He saw David a year or two older, sitting on a vividly labelled trunk at the customs house on the pier.

He saw him riding a bicycle in between brilliant forsythia shrubs and thin naked birch trees down a path with a "no bicycles" sign. He saw him on the edge of a swimming pool, lying on his stomach, in wet black shorts, one shoulder blade sharply raised . . . saw him in one of those fabulous corner stores that have face creams on one side and ice creams on the other, perched . . . at the bar and craning towards the syrup pumps. He saw him throwing a ball with a special flip of the wrist, unknown in the old country. He saw him as a youth crossing a technicoloured campus.

It will be Lolita, a year or two hence, who will sample fountain drinks in American drugstores as Humbert drives her back and forth across the country. But Lolita, too, will never escape into wider life— will not survive to cross a groomed college campus, will not get beyond the looming doom that Nabokov, in these war and just-postwar years, found implied in the vulnerability of childhood.

* * *

MANY OF THE EVENTS of *Lolita* (1955) are set in a fictionalized 1947–48. Among the qualities of the novel that charmed hundreds of thousands of readers, especially American ones, was the comical truth of its settings, which are evoked in a realistic mode. The critic Elizabeth Hardwick observed about the novel, "It is rather in the mood of Marco Polo in China that he meets the (to us) exhausted artifacts of the American scene. Motels, advertisements, chewing-gum . . . for Nabokov it is all a dawn, alpine freshness." Mark Twain's rustic settlements in *The Adventures of Huckleberry Finn* came to American readers with a similar charge in the 1880s: stereotypical settings—Southern river towns, famously sleepy—came into focus as backdrops to events such as the Grangerford-Shepherdson feud, or the Duke and the Dauphin's balderdash connivings. That other American novel of aimless travel was also rich, as *Lolita* is, with the flavors of American speech and the savories of place.

Only in '46 did Nabokov fully take command of English. Early in '47 he wrote Wilson,

> I have not had a word from you for ages. How are you? Did you get my new Russian poem? . . . [*Bend Sinister*] is due to appear in the beginning of June. . . . They sent me a most absurd blurb. . . . I have little hope that [it] brings me any money. I am writing two things now 1. a short novel about a man who liked little girls—and it's going to be called *The Kingdom by the Sea*—and 2. a new type of autobiography—a scientific attempt to unravel and trace back all the tangled threads of one's personality—and the provisional title is *The Person in Question*.

These became wonderful, enchanting books, for many readers Nabokov's best. They were realist in the sense of seeming to be reports of an intelligible world, albeit a world rendered to a degree of detail far from ordinary. Wilson, when he eventually read the manuscript, did not like *Lolita*, but he joined the chorus of praise for the essays that Nabokov began to publish in *The New Yorker*, later to become *Speak, Memory*. Neither the memoir nor the novel is a political fantasy à la *Bend Sinister*, and neither imagines a country that is sort of this way and sort of that.

Neither avoids complicated, allusive writing, but Nabokov's learnedness is semi-masked in *Lolita*. In *Bend Sinister*, the Shakespearean discourse claims most of a chapter and, though intrinsic to the text, interrupts; readers wishing the story to forge ahead have to wait. *Lolita*, by contrast, reads easily, without interpolations; Humbert Humbert's first-person narration goes down very smoothly:

> "Look, make Mother take you and me to Our Glass Lake tomor-row." These were the . . . words said to me by my twelve-year-old flame in a voluptuous whisper, as we happened to bump into one another on the front porch, I out, she in. The reflection of the afternoon sun, a dazzling white diamond with innumerable irides-cent spikes quivered on the round back of a parked car.

> As I lay in bed, erotically musing before trying to go to sleep, I thought of a final scheme how to profit by the picnic to come. I was aware that mother Haze hated my darling for her being sweet on me. So I planned my lake day with a view to satisfying the mother. To her alone would I talk; but at some appropriate moment I would say I had left my wrist watch or my sunglasses in that glade yonder—and plunge with my nymphet into the wood.

The plot is simple: scholarly pedophile makes off with young girl, who escapes. *Bend Sinister*, two-thirds as long, is a labyrinth of plot compared with *Lolita*'s fablelike, mostly chronological unspooling, although the events of the latter are mysterious in a way unknown to the former. The ease of reading is another seduction. Humbert wins us with artful palaver to a position of suspended distaste for his actions ("Oh, my Lolita, I have only words to play with!"), our ease of entry into his view of things complicitous. We should be sufficiently abhorrent of child sexual enslavement to be reading something more improving, but aren't.

Speak, Memory, mandarin in style, is less welcoming to some readers:

> School was taught from the fifteenth of September to the twenty-fifth of May, with a couple of interruptions: a two-week intersemestral gap—to make place, as it were, for the huge Christmas tree that touched with its star the pale-green ceiling of our prettiest drawing room—and a one-week Easter vacation, during which painted eggs enlivened the breakfast table. Since snow and frost lasted from October well into April, no wonder the mean of my school memories is definitely hiemal.

* * *

I see very clearly the women of the Korff line, beautiful, lily-and-rose girls, their high, flushed *pommettes*, pale blue eyes and that small beauty spot on one cheek . . . which my grandmother, my father, three or four of his siblings, some of my twenty-five cousins, my younger sister and my son Dmitri inherited in various stages of intensity.

The book is Proustian—from start to end an excavation of personal memory—but not especially modernist, written in refined, deep-breathing sentences that require attention but do not perplex. Terms like *hiemal* and *pommette* may have sent some *New Yorker* readers to a dictionary, but *Speak, Memory* is the report of a mind awash in clarity, Apollonian, resplendently poised.

Nabokov needed money. Financially "I am rather dejected," he wrote Wilson upon learning that his Guggenheim would not be renewed for a second year. A plan to return west had to be put off for a year, then two, then three. Dmitri had "absolutely nowhere to play out of doors and lives in a neighborhood full of impossible little hooligans," and the family made short trips in summer, one to Newfound Lake, New Hampshire, said to be the cleanest lake in the state today but "filthy" back when Nabokov took his family there. The Nabokovs later told a story about anti-Semitism in New Hampshire, in the wake of the war and reportage of the death camps. In a restaurant with a "Gentiles Only" notice on its menu, Nabokov asked the waitress if she would refuse service to a man and woman and infant son who arrived on a donkey. She had no answer, and they stalked out.

In other versions of the story—which evoke the forthcoming novel and film *Gentleman's Agreement* (both released in 1947)—the New Testament triad arrives in "an old Ford," and in one, Véra is absent but Dmitri brings along a friend, and the boys are deeply impressed by Nabokov's outspokenness. He was psychologically fragile at the time. He had gone to New Hampshire on doctor's orders; exhausted by work on *Bend Sinister* and on a lepidopteral research paper, he'd visited a hospital complaining of heart trouble, ulcers, kidney stones, and cancer. The doctor pronounced him sound but played out. In letters of early 1946, Nabokov described himself as "impotent," most amusingly in a note to Wilson about *Memoirs of Hecate County*, recently published and selling briskly, in part because of daring sexual passages:

There are lots of wonderful things in it. . . . You have given your [character's] copulation-mates such formidable defences . . . that the reader (or at least one reader, for I would have been absolutely impotent in your singular little harem) derives no kick from the hero's love-making. I should have as soon tried to open a sardine can with my penis.

He missed the West, and his feeling of unwellness might have been related to his gaining sixty pounds when he stopped smoking. Beginning in '47, and with hardly an interruption for the next decade and a half, he did go west, mostly to high mountains, where he tramped himself fit. Newfound Lake seemed to him tame, polluted; at the lodge where they stayed, he was sickened by the smell of fried clams drifting in from a Howard Johnson's.

SOMETHING MIRACULOUS HAPPENED. IN the late forties, the émigré who was finally in command of wise, precise, plastic English took a further step. He undertook the American subject as he saw it. As he later explained to *Playboy*, "I had to invent America. . . . It had taken me some forty years to invent Russia and Western Europe, and now I was faced by a similar task, with a lesser amount of time at my disposal." America in his version is marked by fanciful touches—curious, resonant place-names in *Lolita*, for instance, such as "Ramsdale," "Elphinstone," "Beardsley"—but is not fanciful in a metafictional sense, the sense of an arch author signaling the made-up-ness of his text. (Humbert, narrator not author, allows that he has fictionalized here and there but insists on the desperate reality of events.) For scholarly readers who enjoy fossicking in a text, *Lolita*, like the next two American novels, *Pnin* (1957) and *Pale Fire* (1962), offers a rich field of excavation, concocted out of countless literary sources, but Nabokov carefully preserves an illusion of "this world" for readers who wish to enter his story and be carried away.

He had studied America casually, beginning long before he arrived.* At Wilson's urging, he read authors who had escaped his notice, such as

* Nabokov was not yet married to Véra Slonim when he first proposed that they move to America (letter of December 3, 1923). In his late sixties, when an interviewer asked him why he had started writing in English, since he could not possibly have known that he would one day be allowed to emigrate, he said, "Oh, I did know I would eventually land in America."

Henry James (finding him to be a "pale porpoise" who needed debunking). He was conversant with Poe, Emerson, Hawthorne, Melville, Frost, Eliot, Pound, Fitzgerald, Faulkner, Hemingway, and many others, despite being a professor largely of Russian literature and language. Nonliterary evidence also started piling up. In a poem he wrote after an overnight stay at Wilson's, he showed an instinct for the American surreal:

> *Keep it Kold, says a poster in passing, and lo,*
> *loads,*
> *of bright fruit, and a ham, and some chocolate cream,*
> *and three bottles of milk, all contained in the gleam*
> *of that wide-open white*
> *god, the pride and delight*
> *of starry-eyed couples in dream kitchenettes.*

His literary path—until *Lolita*—looked promising without being especially American. Wilson had fashioned an arrangement for him at the *New Yorker*, which guaranteed him a yearly advance in exchange for first look at whatever he wrote, and what he wrote was mainly Russian-inflected. He might have made a small, smart career in *ancien régime* nostalgia, and to a degree the career he did make looks back, revives, lovingly reworks Pushkin, Gogol, and the other Russian forefathers.

He had "a vagabond's sharp-sightedness," however. Thomas Mann, another writer who fled Europe and became American, and who wrote prolifically while in the United States, gave scarcely a hint of his residence in Pacific Palisades, California, and before that in Princeton, New Jersey. Mann wrote about German fascism, about a fictional German composer, about the Ten Commandments and Pope Gregory of the sixth century while in America, but he did not find a way or did not seek a way to represent his American surroundings. Probably the émigré novelist who most closely resembles Nabokov in going American is Ayn Rand, his near contemporary (1905–1982), of a Jewish family similar to Véra Slonim's, a writer of different attainments but, like Nabokov, determined to write for the movies and in the fifties the author of a giant bestseller (*Atlas Shrugged*). Rand was also from St. Petersburg, had also fled the Revolution, and her arrival in the United States began a period of intense self-education and a wholesale embrace of what she took for Americanism.

Nabokov's first short story set in America, "Time and Ebb," looks at the decade of the forties from eighty years later. An old man recalls the

quaint artifacts of 1944—skyscrapers, soda jerks, airplanes—and speaks
to the reader in stiff, fudgy sentences:

> I am also old enough to remember the coach trains: as a babe I
> worshipped them; as a boy I turned away to improved editions of
> speed. . . . Their hue might have passed for the ripeness of distance,
> for a blending succession of conquered miles, had it not surrendered
> its plum-bloom to the action of coal dust so as to match the walls
> of workshops and slums which preceded a city as inevitably as a
> rule of grammar and a blot precede the acquisition of conventional
> knowledge. Dwarf dunce caps were stored at one end of the car
> and could flabbily cup (with the transmission of a diaphanous chill
> to the fingers) the grottolike water of an obedient little fountain
> which reared its head at one's touch.

The nostalgia has a labored, self-pleased quality. Nabokov's model
might have been H. G. Wells, one of his favorite writers as a boy, or
Frederick Lewis Allen, author of the bestselling *Only Yesterday* (1931), a
spry history of the twenties. "Oh—he means those conical little paper
cups they have," a reader thinks after decoding the sprung last sentence,
and the living detail of "diaphanous chill to the fingers" and "flabbily
cup" goes half-astray, being too much worked for.

The story communicates a fondness for American things. In America,
"my most sacred dreams have been realized," he wrote his sister in '45.
"My family life is completely cloudless. I love this country and dearly
want to bring you over. Alongside lapses into wild vulgarity there are
heights here where one can have marvelous picnics with friends who
'understand.' " The American turn was for him a turn of the heart. He
wanted his sister and her son to be here, too, despite the vulgarity. Like
Mann walking his poodle in Palisades Park, Santa Monica, beguiled by
the California light, Nabokov felt safe, he felt hopeful, and in the period
of this gladness he conceived *Lolita*.

9.

As Nabokov began work, Wilson sent him the sixth volume of Havelock Ellis's *Studies in the Psychology of Sex* in its French edition, drawing his attention to an appendix, the sexual confession of a Ukrainian man born around 1870. Of a wealthy family and educated abroad, the man had been initiated into sex at age twelve. He'd become obsessively sexual and failed at his studies, and only by becoming celibate did he manage to qualify as an engineer. On the eve of his marriage to an Italian woman, he encountered some child prostitutes and succumbed to his former obsession. Thereafter he squandered all his money, the marriage fell through, and he became an addict of sex with young girls, exposing himself to them in public. The confession ends with a feeling of hopelessness, of a life ruined by a hunger beyond control.

Nabokov wrote back, "Many thanks for the books. I enjoyed the Russian's love-life hugely. It is wonderfully funny. As a boy, he seems to have been quite extraordinarily lucky in coming across [willing] girls. . . . The end is rather bathetic."

He might have been in that state where everything comes as grist to the mill, the novel in his head finding reflections everywhere. His commitment to writing a sex narrative—a sex narrative likely to invite prosecution for obscenity, as Wilson's *Memoirs of Hecate County* had done for him—seems already quite strong. The tone of his response to Wilson is also notable: his play-it-for-wisecracks approach is already in place, and the critique of his novel that would dominate public discussion—that such compassion as it displays is thin or misplaced, is afforded the degenerate Humbert as much as the ruined little girl—seems implicit.

Nabokov's life in Cambridge was socially rich. He had literary friends, people from Harvard and Wellesley, as well as fellow "sufferers" from the need to chase and study insects. One of his entomology friends was the son of the Harvard museum curator of mollusks; Nabokov had been corresponding with the young man, who was interested in the Blues, since '43. Another young scientist, Charles L. Remington, began haunting the MCZ as soon as he got out of the Army, and he would soon cofound the Lepidopterists' Society, of which Nabokov became a member. Midsummer '46, Remington wrote him suggesting a collecting trip to Colorado. He also wrote to Hazel Schmoll, who owned a nature preserve near Rocky Mountain National Park, inquiring about accommodations. Schmoll, the former Colorado state botanist, usually advertised for guests to her ranch in the *Christian Science Monitor*; Nabokov declined to stay with her when he learned that she favored guests who did not drink.

He did go to Colorado the following summer. The trip became possible with the receipt of an advance of $2,000 for *Bend Sinister*, and in general things were looking up for him financially: his salary from Wellesley was now $3,250, and his MCZ stipend and yearly advance from *The New Yorker* contributed to a respectable total, enlarged by the occasional book-talk fee. The family went west by train. Dmitri was now thirteen and six feet tall; to go west for him meant to go to high mountains again, where he could hike and climb. Nabokov's collecting needs dictated the itinerary. Tips from entomology friends, such as Comstock of the AMNH and Charles Remington, were useful, but by now Nabokov had examined many thousands of specimens, cataloging many of them *de novo*, and his own sense of where to look was astute. The names of North American sites of collection, some of them famous, some not, were sharply present in his mind. Chivington, Independence Pass, and La Plata Peak in Colorado; in Arizona, Ramsay Canyon and Ruby; West Yellowstone; the Tolland bogs; Polaris, Montana; Harlan, Saskatchewan. He had been reading entomological literature for forty years. His MCZ notecards display an astonishing appetite for detail, morphological detail above all—wing-scale counts, sex-organ descriptions, portraits of polytypes—and secondarily the details of discrete moments of capture. "Taken by *Haberhauer* near Astrabad, Persia," he wrote about one insect collected seventy-five years before, "probably in the Lendakur Mts . . . . where in summer 1869 he spent 2½ months, from the 24th of June, 'in a village where shepherds lived only in summer,' *Hadschyabad*, 8000 ft."

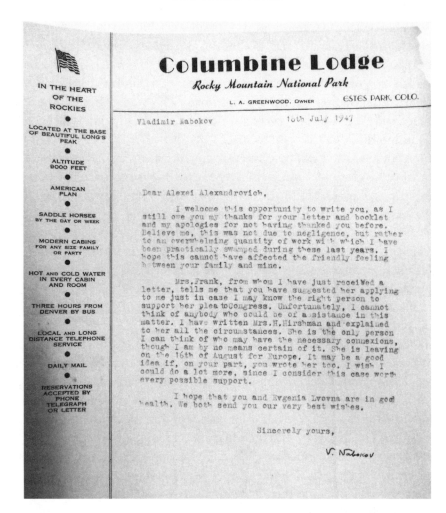

Another notation preserved some suggestive phrasing: "jam of logs [in the Priest River, Idaho] stranded on its sandbars and a scurry of clouds mirrored in the dark water between its high banks." He liked poetic touches—they were part of the specificity that he honored. About *Lycaena aster* Edwards, a copper butterfly, he recorded, "In the summer of 1834 it was nearly as abundant as *Coenonympha tullia* [of] Carbonear Island . . . where every step aroused numbers of these bright little creatures from the grass."

A more typical, substantive notation, showing his precision and alertness to the naturalistic big picture:*

---

* The word *ecology* appears only a few times in his notes. It had been coined only eighty years before, by Ernst Haeckel, the German scientist who also improvised *phylum*, *phylogeny*, and *stem cell*.

N. Colo., Spring Cn. [Canyon] W. of Fort Collins, alt. 52–5500 ft., arid grassy foothills, Upper Sonoran Zone with Transition elements, and 23 miles up Little S. Powder R[iver] Cn. from "The Forks" (alt. 6500 ft), Transition Zone, with Can[yon] Z[one] elements; Bellevue, Larimer Co[unty] alt. 5200 ft. Dry meadows and flats. Three Life Zones . . . noted within a horizontal distance of 6 mi.

In his scientific papers he sounded Nabokovian: artful, expressive, prickly-charming. He wrote,

On a hot August day, from a bridge in Estes Park, Colo., my wife and I watched for almost a minute a striped Hawk Moth (*Celerio*) poised above the water, facing upstream against a swift current, in the act of drinking. The delicate wake produced by the immersion of the proboscis was a special feature of the performance.

In a paper published in *Psyche*:

When the whole [male organ of a Blue] is forced open oysterwise so that its symmetrically extended valves continue to point down . . . the most conspicuous thing . . . is the presence of a pair of formidable semi-translucent hooks . . . facing each other in the manner of the stolidly raised fists of two pugilists . . . with [a hood-shaped feature] lending a Ku-Klux Klan touch to the picture.

He was gracious but argumentative. Fools had made a mess of Lycaenid nomenclature, he said, identifying species falsely, and he campaigned against their influence the way he'd campaigned against "issue" novels and reading for "meaning":

It may well be . . . that a well-marked Washington form near *ssp. scudderi* is disguised as "*Plebeius Melissa* var *lotis*" in Leighton's incredibly naïve paper . . . where utter confusion is achieved by references . . . to Holland's hopelessly unreliable book. In this connection, it is worthwhile repeating that Holland . . . figured . . . the "type" of *Lycaena scudderi* Edwards [as] a male of *melissa samuelis* Nabokov . . . which is one of the reasons I do not attach any importance to Chernock's vague statement . . . that . . . he

Longs Peak, Rocky Mountain National Park, Colorado

found "two males . . . that may be part of the series given to Edwards by Scudder." The confusion . . . runs through the whole literature.

Earlier, in his first papers, he had been warmly charming. He wrote in the tones of the gentleman naturalist of the European nineteenth century, less concerned with scientific rigor than with style:

> I had done no collecting at all for more than ten years, and then quite suddenly a stroke of luck enabled me to visit . . . the Pyrénées Orientales and the Ariège. The night journey from Paris to Perpignan was marked by a pleasant though silly dream in which I was offered what looked uncommonly like a sardine, but was really a tropical moth.

America made him more scientist, less flaneur. It gave him intellectual tools—sex-organ dissection and reliance on the microscope; focus on the Blues—while putting at his disposal the marvelous MCZ. The distance traveled from dreams of sardines to the lab notations of the forties is large:

[*Icaricia icarioides*, Boisduval's Blue] can be defined as a Polyommatus with an Aricia-like organ. There is however one peculiar "American" character which it shares with *shasta neurona*: this is the remarkable glass like thinness . . . of the falx [part of the male organ] which is very wide . . . but tapers almost at once as it goes up producing an impression of atrophy . . . and recalling a piece of pointed candy that has been very thoroughly sucked.

By '47 he had written astute, far-seeing papers, sent copies to close comrades, and become the center of a coterie. Instead of Hazel Schmoll's ranch, with its prohibition on strong drink, he boarded at Columbine Lodge, a forty-year-old hotel-with-cabins mentioned in the 1947 *Western Travel Guide* of the AAA. A number of entomologists from his circle came to see him during his stay there. Charles Remington drove him south to Tolland Bog, a brushy, moist bottomland along South Boulder Creek, at an elevation of nine thousand feet. "I was under the vague impression that he was a writer of novels," Remington would recall forty-five years later; "we never talked about that side of his productivity." Instead they chatted about "recent specimen collecting and

Columbine Lodge, the "Grizzly" cabin, a separate unit reputedly occupied by the Nabokovs, summer 1947

research" that each had done, reveling in their shared obsession. Nabokov was "quite equally passionate" about it—and the real pleasure of the day was the sport of it, the physical effort, feet-on-the-boggy-ground in the Rockies, in the summertime.

Columbine Lodge, four miles from 14,259-foot Longs Peak, offered rooms with bath or without and was deemed "Attractive" by the AAA. Nabokov wrote Wilson, "We have a most comfortable cabin all to ourselves." The lodge was within a half-mile of the better-known Longs Peak Inn and a mile from the popular Hewes-Kirkwood Inn, a storied resort built by Charles Edwin Hewes, author of *Songs of the Rockies* and other works of poetry.* James Pickering, another local author, described the locality at the time of Nabokov's visit:

> It was to the Tahosa Valley that I came as a boy in 1946, following the footsteps of my father. . . . The "cabin," as we called it, was a magical place . . . for a boy from suburban New York. There were two large bear rugs (whose heads and paws still had their teeth and claws) on the floor of the living room in front of the massive two-story moss rock fireplace; a dramatic view of the East Face of Longs Peak . . . and, in the corner, an old wind-up victrola with its collection of raspy dance records. . . . There was no electricity or in-door plumbing, and food was kept in a "cave" just off the back porch, which "Uncle Fred and Aunt Jessie" told us had once been scavenged by a bear, later captured and sent "over the mountain." There were kerosene lamps . . . and a whole stack of paperback novels by Zane Grey and Luke Short.

To Pickering, "this was, surely, the West!" Columbine Lodge looked east to the Twin Sisters, eleven-thousand-foot pyramidal peaks of the Colorado Front Range, and west to Longs and other mountains of the Continental Divide. The valley between these two ranges was high meadow, crisscrossed by streams fed by springs and snowmelt, with beaver dams. Nabokov reported to Wilson that the "flora is simply magnificent," and his family's long stay—late June to early September— allowed them to witness successive wildflower outbreaks. On rising ground, the kinnikinnick gave way to lodgepole pine mixed with ponderosa and juniper, with many aspen stands.

Véra enjoyed the summer, although annoyed that nowhere in Estes Park, the nearest sizable town, could she find a copy of the *Saturday*

* Included in his oeuvre is a 690-page epic in blank verse, *The America* (1941).

Review of Literature, which she and her husband liked to read. Dmitri climbed Longs Peak. Late in July, a collector from Caldwell, Kansas, Don Stallings, made pilgrimage to meet Nabokov in person—they had been corresponding since '43, when a friend at the MCZ had sent Stallings a paper that Nabokov had written (probably "Some new or little known Nearctic *Neonympha*," which recorded his Grand Canyon captures). Stallings, a lawyer, asked Nabokov to help him determine some specimens, offering to pay for the service. Nabokov replied, "I shall certainly be very glad to determine your specimens. There will not be any fee."

In a thank-you letter, Stallings wrote, "I was pleased to note that the wife and I had as a general rule correctly identified these specimens. . . . In the future in your research if we have any specimens that you wish to borrow, please feel free to do so." He added, "Of course I realize that our collection is not as large as some, still it does represent some 10,000 North American Butterflies covering a little over 1100 species— plus a flock of unnamed races which . . . we do not have sufficient material at the present time [to determine]."

This was an enormous personal collection. Within a few years, Stallings, tutored by Nabokov, went into business as "Stallings & Turner, Lepidopterists," furnishing materials to collectors and museums. The correspondence from the beginning had a comradely tone, with tongue-in-cheek sallies. Stallings, from his home on the Oklahoma state line, had ranged throughout the Southwest and into Mexico, and Nabokov relied on him for information on sites; when thinking of going to Alta in '43, he first ran the idea by Stallings.

Vladimir's reliance on the microscope had a galvanizing effect. In a paper he co-wrote for the *Canadian Entomologist*, Stallings said, with the certitude of a new convert,

> This giant race of the species *freija* Thun. was collected along the Alaska Military Highway in British Columbia. In size and wing shape this would appear to be a race of *frigga* Thun. rather than of *freija*, and we have no doubt but that those who depend on external characters only will insist that we are in error; nevertheless gentalic study leaves no doubt as to its true relationship with *freija*.

Stallings prepared for his Alaska trip by studying specimens Nabokov had loaned him from the MCZ. "Yes we'd like to borrow the Alaska Highway specimens," he wrote in April '45, after first declaring,

You will find . . . that in some ways I'm rather lazy—and if another fellow has done something I usually ask him for his results before I dig in myself—hence I'd like to see a rough sketch of yours of the genitalia of *pardalis* indicating where it differs from *icarioides* and you didn't send me any sketches of the innards of the Melissa-scudderi-anna group.

He confessed that "my ideas run along similar to yours—but I always find you about ten good full strides ahead of me." Then, in '46, Stallings wrote, "Also received your latest paper which is more nearly a book. Thanks. I like your genitalic work. Have hopes of . . . doing some of that myself."

Stallings asked Nabokov to teach him the names of genital parts. Soon he was replicating, as far as he could, Nabokov at work at his bench in the MCZ:

Did some dissecting the other evening. A couple of icarioides and one specimen of what I thought was a pardalis, but didn't see any . . . differences, though I haven't made sketches yet of the valves and falax and uncas lobe. I can't get a scope—so am using a borrowed one with 90 power . . . hence I can't do any 300 times looking.

With Stallings, Nabokov engaged in advanced shoptalk. From him he heard of, or heard more about, the concerns of an American man of that time; Stallings wrote that he dreamed of going collecting the following summer "if Uncle Sam doesn't want to send me traveling first," and he also wrote, "Had a letter from my brother-in-law Dr. Turner, he parachuted into France on D-Day and is still going strong. As soon as the war is over . . . we have hopes [of collecting in southern Alaska]."

Near the end of *Lolita*, whose composition Nabokov dated from this time, the heroine, married at seventeen, contacts Humbert Humbert three years after having escaped his captivity. Humbert drives immediately to the city she writes from, a town he calls Coalmont, "some eight hundred miles from New York City" ("not 'Va.,' not 'Pa.,' not 'Tenn.'—and not Coalmont, anyway—I have camouflaged everything," he says). Lolita is pregnant. She asks for a few hundred dollars so that she and her husband, an ex-GI, can move to Alaska to begin a new life. Humbert intends to kill the husband but relents upon seeing how young he is. He implores Lolita to return to him; she refuses. So absolute is the sentence of catastrophe upon everyone in this supposedly comic novel that Lolita, although miraculously intact after her cruel youth, wonderfully seasoned, in fact, and movingly decent in her young womanhood, will soon die in childbirth, and the faint wash of hope in the dark sky of the story comes to bleak nothing.

Stallings also discussed with Nabokov, may have been the first to guide him to, Telluride, Colorado, in the forties a small mining town whose remote location made it a promising site for collecting. Four years later Nabokov made one of the most exciting captures of his life there. According to the afterword he wrote to *Lolita*, Telluride was where he found the female of *Lycaeides argyrognomon sublivens*, on a mountain slope far above the mining village. The "tinkling sounds" of life from below undergo a sea change as they find representation in the novel, becoming, to Humbert's way of hearing, the voices of children at play:

> One could hear now and then . . . an almost articulate spurt of vivid laughter, or the crack of a bat, or the clatter of a toy wagon, but it was all really too far for the eye to distinguish any movement in the lightly etched streets. I stood listening to that musical vibration from my lofty slope . . . and then I knew that the hopelessly poignant thing was not Lolita's absence from my side, but the absence of her voice from that concord.

Stallings invited Nabokov to visit Kansas. Vladimir suggested Estes Park, and there they met at last, with their spouses, late in July. "My family joins me in sending Mrs Stallings and you our kindest regards," Nabokov wrote afterward. "Those two days . . . we had together were most delightful." The first day was hard on Stallings; he was fresh from lowland Kansas, and Nabokov led him high up Longs, making a show of his own ability to caper and bound at a great altitude. The next day Stallings announced, "Today we're going to collect *my* way," and they had better luck hunting *Erebia magdalena*, a Satyr butterfly, at lower elevations on the rocky slopes near timberline that the species favors.

NABOKOV'S FRIENDSHIP WITH DON Stallings continued into the next decade. "I shall never forget your face when I suggested a certain short cut on our way to the *magdalena* ground," Nabokov wrote him—the shortcut was probably a steep one—and Stallings kept their exchange of samples going, responding to Nabokov's interest in *argyrognomon sublivens* by writing, "I am sending you a few of the 'melissa' things that we caught in southern Colorado around Independence Pass and then further south near Lake City and Slumgullion Pass—I don't believe these are your *sublivens* but rather the 'hum drum' race [of *melissa* that resembles *sublivens*]."

Nabokov's years of lepidopteral work were ending. He had wrestled the MCZ collection into shape, meanwhile accomplishing research of a high order that fulfilled dreams of entomological achievement. To his sister he wrote that he was unchanged as an adult—still the boy who had had those dreams. The unity of his world, the persistence of personal themes, was itself a deep subject of *Speak, Memory*, begun in the thirties in France and eventually to appear in American magazines, chapter by chapter. "Some part of me must have been born in Colorado," he wrote Wilson, "for I am constantly recognizing things with a delicious pang." Colorado reminded him of the family estate on the river Oredezh, of mountain slopes in the Crimea where he had collected—the Colorado sky recalled for him the blue of summer mornings at Vyra, on days when he went out hunting.

Two famous passages from *Speak, Memory*, from the butterfly chapter (chapter 6), work a pleasing trick with insects and time, the seven-year-old losing a magnificent swallowtail given him by a servant, only to recapture it "after a forty-year race, on an immigrant dandelion under an endemic aspen near Boulder." At age eleven, exploring across the Oredezh,

> At last I saw I had come to the end of the marsh. The rising ground beyond was a paradise of lupines, columbines, and penstemons. Mariposa lilies bloomed under Ponderosa pines. In the distance, fleeting cloud shadows dappled the dull green of slopes above timber line, and the gray and white of Longs Peak.

The point is that "I do not believe in time," the author tells us. "I like to fold my magic carpet . . . in such a way as to superimpose one part of the pattern upon another." Despite the dislocations of his century—revolution, his father's murder, world war, exterminations—butterflies persist, and, more important, the author by an act of art binds up his realms, unites them, overrules chaos.

He *does* believe in time, though. His protagonists struggle against it, seek to evade or triumph over it, and they must be struggling against something. He also believes in—savors and records—irreducible specificities, and the magic by which the bog bilberry and other marsh flora turn into the flowers of the high Rockies is charming but inexact. "Let visitors trip," he says, and indeed we do trip on the uncharacteristic imprecision of mariposa lilies, which love full sun and rocky ground, growing in piney shade.

In *Bend Sinister* he had blended countries. Then he backed off, in the luminous books of his American prime, downplaying geographical confusions until *Pale Fire*, written in Europe. Some of his iconoclasm regarding geography is strictly lepidopteral; not only are there butterflies, like the swallowtail, that disregard borders, but the *Lycaeides*, the genus of Blues that he most liked to hunt, inhabits

> a lost country of plenty [above and below] the Arctic circle of today; its nurseries are the mountains of central Asia, the Alps, and the Rockies. Seldom more than two and never more than three species are known to occur in a given geographical region, and so far as records go, not more than two species have ever been seen frequenting the same puddle or the same flowery bank.

To his way of thinking, there existed a butterfly supercontinent—the northern half of what is called Pangaea, a supercontinent of three hundred million years ago. Here the small, unshowy Blues fluttered over a domain that subsumed Russia and America and other lands, too.

The books of his American prime disciplined this fancy. He did not lose his interest in geofoolery, but for a period of years the world remained stable in his work, remarkably like the real world; the common reader of the forties and fifties, encountering new books by Nabokov, dealt with many types of ambiguity, but not with wholesale rechartings of the globe.

The flood of American impressions contributed to this (temporary) stability. Needing to earn a living, he taught American undergraduates for twenty years, developing an acute sense of how much disorientation they could take; his acquaintance with students describes a vast opening out, from language classes for three or four to performances in front of three or four hundred, his progress from obscurity to celebrity on campus predicting his writing career. From teaching he took countless impressions:

My most vivid memories concern examinations. Big amphitheater [at Cornell]. Exam from 8 a.m. to 10:30. About 150 students— unwashed, unshaven young males and reasonably well-groomed young females. A general sense of tedium and disaster. Half-past eight. Little coughs, the clearing of nervous throats, coming in clusters. . . . Some of the martyrs plunged in meditation, their arms locked behind their heads. I meet a dull gaze directed at me. . . . Girl in glasses comes up to my desk to ask: "Professor Kafka, do you want us to say that . . .? Or do you want us to answer only the first part of the question?" . . . The shaking of a cramped wrist, the failing ink, the deodorant that breaks down. When I catch eyes directed at me, they are forthwith raised to the ceiling in pious meditation. Windowpanes getting misty. Boys peeling off sweaters. Girls chewing gum in rapid cadence. Ten minutes, five, three, time's up.

Students at Stanford and Wellesley recalled his quick way with slang, his ethnological curiosity. If he had been more like other writers of the emigration—like Bertolt Brecht, for instance, who arrived at about the same time and who had long fantasized a skyscraper America, brutalist and unsentimental—his friendships with Americans would have been few and unimportant. Nabokov immersed himself in the demos. His resemblance as émigré artist is less to Mann or Brecht or other luminaries living in enclaves than to hardworking filmmakers with carry- over reputations: quick studies like Billy Wilder, who had made films in French as well as German before he switched to American, and Henry Koster (*Das Hässliche Mädchen* followed by *One Hundred Men and a Girl*, *The Bishop's Wife*, *Harvey*, *The Robe*, and *The Singing Nun*, among others).

He became fond of a lab volunteer at the MCZ, Phyllis Smith, who prepared specimens for him. They worked together beginning when Smith was seventeen. When she was in her fifties, she recalled "how well he had known me." Nabokov liked to chat at the workbench; he was "sometimes quiet, sometimes *loud*," always "uninhibited and unself- conscious," she remembered. Sometime in the early forties, he read *Moby-Dick*; they then discussed it. He asked her "questions, questions. How-to questions, why questions," savoring the *bizarrerie* of Americans in their native habitats. Smith's parents divorced, and Nabokov consoled her at the time; he asked her many questions about the trouble.

June of '44, he ate "some Virginia ham in a little Wursthaus near Harvard Square and was happily . . . examining the genitalia of a specimen from [California] at the museum, when suddenly I felt a strange wave of nausea." The ensuing bout of hemorrhagic colitis provoked a two-thousand-word account sent to Wilson and McCarthy, graphic and comic and notable for the curiosity he summoned despite projectile vomiting and rectal bleeding:

> By then, I was in a state of *complete* collapse and when the doctor . . . turned up he could find neither my pulse, nor my blood pressure. He started telephoning and I heard him saying "extremely grave" and "not a minute to be lost." Five minutes later . . . he had arranged the matter and . . . I was at the Mt. Aubrey hospital in a semi-private ward—the "semi" being represented by an old man dying from acute cardiac trouble (I could not sleep all night owing to his groans and *ahannement* [panting]—he died towards dawn after telling some unknown "Henry" such things as "My little boy, you can't do that to me. Use me right" etc.,—all very interesting . . .).

After a night and a day on an IV, Nabokov was transferred

> to the general ward, where the radio kept emitting hot music, cigarette ads (in a juicy voice from the heart) and gags without interruption until (at 10 p.m.) I bellowed to the nurse to have the bloody thing stopped (much to the annoyance and surprise of the staff and of the patients. This is a curious detail of American life—they did not actually listen to the radio, in fact everybody was talking, retching, guffawing, wisecracking, flirting with the (very charming) nurses . . . but apparently the impossible sounds coming from the apparatus . . . acted as a "life-background" for the . . . ward, for as soon as it was stopped complete quiet ensued and I soon fell asleep).

He noticed that the dying man panted; also the "juicy voice from the heart." He operated as a writer does, noticing all he can, and this might have helped him negotiate a terrifying and humiliating ordeal. In any event, he was always noticing.

10.

S oon after returning from Colorado, Nabokov heard from a professor
at Cornell, Morris Bishop, informing him of an open position
in Russian literature. Bishop knew of him from stories published in
magazines and because Vladimir's cousin Nicolas had been "the rather
startling Professor of Music" at Wells College, just north of Ithaca.
Bishop published occasional verse in the *New Yorker*, and Katharine
White, hearing of an opening at Cornell, had talked up Nabokov.

He had visited the campus once before. Now he came on a charm tour,
under Bishop's sponsorship; the search committee was leery of hiring
someone without advanced degrees, but Cornell had recently created a
Division of Literature, distinct from other academic departments, and
a Rockefeller grant was tapped to cover his salary (five thousand dollars).

Ithaca became the American base. Here he lived with Véra and
Dmitri (on vacations from school) for eleven years, beginning in the
summer of '48, in houses rented from leave-taking professors. Bishop
and his wife, Alison, became good friends. Bishop's scholarly temperament, leavened with the kind of wit to be encountered in the *New Yorker*
of the Thurber-Perelman era, made him good company, and he was
a faithful institutional protector of Nabokov, in the mold of Wilson
and Comstock. In addition to his poetry and academic writing, Bishop
wrote popular books, including a mystery novel under the name
W. Bolingbroke Johnson. He denied authorship, but a copy found in
the Cornell library bore this inscription in his hand:

> *A cabin in northern Wisconsin*
> *Is what I would be for the nonce in,*

To be rid of the pain
Of The Widening Stain
And W. Bolingbroke Johnson

Nabokov made clear from the outset what could be expected of him as a professor. Though "sorry to disappoint you," he wrote the dean of arts and sciences, "I am entirely lacking in administrative talents. I am a hopelessly poor organizer, and my participation in any committee would be, I am afraid, pretty worthless." At the same time,

> I entirely agree with you that courses in Russian Literature should not be limited to those given in Russian. . . . I know from experience that a course in this subject given in English has a strong appeal for students who have a general interest in literature,—the enrollment in such a course which I am giving currently at Wellesley College . . . is one of the largest in the College.

He was annoyed that Harvard had failed to recruit him. But his Cornell appointment was excellent news—a deep relief. Just on the level of an immigrant's story, his had now become much sunnier. His small boat was being lifted by a postwar tide that produced an enormous expansion in American higher education. Leaving aside his gifts as educator and entertainer, and the undeniable luster he brought to an institution, he had been seeking employment during a long depression that merged with a war, and now that struggle was over.

He worked prodigiously at Cornell. While there, he wrote parts or all of *Lolita*, *Pnin*, and *Speak, Memory*, short stories, poetry, and translations of his own work and others'. He also composed his 1,895-page annotated translation of *Eugene Onegin*, as well as an annotated translation of the Old Slavonic epic *The Song of Igor's Campaign*. In addition, he conceived and began work on *Pale Fire* and *Ada*, his ambitious novels of the sixties. *Pale Fire* is, among other things, an ingenious animation of Ithaca. Almost offhandedly he registers his habitat with a vividness that surpasses in affectionate fidelity the accounts of all other chroniclers. New Wye, the novel's college town, is a place of steep up-and-down topography like Ithaca's, of hardwood forests and drafty old houses above a lake. The winters are snowy and bitter, as Charles Kinbote, the half-cracked, deluded, but not entirely unreliable narrator discovers:

Never shall I forget how elated I was upon learning, as mentioned in a note my reader shall find, that the suburban house (rented for my use from Judge Goldsworth who had gone on his Sabbatical to England) . . . stood next to that of the celebrated American poet whose verses I had tried to put into Zemblan two decades earlier! Apart from this glamorous neighborhood, the Goldsworthian chateau, as I was soon to discover, had little to recommend it. The heating system was a farce, depending as it did on registers in the floor wherefrom the tepid exhalations of a throbbing and groaning basement furnace were transmitted to the rooms. . . . It is true that, as usually happens to newcomers, I was told I had chosen the worst winter in years. . . . On one of my first mornings there, as I was preparing to leave for college in the powerful red car I had just acquired, I noticed that Mr. and Mrs. Shade, neither of whom I had yet met socially . . . were having trouble with their old Packard in the slippery driveway where it emitted whines of agony but could not extricate one tortured rear wheel out of a concave inferno of ice.

Kinbote spies on Shade, the Robert Frost–like poet, and Ithaca/New Wye's prospects assist him:

Windows, as well known, have been the solace of first-person liter-ature throughout the ages. But this observer never could emulate in sheer luck the eavesdropping *Hero of Our Time* or the omnipresent one of *Time Lost*. Yet I was granted now and then scraps of happy hunting. When my casement window ceased to function because of an elm's gross growth, I found, at the end of the veranda, an ivied corner from which I could view rather amply the front of the poet's house. If I wanted to see its south side I could go down to the back of my garage and look from behind a tulip tree across the curving downhill road at several precious bright windows. . . . If I yearned for the opposite side, all I had to do was walk uphill to the top of my garden where my bodyguard of black junipers watched the stars, and the omens, and the patch of pale light under the lone streetlamp on the road below. By the onset of the season here conjured up, I had surmounted . . . private fears . . . and rather enjoyed following in the dark a weedy and rocky easterly projection of my grounds ending in a locust grove on a slightly higher level than the north side of the poet's house.

In a book of tributes to Nabokov published later, Morris Bishop recalled the early sabbatical-house days:

> Most faculty members come from bourgeois, even petty-bourgeois, backgrounds. We have the habit of small economies; we cut our own grass, replace our own washers, paint our own floors. The Nabokovs had known two extremes: first opulence, then privation in mean Berlin furnished rooms. They had had little training in the complacent middle.

Furnished houses, with few duties for upkeep, suited them. Some of the houses were dreary, some splendid, as for example a professor's trim house on Hampton Road in Cayuga Heights, perched atop a hill with a picture-window view of Cayuga Lake. Véra "carried the burdens of everyday life on a small budget in a provincial town," Bishop recalled, and Stacy Schiff exhaustively documents Vera's services to her husband as chauffeur, classroom attendant, housekeeper, house hunter, and amanuensis. She was regal of mien and admired from afar by many, but also pitied, worried over, also from afar:

> The attention-getting part was the distribution of labor. More than a few heads turned when, in the supermarket parking lot, Véra set her bagged groceries down in the snow while she shuffled for her keys, then loaded the trunk. In the car her husband sat immobile, oblivious. A similar routine was observed during a move, when Nabokov made his way into a new home carrying a chess set and a small lamp. Véra followed with two bulky suitcases.

Dmitri's memories of Cornell glow, effuse. He was there off and on; Ithaca became another site of his successful American adjustment, an attachment point for the "cocoon of love and well-being and encouragement in which both my parents always enveloped me," he later wrote. Thinking of Ithaca, he recalled how,

> home for a winter vacation, I would trudge on skis for groceries over Ithaca roads made impassable by a giant snowstorm, or, in spring, drive in our beloved Olds or its successor, the froglike green Buick . . . to the Cascadilla tennis courts for a game with Father.

Each of the houses had "its personal charms, from horseshoes to basement workshops to a splendid cannonball of unknown origin that I dug up in the Hansteens' garden, somehow related in my memory to the expression 'Go over like a lead balloon.' " Evenings passed watching "*The Honeymooners* . . . on one of the sabbatical TVs . . . or Alfred Hitchcock episodes that presaged a collaboration with Hitchcock that was almost to happen [for Vladimir] some years later."

Dmitri was the same age as fictional Dolores Haze. The wash of cozy Americanness was her donnée, too, but made painful and grotesque in her case; the house with Mexican knickknacks where she lived with her mother was where she lost that mother, after having first lost her father, and then the *real* nightmare started. The success of Nabokov's real child—the object of his and Véra's every effort, in a sense—was an accomplishment about which Vladimir, with charming apologies, liked to boast to friends. They had brought their son out of fascist Germany and through many threatful twists had delivered him, un-Englished and wrongly dressed, undernourished-looking, to a bourn of hope. Days after moving to Ithaca, Nabokov wrote his *New Yorker* editor, White, "We are absolutely enchanted with Cornell and very very grateful to the kind fate that has guided us here."

Dmitri was a difficult creation. He was headstrong ("I was not always an easy son"), and his private school tuition, at the Dexter School (attended earlier by John F. Kennedy), St. Mark's (the head there was a "vulgar cad," Véra thought), and the hardy Holderness School, where he learned to ski and went on hikes, cost Nabokov about a third of his Cornell income. "My boarding school career . . . survived some bad skids," Dmitri admitted.

> I . . . lived on the perilous border between success . . . and minor clandestine delinquency: beer in the woods, nighttime excursions, even a first-year episode of petty thievery. . . . A superb teacher named Charles Abbey . . . taught me the rudiments of Shakespeare and guided me to state and New England debating championships. . . . I had already been accepted at [college, when there came] an indignant protest from a group of village mothers. . . . I had volunteered to chauffeur a spastic fellow student on regular visits to the local osteopath [and] discovered that the [doctor had] a flirtatious daughter, and [engaged in] a few groping trysts. Thanks to [the school headmaster] I have been allowed to leave with dignity, [taking] my final examinations on the honor system at home.

The trick was to help him Americanize in positive ways. That the Nabokovs were in a position to reject a school like St. Mark's—elite and renowned, if riddled with favoritism, Nabokov felt—and find a more congenial one, Holderness, testified to their American good fortune.

Lolita also goes to private school. Her predatory stepfather places her in the "Beardsley School," somewhere in New England, after a year of sexual usage on the road. Beardsley has "phoney British aspirations," Humbert says, but is proudly progressive, concerned with " 'the adjustment of the child to group life,' " according to the headmistress. Lolita, cheeky though wounded, her youth profoundly sullied, performs adequately as a student, but Miss Pratt observes certain anomalies: that she " 'is obsessed by sexual thoughts for which she finds no outlet,' " while at the same time she " 'remains morbidly uninterested in sexual matters . . . represses her curiosity in order to save her ignorance and self-dignity.' " She writes an " 'obscene four-letter word which our Dr. Cutler tells me is low-Mexican for urinal with her lipstick on some health pamphlets,' " yet seems not to know about the birds and the bees.

Some of Dmitri's sexual hijinks as a youth, as described in his memoirs, might have colored Nabokov's sketches of hormonal American boys. Humbert jealously guards his captive stepdaughter against such boys, determined that, "as long as my regime lasted she would never, never be permitted to go with a youngster in rut to a movie, or neck in a car," and auto-mad Dmitri seems to lurk behind Humbert's thoughts about "the self-sufficient rapist with pustules and a souped-up car" who comes a-courting. Whatever his qualities, Dmitri had the freedom to explore, to experiment. His intelligent, concerned parents, laboring to put him on the right track, to secure, if possible, an American acculturation in a single generation, leading eventually to happiness and a secure income, both protected and liberated him. Humbert's fathering of Lolita is the dark negation of this.

Bereft of good parents, Dmitri's unlucky sister floats free. Her girlish allure is immense, radioactive:

> Lo, little limp Lo! Owing perhaps to constant amorous exercise, she radiated, despite her very childish appearance, some special languorous glow which threw garage fellows, hotel pages, vacationists, goons in luxurious cars, maroon morons near blued pools, into fits of concupiscence. . . . Little Lo was aware of that glow of hers, and I would often catch her *coulant un regard* in the

direction of some . . . grease monkey, with a sinewy golden-brown forearm and watch-braceleted wrist, and hardly had I turned my back to go and buy this very Lo a lollipop, than I would hear her and the fair mechanic burst into a perfect love song of wisecracks.

Sexually precocious, she travels a dangerous road. To be male would be safer; in one of his few factual misrepresentations, Nabokov, who researched pedophilia carefully, opines,

Ladies and gentlemen of the jury, the majority of sex offenders that hanker for some throbbing, sweet-moaning, physical but not necessarily coital, relation with a girl-child, are innocuous, inadequate, passive, timid strangers who merely ask the community to allow them to pursue their practically harmless, so-called aberrant behavior, their little hot wet private acts of sexual deviation without the police and society cracking down upon them. We are not sex fiends! We do not rape as good soldiers do. We are unhappy, mild, dog-eyed gentlemen. . . . Poets never kill.

They do kill, though. Humbert kills; Clare Quilty, his nemesis, dies by his hand, and Charlotte Haze, his wife, dies in an accident brought on by his acts. Lolita dies, too. After years of his misprotection, she liberates herself by means of a different, stranger captivity, with Quilty. But the mark is upon her: the doomful sex mark. She is American, and for us these things are never simple. Hawthorne seems to attend her as she lights out, Huck Finn style, for the Alaska territory, pregnant with a child who will never be born: hoping to outrun her bad luck, she only manifests the curse more clearly, finds swift destruction.

11.

Nosy Miss Pratt, of the Beardsley School, comically misunderstands Lolita's symptoms, but she gets the main thing right: sex is at the bottom of it all. Concern for " 'the adjustment of the child to group life' " is, to Miss Pratt's way of thinking, concern about sexual development rather than ethical or intellectual growth. As a midcentury American educator who hopes to appear advanced, she puts sex forward—" 'This is why we stress the four D's,' " she tells Humbert: " 'Dramatics, Dance, Debating and Dating.' " The Freudian century is roaring on its way. Freudianism, with its insights into many issues, reduces in the popular mind to a focus on sex. It is Humbert's unusual luck—for good or ill, who knows—to have landed in America in the middle of the century of sex.

Freud did not invent sex, and sex in literature also predates him. Nabokov famously loathed Freud: he maintained his own mental hygiene, he said, by taking "gleeful pleasure every morning in refuting the Viennese Quack by recalling the details of my dreams without using one single reference to sexual symbols or mythical complexes." Yet the popular corruption of Freudianism—that "it's all about sex"—is an attitude consistent with his best novel. His protagonist is surely sex-obsessed. He has been marked for life by a sexual interlude in childhood; Lolita fulfills the dream that infuses that tormented life, gets him excited again. Were there a case that more clearly demonstrates the potency of childhood sexual trauma, it would be hard to make out; Humbert, also an anti-Freudian, an "anarchist" according to his creator, is trapped in a script seemingly dictated by the first psychoanalyst.

Nabokov's earlier novels contain some arousing passages, but sexual fulfillment is usually attended by disaster, as in *The Eye* (1930), *Laughter in the Dark*, *The Real Life of Sebastian Knight*, and other works. His most erotic passages are not accounts of sex acts but descriptions of objects of desire. His protagonists become conduits of enamored perception, connoisseurs of female allure:

> The two sisters resembled each other; the frank bulldogish heaviness of the elder's features was just perceptible in Vanya, but in a different way that lent significance and originality to the beauty of her face. The sisters' eyes, too, were similar—black-brown, slightly asymmetric, and a trifle slanted, with amusing little folds on the dark lids. Vanya's eyes were more opaque at the iris . . . somewhat myopic, as if their beauty made them not quite suitable for everyday use.
>
> *The Eye*

> Albinus taught her to bathe daily instead of only washing her hands and neck as she had done hitherto. Her nails were always clean now, and polished a brilliant red. . . . He kept discovering new charms in her—touching little things which in any other girl would have seemed to him coarse and vulgar. The childish lines of her body, her shamelessness and the gradual dimming of her eyes (as if they were being slowly extinguished like the lights in a theater) roused him to . . . frenzy.
>
> *Laughter in the Dark*

> "What's so attractive about her, after all?" he thought for the thousandth time. "All right, she has those dimples, that pale complexion—that's not enough. Her eyes are so-so, gypsyesque, and her teeth are uneven. And her lips are so thick, so glossy—if one could just stop them, shut them up with a kiss. And she thinks she looks English in that blue suit. . . . As soon as Martin achieved an attitude of indifference toward Sonia, he would suddenly notice what a graceful back she had, how she tilted her head—and her slanted eyes ran across him with a swift chill.
>
> *Glory*

Sex acts abound in some of the books. Yet Nabokov eschews rough language—profanity absolutely—and his visits to the boudoir are Hollywoodish: faux-sophisticated, with shots before the act and after, the act itself undescribed. Sex happens briskly and with an unreal frequency. In *Laughter in the Dark*, Margot, the cruel, taunting mistress, repeatedly has intercourse with Rex, her sociopathic lover, under the nose of Albinus, the man she enjoys betraying; she also has it repeatedly with Albinus. In *Ada*, written thirty years later, the same rabbity automatism undercuts credibility. Sex in Nabokov is mostly odorless and unlubricated, and indirectly realized. The urgent and risky labor that some authors of his era assumed—to imagine and write about sex with expressive power, with nothing left out—was not his duty, not *his* choice.

He wrote well about amorousness: the disposition to become obsessed, to fetishize a lover. In *The Enchanter*, his first *Lolita*-like fiction, he brought his special eye to the task:

> A violet-clad girl of twelve . . . was treading rapidly and firmly on skates that did not roll but crunched on the gravel as she raised and lowered them with little Japanese steps. . . . Subsequently . . . it seemed to him that right away, at that very moment, he had appreciated all of her from tip to toe: the liveliness of her russet curls (recently trimmed); the radiance of her large, slightly vacuous eyes, somehow suggesting translucent gooseberries; her merry, warm complexion; her pink mouth, slightly open so that two large front teeth barely rested on the protuberance of the lower lip . . . her bare arms with the sleek little foxlike hairs.

Nabokov recalled *The Enchanter* as "a dead scrap": "I was not pleased with the thing and destroyed it sometime after moving to America in 1940." Twenty years later, while gathering up manuscripts to give the Library of Congress for a tax break, he found the work and read it with "considerably more pleasure" and decided that it was "a beautiful piece of Russian prose, precise and lucid." Still, he did not say it was a success—that it worked as a story.

Writing about the ravishing of a child challenged him, reduced him to near incoherence. The opening pages are off-putting and opaque. The protagonist, unnamed, in an unnamed European city, anatomizes his attraction to little girls. The writing is full of arch euphemisms. The fifty-five-page piece (in Russian manuscript) holds the subject at arm's length, just as the protagonist holds his own compulsion away, horrified but unable not to speak of it. He is a "thin, dry-lipped" man with a "slightly balding head," closely resembling the dog-eyed, ineffectual men of Humbert's sex-molester profile (rather than Humbert himself, who is "a handsome, intensely virile grown-up" in Lolita's eyes).

The Enchanter reads smoothly after its wan beginning. It differs from *Lolita* in its lack of immediacy (third-person as against first, expository rather than scenic) and in its simplicity, the richly worked allusive style of *Lolita* only hinted at. There are countless similarities, though, from images—Lolita is also described in terms of gooseberries; little girls in both books are said to have a "biscuity" smell—to crucial plot turns, and when the author revisited this material ten years later, no doubt much imaginative work had already been done. Why he returned is the question. The situation of a gentleman pedophile who inherits a child had produced a tale that misfired, in the direction of boredom rather than sensation; it did not seem promising.

Nabokov's personal interest in the material, possibly of a prurient kind, might have brought him back. As a professional writer, he sensed opportunity. Wilson's experience with *Hecate County*—surely not determinative, but concurrent with Nabokov's dusting off of the material—drew attention. This is the kind of frankness that Wilson brought to his audacious novel, his first bestselling book after some twenty American titles:

> But what struck and astonished me most was that not only were her thighs perfect columns but that all that lay between them was impressively beautiful, too, with an ideal aesthetic value that I had never found there before. The mount was of a classical femininity: round and smooth and plump: the fleece, if not quite golden, was blond and curly and soft; and the portals were a deep tender rose like the petals of some fresh flower. And they were doing their feminine work of making things easy for the entrant with a honey-sweet sleek profusion that showed I had quite misjudged her in suspecting . . . she was really unresponsive to caresses.

In another notorious passage, Wilson wrote,

> I remember one cold winter Sunday when Anna had come in the afternoon, a day of blank uptown facades and decorous uptown perspectives, when I had gone down to the deserted museum to look something up in a book, and, returning, it seemed so incongruous to watch her take off her pink slip and to have her in her prosaic brassiere: the warm and adhesive body and the mossy damp underparts . . . between the cold afternoon sheets in the

gray-lit Sunday room; and one evening when I had come home from a party, at which I had made Imogen smile by my tender and charming gallantries . . . and had made love to Anna for the second time, by a sudden revival of appetite after she had put on her clothes to go, by way of her white thighs and buttocks, laid bare between black dress and gray stockings.

Wilson read Henry Miller, whose *Tropic of Cancer* (1934) and *Tropic of Capricorn* (1939) used forbidden terms. *Lady Chatterley's Lover*, according to Leon Edel, the editor of Wilson's compilation *The Twenties* (1975), provided the idea for an American take on class and sex à la Lawrence's. Though Wilson's descriptions seem quiet now, certainly not pornographic, "what we should remember," Edel wrote, "is that . . . in its truth to life and to himself [his frankness] antedated the later avalanche of erotic writings that now colors the creative imagination of America."

The Enchanter, nothing like as bold, does strike one graphic note. At the end of the unnamed subject's torturous encounter with his own pedophilia, rendered in terms of far-fetched conceits ("Never . . . had the subordinate clause of his fearsome life been complemented by the principal one," etc.), we find:

Already his gaze . . . was creeping downward along [the body of a sleeping, half-clothed child]. . . . Finally making up his mind, he gently stroked her long, just slightly parted, faintly sticky legs, which grew cooler and a little coarser on the way down. . . . He recalled, with a furious sense of triumph, the roller skates, the sun, the chestnut trees, everything—while he kept stroking with his fingertips, trembling and casting sidelong looks at the plump promontory, with its brand-new downiness, which, independently but with a familial parallel, embodied a concentrated echo of something about her lips and cheeks.

The book has been reserved so far—and never has the molester succeeded in molesting. Though at last touching her, he ravishes more piercingly with his gaze, and Nabokov's love of fixing specimens and gazing at them "in the wondrous crystalline world of the microscope" comes to mind as his doomed protagonist, who in minutes will die in a road accident, glimpses very heaven.

Possibly what drew him back was the hope that this material, so dangerous-feeling, so uneasy to write about, might compel a breakthrough. Not only a commercial breakthrough, although he longed for that ("All my previous books have been such dismal financial flops," he wrote Katharine White in 1950), but a stylistic one. *The Enchanter*'s disappointments are in the prose. Nabokov's dialogue, which will undergo a liberation in *Lolita*, in the direction of vividness and viciousness, is here stolid, with characters speaking in long, intelligent paragraphs that make women sound like men and men like women and both sound smothered, corseted:

> "Now let's sit down and discuss things rationally," she said a moment later, having descended heavily and meekly onto the newly returned sofa. . . . "First of all, my friend, as you know, I am a sick, a seriously sick, woman. For a couple of years now my life has been one of constant medical care. The operation I had on April twenty-fifth was in all likelihood the next-to-last one . . . next time they'll take me from the hospital to the cemetery. No, no, don't pooh-pooh what I'm saying. Let's even assume I last a few more years."

> "Please, try to understand," he continued. . . . "Even if we pay them for everything, and even overpay them, do you think that will make her feel any more at home there? I doubt it. There's a fine school there, you'll tell me . . . but we'll find an even better one here, apart from the fact that I am and always have been in favor of private instruction."

Nabokov mocks his characters' stuffiness, but his story does not escape the mood. The wickedness of the trick marriage—played for black fun in *Lolita*—is barely exploited. Pedophilia leads swiftly to death, with no stops allowed along the way for demonic riffs, for a savage, Humbertian cutting loose.

IF HE WERE GOING to enter the lists with the other novelists of sex—assuming, for the moment, that Nabokov ever thought of things this way—he would have to mark himself out. And *Lolita* does take astonishing, indelible leaps. The voyeuristic tendency of his sex writing, suggestive of common-garden Peeping Tomism in *The Enchanter*, deepens; in *The Enchanter*, descriptions of the nameless girl tend toward the generic, but Lolita passes before the gaze of a genius of specificity, and her American setting receives similarly lively treatment.

The roller-skating girl was a blur of teeth, curls, and merry cheeks. But Lolita casts an uncanny spell, whereby time slows and her seducer, at first out of his mind with lust, learns to slow down, too. Early on, he reports "an immobilized fraction of her, a cinematographic still" in his mind, as "with one knee up under her tartan skirt she sits tying her shoe." Then comes a flood of recognitions, pitched in various registers—mooncalf, tumescent, scientific, ironic, adoring. It amounts to a kind of Audubon's *Birds of America* about a single child, the type specimen of the taxon *nymphet*:

> The soot-black lashes of her pale-gray vacant eyes . . . five asymmetrical freckles . . . I might say her hair is auburn, and her lips as red as licked candy. . . . Oh, that I were a lady writer who could have her pose naked in a naked light! But I am lanky, big-boned, wooly-chested Humbert Humbert, with thick black eyebrows and a queer accent, and a cesspoolful of rotting monsters behind his slow boyish smile.

The "lady writer" would be able to examine her clinically, therefore more exhaustively, but it is his corrupt, desirous gaze that brings her alive:

> She wore a plaid shirt, blue jeans and sneakers. . . . After a while she sat down next to me on the lower step of the back porch and began to pick up the pebbles between her feet . . . and chuck them at a can. *Ping.* You can't a second time—you can't hit it—this is agony—a second time. *Ping.* Marvelous skin . . . tender and tanned, not the least blemish. Sundaes cause acne. The excess of the oily substance called sebum which nourishes the hair follicles of the skin creates, when too profuse, an irritation that opens the way to infection. But nymphets do not have acne although they gorge themselves on rich food.

> All at once I knew I could kiss her throat or the wick of her mouth with perfect impunity. I knew she would let me do so, and even close her eyes as Hollywood teaches. . . . A modern child, an avid reader of movie magazines, an expert in dream-slow close-ups, might not think it too strange.

Later in the novel—after Humbert has been ravaging Lolita at the rate of three acts of intercourse per day—he continues to discover her.

The rotting monsters of his worse nature do not blind him; indeed, his perceptions grow more complex, more tender:

> She wore her first cloth coat with a fur collar; there was a small brown cap on my favorite hairdo—the fringe in front and the swirl at the sides and the natural curls at the back—and her damp-dark moccasins and white socks were more sloppy than ever. She pressed as usual her books to her chest while speaking or listening, and her feet gestured all the time: she would stand on her left instep with her right toe, remove it backward, cross her feet, rock slightly, sketch a few steps. . . . Above all—since we are speaking of movement and youth—I liked to see her spinning up and down Thayer Street on her beautiful young bicycle: rising on the pedals to work on them lustily, then sinking back in a languid posture while the speed wore itself off; and then she would stop at our mailbox and, still astride, would flip through a magazine she found there, and put it back, and press her tongue to one side of her upperlip.

The pulsing, frightening energy of the novel comes from looking ever deeper at a forbidden thing. For him the captive nymphet is inexhaustible as a subject; then, mysteriously, Lolita the girl is.

That this will be a sex novel announces itself quickly. John Ray Jr., Ph.D., author of the foreword, identifies himself as an authority on "perversions," promising that "platitudinous evasions" will not obscure what's to come. There will be scenes of an " 'aphrodisiac' " nature, so prepare yourself. Ray's foreword, read by most critics as a quick bath in Nabokovian irony, the smug editor daring to think he understands the work he introduces, stands in a proud tradition, that of noted American authors, Whitman and Poe for instance, who reviewed themselves under assumed names. Writing as Ray, Nabokov asserts the supreme value of his work: it is "a tragic tale tending unswervingly to nothing less than a moral apotheosis," he asserts, and though his tongue is in his cheek, this is an argument that his allies (his wife and son, prominently) would advance for the next fifty years:

> A great work of art is of course always original, and . . . should come as a more or less shocking surprise. I have no intention to glorify "H.H." No doubt, he is horrible, he is abject, a shining example of moral leprosy, a mixture of ferocity and jocularity. . . . A desperate honesty that throbs through his confession does not

absolve him from sins of diabolical cunning. He is abnormal. He is not a gentleman. But how magically his singing violin can conjure up a tendresse, a compassion for Lolita that makes us entranced with the book while abhorring its author!

Another shameless American self-promoter—American by naturalization—attending these early pages is Frank Harris, author of the most notorious sex memoir published during Nabokov's lifetime. Humbert, like the Harris of *My Life and Loves* (1922), loses his mother at age three; sexual feelings come soon after (age five for Harris; for Humbert, a bit later, when he observes "some interesting reactions on the part of my organism to certain photographs, pearl and umbra, with infinitely soft partings, in Pichon's sumptuous *La Beauté Humaine*").

Nabokov parodies Harris's and other sex memoirs, but meanwhile he indites one. Sex is not a theme threaded through the story of a life but itself the story, with other elements to clothe it. Unlike Harris, who fancied himself a crusader for a subterranean tradition in English writing, "the one of perfect liberty, that of Chaucer and Shakespeare, completely outspoken, with a . . . liking for lascivious details and witty smut, a man's speech," Nabokov cannot or will not overcome his distaste for profanity. Euphemisms marble this text as they did *The Enchanter*, but here they fail to disguise—often, they perversely underscore—a new directness about physicality, a lurid explicitness:

> Next moment, in a sham effort to retrieve [a magazine they were both looking at], she was all over me. Caught her by her thin knobby wrist. The magazine escaped to the floor like a flustered fowl. She twisted herself free, recoiled, and lay back in the right-hand corner of the davenport. Then, with perfect simplicity, the impudent child extended her legs across my lap.

They are alone in the house together; Mrs. Haze has gone to church. Humbert, wearing a silk dressing gown, "by this time . . . was in a state of excitement bordering on insanity," and he "managed to attune, by a series of stealthy movements, [his] masked lust to her guileless limbs."

Thoughts along these lines were enough to plunge *The Enchanter*'s antihero into a morbid, eventually fatal seizure of guilt. Humbert goes the whole hog. He will not rape the child, but he *will* have his satisfaction:

Talking fast, lagging behind my own breath, catching up with it, mimicking a sudden toothache to explain the breaks in my patter— and all the while keeping a maniac's inner eye on my distant golden goal, I cautiously increased the magic friction . . . between the weight of two sunburnt legs, resting athwart my lap, and the hidden tumor of an unspeakable passion.

Lolita seems oblivious; she chews on an "Eden-red apple." In the frottage piece that follows, the slowing or stretching out of time associated with Humbert's contemplation of a nymphet becomes an entrancement, an instance of sex magic: "I entered a plane of being where nothing mattered," he says, "save the infusion of joy brewed within my body." He loses himself

> in the pungent but healthy heat which like summer haze hung about little Haze. Let her stay, let her stay. . . . What had begun as a delicious distension of my innermost roots became a glowing tingle which now had reached that state of absolute security, confidence and reliance not found elsewhere in conscious life. With the deep hot sweetness thus established and well on its way to the ultimate convulsion, I felt I could slow down in order to prolong the glow.

Soon he begins thinking of seraglios and harem girls. He is describing incidentally a state of *kavla*, to use the Greek term prevalent in the Levant, meaning a state of impending orgasm and the timeless time of its inevitability:

> I was a radiant and robust Turk, deliberately, in the full consciousness of his freedom, postponing the moment of actually enjoying the youngest and frailest of his slaves. Suspended on the brink of that voluptuous abyss . . . I kept repeating chance words . . . as one talking and laughing in his sleep while my happy hand crept up her sunny leg as far as the shadow of decency allowed.

Lolita, too, seems on edge. Humbert touches a bruise on her thigh, and

> "Oh, it's nothing at all," she cried with a sudden shrill note in her voice, and she wiggled, and squirmed, and threw her head back, and her teeth rested on her glistening underlip as she half-turned away, and my moaning mouth, gentlemen of the jury, almost

reached her bare neck, while I crushed out against her left buttock the last throb of the longest ecstasy man or monster had ever known.

Though veiled by his "fancy prose style," this is a transgressive sex act described to the very end. It does not have precedent in Nabokov's oeuvre. It asserts that a child enjoys herself on her abuser's lap; it shows that child in attitudes associated with a grown woman having an orgasm (shrill note, wiggling, head thrown back, teeth biting lip). Nabokov makes happen what formerly he did not or could not. The European gentleman of *The Enchanter* has metamorphosed into a new, rampant type of monster in a common American house, sated, sweaty, "immersed in a euphoria of release," and not at all inclined to commit suicide for shame.

THE COMPOSITION OF *LOLITA* took place over five years. Nabokov's duties at Cornell were lighter than they had been at Wellesley, at least at the start; with a better salary, with *Speak, Memory* appearing serially in the *New Yorker* and attracting readers, with Dmitri doing well at a boarding school his parents liked, Nabokov was set up to undertake a long job of new work.

The writing was arduous. "Once or twice I was on the point of burning the unfinished draft," he says in his afterword; his biographers agree that there were real attempts to destroy the book: one in the fall of '48, as he was starting at Cornell, and another two years later. Véra is the heroine of the burnings. She fished four-by-six cards or pages from a galvanized can in which her husband had started a fire and then she stomped on them, telling him, "We are keeping this," which judgment he accepted.

Burning, rather than throwing away, seemed called for because the book's material was dangerous, explosive. Nabokov destroyed some of his research notes, and today there exists no holograph manuscript of *Lolita* because he burned the cards he composed on when he made a fair copy. The attempts to destroy the work in progress seem contrived, though—dramatic gestures. Véra came to the rescue because she was nearby; he did not start fires when his wife was out of the house.

Though he worried that no publisher in America would touch his new book—especially in light of the prosecution of *Hecate County*—he pushed on. He feared for his novel but also hoped for it. The nature of his difficulties is hard to make out; he blames "interruptions and asides," and indeed there were many claims on his work time in these years. But problems with getting to write usually call for different scheduling, or patience, not for burning. Nabokov also blames age:

> It had taken me some forty years to invent Russia and Western Europe, and now I was faced by the task of inventing America. The obtaining of such local ingredients as would allow me to inject a modicum of average "reality" ... into the brew of individual fancy, proved at fifty a much more difficult process than it had been in the Europe of my youth when receptiveness and retention were at their automatic best.

The evidence suggests, rather than a playing out of energies, a surge in them. In these years he was prodigious, and his move to Cornell inaugurated a working prime not equaled, in terms of quantity and originality of work produced, by any of his contemporaries writing in English. The claim of problems gathering "local ingredients," of lacking the "receptiveness and retention" of youth, is untrue on the face of it— and not interestingly untrue, not another example of Nabokov having us on in a meaningful way. He remained receptive and fully immersed in American materials.

These years of *Lolita* were also the years of some of his most extensive, most joyous wanderings in the West. Places visited—the Corral Log Motel, Afton, Wyoming; Teton Pass Ranch, near Jackson Hole; the "optimistic and excellent Valley View Court," Telluride's only motel in '51; the Chiricahua Mountains, near Portal, Arizona, a "sky island" range isolated in the desert—were ingredients from which he fashioned the locales of the novel. They were also places where he worked on the novel. The idea that his vision of his new book, his "brew of individual fancy," awaited only the injection of local-colorist details— Canadian or Mexican would have served as well—advances an idea that Nabokov liked to propagate, that he was on the Mozartian side of things, his imagination supreme, largely self-contained. In fact the American context was determinative. It fed meaning and amplitude into fancy's brew. The dead scrap he had brought from Europe lived on, revived copiously, in America. The attempted burnings might have been uneasy reactions to how alarming was that growth.

America contributed specifics, and many readers respond with shocked delight to the *en passant* travelogue of their country at midcentury, filmed in period Technicolor as well as in noir black and white. America contributed its Promethean forwardness as well.

Postcard sent by Nabokov to Wilson from Wyoming, summer 1949

America *did* go the whole hog. It had not invented explicitness, but its authors displayed an affinity for going beyond, for bringing into conversation forbidden things. Wilson was a new recruit to sexual frankness in fiction, joining such living predecessors and successors as Henry Miller, William Faulkner of *Sanctuary*, Norman Mailer of *The Naked and the Dead*, Jack Kerouac of *The Town and the City* and *On the Road*, and William Burroughs of *Junkie* and *Naked Lunch*. Nabokov assimilated to this immodest cadre. As he said in his afterword, "I am trying to be an American writer and claim only the same rights that other American writers enjoy." He meant the right to represent

American vulgarity when needed, but also an American disposition to tell, to expose.

He was not a hack, warmly pandering. He was writing the book that had come to him that he felt the need to write. While he wrote, his Russian memoir appeared, and despite its rollout in the *New Yorker* and other magazines, *Speak, Memory* was another "dismal flop" in the market, bringing him "fame but little money," he told his sister. To reach America's mythic mass audience might have begun to seem impossible.

America contributed a cathexis as well. In France in the fall of '39, when he wrote *The Enchanter* and then read it one night to four friends, a pedophile's story, complete with description of desperate flight with child, did not live on the page. In America, the resonance was different. Like the author of a story about bulls and capes who changes the setting to Spain, Nabokov inherited a stage, and the sad, abbreviated flight in *The Enchanter* became as large as he was able to make it. Mark Twain, another writer he hardly deigned to notice ("in the matter of the American Academy . . .," he wrote Wilson at about this time, "I know nothing whatsoever . . . and at first confused [the Academy] with a Mark Twain horror that almost obtained my name"), was the acknowledged master of *that* literary domain. Twain wrote within a tradition of slave narratives, as well as the genre of Indian abduction accounts, stories of frontier settlers taken and carried away. The white captives were often female. The first popular book of the kind was Mary Rowlandson's *The Sovereignty and Goodness of God*, about a Massachusetts wife taken by Narragansett Indians during King Philip's War (1675–78). It became the first American bestseller and appeared in thirty editions over the next 150 years. By 1800, seven hundred captivity narratives had been published, and early American novelists, such as Susanna Rowson and Charles Brockden Brown, worked the theme ingeniously. Sexual exploitation was always a subtext. Nabokov's interest in such accounts—at any rate, his acquaintance with the genre—follows from his reading of Pushkin, who in 1836 wrote a long, enthusiastic review of the French translation of a book called *The Narrative of John Tanner* (a.k.a. *The Falcon: A Narrative of the Captivity and Adventures of John Tanner during Thirty Years Residence among the Indians in the Interior of North America*). Writing in a Russian journal he co-edited, Pushkin told the story of an American child abducted by Shawnee at age nine, then sold to an Ottawwaw woman whose son had died. The "absolute artlessness and humble simplicity of the narrative vouch for its truth," Pushkin said, and he liked especially the description of an animal called "the moose," which he identified as "the American reindeer."

The Leatherstocking Tales, cover art by C. Offterdinger

Nabokov's immersion in Pushkin was lifelong but reached its height in the years when he worked on *Lolita*, when he was also translating *Eugene Onegin*. He might have read Fenimore Cooper's *The Last of the Mohicans*, the best of the Leatherstocking Tales, as Pushkin had done; like Mayne Reid, who wrote a novel called *The White Squaw* (1868), Cooper embroidered the female abduction theme. Probably Nabokov's path to channeling this mode is best explained, however, not by examining literary influences but by invoking the imponderables of inspiration. As quick as he was to pick up American slang, or to become knowing about American locales, he was intuitive and subtle in knowing what tale to tell—a very old tale, as it happened, provocative, formally simple, and outward-facing, toward the American vastness.

SUMMER OF '49, HE TRAVELED to Salt Lake City to take part in a writers' conference. His fellow panelists included Wallace Stegner, the Western novelist best known for *The Big Rock Candy Mountain* (1943), and Dr. Seuss (Ted Geisel), former political cartoonist and author of *And to Think That I Saw It on Mulberry Street* (1937) and *Bartholomew and the Oobleck* (1949). John Crowe Ransom, editor of the *Kenyon Review*, was also there; Nabokov found him smart and likable, and he was taken also with Dr. Seuss. The Nabokovs stayed at a sorority house on the University of Utah campus. They had driven west in their own car, a '46 Oldsmobile, their first cross-country drive since the trip to Stanford. Véra had taken lessons in Ithaca. She was nervous about driving across herself, so they hired one of Nabokov's Cornell students, a nineteen-year-old named Richard Buxbaum, to spell her at the wheel.

Buxbaum was brought along also to keep Dmitri company. The boys spent time talking about girls. At the conference, each proposed to pick out a girl "to have for the duration" of their stay in Salt Lake. Buxbaum drove more than Véra did, with Dmitri or Véra beside him in the front seat; Nabokov was always in back with his notebook. The route they took was direct, resembling the route taken by Humbert Humbert on his second long journey with Lolita, from the Northeast across Ohio, then "the three states beginning with 'I,' " then Nebraska—"ah, that first whiff of the West!" Humbert enthuses, his ultimate goal being California, where he intends to spirit Lolita across the Mexico border. The nonfictional travelers stayed at motels, as do the fictional ones; the boys shared a room, the grown-ups another—the grown-ups, Buxbaum noted, preferring rooms with separate beds.

"We traveled very leisurely," it says in the novel, and Nabokov and his party took eleven days to reach Salt Lake, a moderate pace at the time. Lolita "passionately desired to see the Ceremonial Dances" along the Continental Divide, Native American dances; unbeknownst to Humbert, she plans to escape there, into the custody of Quilty, her other pedophile suitor. They are welcomed to motels by signs that read,

"We wish you to feel at home while here. All equipment was care-fully checked upon your arrival. Your license number is on record here. Use hot water sparingly. We reserve the right to eject without notice any objectionable person. Do not throw waste material of any kind in the toilet bowl. Thank you. . . . We consider our guests the Finest People of the World."

Humbert recalled paying "ten for twins," that "flies queued outside at the screenless door and . . . scrambled in," that "the ashes of our predecessors still lingered in the ashtrays" and "a woman's hair lay on the pillow." Fictional '49 probably resembled real, and vice versa; Humbert registers a contemporary change in roadside architecture, that "commercial fashion was [for] cabins to fuse and gradually form [a] caravansary, and . . . a second story was added, and a lobby grew in, and cars were removed to a communal garage."

Buxbaum found Véra fascinating. She was a graceful woman with "beautiful bones—a lovely person, lovely." Nabokov reminded him of other Eastern European gentlemen he had known, with savoir faire and languages. (Buxbaum's family were German-speaking Jews who had arrived in '39. His father was a doctor in Canandaigua, New York; he worked at a Mohawk reservation on the Quebec border.)

The conference over, the group headed for the Tetons, where Nabokov had some collecting he wanted to do. In advance, he had conferred with Alexander B. Klots, a lepidopterist at the AMNH; Klots sought to allay Véra's fears of grizzly bear encounters, warning, though, that moose could be aggressive and "I would rather meet ten bears with cubs." South of the Tetons, where the Hoback River joins the Snake, they traveled east and stayed at the Battle Mountain Ranch, where Nabokov busily collected. They stayed longer, for more than a month, at the Teton Pass Ranch, in Wilson, Wyoming, seven miles west of Jackson and south of the high mountains. Buxbaum left them here, to hitchhike back east, but first the two boys tried to climb Disappointment Peak, a subsidiary summit of the Grand Teton. They failed but had an adventure. They wore tennis shoes and began climb-ing the shattered rock of the mountain without mountaineering equip-ment. Somewhere short of the nearly twelve-thousand-foot summit, they were afraid to climb any higher but faced a jump from one ledge to a lower one in order to descend, with a misstep promising death. It took two hours for one of them to summon the nerve, the other then following.

Disappointment Peak, Teton Range, Wyoming

Buxbaum sensed Nabokov's anger when they emerged from the woods several hours late. Nabokov seethed but did not voice his anger. Both parents had been out of their minds with worry.

Nabokov wrote Wilson on August 18, "We have had some wonderful adventures . . . and are driving back next week. I have lost many pounds and found many butterflies." They crossed into Canada on the way back, traveling just north of the Great Lakes. The previous spring, after a car trip with Véra, he had described to Wilson the "lovely soft-bosomed scenery" they saw between Ithaca and Manhattan; his wife had driven him "beautifully," he said. They were Americans now, able to go where they wanted in their own car, when they wanted. Their automobiles—a 1940 Plymouth, never in very good shape; the Oldsmobile; a new green Buick Special bought in '54; an "amazing white [Chevrolet] Impala" rented while they lived briefly in Los Angeles—became markers of periods in their lives and of their modest financial ascent. The Olds was the *Lolita* car, the one Véra parked in the shade of roadside trees when Vladimir wanted a quiet, upholstered place to write. The famous photo of him writing in a car, taken by Carl Mydans of *Life*, dates from '58 and is a staging; the car is the two-door Buick, not the legendary Olds, and the location is a roadside near Ithaca.

12.

During their next trip west, in 1951, Nabokov was still constantly taking notes. His American researches were extensive. They bespeak a desire to get things right and also an anxiety about his subject; he recorded information on the habits and physiques of pubescent American girls, on the average age of menstruation onset, on attitudinal changes, on the proper method of inserting an enema tip into a rectum. He collected girlish slang from teen magazines, his Russianness, notwithstanding his long acquaintance with formal English, helping such phrases as "It's a sketch" or "She was loads of fun" to emerge from colloquial invisibility.

As a writer he took off, felt liberated to create, when he knew hard facts. No author of his century was so punctilious about demonstrable, testable reality and simultaneously so agnostic toward it, if we take his warnings about its provisionality seriously. He rode on buses to hear teenagers speak, and for the scene with Miss Pratt, head of the Beardsley School, he interviewed a real school principal and pretended to have a daughter who sought admission.

Late in March 1950, he read newspaper reports of a sensational crime. An unemployed auto mechanic, Frank La Salle, had abducted an eleven-year-old girl named Sally Horner and kept her for two years as his sex slave, traveling from New Jersey to California by way of Texas, before being apprehended in a San Jose auto court. La Salle was described as a "hawk-faced . . . sex criminal" with "a long record of morals offenses," and Sally as a "plump little girl" and "a nice looking youngster, with light brown hair and blue-green eyes." The second part of *Lolita*, the schema for it, had been handed him. Sally's captivity lasted for twenty-one months, included attendance at school, and concluded when she confided her secret to a classmate, who told her that what was happening was wrong. Lolita, similarly, travels for twenty-one months before being placed in the Beardsley School, where Humbert fears that she has spilled the beans to a classmate, who has advised her on how to run away. La Salle controlled Sally by claiming to be an FBI agent who would send her to "a place for girls like you" unless she did his bidding. Humbert, taking pointers, reminds Lolita that, as a child whose birth parents are both dead, she would end up in a "detention home, or one of those admirable . . . protectories where you knit things" if her stepfather were to go to jail.

La Salle abducted Sally after watching her commit a crime (shoplifting), hence the threat about sending her to "a place for girls." This may be Nabokov's crucial borrowing; Humbert also persuades Lolita that she has broken the law, has "impaired the morals of an adult in a respectable inn" by inviting him "to know her carnally" when they spent the night at the Enchanted Hunters hotel. Precocious and in many ways bright, Lolita is finally just a child. She can be gulled. Nabokov's other borrowings from the Horner case include the girls' resemblance ("nice-looking . . . light brown hair and blue-green eyes") and Lolita's fate, which is prefigured in the short life of Sally, who two years after being rescued from her captivity died in a highway accident, as Lolita will die in childbirth. For both of them, an extinguished childhood and early sex are doomful; no matter their hopes and apparent second chances, they have been marked.

NABOKOV'S JOURNAL FOR '51, the notes he kept as he traveled, show him wide awake and questing. "Sunday, June 24 . . . started 7:30 p.m. Mileage 50.675 clover in bloom, low sun in platinum haze, warm, peach upper contour of one dimension pale grey cloud fusing with distant mist." The landscape of upstate New York reminded him of "oilskins . . . with pictures, hung on wall above washstand [with] these kind of curly trees, this kind of green, these farms and cows," from his Russian boyhood. With pleasure he realized that his first images of America had been "imported from here!"—from rural upstate New York or somewhere similar.

This recognition made its way into *Lolita*. "Not only had Lo no eye for scenery," Humbert writes about their first, yearlong ramble cross-country, "but she furiously resented my calling her attention to this or that enchanting detail of landscape." He continues,

By a paradox of pictorial thought, the average lowland North-American countryside [was] something I accepted with a shock of amused recognition because of those painted oilcloths which were imported from America in the old days to be hung above washstands in Central-European nurseries . . . opaque curly trees, a barn, cattle, a brook . . . and perhaps a stone fence or hills of greenish gouache.

The "pale grey cloud" gets into the famous description of a "two-dimensional, dove-gray cloud" turning peach as the sun sets. In real-life Missouri, outside a restaurant, where "the bill was delicately placed by waitress under the rolls," Nabokov noted another sky, this one containing "Lorrain's clouds . . . fading into misty azur . . . parts of them . . . projected out of neutral background." In *Lolita* we read of

a line of spaced trees silhouetted against the horizon, and hot still noons above a wilderness of clover, and Claude Lorrain clouds inscribed remotely into misty azure with only their cumulus part conspicuous against the neutral swoon of the background. Or again, it might be a stern El Greco horizon, pregnant with inky rain.

Over and over his journal jottings find their way into the text. Quite possibly it was not a case of him being inspired by something seen, which then prompted him to write a passage now to be found in *Lolita*, but rather of him actively seeking some detail to solve a problem in his writing. He looks at the sky in coming days or on the very day of arriving at a problem, discovering something that he can use; to say that the landscape has inspired him is to romanticize the process.

He provides what he needs, shaping what he finds; he is "inventing America," as he claimed, by looking at it creatively and with many words ready to be summoned—indeed, with words inseparable from the looking. The sky on a particular day, like the philosopher's tree that falls or maybe does not fall in the forest, suddenly arrives at existence. In biographical terms, he may be recording a process of learning to read America. He imputes this process, or an approximation of it, to Humbert. There is at first a tendency to see scenes as stereotypes (the oilcloth images), along with an attitude of uninterest or condescension, but the "inutile loveliness" begins to work on Humbert, and though Lolita remains resistant, "I myself learned to discern [the landscape] . . .

after being exposed for quite a time" to it, to "the delicate beauty ever present in the margin of our undeserving journey."

What Nabokov saw, other than instances of the picturesque, is not the immediate concern of his novel. Still, his protagonist registers moods and reaches conclusions. The year of madcap moteling (August '47 to August '48) began with

> a series of wiggles and whorls in New England, then meandered south, up and down, east and west; dipped deep into *ce qu'on appelle* Dixieland, avoided Florida . . . veered west, zigzagged through corn belts and cotton belts . . . crossed and recrossed the Rockies, straggled through southern deserts where we wintered; reached the Pacific, turned north through the pale lilac fluff of flowering shrubs along forest roads; almost reached the Canadian border; and proceeded east, across good lands and bad lands.

They had been almost "everywhere." Yet, "We had really seen nothing," Humbert decides. He means that the greed and dishonor of what he's done to a child cancel other values. Their "long journey had only defiled with a sinuous trail of slime" the dreamy American vastness; what remained were "dog-eared maps, ruined tour books," and the child's "sobs in the night—every night, every night—the moment I feigned sleep."

Humbert and Lolita lose reality themselves as they travel. Even at "our very best moments," he writes,

> when we sat reading on a rainy day . . . or had a quiet hearty meal in a crowded diner, or played a childish game of cards, or went shopping, or silently stared, with other motorists and their children, at some smashed, blood-bespattered car with a young woman's shoe in the ditch . . . I seemed to myself as implausible a father as she seemed to be a daughter.

They are not father and daughter—they are pedophile and captive. They pretend; each has reasons to do so, and doing so awakens in one of them a sensitivity to a cognate quality in the passing scene, an undertone of enigma. "And sometimes trains would cry in the monstrously hot and humid night," Humbert records, sounding Allen Ginsbergian. The train whistles have a "heartrending and ominous plangency, mingling power and hysteria in one desperate scream." He takes Lolita to a "dusk-mellowed, mysterious side-road" for some fondling; a little later, tall trucks studded with colored lights, like dreadful giant Christmas trees, loomed in the darkness and thundered by [our] little sedan. And again next day a thinly populated sky, losing its blue to the heat, would melt overhead, and Lo would clamor for a drink . . . and the car inside would be a furnace when we got in again, and the road shimmered ahead, with a remote car changing its shape mirage-like in the surface glare.

The mirage car predicts the one that Humbert will see following them later on; his pedophile shadow self, Clare Quilty, may be at the wheel. Mirages grow from this landscape. Humbert notes "the mysterious outlines of table-like hills" as they get farther west, and then "red bluffs ink-blotted with junipers, and then a mountain range, dun grading into blue, and blue into dream."

An impostor, he roams a land of equivocal sights. The freedom to move at will, to cover hundreds of miles in a day, to stay under assumed names (as Quilty does) in interchangeable motels: this is the man-made anonymous world, laid upon a landscape already given to mystery. The more Humbert peers at America, the stranger it appears. Illusions hatch there, as do vision seekers and con artists. Humbert's paranoia grows rather than diminishes as he becomes an experienced traveler on American roads. At first these promise fun: "I have never seen such smooth amiable roads as those that now radiated before us," he writes, "across the crazy quilt of forty-eight states. Voraciously we consumed those long highways, in rapt silence we glided over their glossy black dance floors." A day's travel often ends in disorientation, though:

And the desert would meet us with a steady gale, dust, gray thorn bushes, and hideous bits of tissue paper mimicking pale flowers among the . . . wind-tortured withered stalks all along the highway; in the middle of which there sometimes stood simple cows, immobilized in a position . . . cutting across all human rules of traffic.

Quilty, who *does* pursue them and who *is* a fiendishly clever tormentor, belongs among the withered stalks and snagged toilet paper. He resembles Humbert in his degeneracy and his witty wordplay but differs as regards the moral sense. Humbert lacerates himself as he debauches his captive; he anguishes over the state of what might be his soul, while

Quilty is more hipster-lecher, rotten with boredom yet everywhere active, a con man on the order of the central character of Melville's *The Confidence-Man* (1857), an arch manipulator, a deep devil of deceit. Quilty also recalls Chichikov, in Gogol's *Dead Souls*, but Chichikov was a lower order of devil, less conscious, more buffoon. Quilty is, in some reprehensible way, an artist, a magician of style.

Nabokov liked to mock commentary that found larger meanings in *Lolita*. "Although everybody should know that I detest symbols and allegories" by now, "an otherwise intelligent reader who flipped through the first part described *Lolita* as 'Old Europe debauching young America,' while another flipper saw in it 'Young America debauching old Europe.' " Readers can take from a text whatever meanings they wish; novels have mythic dimensions because readers perceive them. *Lolita* invites interpretation coquettishly. It describes a journey across the whole "crazy quilt," Whitmanesquely embracing all America, meanwhile focusing its attention on the growth edge of the enterprise, as represented in the magazines and television of the time: the suburbs. Wittily it engages in the sort of pseudo-analysis that Nabokov liked to mock, shuffling everything into categories:

> We came to know—*nous connûmes*, to use a Flaubertian intonation—the stone cottages under enormous Chateaubriandesque trees, the brick unit, the adobe unit, the stucco court. . . . The log kind, finished in knotty pine. . . . We held in contempt the plain whitewashed clapboard Kabins, with their faint sewerish smell. . . . *Nous connûmes* (this is royal fun) . . . all those Sunset Motels, U-Beam Cottages, Hillcrest Courts, Pine View Courts, Mountain View Courts. . . . The baths were mostly tiled showers, with an endless variety of spouting mechanisms.

He categorizes people, too:

> the various types of motor court operators, the reformed criminal, the retired teacher and the business flop, among the males; and the motherly, pseudo-ladylike and madamic variants among the females. . . . We came to know the curious roadside species, Hitchhiking Man . . . with all its many subspecies and forms: the modest soldier, spic and span, quietly waiting, quietly conscious of khaki's viatic appeal; the schoolboy wishing to go two blocks; the killer wishing to go two thousand miles; the

mysterious, nervous, elderly gent, with brand-new suitcase and clipped mustache; a trio of optimistic Mexicans; the college student displaying the grime of vocational outdoor work . . . the clean-cut, glossy-haired, shifty-eyed . . . young beasts in loud shirts and coats . . . priapically thrusting out tense thumbs to tempt lone women or sadsack salesmen.

If he is not writing a novel of midcentury America, what *is* he writing? A massive body of critical scholarship, beginning with Page Stegner's *Escape into Aesthetics: The Art of Vladimir Nabokov* (1966) and amounting now to hundreds of books and thousands of scholarly articles, largely seeks to answer that question. Readers continue to take him at face value, even so. They encounter his lists of American types and think they recognize someone or something they know. His period slang is engagingly accurate (in the passage above, "business flop," "spic and span," "brand-new," "sadsack"), and the details he forefronts recall a time that Americans feel as if they have lived through, no matter when they were born:

> [Lolita] it was to whom ads were dedicated: the ideal consumer, the subject and object of every foul poster. And she attempted . . . to patronize only those restaurants where the holy spirit of Huncan Dines had descended upon the cute paper napkins and cottage-cheese-crested salads.

> I was not really quite prepared for her fits of disorganized boredom, intense and vehement griping, her sprawling, droopy, dopey-eyed style, and what is called goofing off—a kind of diffused clowning which she thought was tough in a boyish hoodlum way.

Independent of the novel's allusions—references to, or parodies of, Poe, Dante, Dostoevsky, Lewis Carroll, Freud, Baudelaire, Flaubert, T. S. Eliot, Chester Gould's *Dick Tracy*, *Tristram Shandy*, *Dr. Jekyll and Mr. Hyde*, *Don Quixote*, and John Keats; Hans Christian Andersen, Proust, the Brothers Grimm, Shakespeare, Mérimée, Melville, Bacon, Pierre de Ronsard, lepidoptery, and the literature of the double; Aubrey Beardsley, Sherlock Holmes, Catullus, Lord Byron, Goethe, Rimbaud, Browning, Nabokov himself—the basic story of abduction and flight, and the sexual exploitation of a child, moves logically forward, in a detailed American context. The book itself is a parody. It is Humbert's parody of the Romantic confessional novel of an earlier century, telling of a hopeless and obsessive love. According to the able scholar Alfred Appel Jr., Nabokov found ways to make parody play for pathos as well as for laughs; *Lolita* is "a parody . . . with real suffering in it," he says. The novel has it "both ways,"

> involving the reader . . . in a deeply moving yet outrageously comic story, rich in verisimilitude, [while] engaging him in a game made possible by the interlacings of verbal figurations which undermine the novel's realistic base and distance the reader from its dappled surface.

Many readers do not feel distanced. American or not, they recognize something like the America they know or believe they know. Half-aware of hints being dropped, skimming the many uncommon French terms (*frétillement, grues, poser un lapin, arrière-pensée,* etc.), sensing an author a bit on the solipsistic side, one whose tale of a self-absorbed but sympathetic pervert is a working out, on some level or in some sense, of personal issues, they read on. Humbert is just amusing enough to not be unbearable. What he does to the girl child is hateful but—if we can be frank here—lasciviously compelling, at least in the early chapters. And the book is suspenseful. Readers of mysteries and fans of film thrillers of the kind made by Alfred Hitchcock in the same years— *Rebecca* (1940), *Suspicion* (1941), *Notorious* (1946)—undergo the same compulsion to find out, to follow through to the end, when they embark on *Lolita.* The "undermining of the novel's realistic base" may mean one thing to a scholar of an ontological bent; to a reader who begins to sense, along with Humbert, that something's not quite right, that someone is playing tricks on a poor foreign-born pedophile, it means another.

The book is *decidedly* about Europe, in the person of a perverted sophisticate, debauching a child who decidedly symbolizes America. Nabokov conceived of a way to make quotidian reality compelling: that reality was so concerned for order, so conventional and outwardly prim, that if one entered it via the back door, off the dark alley under the awful sign THE RAPE OF CHILDREN, one set off profound reverbera-tions. Efforts to suppress the book attended its U.S. publication three years after its Paris debut, and those efforts continue to this day. The turmoil over the sexual abuse of children in 1980s–90s America, a kind of neo-Salem-witch-trials hysteria, suggests how invested with meaning the issue remained and remains. Nabokov sensed that depth of meaning, or luckily stumbled on it. One would have to believe, as no one does seriously anymore, that a novel can affect an entire culture—can focus its darkest dreams, its foulest fantasies—to say that *Lolita* led directly to the contemporary redefinition of sexual abuse as soul murder, as a crime as vile as any. No doubt the reckoning with child abuse in America would have taken place regardless, but *Lolita* gave it faces: it was *this* little girl, a child born Dolores Haze, whose youth was being pillaged, and *this* handsome, over-intellectual foreigner who was raping her every day—every day.

13.

Humbert, in the period before Lolita at last gets away from him, by means of a smart plan devised by her and Quilty ("the Beast," as Humbert calls him), goes far into full-on paranoia, or "persecution mania," as he has it. Just before his worst imaginings come true, this mania relaxes:

> After all, gentlemen, it was becoming abundantly clear that all those identical detectives in prismatically changing cars were figments . . . images based on coincidence and chance resemblance. *Soyons logiques*, crowed the cocky Gallic part of my brain—and proceeded to rout the notion of a Lolita-maddened salesman or comedy gangster, with stooges . . . hoaxing me, and otherwise taking riotous advantage of my strange relations with the law.

They are in the mountain town of Elphinstone, in a western state. The previous days have been a nightmare, Humbert enduring a heart attack (among other woes) as their journey offers hints of a conspiracy against his hopes. He is on the verge of a kind of revelation. That revelation attends the collapse of his plans for continued ownership of a child, continued sexual access to her; in possibly his most loathsome musing, Humbert has earlier thought that

> around 1950 I would have to get rid somehow of a difficult adolescent whose magic nymphage had evaporated [but that] with patience and luck I might have her produce eventually a nymphet

with my blood in her exquisite veins, a Lolita the Second, who would be eight or nine around 1960, when I would still be *dans la force de l'âge*; indeed, the telescopy of my mind . . . was strong enough to distinguish . . . salivating Dr. Humbert, practicing on supremely lovely Lolita the Third the art of being a granddad.

He is being facetious—isn't he? But in certain moods, Humbert does conceive of monstrous things. The "sleepiness" and sheer size of America have induced in him fantasies of godlike control, extending even to the breeding of future slaves. Promethean schemes go with the land. America has a bad history of this, one of the most powerful fictional representations of it to be found in *Absalom, Absalom!* (1936), Faulkner's ninth novel, by some reckonings his last great novel, a fierce account of racialism and monomania. Nabokov nowhere mentions that work, but the story of a mad patriarch breeding offspring into the incestuous future performs Humbert's fantasy very closely, against the backdrop of an historic horror. (The high Southern gothic of the novel would no doubt have awakened his ridicule, always poised to be applied to Faulkner.)

The trip in '51 brought him to Telluride. It is a few miles outside fictional Elphinstone, after Lolita's escape, that Humbert has his revelation:

An attack of abominable nausea forced me to pull up on the ghost of an old mountain road that now accompanied, now traversed a brand new highway. . . . After coughing myself inside out, I rested a while on a boulder, and then, thinking the sweet air might do me good, walked a little way toward a lone stone parapet on the precipice side of the highway.

In a letter to Wilson, Nabokov set the actual scene:

I went to Telluride (*awful* roads, but then—endless charm, an old-fashioned, absolutely touristless mining town full of most helpful, charming people—and when you hike from there, which is 9000′, to 10000′, with the town and its tin roofs and self-conscious poplars lying toylike at the flat bottom of a *cul-de-sac* valley running into giant granite mountains, all you hear are the voices of children playing . . .).

"A steep slope high above Telluride," looking down upon the mountain town

Don Stallings, his collector friend, had had good luck around Telluride, and so did Nabokov:

> My heroic wife . . . drove me through the floods and storms of Kansas [for the purpose] of obtaining more specimens of a butterfly I had described from eight males, and of discovering its female. I was wholly successful in that quest, finding all I wanted on a steep slope high above Telluride—quite an enchanted slope, in fact, with hummingbirds and humming moths visiting the tall green gentians that grew among the clumps of a blue lupine, *Lupinus parviflorus*.

Humbert, poised on his parapet, contemplates the drop:

> Small grasshoppers spurted out of the withered roadside weeds. A very light cloud was opening its arms and moving toward a slightly more substantial one belonging to another, more sluggish, heaven-logged system. . . . I grew aware of a melodious unity of sounds rising like vapor from a small mining town that lay at my feet, in a fold of the valley. One could make out the geometry of the streets

between blocks of red and gray roofs, and green puffs of trees, and a
serpentine stream, and . . . behind it all, great timbered mountains.

Here the pedophile has his epiphany. Those are children's voices,
children making that harmony. He is heartbroken and heart-diseased
but not self-pitying now—ruing not the loss of his slave so much as what
he has done to her. He perceives a quality "divinely enigmatic" in the
voices, and the man prepared to breed more captives with a stolen
child's body seems far away—if you can believe him.

The notes of heavenly unison, unusual in Nabokov, place us close to
another tradition. Nabokov would not have agreed with—probably
would have parodied—Emerson's claim that "every natural fact is a
symbol of some spiritual fact," but Humbert mourns and moons with a
full failing heart, his position above an earthly paradise, bathed in the
music of childish goodness, securing for him rare moments of full
humanity. They are transcendental moments, transcendental in the
sense of time-tethered, changeable, worldly facts giving rise to ideas of a
realm of value that does not change, that achieves perfection. Humbert
joins himself briefly to that realm—then, when he leaves his enchanted
hillside, *Lolita* plunges into its tragic final act.

NABOKOV'S TRAVELS OF '51 and '52 (a little less so '53), full of
pleasure and diversion, good insects, weeks of doing exactly what he
wanted, represent a kind of apotheosis. He was married to a woman
he loved and who loved him, their child was turning out well,
showing signs of unusual talent (singer, debater), and the Oldsmobile
was ever ready to take them farther on America's amiable roads.
This happy phase, a testament to his ability to be comfortable in
his own skin, in whatever surroundings, is part of the lore of *Lolita*. He
was not a tortured artist writing a masterwork in a garret; no, he was a
family man, an eater at common lunch counters, a man like you
or me.

Leaving that improbable conclusion aside, his passage, in his fiction,
through places that betray an up-front Americanness—a quality, often,
of cheapjack vulgarity, of corny coziness packaged for sale (with, in
the background, mystic meadows and mountains)—transforms those
places. The transformation is again in an American direction. As he
reflects reality back at readers, he renders it as deep and full of
mystery; the forest surrounding the town in the first great American
short story, Hawthorne's "Young Goodman Brown," is this kind of

place, too, pulsing with demons and trickery, a gloomy breeding ground of conspiracy and paranoia, possibly illusional. Stories of evil and of compromised innocence are not rare in American literature, nor are stories of a belief that deforms reality. The brooding, enigmatic something that Nabokov finds at large has spoken to others, too.

His summer contentment, noted in letters to friends, coexisted with anxieties. Dmitri would soon be at college. "I want to ask your advice," he wrote Harry Levin of Harvard:

> Dmitri has set his heart on [your university]. He is in his junior year of prep school now and so will be ready to enter . . . in spring 1951. I believe *démarches* are made by fathers at the end of the junior year and would be very grateful to you for any advice you could give me as to the customary procedure.

Levin did not acknowledge any impropriety in this approach—itself a subtle *démarche*. He replied,

> It's always a pleasure to get your annual letter. It's also a pleasure to think that Dmitri—to whom we took a great liking, when we glimpsed him last fall in his new and semi-adult phase—is likely to be at Harvard fairly soon. I have his cousin Ivan, also a nice and bright boy, in one of my freshman classes. . . . The person to address about Mitya's application is Dr. Richard M. Gummere, Director of Admissions. . . . If any references are required, I should be honored to stand as an enthusiastic godparent.

That was how things were done in America! Dmitri was duly admitted to Harvard, although without a scholarship. Nabokov wrote Roman Grynberg, who often loaned him large sums, that he was worried:

> I'll tell you in complete honesty, the thought that I would not be able to afford his Harvard education takes a lot out of me. I just sent a story to the *New Yorker* and if they take it . . . then it'll be just enough to pay in December around five hundred for his education, and for ourselves to scrape out of the sludge we've become trapped in. But if it doesn't sell then for at least some of the sum I will turn to you.

The *New Yorker* did take the story, "Lance," Nabokov's last short story, which is about, among other things, the fear felt by the parents of an adventurous young man who climbs mountains and travels to other planets. Harold Ross, the *New Yorker* editor in chief, complained that he could not understand it, but Katharine White argued for it, and the magazine published it after Ross's sudden death.

Restored by his vacations, Nabokov was also impoverished by them. His western trips represented the re-embrace of an avocation that had never earned him much, and over the years he noticed that summer was often a time of feeling especially broke. Though appreciating Cornell, he soon complained of being underpaid. He asked for advances against his salary, and he began looking for other positions—at Harvard, Johns Hopkins, and Stanford. *Speak, Memory*, not selling well, had "already brought me 13–14 thousand" from magazine excerpts, he told Grynberg, but his new novel could not be published that way—too scandalous. In any case, the magazine money was "long since spent."

At midcentury, Nabokov was half a century old. He had dentures top and bottom. In May '50 he wrote, "I have to go to Boston to have six lower teeth extracted. My plan is to go thither . . . Sunday the 28th, grunt at the dentist's . . . Monday and Tuesday and perhaps Thursday . . . then mumble back, toothless, to Ithaca." When returning from his summers, he glowed with good health, but there were collapses. "I am ill," he wrote Wilson upon his return in September '51.

> The doctor says it is a kind of sunstroke. Silly situation: after two months of climbing, shirtless, in shorts, in the Rockies, to be smitten by the insipid N.Y. sun on a dapper lawn. High temperature, pain in the temples, insomnia and an incessant, brilliant but sterile turmoil of thoughts and fancies.

He often complained of poor sleep, and the separate bedrooms he and his wife kept were at least in part so he could pace or write in the middle of the night. He was under great pressure. It was mostly self-generated: to write wonderful things, to do so now. He had the beginnings of a devoted audience, mostly via *The New Yorker*; as he told Wilson, "The letters from private individuals I get are, in their wild enthusiasm, ridiculously incommensurable" with the treatment he got from publishers, who failed to push his books. Great things, and great success, were possible. In '51, he witnessed the extraordinary breakout of another *New Yorker* writer, J. D. Salinger, who in '46 had published "Slight Rebellion Off Madison," a story introducing a character called Holden Caulfield. Salinger was the rare author of his time of whom Nabokov did not speak with disrespect. Stories published by Salinger, in various magazines, introduced his signature concern for adolescence and for young men entranced by younger girls; among aspects of his style that might have appealed to Nabokov are his shaggy-dog plots and his quirky, imaginative accounts of the flow of thought. His use of slang, like Nabokov's, is choice. Both authors venture into sex talk, and both find a fertile subject in postwar teenagerhood.

Nabokov's emergence, its crucial stage, coincided exactly with Salinger's. Eleven chapters of the future *Speak, Memory* appeared in the *New Yorker* just in the years (1948–50) when Salinger was publishing "A Perfect Day for Bananafish," "Uncle Wiggily in Connecticut," "Just Before the War with the Eskimos," and "For Esmé—with Love and Squalor," the run of stories that made him a coming star. In '48, the magazine offered Salinger a first-refusal deal of the kind Nabokov had gotten in '44. Salinger worked on *The Catcher in the Rye* (1951), as Nabokov did *Lolita*, off and on for years. Each book seems vaguely aware of the other. Both invoke an America in which to write about magical young girls is somehow a necessary thing—a key to what is.

Holden's sister, Phoebe, is the object of her brother's immense, protective devotion:

> She has nice, pretty little ears. In the wintertime, her [red hair is] pretty long. . . . Sometimes my mother braids it and sometimes she doesn't. It's really nice, though. She's only ten. She's quite skinny, like me, but nice skinny. Roller-skate skinny. I watched her once from the window when she was crossing over Fifth Avenue to go to the park, and that's what she is, roller-skate skinny. You'd like her. I mean if you tell old Phoebe something, she knows exactly what the hell you're talking about.

Holden's voice is the marrow of his novel. Just so Humbert's. Among the attractions of Humbert's is that he describes people without common decency or restraint; Holden, too, is funny when most harsh, usually about adults. Scholars have so far failed to detect parodies of *The Catcher in the Rye* in *Lolita*, but Holden's ambling, self-reflexive, morally troubled voice, an instrument for negotiating a way out of sexual fear, among other things, suggests Humbert's gleeful sexual ravenousness turned on its outrageous head:

The only trouble is, she's a little too affectionate sometimes. She's very emotional, for a child. . . . Something else she does, she writes books all the time. Only, she doesn't finish them. They're all about some kid named Hazel Weatherfield—only old Phoebe spells it "Hazle." Old Hazle Weatherfield is a girl detective. She's supposed to be an orphan, but her old man keeps showing up. Her old man's always a "tall attractive gentleman about 20 years of age." That kills me. Old Phoebe. I swear to God you'd like her.

Late in the story, Holden returns from boarding school and sneaks into his sister's room. The mention of Phoebe having a part in a school play, as does Lolita Haze—like the name "Hazle" for Phoebe's alter ego, an "orphan" whose "old man keeps showing up"—and the length of the bedroom scene, a morally glowing inversion of the morally appalling bedroom scene in *Lolita* at the Enchanted Hunters, suggest that Nabokov read Salinger or in some way imbibed his novel's vapors. Holden watches his sister asleep:

She was laying there . . . with her face sort of on the side of the pillow. She had her mouth way open. It's funny. You take adults, they look lousy when they're asleep and they have their mouths way open, but kids don't. Kids look all right. They can even have spit all over the pillow and they still look all right.

Humbert gazes upon *his* little girl:

Clothed in one of her old nightgowns, my Lolita lay on her side with her back to me, in the middle of the bed. Her lightly veiled body and bare limbs formed a Z. She had put both pillows under her dark tousled head; a band of pale light crossed her top vertebrae.

He has given her a sleeping potion. But it isn't strong enough:

The whole [drug-giving] had had for object a fastness of sleep that a whole regiment would not have disturbed, and here she was staring at me, and thickly calling me "Barbara." Barbara, wearing my pajamas which were much too tight for her, remained poised motionless over the little sleep-talker. Softly, with a hopeless sigh, Dolly turned away, resuming her initial position.

Humbert soon does to Dolly something that Holden, in his fragile emotional state, might have found unbearable to hear or even think about. For both, a certain period of childhood—nymphethood for Humbert, and for Holden those years when a child comes out with things that "just kill" you—is a window upon radiance. If it makes sense to speak of an American zeitgeist, then these two seem to have partaken of something within it, maybe of the same thing—each, of course, in his own way.

SALINGER OFFERS A TART account of Holden's boarding school, called Pencey Prep. Nabokov, generating new book ideas even as he labored at *Lolita*, made a mental note to write about St. Mark's, Dmitri's un-favoritest school, in the second volume of autobiography he was contemplating. While *Lolita* was under way, he also applied for a Guggenheim to finance the translation of *Eugene Onegin*. This work, with scholarly notes, would take him a little over a year to complete, he confidently told Henry Moe, of the foundation.

His friend Mikhail Karpovich, of the skunk-and-moth-rich Vermont farm, was going on sabbatical, and he asked Nabokov to take over his classes at Harvard for the spring of '52. In Cambridge they sublet a house from the memoirist May Sarton, who remembered them afterward for their kindness to her old cat, which had health problems, and for breaking a number of dishes. Véra audited a course in which Dmitri was also enrolled, and she was upset to see how often he was late to class or simply didn't show up.

Nabokov had first read *Eugene Onegin* at nine or ten. Modern Russian literature comes "out from Gogol's 'Overcoat,' " Dostoevsky is supposed to have said, but others thought it came from Pushkin's dueling pistol; Nabokov had no doubt that in writing a readable translation of Pushkin's intoxicating novel in verse he would be introducing a supreme work of art, also furthering his project of Russifying the Anglophones. While at Harvard he learned that he had been awarded the Guggenheim. Thus he could take a second semester away from Cornell (spring of '53), and his researches, as he investigated the social and literary context of Pushkin's work, expanded.

"Being at heart a pedant," as he said of himself, he battened on the deep research. "For two months in Cambridge," he wrote Wilson, "I did nothing (from 9 A.M. to 2 A.M.) but work on my commentaries to *E.O.* The Harvard libraries are wonderful." The story of Onegin, jaded Russian nobleman of the 1820s who retreats to the country, where he befriends a mediocre young poet, Lenski, whom he later kills in a duel, for Nabokov as for other Russians was a giant leap forward in sophistication, wit, and self-awareness in a work of art. Onegin does not invent the attitude of "weary negligence"—a pose first named, perhaps first identified, by Shakespeare, in *King Lear*—but he bodies it forth ably, and for Nabokov the way that attitude and Onegin's whole character are constructions out of the books he has read—lots of Byron, for example—was a fruitful idea.

Tatiana, the novel's heroine, falls in love with Onegin. She writes him a rash letter, impassioned, frank, self-compromising:

> 'Tis now, I know, within your will
> to punish me with scorn.
> But you, for my unhappy lot
> keeping at least one drop of pity,
> you'll not abandon me.
> At first, I wanted to be silent;
> believe me: of my shame
> you never would have known
> if I had had the hope,
> even seldom, even once a week,
> to see you at our country place,
> only to hear your speeches,
> to say a word to you, and then
> to think and think about one thing,
> both day and night, till a new meeting.

A retired rake, Onegin refuses her—not unkindly, but he does refuse. He is a man of "sharp, chilled mind." Pushkin, who portrays himself as Onegin's close friend in the poem, explains that there were "no more enchantments" for Onegin, that he had burned out early:

> him does the snake of memories,
> him does repentance bite.
> All this often imparts
> great charm to conversation.
> At first, Onegin's language
> would trouble me; but I grew used
> to his sarcastic argument

and banter blent halfwise with bile
and virulence of gloomy epigrams.

So disenchanted is Onegin that, while still young, he gives up reading. Formerly he had been, like the poem's translator, a quotating pedant, with scraps of Juvenal, Virgil, *Childe Harold's Pilgrimage*, and Rousseau salting his table talk. Now in his rustic retreat he buys books, but

without avail:
here there was dullness; there, deceit and raving;
this lacked conscience, that lacked sense;
on all of them were different fetters;
and the old had become old-fashioned,
and the new raved about the old.
As he'd left women, he left books.

Pushkin was likewise made of books, of words. Nabokov's scholarly apparatus—more than a thousand closely printed pages, notes on everything from the first word of the poem's French epigraph (*Pétri*, meaning "steeped in," "consisting of") to several pages on the precise shade of red of a woman's fashionable beret—shows him drunk on words, drunk on research, joyously drunk on the task of tracking down antecedents to Pushkin's every thought or phrase. Russian verse was less than one hundred years old at the time, Nabokov tells us, and the new literature had been born through shameless borrowing—mostly from French but also from English, German, Italian, and classical Latin literatures.

"Pétri" appears in an epigraph that Pushkin made up, after the manner of other fictionalizing epigraphers. Nabokov tells us,

The idea of tipping a flippant tale with a philosophical [quote] is obviously borrowed from Byron. For the first two cantos of *Childe Harold's Pilgrimage* . . . Byron sent [his publisher] . . . a motto beginning: "L'univers est une espèce de livre, dont on n'a lu que la première page," [taken] from Louis Charles Fougeret de Monbron's *Le Cosmopolite* (London, 1750), p. 1.

The oblique epigraph was a great favorite with English writers; it aimed at suggesting introspective associations; and, of course, Walter Scott is remembered as a most gifted fabricator of mottoes.

Pushkin's Russian—like the Russian of other poets he salutes, parodies, or otherwise makes use of—was bursting with Gallicisms. The brains of Russians had been so colonized by French that even Tatiana, a semi-educated landowner's daughter stuck off in the provinces, composes her love letter in that language. The plain speech of the heart had been learned not from life but from books. When Tatiana writes,

> Why *did you visit us?*
> *In the backwoods of a forgotten village,*
> *I would have never known you*
> *nor have known bitter torment.*
> *The tumult of an inexperienced soul*
> *having subdued with time (who knows?),*
> *I would have found a friend after my heart,*
> *have been a faithful wife*
> *and a virtuous mother*

she is borrowing, unconsciously, from the literature of the day, where the phrase "an inexperienced soul" is a commonplace. She might have married another, but never would she have *loved* another. "Another!" she exclaims:

> *No, to nobody [else] on earth*
> *would I have given my heart away!*
> *That has been destined in a higher council,*
> *that is the will of heaven: I am thine;*
> *my entire life has been the gage of a sure tryst with you;*
> *I know, you're sent to me by God.*

She is replicating, or Pushkin is, a formula common in the romances of the time, as for example in French poet André Chénier's *Les Amours* (*"Un autre! Ah! je ne puis"*) or in Byron's *The Bride of Abydos* ("To bid thee with another dwell: Another!").

A year after Tatiana's letter—after Onegin has killed Lenski in the duel—Tatiana one day sets out for his manor house, now deserted. In his empty rooms she finds some books he left behind, with notes ("the dashes of his pencil"):

> *And by degrees begins*
> *my Tatiana to understand*

more clearly now—thank God—
the one for whom to sigh
she's sentenced by imperious fate.
A sad and dangerous eccentric,
creature of hell or heaven,
this angel, this arrogant fiend,
who's he then? Can it be—an imitation,
an insignificant phantasm, or else
a Muscovite in Harold's mantle,
a glossary of other people's megrims,
a complete lexicon of words in vogue? . . .
Might he not be, in fact, a parody?

In his charming, loquacious commentary, Nabokov explains,

At this point the reader should be reminded of the fascination that Byron exercised on Continental minds in the 1820s. His image was the romantic counterpart of that of Napoleon, "the man of fate," whom a mysterious force kept driving on, toward an ever-receding horizon of world domination. Byron's image was seen as that of a tortured soul wandering in constant quest of a haven beyond the haze.

The man who so captivated her was but a copy. Not that this makes Tatiana love him any less; as Pushkin writes,

Tatiana with soft-melting gaze
around her looks at all,
and all to her seems priceless,
all vivifies her dolent soul
with a half-painful joyance.

There is a painting of Byron in the room, and even a little "puppet"—a statuette showing a man "under a hat, with clouded brow / with arms crosswise compressed" (possibly inspired by the 1813 oil, by Thomas Phillips, of Byron in ethnic Albanian dress).

The *Onegin* took Nabokov not one year to complete, but seven. He poured into it the literary equivalent of his lepidopteral passion, summoning the skills of a philologist and entering into debate with generations of Pushkin scholars, just as he had addressed, befriended, denounced, and embraced the butterfly men in his museum work. His commentary is itself parodic. Sounding like himself, but also like émigré scholars of the day, such as Leo Spitzer and Erich Auerbach, he is exhaustless in his hunt for influence; his approach is to read everything Pushkin and his characters have read or might have, in the original language or in contemporary translation.

The commentary, like the poem, hails *Lolita* at many points. *Onegin* is a story of an obsessive love complicated by fate, as is the novel. Tatiana's letter, cliché-ridden but from the heart, is treated more kindly by Onegin than is Charlotte Haze's to her boarder in Ramsdale, USA, but Charlotte's has the same tone of abject vulnerability:

> This is a confession. I love you. . . . Last Sunday in church . . . when I asked the Lord what to do about it, I was told to act as I am acting now. You see, there is no alternative. I have loved you from the minute I saw you. I am a passionate and lonely woman and you are the love of my life.
>
> Now, my dearest, dearest, *mon cher, cher monsieur*, you have read this; now you know. So will you please, *at once*, pack and leave. . . . Go! Scram! *Departez*! I shall be back by dinnertime, if I do eighty both ways and don't have an accident (but what would it matter?).

Lolita's plot grows from this letter as *Onegin*'s does from Tatiana's. And Humbert closely resembles Onegin. There are important points of difference—pedophilia, for one—but a strong genotypic similarity, and Nabokov the scholar traces the Byronic lineage both pre– and post–*Childe Harold*, discerning its outline in Romantic novels such as Chateaubriand's *René* (1802), which he deems "a work of genius," and Benjamin Constant's *Adolphe* (1816), "a contrived, dry, evenly gray, but very attractive work." Constant's hero, like Humbert, blends "egotism and sensibility":

> His is a checkered nature, now knight, now cad. From sobs of devotion he passes to fits of infantile cruelty, and then again dissolves in saltless tears. Whatever gifts he is supposed to possess, these are betrayed and abolished in the course of his pursuing this or that whim and of letting himself be driven by . . . vibrations of his own irritable temper.

Midway in the dark wood of his novel, Nabokov drinks deeply from exotic sources. He needs to be reminded of his idol Pushkin, needs to think of Chateaubriand, "the greatest French writer of his time," the first foreign novelist to travel in America and to write suggestively of its wild landscape. Nabokov is, as always, putting out product for the market, writing because he needs to publish, to make his way, but his deep immersion in Pushkin is a necessary detour, allowing something in the novel to ripen. In the period 1951–53, he refreshed himself by going often to a great library, by preparing to write scholarly articles, and by sometimes writing on subjects that were neither *Onegin*- nor *Lolita*-related. Some months he even wrote nothing. In the way of a professional managing his energies and hopes, he found ways to continue to work on a novel that he also kept wanting to burn.

"IN MY BOYHOOD I was an extraordinarily avid reader," Nabokov told an interviewer in the mid-sixties.

> By the age of 14 or 15 I had read or re-read all Tolstoy in Russian, all Shakespeare in English, and all Flaubert in French—besides hundreds of other books. Today I can always tell when a sentence I compose happens to resemble in cut and intonation that of any of the writers I loved or detested half a century ago.

He is not like us—us Americans. Not because he reads a lot, and not because he reads in three languages, but because he hears his sources as he writes.* He makes that recognition part of the story. Resemblance made conscious becomes homage—or parody. He might have said, "I write by borrowing, by pretending to be someone else in many lines that I compose—and I catch myself in the act of pretending."

---

* Americans have historically spoken, thought, and written out of any number of texts, but especially religious ones, and most especially the Bible. A masterful piece of American rhetoric like the Reverend Dr. Martin Luther King Jr.'s "I Have a Dream" speech is continually allusive but unpedantic. The density of its culture may be hidden to American ears yet is a prime source of its power. Among the sources melded and worn plainly but veiled by familiarity in that speech are the American Negro spiritual ("Free at last"), the Gettysburg Address, the Declaration of Independence, "My Country, 'Tis of Thee," Langston Hughes's "Let America Be America Again," Exodus, Galatians, Isaiah, Amos, *Richard III*, "This Land Is Your Land," and W. E. B. Du Bois's *Autobiography* ("this is a wonderful America, which the founding fathers dreamed").

Novels that proceed in this way are rare in America. Often they fail to attract many readers. Eliot and Pound, not favorites of Nabokov's, and not novelists, founded their modernism on a similar approach, but Melville is probably the American writer of whom Nabokov was aware whose literary sources likewise seem to give birth to his prose— not only add meaning or pedigree to it but seem often to generate the lines themselves.

Moby-Dick (1851), which Nabokov might have never read to the end, evinces a wide literary culture—"all Shakespeare in English," plus the King James Bible, Greek and Roman mythology, Seneca and other Stoics, Byron, Burke, Spinoza, Plato, Kant, Dante, Pascal, Rousseau, Coleridge, many others. Much of this wide culture Melville came to late, when, having written adventure books based on his youthful years at sea, he awakened to a philosophical potential in the novel, its ability to sound deep chords. About *Mardi* (1849), a kind of trial run at *Moby-Dick*, Melville's beloved friend Hawthorne wrote that it had depths that "here and there . . . compel a man to swim for his life," and there is already some of the stylistic mashing up in *Mardi* that made *Moby-Dick*, when it had been nearly forgotten in America, a sensational rediscovery for modernist critics.

Nabokov nods, slyly, toward Melville. In a letter to the editor in 1971, he compared hunting for the sexy parts in *Lolita* to "looking for allusions to aquatic animals in *Moby Dick*," and in an interview he joked about "Melville at breakfast feeding a sardine to his cat." Humbert, early in *Lolita*, joins an expedition to the Canadian Arctic that builds a weather station at "Pierre Point, Melville Sound," *Pierre* being Melville's last published novel.

At Harvard, Nabokov might well have lectured on *Moby-Dick*, which was usually on the syllabus for Karpovich's survey course, but he decided not to. His preference was to teach books he had already worked up at Cornell. *Moby-Dick*, like other works of the American Renaissance—*The Scarlet Letter*, by Hawthorne; Poe's last published poem, "Annabel Lee"; and Poe's *The Narrative of Arthur Gordon Pym of Nantucket*, which broods behind that trip to the Arctic (although Pym voyaged toward the South Pole, not the North)—is a ghostly source, a distant touchstone, and maybe to find its influence is only to exemplify a dictum of Borges, that "great writers create their precursors." Borges meant that a work of sufficient power casts light backward as well as ahead, so that a novel about a young girl used for sex along the American road of 1947 can seem to be prefigured in a story of the Puritan seventeenth century

Dmitri, mid-1950s, in the first of two MG TCs

where another lustrous, capricious child is the Pearl at the very heart of things. *Moby-Dick*, whether or not Nabokov read every page (and if he did not, he would only be following Melville's method, which was to read enough of a book to catch its "idea"), shares with *Lolita* an immense anxiety about the world. Ahab tries to fix the world in place with a harpoon. Likewise Stubb, the second mate on the *Pequod*, muses, during a rainy night watch, "I wonder, Flask, whether the world is anchored anywhere; if she is, she swings with an uncommon long cable, though."

Melville throws many types of rhetoric at the world. There is Puritan sermon, scientific treatise, legal brief, and Miltonian thunder in his book, not to mention comedy, drama, and classical argument. His use of a rough sort of Shakespeare-speak achieves an earnestness beyond parody:

THE OLD MANXMAN
Sir, I mistrust it; this line looks far gone,
Long heat and wet have spoiled it.

AHAB
    Twill hold,

Old gentleman. Long heat and wet, have they
Spoiled thee? Thou seem'st to hold. Or, truer
Perhaps, life holds thee; not thou it.

OLD MANXMAN
    I hold
The spool, sir. But just as my captain says.
With these gray hairs of mine 'tis not worth while
Disputing, 'specially with a superior, who'll
Ne'er confess.

AHAB
    What's that? There now's a patched
Professor in Queen Nature's granite-founded
College; but methinks he's too subservient. Where
Wert thou born?

OLD MANXMAN
In the little rocky Isle of Man, sir.

AHAB
Excellent! Thou'st hit the world by that.

Nabokov's parodies are more sarcastic. But both novels record a failure to tame the world with words. They are incommensurate, words and the world: the analogy may be to Job's feeble, pious prayers as against the voice out of the whirlwind, or the whirlwind itself.

Nabokov does not attempt Shakespeare-speak, but *Lolita* is spotted with Shakespearean allusions, and a device central to the novel is borrowed from *Hamlet* and *A Midsummer Night's Dream*: the play within a play. Boyd shows that the novel's play, a work by Clare Quilty, Humbert's nemesis, in which Lolita wins a part, is unpersuasive; Quilty describes events that he could not possibly have known about, nor could he have known that Humbert would bring his captive child to the New England town of Beardsley, there to enroll her in a school that happens to be putting on the play in question. But never mind. *Lolita*'s story of a selfish monomaniac imposing a scheme on others that leads to general doom evokes Captain Ahab's in its essence. Faulkner, whose Sutpen saga grows from a similar root, said of *Moby-Dick*,

The Greek-like simplicity of it: a man of forceful character driven by his sombre nature and his bleak heritage, bent on his own . destruction and dragging his immediate world down with him with a despotic and utter disregard of them as individuals . . . a sort of Golgotha of the heart become immutable as bronze in the sonority of its plunging ruin; all against the grave and tragic rhythm of the earth in its most timeless phase: the sea.

What's missing from *Moby-Dick* is an enchanting child. But there *is* a child, and he *is* enchanting. Ahab's grimness is tempered by his love for the ship's boy Pip, who loses his mind from fear after being left awhile afloat in the open ocean. Like Lear's fool, Pip speaks cracked wisdom, and Ahab adopts him, explaining, "Thou touchest my inmost centre, boy; thou art tied to me by cords woven of my heart-strings."

One of three blacks (one African, two African American) aboard the ship of all men, Pip wonderingly strokes the captain's hand, musing,

What's this? here's velvet shark-skin. . . . Ah, now, had poor Pip but felt so kind a thing as this, perhaps he had ne'er been lost! This seems to me, sir, as a man-rope; something that weak souls may hold by. Oh, sir, let old Perth [ship's blacksmith] now come and rivet these two hands together; the black one with the white, for I will not let this go.

Ahab, along with everyone but Ishmael, will not escape his fate by this turn to fatherly love. But the novel escapes some of its grimness thereby. Ahab has set his course and will follow it, but his diabolical arrogance partly drops away. The grimness of a story of mechanical, three-times-a-day rape of a child was the great challenge to Nabokov, and he wrapped it in brilliant wordplay and other diversions, but finally there it was, unbearably, unmistakably. Like Melville, whose Greek-like tragedy was all too plainly built and dark, Nabokov added colors of the heart, facetiously or not, to his story, especially to its final act. We see the monster coming to love, treasuring the worn seventeen-year-old girl with her "adult, rope-veined narrow hands" when Humbert visits her in Coalmont, and his untrustworthy words need to be trusted, so that we, his readers, can feel the deepest pity stir in us:

Unless it can be proven to me . . . that in the infinite run it does not matter a jot that a North American girl-child named Dolores Haze had been deprived of her childhood by a maniac, unless this can be proven (and if it can, then life is a joke), I see nothing for the treatment of my misery but the melancholy . . . palliative of articulate art.

14.

One of Nabokov's favorite spots to stay, with an inexpensive roof over his head, was Afton, Wyoming, a small Mormon town along the meandering Salt River. Here Vladimir and Véra spent some weeks in '52 and '56, in a motor court on the edge of town called the Corral Log Motel. East of town rises the Salt River Range, part of a national forest. In a chatty entomological paper called "Butterfly Collecting in Wyoming, 1952," Nabokov remembered "spending most of August in collecting around the altogether enchanting little town of Afton," which was reached by a paved road close to the Idaho state line.

The Nabokovs had their own unit with bath. Gathered around a central space, like encircling Conestoga wagons, the cabins were built in Broadaxe Hewn Log style, with compound dovetail corners (each log end extending beyond the meeting of walls). The logs were debarked and varnished, the chinks filled with mortar and covered with battens. Several creeks flow west from the mountains near Afton. Nabokov's method was to follow the creeks upstream, taking specimens in the riparian brush. "In early August," he wrote in his paper, "the trails in Bridger National Forest were covered at every damp spot with millions of *N. californica* Boisd. in tippling groups of four hundred and more, and countless individuals were drifting in a steady stream along every canyon."

He had been working on *Lolita* at that point for three years. Most of that work had been preparatory, what he called "palpating in my mind," with much note-taking. During his semester at Harvard in spring '52 he might have begun writing a draft, but during that summer he in fact wrote little or nothing.

Corral Log Motel, Afton, Wyoming

He enjoyed his usual vacation bloom of health. The years of work on the book were, on the whole, a time of health crises: dental dramas, and in '50 a recurrence of intercostal neuralgia, a painful inflammation of the nerves of the ribs, which can make breathing torturous. He told Wilson,

> I spent almost two weeks in a hospital and have been howling and writhing since the end of March when the influenza I caught at that somewhat dingy [*New Yorker*] party tapered to the atrocious point of intercostal neuralgia, the symptoms of which, the wracking, unceasing pain and panic, mimic diseases of the heart and kidney, so that for days on end I was experimented upon by doctors. . . . I am not quite well yet, had a little relapse to-day and am still in bed, at home.

When at home he was able to write undisturbed. Véra delivered his lectures in his stead, and other annoying duties temporarily dropped away.

Dmitri, who had faltered at Harvard—his freshman year "began tempestuously," Nabokov told Wilson—soon righted himself. He was distractable but able "to focus briefly on a page [and have] it register photographically," he later wrote of himself, and in the end he graduated with honors, to his parents' delight. Nabokov told his sister that Dmitri was "interested, in the following order, in: mountain climbing, girls, music, track, tennis, and his studies." Vladimir's semesters at Harvard were for purposes of close monitoring as well as research; Véra and he imposed a regime whereby Dmitri had to earn his own pocket money, and he worked as a dog walker, a mailman in Harvard Yard, and a "partner for tennis and French conversation to an odd, ruddy-faced Bostonian bachelor" who picked him up in a Jaguar.

He joined the Harvard Mountaineering Club. This organization has been associated with ascents of imposing mountains since its founding, in 1924, and Dmitri came to the club during a postwar golden age. Harvard climbers went to Alaska, Peru, Antarctica, the Himalaya, the Canadian Rockies, and western China. (A peak in the Amne Machin Range was rumored to be taller than Everest.) The most influential American climbers of the fifties were Harvard men. They included Charles Houston, leader of the 1953 K2 expedition, on which Art Gilkey died; Ad Carter, editor of the *American Alpine Journal*, the world's leading mountaineering journal; and Brad Washburn, whose aerial photos of Mount McKinley and other peaks made accurate mapping possible. Dmitri did not climb on a rope with them, but he rubbed shoulders with these men, and he hungrily assimilated the club ethos, moving from beginner to leader on first ascents. In '54 he published an article in the *Alpine Journal*, "Mt. Robson from the East," describing a climb of the East Face of the highest peak in the Canadian Rockies, a two-day ascent that included sleeping out in a crevasse. On this same trip he led the first ascent of Gibraltar Mountain, in the Canadian Selkirk Range. His team drove into Canada in "an elderly Packard hearse whose motor we lovingly rebuilt . . . and which we equipped with bunks" and war-surplus B-25 tires.

"I doubt if we shall ever get used to it," Nabokov wrote his sister Elena, referring to his son's risk taking. Several Harvard climbers died. Dmitri was mad for speed as well as summits, and by September '53 he had run "his third car into the ground," his father reported, "and is getting ready to buy a used plane." He "worked building highways in Oregon [in the summer of '53] and handling a gigantic truck," while his father and mother, traveling here and there to rendezvous with him, often worried.

For a while they lodged in the town of Ashland, Oregon. Like Afton, and like Estes Park and Telluride, Ashland sits in the lee of mountains, in this case the Siskiyous, with nearby streams, lakes, and marshy meadows. ("There is no greater pleasure in life than exploring . . . some alpine bog," Vladimir told Wilson.) The town had a commercial district and modest wooden houses for rent. Ashland in the summer is full of blooming roses. Here Nabokov dictated much of *Lolita* in its final form.

Corral Log Motel (interior)

Upon returning to Ithaca that September he told Katharine White that he had "more or less completed" his "enormous, mysterious, heart-breaking novel," a novel requiring "five years of monstrous misgivings and diabolical labors." It had cast on him an "intolerable spell" and was "a great and coily thing [with] no precedent in literature. In none of its parts will it be suitable" for her magazine.

He had sent White something else instead, a story about Pnin, a Russian-born professor, which *was* suitable. Writing that and writing the installments of *Speak, Memory* had been "brief sunny escapes" from the other book, the one that had tortured him. Nabokov both wanted and did not want to show White *Lolita*. He was obliged to, under their contract, and he hoped that she would declare it a work of genius despite its treatment of depravity, of such incomparable merit that all worries about public revulsion or possible prosecution could be forgotten. White was not charmed, however, by the unsigned manuscript that Véra hand-carried to New York a few months later, at the end of '53. The *New Yorker's* head editor, William Shawn, was not to be shown it by any means, Véra insisted to White—Shawn was more shockable than she was.

The writing of a classic novel thus passed, was accomplished, marked by a few comments to an editor ("heartbreaking," "enormous") and by a hint or two to friend Wilson ("quite soon I may show you a monster"). White had no doubt heard this sort of thing before: writers often think their latest work their greatest. He continued dictating that fall, recording only on the sixth of December that he was truly finished. "The theme and situation are decidedly sensuous," he told Wilson, but "its art is pure and its fun riotous." It was his "best thing in English." One of the first editors to see the manuscript warned him, however, that "we would all go to jail if the thing were published. I feel rather depressed about this fiasco."

The publication of *Lolita*, like its composition, was long and tormenting. At times it seemed unlikely to be accomplished. Nabokov acted as his own agent, as Wilson had taught him to. Viking rejected it first, an editor warning that publication under a pseudonym, Nabokov's initial plan for the book, would invite prosecution, reluctance to affix an author's real name suggesting awareness of pornographic content. Simon & Schuster rejected it next, editor Wallace Brockway blaming the decision on prudish colleagues. In October '54, J. (James) Laughlin, bold avant-gardist not afraid to challenge obscenity statutes, said no for New Directions. Farrar, Straus & Young declined out of fear of a court battle they could not win. Jason Epstein, of Doubleday, had been tipped to the book by Wilson, who was given a manuscript in late '54; like Pascal Covici, the Viking editor, and like Brockway, and like Roger Straus of Farrar, Straus, Epstein esteemed Nabokov's writing but was unable to persuade his colleagues to publish the new book, and in a memo he expressed some literary reservations but also a feeling that *Lolita* was somehow and not in a trivial way, brilliant.

Laughlin and Covici thought it might have a better chance overseas. Nabokov therefore sent it to Doussia Ergaz, his agent in Paris, and started looking around for an American agent to do what he had been unable to—he was willing to part with 25 percent of earnings, he told Brockway.

This complicated process, which did lead eventually to a foreign first publisher (Olympia Press) and finally to an American one (Putnam's), seems in retrospect fated to have worked out. The book was sexual but demure: free of forbidden words. It was highly readable. It appeared at a good moment, when the enforcers of public morality were coming to seem completely absurd. Joyce's *Ulysses*, widely acknowledged as an iconic work, possibly the greatest of the century, had been under attack by moral guardians since before it was even a book. (A first excerpt, published in 1918, brought convictions for obscenity for the two editors of the *Little Review*.) A long line of other works, condemned, confiscated, and burned, including Lawrence's *Women in Love*, *The Well of Loneliness*, by Radclyffe Hall, *Tropic of Cancer*, *Tropic of Capricorn*, *Naked Lunch*, Ginsberg's "Howl," Dreiser's *An American Tragedy*, Erskine Caldwell's *God's Little Acre*, Lillian Smith's *Strange Fruit*, and *Memoirs of Hecate County*, had pre-dug Nabokov's rose garden. Just in the years between his book's first rejections ('54) and its acceptance by an American house ('58), the censorship effort in America went from weak to moribund, and by '59 *Lady Chatterley's Lover*, the most suppressed novel of the century, had appeared in paperback from Grove Press, and in '61 *Tropic of Cancer* also appeared, also from Grove.

It was fated to work out for other reasons, too. Though Nabokov told Katharine White that *Lolita* was "a great and coily thing" without precedent, it was not a formal breakthrough on the order of *Ulysses* or *The Sound and the Fury*, or *As I Lay Dying* (or *Moby-Dick*, for that matter). It did not present difficulties for readers like those to be found in Djuna Barnes's *Nightwood* or Andrei Bely's *Petersburg* or, to name works only of *Lolita*'s own decade, Beckett's *Molloy*, *The Voyeur*, by Robbe-Grillet, *The Recognitions*, by William Gaddis, or Michel Butor's *Second Thoughts*. Within Nabokov's own canon it was easier to enter than *The Gift* or *Bend Sinister*. If by "without precedent" he had meant the theme of sex with children treated openly, on that score he would have been exaggerating his book's originality; disturbing accounts had appeared before, in works by the Marquis de Sade (*The 120 Days of Sodom*, *Incest*) and others. Nabokov meant something else by "without precedent." Probably he meant the coily, intricate skein of correspondences half-buried in the text, hints whereby Humbert becomes aware of Quilty, whose string pulling mirrors his own but on a level suggestive of devilish intriguing, of a universe of mocking gods, with a Master Pratfall Designer up there somewhere, ensnaring everyone in a stupendous gag.

Whatever he meant, he had written a novel for readers: ordinary readers. It was decked with gaudy allures, wickedly funny, sure to offend, but with its doors wide open. Altagracia de Jannelli would have approved. She had wanted him to write something right over the American plate. In all his magpie gleaning of period objects and attitudes he had managed not to overlook simplicity and emotion as American preferences. The book sold well for Olympia, despite legal challenges in Britain and France, and for Putnam's and later American publishers it sold extremely well—phenomenally well, in the hundreds of thousands in just its first year, and in ensuing decades in the many, many millions.

SOME OF NABOKOV'S STRUGGLE as he wrote came from fear that his new book would be stillborn—would be suppressed, kept from all those readers. Writers are a varied bunch, some concerned about readership, some indifferent, but even the indifferent ones write with at least one reader in mind, working to entice and seduce and impress themselves. To give up five years of professional prime and his best work in English, as he decreed *Lolita* to be—to carry the child full-term, knowing that it might already be dead—that was indeed anguishing.

His superciliousness, his scorn for all that was popular and midmarket, was an authentic attitude with him but also a deception. His novel *Pnin* was valuable and justified as a work of art because "what I am offering you," he told one publisher who became interested in it, "is a character entirely new to literature . . . and new characters in literature are not born every day." Novelty was what justified *Lolita*, too, he felt—being without "precedent in literature." Luckily, to have the sense of originality he needed in order to write did not require an *As I Lay Dying* type text, structurally strange and forbidding to mainstream readers. He had written such books, plentifully forbidding ones—*Bend Sinister* was his modernist American swan song, unfriendly to many reader expectations, and some of his Russian novels, such as *Invitation to a Beheading*, rejoice in narrative discontinuities and redressings of reality.

Reality, identified by Nabokov as "one of the few words which mean nothing" without quote marks around them, signified something new in the New World. Reality was vital and vulgar here. It provided Nabokov with "exhilarating" opportunities for burlesque, for extended high-flying parodies, and the books of his American prime are excited even when dark. Readers puzzled or disgusted by the high spirits of *Lolita*, which he himself deemed a tragedy, were not misperceiving it; the energy of discovery—the pleasure in claiming new writerly territory—skews the representation. But that reality is also fairly stable. In *Pnin* the quote marks around it have been all but erased, and a reader of *Lolita*, especially of the road-trip parts, might almost have used it as a Baedeker. In *Ada*, written after his self-exile to Switzerland, the reality of countries and continents is an idea again under interrogation. Use *Ada* as Baedeker at your peril.

Summer of '54, the Nabokovs had a rare bad western trip: a cabin they rented turned out to be a mess—it was ten miles north of Taos, New Mexico, "an ugly and dreary town," Nabokov wrote White, with "Indian paupers placed at strategic points by the Chamber of Commerce to lure tourists from Oklahoma and Texas." Then Véra found a lump in her breast. A local doctor said it was cancerous, and she rushed east by train, to a doctor in New York who removed the lump and found it to be benign. Before this, which put an end to the New Mexico trip, Vladimir had asked a local man to introduce him to Frieda Lawrence, D. H. Lawrence's notorious widow, who lived on a ranch nearby. Véra refused to go with him; she had no interest in meeting such a woman, and she discouraged him from going on his own. The Lawrence ranch, where the writer's ashes had been brought after his death in southern France, had been given to Frieda by the arts patron Mabel Dodge Luhan, and it had become a place of pilgrimage for devotees, who ventured to it as to a shrine. Nabokov's attentions to graves and writers' widows are little known—in America, this appears to have been his only attempt to pay such respects.

He worked hard the year *Lolita* was being rejected. Among his projects was a translation into Russian of *Speak, Memory*, a "most harrowing" task, he informed White. "I think I have told you more than once what agony it was . . . to switch from Russian to English. . . . I swore I would never go back, but there I was, after fifteen years . . . wallowing in the bitter luxury of my Russian." He continued working on *Eugene Onegin*, translating the other direction. He wrote a second chapter of *Pnin*, deemed "unpleasant" by the *New Yorker* and rejected; Viking had acquired book rights, but his editor there felt unsure after reading the early chapters and disagreed with Nabokov's overall plan, which ended in death for "poor Pnin . . . with everything unsettled and uncompleted, including the book Pnin had been writing all his life." Speaking Jannellian market wisdom, the editor, Pascal Covici, urged an outcome a little less hopeless, and Nabokov took this advice: he changed his plan.

Pnin shows him performing as an alert professional, writing about a Russian in America after the death of Stalin and during Joseph McCarthy's hunt for Soviet moles—a time of unusual focus on things Russian. The book is of the early fifties as *Lolita* is of the late forties and a bit later. Michael Maar, a German scholar, notes that "the mushroom cloud over Hiroshima" makes its way into the text, Professor Pnin reminded of it when he sees a thought bubble in a cartoon, and in general, "no other work by Nabokov lets so much contemporary history pass through its membranes." The writing is social comedy of an exalted sort. Mary McCarthy had published *The Groves of Academe* in '52, and Nabokov read it and pronounced it "very amusing and quite brilliant in parts." *Pnin* is, like hers, a campus novel, but Nabokov, although he holds some characters up to ridicule, and though he takes aim at a discrete social world, writes a few degrees off true north of social satire, not much concerned to shape a thoroughgoing critique of anything. Pnin is a good soul and an honorable man. He patronizes a local restaurant, the Egg and We, out of "sheer sympathy with failure," and his byword is kindness. He has been through the century's wringer. Now he finds himself in a land of excellent washing machines:

> Although forbidden to come near it, he would be caught trespassing again and again. Casting aside all decorum and caution, he would feed it anything that happened to be at hand, his handkerchief, kitchen towels, a heap of shorts and shirts smuggled down from his room, just for the joy of watching through that porthole what looked like an endless tumble of dolphins with the staggers.

Like his author, he hails from St. Petersburg, but unlike him he is oddlooking and hopeless with English:

> Whereas the degree in sociology and political economy that Pnin had obtained . . . at the University of Prague around 1925 had become . . . a doctorate in desuetude, he was not altogether miscast as a teacher of Russian. He was beloved not for any essential ability but for those unforgettable digressions of his, when he would remove his glasses to beam at the past while massaging the lenses of the present.

Nabokov shapes his story as professional writers do, ending segments with cliffhangers (chapter 2, part 4; chapter 6, part 4). Pnin's speech is a source of fun. Not masterful as a writer of dialogue, Nabokov works hard to present Pnin-speak as comical; when Pnin inspects a room for rent, the room, and the fragment of winter afternoon, are what are memorable:

> "Well, to make a long story very short: habitated in Paris from 1925, abandoned France at beginning of Hitler war. Is now here.

Is American citizen. Is teaching Russian and such like subjects at Vandal [Waindell] College. From Hagen, Head of German Department, obtainable all references." . . .

Pnin peered into Isabel's pink-walled, white-flounced room. It had suddenly begun to snow, though the sky was pure platinum, and the slow scintillant downcome got reflected in the silent looking glass. . . . He held his hand at a little distance from the window.

Based partly on another Cornell professor, émigré historian Marc Szeftel, the character Pnin draws on elements of Nabokov's own biography, parts not fitted into other American books. There is the matter of bad teeth. Before his room inspection, Pnin tells his prospective landlady, "I must warn: will have all my teeth pulled out. It is a repulsive operation." But like Nabokov, Pnin experiences liberation, uncanny joy, following dental surgery:

During a few days he was in mourning for an intimate part of himself. . . . And when the plates were thrust in, it was like a poor fossil skull being fitted with the grinning jaws of a perfect stranger. . . . Ten days passed—and suddenly he began to enjoy the new gadget. . . . At night he kept his treasure in a special glass of special fluid where it smiled to itself, pink and pearly. . . . The great work on Old Russia . . . which for the last ten years or so he had been fondly planning, now seemed accessible.

Speak On, Memory, Nabokov's intended second memoir, became less likely now. Into *Pnin* went an account of a St. Mark's-like boarding school, which Victor Wind, the teenaged son of Pnin's ex-wife, attends. Likewise Vladimir's plan to write, in a memoir, about his tour of southern colleges yielded to the comic possibilities of putting Pnin on a similar tour. As the book begins he is headed for a distant town to speak to a women's club, but "now a secret must be imparted," Nabokov tells us. "Professor Pnin was on the wrong train." Like several of his other novels, this one employs dramatic irony of the most extreme kind, the protagonist absurdly unaware of what a reader sees thumpingly to be the case. Nabokov's reputation for cruelty—for creating situations in which his characters mistake reality to an elephantine extent—would have been validated but for his affection for his hero, nor is it an exaggeration to say that he *loves* his hero, in the way of a friend realizing, as he tries to describe them, the deep goodness and mysterious idiosyncrasy of another.

The book's narrator, whom Nabokov calls "VN," is not quite V. Nabokov. VN knew Pnin in St. Petersburg, and he offers an account of their boyhood. Nabokov, who by his own confession was a bully when young, who needed to triumph in all encounters and who disdained weakness, lends this shading of his personality to VN, whose roguish way with women includes a casual conquest of Pnin's future wife, who, Tatiana-like, throws herself at VN's feet. On the rebound she marries Pnin, telling him "everything" about the affair.

The novel's set piece—a housewarming—appeared as a *New Yorker* story on November 12, 1955. Nabokov was by then the veteran of ten years of close editing by the magazine. He had fought strenuous attempts to improve him, and as recently as the year before he had made himself count to ten before replying to Katharine White's rejection of *Pnin*'s chapter 2 ("I intended to answer—and refute—your criticism point by point; but . . . the five-month delay has dulled that urge"). White's changes to "Pnin Gives a Party" imposed *New Yorker* house style, inserting commas that seemed intended to correct, as a teacher corrects a wiggling student, a fondness for unfettered movement. Thus, "All of a sudden he experienced an odd feeling of dissatisfaction as he checked the little list of his guests" became "All of a sudden, he experienced an odd feeling of dissatisfaction as he checked, mentally, the little list of his guests." "The good doctor had perceptibly aged since last year but was as sturdy and square-shaped as ever" became "The good Doctor, a square-shouldered, aging man . . ." Nabokov had learned not to fight over everything. Exposure in the magazine's pages was valuable, and he was being well paid. Still, "Pnin Gives a Party" is incomparably less as short story than as chapter in a book. The description of the doctor—a German professor who is fond of Pnin, who protects him when others try to fire him, but who is himself about to leave Waindell for a better job—continues in the novel, "with his well-padded shoulders, square chin, square nostrils, leonine glabella, and rectangular brush of grizzled hair that had something topiary about it." White edited the chapter to article length, cutting out of necessity. A quality of uncanny heartbreak went out of the prose, and it became a sophisticated amusement, whereas before it had been that but also a mortal plaint, a cry.

Unaware of his impending firing, Pnin hopes to buy the house he rents. "The sense of living in a discrete building all by himself," VN explains, was to Pnin something singularly delightful and amazingly satisfying to a . . . want of his innermost self. . . . One of the sweetest things about the place was the silence—angelic, rural, and perfectly secure, thus in blissful contrast to the persistent cacophonies that had surrounded him from six sides in the rented rooms of his former habitations.

The house is "cherry-red brick, with white shutters and a shingle roof." It is definingly a house of the era. Nearby is a cornfield; across Todd Road, where the house sits, are spruce trees and old elms, and the nearest neighbor is half a mile away, which accounts for the silence. Pnin thinks of it as "suburban," possibly because outlier houses invaded farmland in advance of suburbs in America. In back is some remnant raw nature: a cliff surmounted by brush. Late in his party, Pnin takes two friends upstairs, and from his bedroom windows they see "a dark rock wall rising" only fifty feet away from the house. One friend is moved to say, as if understanding author Nabokov's own love of cliffs, "At last you are really comfortable."

We know he will lose the house before he can possess it. We know that the friends of his Waindell years—some of them more than casual, some who love him—will be lost to him. The comedy of being on a wrong train is missing here—again a Nabokovian hero labors under absurd misconceptions, but there is little humor in it. The party is nevertheless lovely, a success. Academics and their wives, existing as broad types but also as cherishable individuals, hold forth in ways that make a reader want to say, *Yes, they* would *sound like that,* but also, *Wait a minute, I know that man (or woman).* All come under a shadow, their vividness instinct with impermanence. One of the guests, an English lit professor, channels the mood. He is "an obvious figure," Nabokov explains:

> If you drew a pair of old brown loafers, two beige elbow patches, a black pipe, and two baggy eyes under heavy eyebrows, the rest was easy to fill out. Somewhere in the middle distance hung an obscure liver ailment, and somewhere in the background there was Eighteenth-Century Poetry, Roy's particular field, an overgrazed pasture, with the trickle of a brook and a clump of initialed trees.

The professor has a secret. He is a Pepys-style chronicler who keeps "a detailed diary, in cryptogrammed verse, which he hoped posterity would someday decipher and, in sober backcast, proclaim the greatest literary achievement of our time." Sent to fetch his wife's purse, he

blundered from chair to chair, and found himself with a white bag, not knowing really where he picked it up, his mind being occupied by the adumbrations of lines he was to write down later in the night:

We sat and drank, each with a separate past locked up in him, and fate's alarm clocks set at unrelated futures.

An earlier chapter, number 3, begins,

During the eight years Pnin had taught at Waindell College he had changed his lodgings . . . about every semester. The accumulation of consecutive rooms in his memory now resembled those displays of grouped elbow chairs on show, and beds, and lamps, and inglenooks which, ignoring all space-time distinctions, commingle in the soft light of a furniture store beyond which it snows, and the dusk deepens, and nobody really loves anybody.

The writing is plain, less worked than *Lolita*'s prose of high allusion. To a degree the book is an un-*Lolita*, designed to charm not scare away publishers, and Pnin is a non-Humbert, a radiant soul rather than a destroyer of childhood.

Pnin is also almost a stepfather. He warms to his ex-wife's fourteen-year-old son, Victor, who visits him in Waindell. This remarkable boy, tall and magnetically self-possessed, like Dmitri, can perceive the Pninian radiance, and one of the disappointments of the novel is that Nabokov does not arrange for them to linger longer together onstage, packing the boy off to California and Pnin to a Karpovich-like summer camp with Russians. Humbert gave his stepdaughter presents to win sex from her. Pnin also gives Victor gifts, but gifts that misfire: a soccer ball when Victor has no interest in sports, a book of Jack London stories when he reads at a higher level. The most remarkable gifting happens the other way, when Victor sends Pnin a "large bowl of brilliant aquamarine glass with a decorative design of swirled ribbing and lily pads." The bowl arrives the day Pnin begins planning a party. One of his guests will exclaim, "Gracious, Timofey, where on earth did you get that perfectly divine bowl!" He fills it with wine punch.

The bowl cannot help but symbolize: it suggests the fragile world of friendship and amusement, caught in time; Victor's affection for Pnin; many things possibly not necessary to spell out—while being also exceptional, eye-catching, eerie. Around the blue bowl, which is a kind of cocktail-party version of James's burdensomely meaningful golden bowl, the gathering of well-lubricated friends, each with a separate past and living to the ticking of an unknown alarm, ascends into a realm of heightened here-and-nowness—the novel itself seems to exist within quotation marks for a page or two, not the quotes of ironic distance but quote marks in their original sense, simple signs setting off true speech, the living words for things.

Later the bowl appears to crack, like James's crystal bowl with its flaw. Pnin has received the bad news, from his academic protector, that his sanctuary is built of wind, and in his distress he mishandles the bowl in a sinkful of sudsy water. But no, better not go that way, Nabokov seems to decide: recalling his editor's strictures on bleak endings, possibly, he makes it an unimportant wineglass that breaks. ("The beautiful bowl was intact. He took a fresh dish towel and went on with his household work.")

Pnin's tale briskly concludes thereafter. Not only is he to be fired, but the English department "is inviting one of your most brilliant compatriots" to Waindell, and this man is none other than VN, the novel's narrator, the man who seduced Pnin's beloved years ago. Pnin can stay on but at this rival's sufferance. He declines to stay.

Viking had second thoughts when Nabokov sent them the full manuscript on August 29, 1955. The book was too short, they thought. It had other problems, the main one being that it failed to cohere, was mere sketches. Nabokov had worked hard to make it come together, and he was offended. The story begins with a trip to a women's club, and it ends with a faculty wag about to retell that story. Michael Maar argues that the book is built as a perfect mirror construction, seven chapters arranged along a "central axis of symmetry," the axis being chapter 4, about Victor and Pnin. A homely rodent, the American tree squirrel, appears in every chapter. Squirrels are so plainly stitched into the American scene that only a foreigner might be expected to notice them. They remind Pnin of a kind, incandescent girl he loved in St. Petersburg, a Jewish girl who fled Russia and died in Buchenwald. She was called Mira Belochkin— Belochkin echoing *belochka*, a diminutive of *belka*, Russian for "squirrel."

In one of the era's regrettable editorial misjudgments, Viking declined to publish *Pnin*. Literary values aside, they thus failed to nail down a relationship with an author who was soon to become world famous. *Pnin* was not the book that made Nabokov, but it was a title that a publisher would long feel fortunate to have on its list. Appearing from Doubleday in March '57, it had remarkable sales, sales that a book by Nabokov had never enjoyed before. *Lolita* was a cause célèbre by then, available only in the raffish Olympia edition, which was hard to find.

Much of the writing is splendid. When Pnin first attaches a pencil sharpener to his desk, it is "that highly satisfying, highly philosophical implement that goes ticonderoga-ticonderoga, feeding on the yellow finish and sweet wood, and ends up in a . . . soundlessly spinning ethereal void." About the college's self-satisfied nowhereness, VN says,

> Pnin walked down the gloomy stairs and through the Museum of Sculpture. Humanities Hall, where . . . Ornithology and Anthropology also lurked, was connected with another brick building, Frieze Hall, which housed the dining rooms and the Faculty Club, by means of a rather rococo openwork gallery: it went up a slope, then turned sharply and wandered down toward a routine smell of potato chips and the sadness of balanced meals.

The college president

> had started to lose his sight a couple of years before and was now almost totally blind. With solar regularity . . . he would be led every day by his niece and secretary to Frieze Hall; he came, a figure of antique dignity, moving in his private darkness to an invisible luncheon . . . and it was strange to see, directly behind him on a [large mural], his stylized likeness in a mauve double-breasted suit and mahogany shoes, gazing with radiant magenta eyes at the scrolls handed him by Richard Wagner, Dostoevski, and Confucius.

The tone is tongue-in-cheek, with overtones of self-regard. Nabokov's standard table talk—mockery of psychoanalysis, of inferior writers, of au courant scholars; praise of authentic geniuses like himself; savage scorn for the Soviets—forms the book's substrate. The anti-Bolshevik writing is of a high order, tuned to fit with anti-Communist sentiments of the day. Senator McCarthy comes in for mention but is neither endorsed nor condemned, and Nabokov mourns the Russian intelligentsia oppressed under the tsar and obliterated by the Soviets. What is missing is plot. When Victor, who loves Pnin instinctively, enters the story and his need for a father begins to touch us, it seems that the story has found its point, but, as Covici lamented, Nabokov disdains to develop that feeling. He seems to have wanted to but to have been unable. "We can't know more about Victor," he replied, answering an editorial letter full of doubts as well as praise. "Throughout the years I worked at this book, I discarded many vistas that opened before me, abandoned many alluring but unnecessary sub-plots . . . eliminating everything that was not strictly justified in the light of art." In general he derogated plot—plottedness was a characteristic of lesser work, he thought. He was not good at plots, although he was good at schematics, at working within a set of arbitrary preconditions, making things come out neatly. A plot of the kind that Covici seems to have wanted takes a story in unexpected but convincing directions, while expressing emotions to a degree uncommon in life outside of books. Many readers, not the readers Nabokov was most comfortable catering to, read to feel the breaking of "the frozen sea inside us" that Kafka wrote about in his famous letter to a school friend. Nabokov knew this, might even have wished to please such readers—witness his "many discarded vistas"—but could not.

Edmund Wilson enjoyed *Pnin* moderately. About the first excerpt to appear he wrote, "Elena [his new, fourth and final, wife] loved your . . . short story. . . . I liked it, too, but expected more of a wow at the end." He was more positive when the full book came out, saying, "I think it is very good, and also that you may at last have made contact with the great American public. . . . The reviews I have so far seen all say exactly the same thing: this shows that no one is puzzled, they know how they are meant to react." He offered corrections, some picayune. It was important for him to praise *Pnin*. *Lolita* had left him cold, repulsed. "Now, about your novel," he had written three years before, after reading a copy of the *Lolita* manuscript:

I like it less than anything else of yours I have read. The short story that it grew out of was interesting, but I don't think the subject can stand this very extended treatment. Nasty subjects may make fine books; but I don't feel you have got away with this. It isn't merely that the characters and the situation are repulsive . . . but that . . . they seem quite unreal. The various goings-on and the climax . . . become too absurd to be horrible or tragic, yet remain too unpleasant to be funny. . . . I agree with Mary that the cleverness sometimes becomes tiresome."

It is remarkable that the friendship survived this response. Nabokov, who was undoubtedly wounded, nevertheless replied, only a few months later, with unequivocal praise for a Wilson article in the *New Yorker*: "Bunny, I liked *very much* your Palestine essay. It is one of your best pieces." Wilson was too needed a friend—too close, too simpatico—to lose over this. When he came to feel, erroneously, that Wilson had not read the full manuscript (he had wished to hand it on to publishers as soon as possible; also he was sharing pages with Elena and with Mary McCarthy, therefore he read it quickly), Nabokov was hurt anew. He wrote, "I have sold my LOLITA [in France]. . . . I would like you to read it some day," and when publishers in America still shunned the book,

> It depresses me to think that this pure and austere work may be treated by some flippant critic as a pornographic stunt. This danger is the more real to me since I realize that *even* you neither understand nor wish to understand the texture of this intricate and unusual production.

Wilson tried to express what had disappointed him. "I think that the time is approaching," he wrote Véra in '52, "when I am going to read his complete works and write an essay on them that will somewhat annoy him." Two years later, he was still promising an *étude approfondie*, a view of the whole oeuvre to date, but it never came together. Friendship might have prevented a frank assessment. Nabokov in '52 or even into '57 was still a little-known immigrant author subsisting on a professor's salary, and Wilson might have feared damaging him. When he did speak at last in a full-throated way it was ten years later, and it was only about the translation of *Eugene Onegin*, which he disliked for stylistic and scholarly reasons. By then, 1965, Nabokov was a titan, very nearly a literary immortal, and to challenge him risked damage to Wilson's reputation more than Nabokov's.

Only at the end of his life—succumbing to strokes and beset by other health problems—would Wilson write something like a general assessment. In a volume called *A Window on Russia*, published the year he died (1972), he presents a summing up only seven pages long. He has gone back and read the early novels, he says. On the whole he has not been carried away. "The heroes of these stories," he writes, "were almost always . . . surrounded by rather absurd inferiors; they, however, possess an inalienable distinction and at moments a kind of communication with a higher world."

> Mr. Nabokov has gone on record . . . as explaining that he regards a novel as a kind of game with the reader. By deceiving the latter's expectation, the novelist wins the game. But the device exploited in these novels is simply not to have anything exciting take place, to have the action peter out. . . . In *King, Queen, Knave*, the lover and his mistress are discouraged from murdering her husband. In *Invitation to a Beheading*, [the hero] is not executed but, dissociating himself from his accusers, simply gets up and walks away. (It is curious to contrast this ending with one of Solzhenitsyn's prison camps from which there can be no escape.)

Perhaps forgetting his own subtle early readings, his appreciation for stand-alone worlds of art, Wilson loses patience with the undeveloped plots, with actions that dissipate. He finds "sado-masochism" present and associates Nabokov with people "who enjoy malicious teasing and embarrassing practical jokes" but get "aggrieved and indignant" when someone turns the tables.

Pnin, he says, in his summing up, shows Nabokov importing himself into a story, for reasons mainly related to this sado-masochism. He can more directly "humiliate . . . his humble little Russian professor, who dreads Nabokov's brilliance and insolence," i.e., the character VN's insolence. Pnin is "somewhat sentimentalized," Wilson continues. "The sadist, here as often, turns out to have an underside of sentimentality." Wilson misses badly on this matter of VN entering the story. Not to humiliate more, but to display refinements of soul in Pnin—to distinguish between him and VN in ways readers can put together but that VN, largely, cannot—is why the narrator invades his text.

On the question of sentimentality, Wilson was more useful. The moral center of the book is underdeveloped. It is Mira, the young woman who died at Buchenwald, the girl Pnin had been in love with long ago; he remembers her in a reverie brought on by a cardiac event (possibly a heart attack), and he thinks of her in terms familiar from other Nabokovian evocations of fetching young girls ("the warm rose-

red silk lining of her karakul muff," "the slenderness of arm and ankle").
Here, almost uniquely in his writings, Nabokov makes explicit mention
of the Holocaust and a known site of extermination. His approach,
usually, is to broadly fictionalize, as if to name the horrors of his own
century would be to endorse them. Better to write of them in code, in
contexts insistently unreal, thus to keep the foulness at a remove.

This approach is understandable. The danger is that characters such
as Krug in *Bend Sinister*, Kinbote in *Pale Fire*, and even Humbert may
be allowed to dress themselves in the robes of unmentionable suffering,
entering special pleas on account of the darkness of their times. Even
noble Pnin seems to do this, since Nabokov does not fully dramatize
the connection with Mira. She is a fey angel, that's all; Pnin remembers
her "gentle heart," her "graceful, fragile, tender" young womanhood,
but, as with stepson Victor, the author's plan for his book rules out an
exploration via plot. Pnin hurries from lovelorn thoughts to visions of
Mira dying "a great number of deaths," being "inoculated with filth,
tetanus bacilli, broken glass, gassed in a sham shower bath with prussic
acid, burned alive in a pit," etc. Nabokov himself seems to hurry,
pushing her offstage. She is made into a paragon, an Anne Frank figure;
without benefit of enriching, complicating scenes that have a flavor of
tricksome life, she is sacralized, sent straight to the higher realms.

15.

Wilson's criticisms of *Pnin* and other works have been seen by some Nabokov scholars as proof, on a deep level, of envy. An upstart crow arrives, not even speaking the language well, and carries off all the loot; a man who needs to be top dog—not Nabokov, Wilson—turns against a former protégé, now blown up far too high. Envy probably played some part. But Wilson's words expressed critical reservations of the kind that was his métier, with which normally he took great care. He might have been blind or philistine or so weakened near the end as to be incapable of judging well, but probably he was not corrupted by envy in a simple way. Something did not persuade him in Nabokov's work. He had voiced objections for years. Even books he liked, such as *Nikolai Gogol*, annoyed him, and the one novel he enthused about, *The Real Life of Sebastian Knight*, also had important flaws, in his view.

Wilson made a fetish of his independence and incorruptibility. This might have fooled him—led him not to recognize the tribute to their friendship written into *Bend Sinister*, for instance. For all his devoted reading of whatever Nabokov sent his way, Edmund did not read him professionally. He did not take extensive notes on—possibly did not remember—important aspects of the work. In '53 he wrote, "Is there any chance of your publishing a book any time before the fall after next? I hope so, for it would give me a pretext to do a long *New Yorker* article about you and include it in a book that is supposed to come out." He *wanted* to read him, sought grounds for a professional appraisal. He added, "I have been aiming to make you my next Russian subject after Turgenev."

An enduring difference was political. Scholars friendly to Nabokov cast the Russian as immensely more knowledgeable about history, as someone who had not only experienced it but had thought hard about it. In *The Gift*, according to Simon Karlinsky, a careful and persuasive Nabokov scholar who was also an émigré, the writer "dealt with the roots of totalitarianism in the ostensibly libertarian but actually dogmatic and fanatical ideologies" of the Russian reformers who predated the Bolsheviks. Wilson, to his misfortune, never read *The Gift*—his Russian wasn't up to it, and an English translation appeared only in '63. Thus he could write ignorantly, indeed insultingly, to Nabokov when *Bend Sinister* came out, advising him to avoid all "questions of politics and social change," since "you aren't good at this."

Had Wilson read *The Gift*, he might have been persuaded that the reformers had given birth to the murderous, ingenious Bolsheviks, and that literature written to advance a social agenda, even worthy-seeming literature, can be dangerous. But equally, he might have felt that Nabokov *still* did not understand. Nikolai Chernyshevsky, the bad novelist who is subjected to an amusing biographizing in *The Gift*, foisted materialist utilitarianism on literature, judging Pushkin to be a writer of aesthetic trifles. But Chernyshevsky, who spent twenty years in prison and exile, was like Nabokov's poet hero, Fyodor, and like Nabokov himself, decisively on the mind side of things, the ideational side, his strict materialism to the contrary notwithstanding. (All is matter, and there is only material reality, but this idea is itself the lever of the future: the man who possesses it will move the world.) Wilson was less idealist. The questions he asked about situations of social conflict were on the order of *Who is suffering here? Who possesses real power? Whose lives are being crushed?* Had he read *The Gift* he might have agreed with Nabokov, who believed it to be his best work in Russian. But also he might have dismissed it. The young hero, Fyodor, is fascinated by his own creative process—ravished by the beauty of his mind. His own inspirations thrill him; they constitute the drama of his life in shabby thirties Berlin:

> When in the mornings I entered this world of the forest, whose image I had raised as it were by my own efforts above the level of those artless Sunday impressions (paper trash, a crowd of picnickers) out of which the Berliners' conception of "Grunewald" was composed; when on these hot, summer weekdays I walked

over to its southern side, into its depths, to wild secret spots, I felt as much delight as if this was a primeval paradise.

Fyodor climbed aboard [a bus], and the conductor, on the open top deck, smote its plated side with his palm to tell the driver he could move on. Along this side and along the toothpaste advertisement upon it swished the tips of soft maple twigs—and it would have been pleasant to look down from above on the gliding street ennobled by perspective, if it were not for the everlasting, chilly thought: there he is, a special, rare and as yet undescribed and unnamed variant of man, and he is occupied with God knows what, rushing from [poorly paid language] lesson to lesson, wasting his youth on a boring and empty task.

In sometimes exciting passages—flaneur reportage of a high order—Fyodor creates a Berlin, and though these are dire times, portentous for the entire world, German fascism hardly figures in the portrait. Only near the end do we read, "A truck went by with a load of young people returning from some civic orgy, waving something or other and shouting something or other." Wilson, to presume to speak for him, would have noticed more amply. The author is making a familiar point about realms of the imagination being open to the artist, who lives and suffers in historical time but can sometimes transcend it, but *why* is Nabokov's Berlin novel so contentedly, so entertainingly unempathic? Did social reform ideas of the Russian 1860s really create Bolshevism? What about serfdom and its imperfect eradication, continuing the beggaring of the peasantry? What about outbreaks of violence against landowners going back hundreds of years, or the dislocations of primitive Russian industrialization, or the rate of infant mortality? Nabokov's most autobiographical novel has no responsibility to address those matters, nor to acknowledge historical forces as commonly understood, but it does present itself as saying something pertinent about Bolshevism, and what it says, at unusual length, is not persuasive.

In his response to *Bend Sinister*, Wilson had written, "You have no idea why or how the [dictator] Toad was able to put himself over," and here is the crux of their disagreement. For Nabokov, dictators are beneath notice, even when they murder you. For Wilson, the suffering of classes of people is a commanding truth, and the means by which they connive in their own enslavement needs to be understood. The novel was not the best place to seek that understanding, but for Wilson, a rejection of the whole topic by an author was telling. Too often he found in his friend's work a giggling pleasure in suffering. Maybe more important, the novels, with their clever schematic premises, held to with impressive rigor, did not relax and breathe and give him a feeling of life profoundly opened to and understood, a feeling he got from novelists Nabokov disdained—Malraux, Faulkner, Pasternak—as well as some he respected—Gogol, Tolstoy. An art of narcissism, of exultant, trumpeted ego: this was a possible description of Nabokov's art, and for Wilson that was a disappointment.

IN DECEMBER '55 A break: novelist Graham Greene named *Lolita*, still available only in the Olympia Press edition, one of the three best books of the year. This mention in the London *Sunday Times* led a columnist, John Gordon of the London *Sunday Express*, to declare the novel "the filthiest book I have ever read. Sheer unrestrained pornography. . . . The entire book is . . . utterly disgusting. . . . It is published in France." An item in Harvey Breit's book-chat column in the *New York Times* noted the London controversy; till then, *Lolita* had not been mentioned anywhere in the U.S. press.

Pnin had just been rejected by its publisher. It took Nabokov time to realize his good fortune: "I am extremely irritated by the turn my nymphet's destiny is taking," he wrote Wilson, and, "although I foreglimpsed the situation, I have no inkling how to act" in regard to the British controversy. He did not need to act. A perfect Rube Goldberg machine of promotion had been jiggered into action, with Greene forming a John Gordon Society to identify "all offensive books, plays, paintings, sculptures and ceramics." The society actually met, leading to amusing press coverage. Nabokov's reputation for magical English prose, a reputation won through hard work over fifteen years, made what he feared for *Lolita* unlikely. His American professional cohort— book editors, magazine editors, reviewers, literary scholars, and writers who read him with joy and amazement—made it difficult to dismiss him as a hack (or a pornographer). A second column by Breit quoted reactions from that cohort:

"[*Lolita*] shocks because it is great art, because it tells a terrible story in a wholly original way." . . . "The actual theme of the book—which has long held a powerful appeal for our most important writers—is the corruption of innocence, as now envisioned through the imagination of a European intellectual in quest of his private America." . . . "Readers may find something of Nathanael West in it. Its closest analogues are *Notes from the Underground* and *The Possessed*." . . . "Something of its bedazzlement might be suggested by a composite impression of *Daisy Miller* and *The Possessed*—or perhaps, again, of *The Captive* and *Tender Is the Night*."

What Nabokov called a "foul little flurry" in London secured *Lolita*'s future. Gallimard, the esteemed French house, acquired rights for a French-language edition, and the *Nouvelle Revue Française* arranged to run an excerpt. Some American publishers now contacted Nabokov—none was able to bring the book out in the end, but that there would be an American *Lolita* edition was looking more likely.

Spring of '56, Nabokov took leave from Cornell and spent three months at Harvard, further researching *Eugene Onegin*. Dmitri was in Cambridge, too, studying music at the Longy School, a Harvard-connected conservatory. In his memoir Dmitri says,

> My first MG has been wrecked, and I drive my second. It was bought used, has been modified to go fast, and possesses no top or windshield wipers. It is often parked near Harvard Square, and usually contains, amid sports paraphernalia and snow, an open copy of the first book I shall translate: Lermontov's *Hero of Our Time*. Father . . . comes upon the car [and] carefully notes the page number to see how far I have progressed, and reproachfully reports it to me in the evening.

His parents, nervously supporting his hopes for an operatic career, had hatched a backup plan. Vladimir had proposed to Viking a retranslation of the Lermontov novel, offering "a very wonderful young translator" to do the work. The wonderful translator's father would supervise him. That Dmitri knew of this only vaguely in advance is suggested by a note from Véra:

> I have a piece of very good news for you: it appears almost certain that you will be entrusted with the translation of THE HERO OF OUR TIME. . . . One of the Doubleday editors flew over last

Monday for lunch and after a long conference with father became interested in this idea. To-day he has written and offered to go ahead with the contract.

By then a Harvard graduate, accepted at Harvard Law (but without interest in attending), Dmitri still seemed dangerously unmoored, if we can read between the lines of Véra's letter:

> The contract (if passed) will be between you and Doubleday. The book has about 200 pages. . . . This means good, thorough, conscientious work, up to an hour and a half to a page, and at least 3–4 pages a day. . . . You should have about one half of the book done before [you start at Longy]. After that you will progress at a slower rate, but you will still have to work every day (no holidays) for as many hours as you can squeeze in. . . . It is very enjoyable work but it is also quite exacting and above all it has to be followed up with the utmost perseverance.

Something in her American son frightens her—maybe several things. "Your father, who never can say no," as Véra described Vladimir, "expects of you" a good job, and declining the opportunity seems not to have been an option. When Dmitri failed to carry through on the work as expected, his parents did most of it themselves. "Dismiss all thought of things such as car racing," Véra warned him a year later, summer of '56.

> Also, please review your financial life of the past year: You received (and sent down the drain) a very important sum ($1.000) from Doubleday, only one third of which you have more or less earned; you "borrowed" from your father an additional substantial sum which still has to be repaid; you borrowed from the bank; you spent every cent you earned; you were all the time short of money. . . . Instead of taking a good rest, your father and I have been working all [summer] on the "Hero," and shall be saddled with this job to the end of our vacation. Is this fair? Ponder it, son, ponder it, it's time to grow up!

Dmitri had come to resemble Toad—not the dictator in *Bend Sinister* but the madcap in *Wind in the Willows*. He had always had a "passionate love for moving things," but "so much more intense" than other children, Véra wrote. His habits began to look like a death wish. Nabokov's stories written in America have a persistent theme of the death of a child—not only *Lolita* and *Bend Sinister* but also the short stories "Signs and Symbols" and "Lance," and the poem "Pale Fire," in the novel of that name, is centrally about the death of a daughter.

Sylvia Berkman, a friend from the Wellesley years, saw them during their spring at Harvard.* She was one of Véra's intimate correspondents and author of a critical study of Katherine Mansfield. At Wellesley Berkman had sometimes found Vladimir hard to bear, his playfulness exhausting, but by the mid-fifties she was a wholesale admirer and something of a protégé. "She is one of our most subtle and sensitive women writers," Vladimir (or maybe Véra) wrote to the University of Iowa when Berkman applied to the Writers' Workshop in '55. "I see a radiant future. . . . Her method of writing, with its artistic care for wording and vivid detail, demands some leisure," i.e., paid time off from Wellesley.

Nabokov put her name forward for the Guggenheim. When a book of Berkman's stories came out, he urged the publisher, who was also one of his publishers, to get behind it. Berkman read everything by Nabokov that saw print, and though she was in a position where a tone of worship could be said to have been in her interest, she *was* worshipful, authentically in awe of him.

Writing about *Pnin* she said, "I think the . . . installments are superlative—all permeated with a wise mellow humor and astringent wit, the sharpest kind of exact presentation, and the constant melancholy sense of . . . things . . . never again to be reached." *Pnin* as a campus novel especially engaged her. "This is the absolute location in the college world I think (it makes 'The Groves of Academe' shrivel to a waspish hum), because while it is unsparing in its utter accuracy it is yet genial, and allows . . . that bores may at the same time be well meaning."

Berkman walked in the master's steps when possible. She spent a summer at Stanford, socializing with some of the same friends the Nabokovs had made there in the forties. Traveling Nabokov style, but by Greyhound bus rather than by car, she made an adventurous exploration out of her trip west, "all the way South and into the Southwest on my way [out] then up into the Pacific Northwest and down through the States to Colorado," staying at cheap lodgings. *Lolita* had just come out in its

---

* They also saw Harry Levin and his Russian-born wife, Elena, who introduced them to the novelist John Dos Passos; the Mikhail Karpoviches; Arthur and Marian Schlesinger; and the painter Billy James, son of the philosopher William and nephew of novelist Henry.

American edition. Long, open-road explorations by writers made up a distinct genre in the late forties and fifties: Berkman, whether or not she read them, was traveling and experiencing the country in the style of Henry Miller's *The Air-Conditioned Nightmare* (1947), Simone de Beauvoir's *America Day by Day* (1948), and Jack Kerouac's *On the Road* (1957) and *The Dharma Bums* (1958), as well as Humbert Humbert's saga. Her ability to take from the master was limited, however. "What I . . . learn from [him] most," she wrote Véra, "is the clear, condensed particularity, residing always in the sharp word chosen rather than the indifferent ordinary one." She could write with bracing accuracy herself, rendering equivocal perceptions well, but, like other gifted psychological realists, she found Nabokov problematic as a model. His example led to despair:

> I've been delighted to see all the fine notice of *Pnin* in the English newspapers and reviews. . . . *Lolita* I think is the most brilliant and extraordinary novel of this century. It has been very much commented upon I know in the reviews and quarterlies, and I add my bedazzled admiration and enormous pleasure to all that has been said. Why does anyone else even attempt to write in the face of work like this? It meets what I consider a primary test in that one wants to read it again and again.

Nabokov was supreme, and his courage to write as an exercise of arrogant self-awareness, in defiance of Bolsheviks and Nazis and any others who would subsume art to their purposes, made his example stirring. But particularity and *le mot juste* were just the beginning for him. In a letter to Wilson that has become famous, in which he speaks of "the specific detail . . . the unique image, without which . . . there can be no art," he has not explained his aesthetic but only a *sine qua non* of good work. What follows from precision is large—is larger. Reality vibrates like an icicle tapped with a cane in passages of his characteristic descriptive prose. From *Laughter in the Dark*:

> It really was blue: purple-blue in the distance, peacock-blue coming nearer, diamond-blue where the wave caught the light. The foam toppled over, ran, slowed down, then receded, leaving a smooth mirror on the wet sand, which the next wave flooded again. A hairy man in orange-red pants stood at the edge of the water wiping his glasses.

* * *

A large bright ball was flung from somewhere and bounced on the sand with a ringing thud.

"The water is wet!" she cried, and ran into the surf. There she advanced swinging her hips and her outspread arms, pushing forward in knee-deep water.

From *Lolita*:

Under the flimsiest of pretexts . . . we escaped from the café to the beach, and found a desolate stretch of sand, and there, in the violet shadow of some red rocks forming a kind of cave, had a brief session of avid caresses, with somebody's lost pair of sun-glasses for only witness. I was on my knees, and on the point of possessing my darling, when two bearded bathers, the old man of the sea and his brother, came out of the sea with exclamations of ribald encouragement, and four months later she died of typhus in Corfu.

The vibration, to readers responsive to such things, occurs seemingly within the reader's own mind. The author comes intimately close, saying just those words that cause an apprehension. The phrases please and may be comic but are not necessarily "aesthetic"—often they are very simple. They evoke a specific thought, and the whole process is attended by a feeling of *I knew that—I've seen such things before, I just never put them into words.*

A writer like Berkman—or like John Updike, Dmitri's near classmate at Harvard and a great champion of Nabokov in the coming generation—practices precision, refines and furthers it, but does not necessarily take a step beyond, the step whereby the hyperreal begins to dissolve. Mary McCarthy, another realist writer, objected to that next step; writing to Wilson, when both were reading the *Lolita* manuscript, she praised "all the description of motels and other U.S. phenomenology" but felt the novel "escaped into some elaborate allegory or series of symbols. . . . You felt all the characters had a kite of meaning tugging at them from above." The writing was "terribly sloppy" as a result, "full of what teachers call *haziness,* and all Vladimir's hollowest jokes and puns. I almost wondered whether this wasn't . . . part of the idea."

It was part. Reality showed itself to be ambiguous, self-undermining around the edges; it donned quotation marks and at that point became more interesting for Nabokov, opened upon something magical, an encounter with the *primam causam*, with the author himself. In *Pale Fire* (1962), the reader learns that "somehow Mind is involved as a main factor in the making of the universe," and this capitalized Mind, possibly the mind of God, is, on the evidence of *Pale Fire* itself, a trickster consciousness besotted with puns, doublings, misperceptions, and literary texts that acknowledge one another. *Pale Fire*, like *Pnin* but unlike *Lolita*, is esoteric and spiritualistic; it does many things, but notably it makes a case for a higher realm. The existence of such a dimension is implied by anomalies of this world we inhabit; the Great Mind that decrees a world of doubles, riddling coincidences, and secret correspondences is, by a curious coincidence, the very model of the mind that can understand it.

This spiritual project is an old one in American letters. Emerson, Hawthorne, Whitman, and Dickinson, along with many lesser-known authors, make up one cohort of spirit seekers; others had come before them and others would come later, but by the end of the nineteenth century metaphysical speculation had fallen somewhat out of favor, authors such as Twain, James, and Howells positing a world more or less without godly overtones. Some of Nabokov's distaste for James may represent unease with the older writer's ordinary epistemology. The world around us, especially in its social aspects, is complex and devious but not unknowable for James, and knowledge consists in perceptions tested against those of other people. Nabokov, although he writes of the comedy of getting things horribly wrong—thinking yourself a king of a foreign land, for instance, while being in fact an obscure refugee academic, like the main narrator of *Pale Fire*—claims for himself such powers of clairvoyance as to remove any need to consult with other minds. That they are *his* metaphysical insights and riddles is supreme validation: the mind that can make worlds is the final fascination.

LIKE OTHER OF NABOKOV'S best works, *Pale Fire* is a second attempt, a reboot. Important parts were already present in *Pnin* (and the character Pnin himself reappears in *Pale Fire*: readers troubled by his loss of a job find him securely placed in the later story). In the winter of 1939–40, after writing *The Enchanter*, *Lolita*'s precursor, Nabokov had written two chapters of a never-to-be-completed novel that prefigure *Pale Fire*. There is a fantasia on the theme of a lost kingdom; there is an artist grieving over a loss, hoping for personal contact beyond the grave. Now he began to feel the stirrings of a new book, new but old, in those same miraculous few years when he completed *Lolita* but could not yet get it published as he wanted, when he wrote *Pnin*, when he dove ever deeper into the scholarship of *Eugene Onegin* and translated it several times, only by the painful process of rejecting his own work arriving at last at a version he felt did Pushkin honor. And now something more: in October of '56, Véra wrote Sylvia Berkman that Vladimir's teaching was interfering "with his literary work, for apart from going ahead with the Pushkin book, he is trying to write a new novel."

Pale Fire brewed for a long while. Between the first stirrings and the actual writing (early sixties, when he was back in Europe) occurred what the Nabokovs referred to as "Hurricane Lolita," an enormous upheaval on all fronts. In March '57 Vladimir sent Doubleday editor Jason Epstein a preview of a projected, post-*Lolita* novel: it would involve "some very sophisticated spiritualism," he wrote, adding, "My creature's quest is centered in the problem of heretofore and hereafter, and it is I may say beautifully solved."

Pale Fire would be metaphysical although "completely divorced from so-called faith or religion." There would be "an insular kingdom" where "a dull and savage revolution" ousts a king, who escapes to America. Nabokov signals an intention to play with geography in a way hinted at in earlier books. The Hudson River will flow "to Colorado," and the border between upstate New York and "Montario" will be "a little blurry and unstable," but overall, "the locus and life-color are what a real-estate mind would call 'realistic.' "

The novel's central conceit—that a man called Charles Kinbote is annotating a poem by a man called John Shade—is not described in the Epstein letter. Brian Boyd, for whom *Pale Fire* may be "the most perfect novel ever written," wonderfully describes a reader first trying to enter the book:

> Two pages into the foreword, Kinbote tells us that his poor friend Shade proclaimed to him on the last day of his life that he had reached the end of his labors [on the long poem]. Kinbote adds: "See my note to line 991." At this point we can either continue with the foreword, and catch the note when we come to it, or trust the author enough to suppose there is some reason . . . and turn to the note. If we take the second course, we can witness at once Kinbote's curious attachment to Shade. As he returns home, Kinbote . . . finds Shade on "the arborlike porch or veranda I have mentioned in my note

to lines 47–48." Do we continue the note to line 991 . . . or do we divert to the earlier note? If we do, we are referred forward almost at once to the note to line 691, and though we are running out of fingers to insert as bookmarks . . . we may agree to one last try.

Nabokov works hard to entertain his reader. There is also a subtle humbling. Between 1956, when the book first stirred in him, and the early sixties, novels of which Nabokov was aware, some of which he praised—for instance, works by Alain Robbe-Grillet and Raymond Queneau, stalwarts of, respectively, the *nouveau roman* and the French literary movement *Oulipo*—appeared and acknowledged, in some ways superseded, Nabokov's formally most innovative work. He might have felt inspired to move further in an experimental direction. The humbling was of the common reader. As his follow-up to a smash bestseller, Nabokov was offering a novel with no certain way to be read. Kinbote tries, in his way, to be helpful:

> Although these notes, in conformity with custom, come after the poem, the reader is advised to consult them first and then study the poem with their help, rereading them of course as he goes through its text, and perhaps, after having done with the poem, consulting them a third time so as to complete the picture.

No question which part the commentator hopes will not be missed! Possibly in a bid to double book sales—akin to the astute copywriter who first printed on a bottle of shampoo, "Rinse and Repeat"—he confesses that he finds it

> wise in such cases as this to eliminate the bother of back-and-forth leafings by either cutting out and clipping together the pages with the text of the thing, or, even more simply, purchasing two copies of the same work which can then be placed in adjacent positions on a comfortable table.

The book's focal text, Shade's long poem "Pale Fire," is old-fashioned: rhymed and metered. Boyd calls it "a brilliant achievement in its own right," adding that "English poetry has few things better to offer than 'Pale Fire.' " It derives its form from the verse of Alexander Pope, although other writers are also echoed, among them Milton, Goethe, Wordsworth, Housman, and Yeats. John Shade, a college-dwelling author of the fireside sort, is a medium-famous northeastern poet, or as he puts it in "Pale Fire," "my name / Was mentioned twice, as usual just behind / (one oozy footstep) Frost." Nine hundred ninety-nine lines long, his poem is not frank doggerel, but it does have a wearying singsong quality, and the self-satisfied mastery of eighteenth-century heroic couplets—rhyming pairs of lines of iambic pentameter—produces an effect of contented neatness:

> *Maud Shade was eighty when a sudden hush*
> *Fell on her life. We saw the angry flush*
> *And torsion of paralysis assail*
> *Her noble cheek. We moved her to Pinedale,*
> *Famed for its sanitarium. There she'd sit*
> *in the glassed sun and watch the fly that lit*
> *Upon her dress and then upon her wrist.*
> *Her mind kept fading in the growing mist.*

The rhyme-and-meter-driven ordering of sense that Nabokov had weaned himself from in his translations of *Eugene Onegin*—sacrificing everything to strict literal fidelity—here wins out. Early on, Shade describes a strange episode of his youth:

> *One day,*
> *When I'd just turned eleven, as I lay*
> *Prone on the floor and watched a clockwork toy—*
> *A tin wheelbarrow pushed by a tin boy—*
> *Bypass chair legs and stray beneath the bed,*
> *There was a sudden sunburst in my head.*
>
> *And then black night. That blackness was sublime.*
> *I felt distributed through space and time:*
> *One foot upon a mountaintop, one hand*
> *Under the pebbles of a panting strand,*
> *One ear in Italy, one eye in Spain,*
> *In caves, my blood, and in the stars, my brain.*

The episode recalls the hero's heart trouble in *Pnin*, when he has visions of Mira Belochkin. The poem is like Wordsworth's *The Prelude*, about "the growth of my own mind;" it is the story of a mental crisis with a spiritual dimension, in the manner of other works of the canon as well (Augustine's

Confessions, Dante's *Divine Comedy*, Whitman's "A Word Out of the Sea" and parts of "Song of Myself"). "Pale Fire" contains many of Nabokov's own beliefs. As he told an interviewer in the sixties, "It is . . . true that some of my more responsible characters are given some of my own ideas. There is John Shade. . . . He does borrow some of my own opinions."

These include musty crotchets: "I loathe such things as jazz" and also bullfighting, a "white-hosed moron torturing" an animal. Like his creator, Shade detests

> *abstract bric-a-brac;*
> *Primitivist folk-masks; progressive schools;*
> *Music in supermarkets; swimming pools;*
> *Brutes, bores, class-conscious Philistines, Freud, Marx,*
> *Fake thinkers, puffed-up poets, frauds and sharks.*

Shade develops the nonreligious metaphysic that Nabokov hints at in some other books. In *Pnin* the hero reflects that he "did not believe in an autocratic God. He did believe, dimly, in a democracy of ghosts. The souls of the dead . . . formed committees, and these, in continuous session, attended to the destinies of the quick"—as Mira, the murdered girl, does, sending antic squirrels into the world to cheer Pnin.

Speak, Memory is partly a communion with the dead, and while portraying his own life, explaining the development of his artistic consciousness, Nabokov reveals how it all makes sense for him. "The cradle rocks above an abyss, and common sense tells us that our existence is but a brief crack of light between two eternities of darkness." He has made "colossal efforts to distinguish the faintest of personal glimmers" in the darkness, and though séances did not work for him, nor did "ransack[ing] my oldest dreams for keys and clues," he rejects the "common sense" view—common sense by its very commonness being displeasing. There is a realm of timelessness, he confidently asserts. He can access it through his imagination, a feature of artistic imagination being the ability to feel "everything that happens in one point of time." The poet, lost in creative thought,

> taps his knee with his wandlike pencil, and at the same instant a car (New York license plate) passes along the road, a child bangs the screen door of a neighboring porch, an old man yawns in a misty Turkestan orchard, a granule of cinder-gray sand is rolled by the wind on Venus . . . and trillions of other such trifles occur—all

forming an instantaneous and transparent organism of events, of which the poet (sitting in a lawn chair, at Ithaca, N.Y.) is the nucleus.

John Shade, writing "Pale Fire" in fictionalized Ithaca ("New Wye"), has authentic powers. Some lines of his poem attest to it, and Nabokov, although having fun at his expense (Shade is "behind" Robert Frost, and Frost is himself no Pushkin or Shakespeare), seems present in Shade. "Pale Fire" as a whole is a demonstration, an instance of the "plexed artistry" that Shade, speaking for himself but also for Nabokov, finds meaningful, because in the artist's ability to master time, to unite a childhood memory with the old man in Turkestan, and with other events of this specific instant, also with a likely future (one that includes a book in which the verse will appear), there is a richness far beyond the brief crack of light. Shade feels that he understands

> *Existence, or at least a minute part*
> *Of my existence, only through my art,*
> *In terms of combinational delight;*
> *And if my private universe scans right,*
> *So does the verse of galaxies divine*
> *Which I suspect is an iambic line.*
> *I'm reasonably sure that we survive*
> *And that my darling somewhere is alive,*
> *As I am reasonably sure that I*
> *Shall wake at six tomorrow, on July*
> *The twenty-second, nineteen fifty-nine,*
> *And that the day will probably be fine.*

As it happens, he shall not awake then. He is shot to death the evening before.

Shade's darling is his late daughter, Hazel. The poet's life has been harrowed by, has been obsessed with, death:

> *There was a time in my demented youth*
> *When somehow I suspected that the truth*
> *About survival after death was known*
> *To every human being: I alone*
> *Knew nothing, and a great conspiracy*
> *Of books and people hid the truth from me.*

> *There was the day when I began to doubt*
> *Man's sanity: How could he live without*
> *Knowing for sure what dawn, what death, what doom*
> *Awaited consciousness beyond the tomb?*
>
> *And finally there was the sleepless night*
> *When I decided to explore and fight*
> *The foul, the inadmissible abyss,*
> *Devoting all my twisted life to this*
> *One task.*

Hazel, dying young, is a pitiable case. Shade presents her in terms mostly of her unattractiveness: she is heavy-limbed, her eyes are funny, etc. "She may not be a beauty, but she's cute," the parents tell each other, fearing it isn't so.

"It was no use, no use," the poet laments. "And like a fool I sobbed in the men's room," his tears provoked by seeing his daughter in a Christmas pageant. Appearance means much, if not everything. In a poem that tries to speak of ultimate matters, to offer plainness as a tragic fate seems ill considered. "Alas, the dingy cygnet never turned / Into a wood duck," Shade writes, and the girl becomes a depressive, with wounds that cannot heal:

> *And still the demons of our pity spoke:*
> *No lips would share the lipstick of her smoke;*
> *The telephone that rang before a ball*
> *Every two minutes in Sorossa Hall*
> *For her would never ring; and, with a great*
> *Screeching of tires on gravel, to the gate*
> *Out of the lacquered night, a white-scarfed beau*
> *Would never come for her.*

Hazel has a blind date. The young man, upon first seeing her in person, remembers he has something else to do. This is the last straw. She goes directly to a half-frozen lake and throws herself in. The unwitting parents are channel-surfing at home at the time, finding not much on, already the artistry of fate throwing forth unrecognized signs, ironies:

> *"Are we quite sure she's acting right?" you asked.*
> *"It's technically a blind date, of course.*
> *Well, shall we try the preview of* Remorse?*"*

And we allowed, in all tranquility,
The famous film to spread its charmed marquee;
The famous face flowed in, fair and inane . . . .

Your ruby ring made life and laid the law.
Oh, switch it off! And as life snapped we saw
A pinhead light dwindle and die in black
Infinity.

This contrapuntal movement—daughter drowning while parents watch TV—is echoed in several parts of the novel. Disparate stories reflect one another. The most disparate, and the source of most of the mad humor of the book, is Kinbote's commentary to the poem and how it appears to us: Kinbote's scholia are insanely off, a classic case of a reader stealing a text for his own purpose, and it seems that we are in the presence of another absurd Nabokovian solipsist, like Hermann of the early novel *Despair*, who kills a man he doesn't resemble, thinking that he is his exact double, or Humbert, or the scheming lovers of *King, Queen, Knave*, or Albinus of *Laughter in the Dark*, a man so blind that he does go blind.

Kinbote believes himself to be—may even be—not an unhappy, lonely language instructor at a Cornell-ish university but Charles Xavier Vseslav, "The Beloved," the last king of Zembla, a "distant northern land" near Russia. He has come to America to escape the revolutionaries who deposed him, who want to murder him. A devotee of Shade's poetry, which he tried once to translate, he attaches himself to the poet in the last months of Shade's life. Together they ramble of an evening in New Wye, in a neighborhood like Ithaca's professor ghetto, Cayuga Heights. Kinbote feeds the poet story lines from the life of Charles II. Shade, he hopes, will feature them in his poem in progress.

"Pale Fire" may end up cluttered with "sundry Americana," Kinbote knows. But Zembla will dominate:

Oh, I did not expect him to devote himself *completely* to [my] theme! . . . But I was sure his poem would contain the wonderful incidents I had described. . . . [But once he reads the actual poem] nothing of it was there! . . . Instead of the wild glorious romance— what did I have? An autobiographical, eminently Appalachian, rather old-fashioned narrative in a neo-Popian prosodic style . . . void of my magic, of that special rich streak of magical madness which I was sure would run through it.

The novel, like the poem, is solidly American—replete with *Lolita*-style, *Pnin*-style imagery, offering reports on scenes of contemporary academic life, summoning the natural surroundings with affectionate precision. All of the poem, and all of the novel, grow out of an image of a common perching bird seen year-round in Ithaca yards:

> *I was the shadow of the waxwing slain*
> *By the false azure in the windowpane;*
> *I was the smudge of ashen fluff—and I*
> *Lived on, flew on, in the reflected sky.*

Birds fly head-on into picture windows: sad, but true. Shade's parents were ornithologists. Like Nabokov, and like Fyodor, hero of *The Gift*, Shade has inherited a semi-scientific way of looking at the world:

> *All colors made me happy: even gray.*
> *My eyes were such that literally they*
> *Took photographs. Whenever I'd permit,*
> *Or, with a silent shiver, order it,*
> *Whatever in my field of vision dwelt—*
> *An indoor scene, hickory leaves, the svelte*
> *Stilettos of a frozen stillicide—*
> *Was printed on my eyelids' nether side . . . .*
>
> *How fully I felt nature glued to me*
> *And how my childish palate loved the taste*
> *Half-fish, half-honey, of that golden paste!*

The cedar waxwing announces that doubling worlds exist, that they interpenetrate, project upon each other:

> *And from the inside, too, I'd duplicate*
> *Myself, my lamp, an apple on a plate:*
> *Uncurtaining the night, I'd let dark glass*
> *Hang all the furniture above the grass,*
> *And how delightful when a fall of snow*
> *Covered my glimpse of lawn and reached up so*
> *As to make chair and bed exactly stand*
> *Upon that snow, out in that crystal land!*

Kinbote declares that he has "no desire to twist and batter an . . . *apparatus criticus* into the monstrous semblance of a novel"—no, absolutely not. But he does have an ungovernable urge to comment. He tells his tale by ventriloquizing the poet and by composing just such an independent apparatus. In the end, the question of whether he is Charles II or a delusional paranoid is undetermined. On the side of believing him, in addition to narrative passages that enthrall and are logical and detailed, is his blithe kingliness, the majestic manner of his condescension and of his confident, ever active homosexuality:

> I turned to go. . . . I explained I could not stay long as I was about to have a kind of little seminar at home followed by some table tennis, with two charming identical twins and another boy, another boy.

> We shall now go back from mid-August 1958 to a certain afternoon in May three decades earlier. . . . He had several dear playmates but none could compete with Oleg, Duke of Rahl. In those days growing boys of high-born families wore on festive occasions . . . sleeveless jerseys, white anklesocks with black buckle shoes, and very tight, very short shorts. . . . [Oleg's] soft blond locks had been cut since his last visit to the palace, and the young Prince thought: Yes, I knew he would be different.

How *would* a deposed king, homosexual to boot, forced to flee and hide alone on a distant continent, conduct himself? The combination of fear and superiority is finely calibrated, and Charles the Beloved replies to sometimes savage mockery, often based in homophobia, with the sweaty aplomb of an out-of-shape fencer:

> Well did I know that among certain youthful instructors whose advances I had rejected there was at least one evil practical joker; I knew it ever since the time I came home from a very enjoyable and successful meeting of students and teachers (at which I had exuberantly thrown off my coat and shown several willing pupils a few of the amusing holds employed by Zemblan wrestlers) and found in my coat pocket a brutal anonymous note saying: "You have hal. . . . . s real bad, chum," meaning evidently "hallucinations."

> One day I happened to enter the English Literature office . . . when I overheard a young instructor in a green velvet jacket,

whom I shall mercifully call Gerald Emerald, carelessly saying in answer to something the secretary had asked: "I guess Mr. Shade has already left with the Great Beaver." Of course, I am quite tall, and my brown beard is of a rather rich tint and texture; the silly cognomen evidently applied to me, but was not worth noticing, and . . . I contented myself on my way out with pulling Gerald Emerald's bowtie loose.

From Kinbote's arch, circumlocutory speech, images leap to the reader. His style is one source of fun: it recalls Humbert Humbert's brainy, lurid speech but with more cluelessness. Only a few days in town, Kinbote meets Shade for the first time at the faculty club:

His laconic suggestion that I "try the pork" amused me. I am a strict vegetarian. . . . Shade said that with him it was the other way around: he must make a definite effort to partake of a vegetable. . . . I was not yet used to the rather fatiguing jesting and teasing that goes on among American intellectuals of the inbreeding academic type and so abstained from telling John Shade in front of all those grinning old males how much I admired his work lest a serious discussion of literature degenerate into mere facetiation.

Kinbote is under stress, despite his poise. Desperate words escape him: "Dear Jesus, do something," he exclaims at the end of a lyrical description of the college grounds. He is above all things confessional: hungry to contact a listener, a reader, to do so intimately. "There is a very loud amusement park right in front of my present lodgings," and later, "damn that music," he says, fairly tearing his hair. Though a king, he frequently stoops. The combination of Old World formality, incomprehension of the New, fear, desperate purpose, and sadness makes him appealing despite his unreliability. Shade, if Kinbote's reports of him can be trusted, treats him with simple kindness. They often walk together. Shade is a university poet but not quite academic: his final work, the poem that he writes in the last weeks of his life, struggles to break through, to speak with a full throat, to consummate. Yet he chooses Popian prosody as his vehicle, the very mode of learning-stuffed, intellectualized verse that Wordsworthian effusions came into being to supersede. With his scientific precision he cannot quite conquer heaven, after all. The poem finds wisdom in its own failure; there can be no fiery word from on high, no communication with the other side, but the poet's creation, in the intricacy of its correspondences, suggests the structure of the cosmos.

Kinbote is no Pope. "I notice a whiff of Swift in some of my notes," he confesses, but on balance his temperament is more Romantic than Augustan. Though a "desponder" by nature, with "frozen mud and horror" in his heart, he also has "moments of volatility and *fou rire*." Early on, thrilled to be knowing Shade, he says,

> My admiration for him was for me a sort of alpine cure. I experi-
> enced a grand sense of wonder whenever I looked at him . . .
> enhanced by my awareness of [other people] not feeling what I felt,
> of their not seeing what I saw, of their taking Shade for granted,
> instead of drenching every nerve . . . in the romance of his presence.

Shade is an artist: while he stands there chewing a piece of celery, he is taking in and recombining impressions so as to produce "an organic miracle, a fusion of image and music, a line of verse" at some later time. After Shade's murder, Kinbote is still in awe:

> Clink-clank, came the horseshoe music from [a nearby game].
> In the large envelope I carried I could feel the hard-cornered,
> rubberbanded batches of index cards [of Shade's final manuscript].
> We are absurdly accustomed to the miracle of a few written
> signs being able to contain immortal imagery. . . . In a sense,
> by the very act of brutish routine acceptance, we undo the work
> of the ages, the history of the gradual elaboration of poetical
> description and construction, from the treeman to Browning,
> from the caveman to Keats.

Deeply respectful of this lineage, he goes on:

> Solemnly I weighed in my hand what I was carrying under my
> left armpit, and for a moment I found myself enriched with an
> indescribable amazement as if informed that fireflies were making
> decodable signals on behalf of stranded spirits, or that a bat was
> writing a legible tale of torture in the bruised and branded sky.

Kinbote resembles his author, who also is prone to wonderment. Upon first coming to America—parachuting into a field near Baltimore— Kinbote looks around him with "enchantment and physical wellbeing."

The commentary is seeded with Nabokov's enduring love of mountains. Zembla is a high kingdom, a peninsula with a mountain range forming its spine, and the king escapes only by climbing into that range and then down the other side. At an "eerie altitude, in the heady blue," he enters the mental zone "where the mountaineer becomes aware of a phantom companion"—a friend, an imaginary ally, who can lead him to safety.*

Shade is such a friend to Kinbote. Shade's poem, incorporating Zemblan material, is casually mountain-minded, making reference to famous peaks (Mont Blanc, the Matterhorn) and making much of a confusion between a mountain and a fountain. "How serene were the mountains, how tenderly painted on the western vault of the sky," Kinbote enthuses, and the commentary, as it relates the king's escape, paints in all manner of alpine life, from "the first full cowbell of dawn" to the "lacy resilience" of bracken underfoot, to dangerous boulderfields ("Mr. Campbell had once twisted an ankle and had to be carried down, smoking his pipe, by two husky attendants") to mountain huts where exhausted climbers are saved by friendly rustics who provide them with nourishing food, a "bowl of mountain mead" thrown in, and whose unwashed daughters lead them on tricky parts of the route and then strip naked, offering themselves.

Motifs of the poem, many, appear again up high, transformed, as believable parts of the mountain world. The "pinhead light" of the TV becomes a "pinhead light" from a distant hut. A butterfly that skelters through the poem, called "dark Vanessa" by Shade and associated with his wife, Sybil, greets the king as sunlight reaches him on a dawn mountainside. His journey to freedom evokes Wordsworth's "Tintern Abbey," about ecstasies had in nature ("I came among these hills; when like a roe / I bounded o'er the mountains"); and a beautiful passage from "Pale Fire," a borrowing from Goethe's "The Erlking," expressing Shade's grief over his daughter's death, is echoed by Charles's repetition of similar lines as he tries to escape.

Maybe Shade *was* writing about Zembla, after all. Or maybe Kinbote, the sole possessor of the manuscript following the poet's death (at the hands of a misfiring assassin, à la Nabokov's father), is inspired to write a fantastic gloss that takes off from Shade's poem and that begins with

---

* This well-documented delusion among climbers is usually associated with extreme exhaustion. Dmitri may have told his father about it. The son writes in his memoir that he "read of the ghostly 'third man' that accompanied early Himalayan climbers at high altitudes."

the useful fiction that the inspiration went the other way, critic to poet. Kinbote says of himself,

> I am capable, after long dabbling in blue magic, of imitating any prose in the world (but singularly enough not verse—I am a miserable rhymester). . . . I do not consider myself a true artist, save in one matter: I can do what only a true artist can do—pounce upon the forgotten butterfly of revelation, wean myself abruptly from the habit of things, see the web of the world, and the warp and the weft of that web.

Nabokov might have said this about himself. To see things fresh, to combine freely: this was his artistic way. The result is a body of work full of metaphor and comparison. *Pale Fire*, deriving Zembla from staid transcendental verses, is itself a metaphor, one thing for another, a conjunction absurd on its face but enchanting, if read a certain way. Kinbote spells that out:

> Gradually I regained my usual composure [after a first look through the manuscript]. I reread *Pale Fire* more carefully. I liked it better when expecting less. And what was . . . that dim music, those vestiges of color in the air? Here and there I discovered . . . echoes and spangles of my mind, a long ripple-wake of my glory. I now felt a new, pitiful tenderness toward the poem.

The book shows other aspects, intimate aspects, of Nabokov. Whether in Shade's costumery or in another's, the author seems helpless not to portray himself:

> A large, sluggish man with no passions save poetry, he seldom moved from his warm castle and its fifty thousand crested books, and had been known to spend two years in bed reading and writing after which, much refreshed, he went for the first and only time to London, but the weather was foggy . . . and so went back to bed for another year.

As the commentary literally overcomes the poem—seventy-five thousand words to a mere seventy-five hundred—the romantic impulse overwhelms the transcendental. The grounds for metaphysical belief that Shade had advanced, developing a cosmology based on the artist—who alone senses the workings of creation, who alone resembles the Creator—come to seem paltry. Many mortals who believe fervently do so with a sense of inadequacy, not with exultant superiority. Often terrified or disheartened, they seek mercy, not recognition; are moved not by their own genius so much as by acts of compassion, tales of martyrs' sufferings. Kinbote seems to be of this humble, numerically vast human category at times. He disagrees with Shade's skepticism about sin and God. He is a churchgoer, a serious churchgoer, and one Sunday he strolls home "in an elevated state of mind" after having prayed in not one but two congregations (feeling "in my bones that there is a chance yet of my not being excluded from Heaven"). He hears a disembodied voice in the summer air, Shade's voice seemingly, speaking to him, saying something that moves him very much: "Come tonight, Charlie," meaning, *Come over for a walk and some friendly talk.* Later, speaking to Shade on the phone, Kinbote "all at once, with no reason at all, burst into tears"—he is an emotional man; he needs this friend and his simple kindness. They are, after all, connected.

16.

In their last years in America, the Nabokovs traveled west faithfully, as if trying to visit every corner of the country, to tick off all the attractive areas (all those promising for collecting, that is). Vladimir amassed a library of maps and guides, with his notes scribbled in. He could tell that there would come a time when he would want to read them again and remember.

After they moved to Switzerland in late 1960, a "well-meaning maid would empty forever a butterfly-adorned gift wastebasket of its contents," Dmitri later recorded. The wastebasket's treasures included "a thick batch of U.S. roadmaps on which my father had meticulously marked the roads and towns that he and my mother had traversed. Chance comments of his were [noted] there, as well as names of butterflies and their habitats."

Nabokov's *Speak On, Memory*, the continuation volume to *Speak, Memory*, thus had an unlucky fate. There are other reasons to think that he would never have written it, though. He told first biographer Andrew Field that he had had a plan in mind for twenty years but that when he sat down to write it, the book turned into a mere collection of anecdotes, something that promised "not . . . violins but trombones." The only parts still attended by throbs of inspiration for him were the MCZ period and his butterfly adventures in the Rockies.

In '56, the Nabokovs had a long, pleasant trip, starting in late spring and extending into August. Véra had rented a cabin in Utah, a log-and-stone summer house built by the Western artist Maynard Dixon outside the village of Mount Carmel, along a fork of the Virgin River. Zion National Park was twenty miles west. Bryce Canyon National Park was

Maynard Dixon cabin, Mt. Carmel, Utah

Dixon cabin (interior)

thirty miles northeast, and an alpine zone of conifers and canyons called the Cedar Breaks was about the same distance northwest. The immense variety and rugged separations of landforms promised good collecting. Neither Nabokov seems to have known who Maynard Dixon was. He was an ex–San Francisco bohemian, the illustrator of Clarence E. Mulford's Hopalong Cassidy novels, who became an easel painter and muralist, a light-struck, self-taught master of desert atmospherics, of big vistas and dry hazes, a perpetrator of nostalgic cowboy art à la Frederic Remington but also of landscape abstractions through which Cézanne and Braque seem to roam, wearing cowboy hats. It was Dixon's widow, Edith Hamlin Dale, a former WPA muralist herself, who rented them the cottage. Like other lodgings of theirs, this one was close to a town but not too close. The floodplain of the Virgin is a miles-long meadow, adjacent to sandy sagebrush country. Two hours' drive to the southeast is the Grand Canyon's North Rim, and they collected there, too.

From Utah they migrated north as summer progressed, arriving in Afton in time for the hatches they had found there four years before. They had been traveling the West now for fifteen years. They did not stop to see people they knew or had collected with; if they stayed at the Corral Log Motel again, it was for the same reasons as before: convenience and low rates. Their lives during the rest of the year, bringing them in contact with hundreds of people they needed to deal with but did not necessarily want to know, made the emptiness of the West tonic. In 1950, the middle year of their American period, Colorado was the only Rocky Mountain state with a population greater than one million. Wyoming, their favorite state, was famously empty, the least populous per square mile next to Nevada.*

The European semi-isolation of their last years, lived in a suite of rooms in a grand hotel on Lake Geneva, was a sedentary version of their American vacationing. Vladimir needed protected time alone, to write, to read, to think, to recuperate. Véra was not markedly more social than he, nor was either of them really reclusive; they treasured visits from good friends, as long as they could control the timing and length of those visits. They were well matched in this regard, unlike Pushkin and his alluring wife, whose warm response to the attentions of a rakish

---

* And soon to fall behind Nevada as the population of Las Vegas boomed. Wyoming was also the American mountain heartland, another reason that it thrilled the Nabokovs: the Tetons include the most totemic and challenging mountaineering peaks to be found in the American Rockies.

Chevalier Guard of Tsar Nicholas I led to the poet's death in a duel. Nabokov had married well—he also married for love. Just as his careful study of Gogol had taught him how not to act should one of his books ever achieve immense success, Pushkin's fate might have telegraphed the utility of marrying someone devoted who was also equipped to help him in his career.* That Véra Evseevna had a splendid mind and literary sense was the best of his many lucky breaks.

The loneliness of the West, full of waste places emblematic, for many, of a cosmic emptiness, is a feature missing from Nabokov's writing. Humbert and Pnin feel lonely and beset, but not because the New World horizon is too far. At the end of his book, Pnin rides off into that unknown, in a car stuffed with belongings and a little white dog, his American life in tatters, but he is unintimidated and not without hope:

> The air was keen, the sky clear and burnished. . . . Then the little sedan boldly swung past [a truck in front of it] and, free at last, spurted up the shining road, which one could make out narrowing to a thread of gold in the soft mist where hill after hill made beauty of distance, and where there was simply no saying what miracle might happen.

Humbert, too, though he endures torments in Western settings, meanders through. Social traps are what he fears more: neighborhood snoops, progressive schools with nosy heads, the police.

In '57 the Nabokovs did not travel. But in '58 they put eight thousand miles on their car in seven weeks, and the next year, their last of American voyaging, they probably drove even farther, across the country and back by meandering routes. Véra made a document of the last years' trips; for this purpose she took over a page-a-day diary that dated from 1951, in which Vladimir had jotted early notes, and on the unwritten-upon pages she interposed entries that belong to 1958–59. The notebook begins with a quick sketch of everything that happened to them: all that had come to them in America, from the start. "We arrived . . . on the Champlain," and Dmitri's schools, Vladimir's first writing jobs, summer camps, Wellesley, Stanford,

---

* From Gogol, who was badly thrown off by the success of *The Government Inspector* and of *Dead Souls*—disturbed by the critics who misunderstood his work—Nabokov learned to be willing to disappoint, willing to confound readers who had loved him perhaps too much, or for the wrong reasons—always to push on and not to apologize.

parties at which Véra found it "difficult to follow many-pronged conversations in English," the Alta summer with Laughlin, friends Vladimir made among the entomologists: everything gets a mention. The rental addresses, eleven in Ithaca alone. That the trip to Colorado had been "by train both ways, caught in floods, re-routed." The books her husband wrote while living at Craigie Circle, Cambridge. Where Dmitri roomed as a Harvard freshman.

Like real Americans, they denominate periods by the cars owned: first the Oldsmobile and then the '54 Buick, and meanwhile Dmitri has been living his own car-inflected history, driving what Véra called a "Ford-Keyser" (actually a '31 Model A Ford, dark blue) and later a '38 Buick, which took him to the Tetons. Dmitri the madcap has by August 21, 1958, when Véra wrote many of these notes, become Harvard graduate Dmitri, aspiring performer Dmitri, a young man with "a wonderful job, excellent singing teacher," and a "charming apartment of his own, which he keeps meticulously clean." In '57 he was drafted into the Army. After six months of training he joined a reserve unit that met weekly in Manhattan and for two weeks each summer out of town. "Dmitri went today to Camp Drum," Véra wrote on August 7, 1958, noting that he sounded "cheerful, reasonable, tenderly interested in everything" on the phone.

An event was approaching that, like a celestial happening—a gigantic comet, say, swooping close to the earth, causing explosions and a wobble

Near Ithaca, New York, September 1958 (Photo by Carl Mydans, *Life* magazine)

in the planetary orbit itself—would alter whatever it could. The Nabokovs were as solid and well prepared for big change as can be imagined; they were deeply in love, partners in an enterprise—the advancement of the husband's writings—that seems never to have awakened envy in the wife; neither had a drinking problem or at this point was prone to stray; and the husband's oft-expressed belief in his own genius, which once might have hinted at underlying uncertainty, the recognition that the best creators are often plowed under regardless, graced only with the world's forgetting, had, like Vladimir himself, only grown stouter.

He was not played out as Hurricane Lolita, the American publication of his novel, hit. He was in the conceiving stage of his last great book (*Pale Fire*), had nearly finished annotating *Eugene Onegin*, and, as final inoculation against any warping effects, was just completing another translation, his Englishing of the twelfth-century *The Song of Igor's Campaign*. When he suddenly became famous on a scale that he had long hoped for, lifelong habits that included their yearly travels, the low-rent, free-range recuperations out west, put a barrier between them and what might have turned other people's heads.

Still, the Lolita event was a bomb, and it was the force of it that Véra tried to record. "Dinner at the Bishops," she writes for May 20, 1958, and then her husband, as if looking over her shoulder, calmly pencils in, "Spread Wyoming butterflies, batch taken in 1952 . . . West Wyoming." They trade off entries for a while; the Putnam American edition is scheduled for August, they can feel it coming. "Dmitri telephoned. In raptures. . . . Sang (audition) for Opera group, got enthusiastic praises. Loves his apartment." Maybe Dmitri is what they are both most worried about. Whatever is coming, it will mean something also for a reckless, uncertainly artistic child who is subject to raptures. Dmitri told his barracks mate, a New Yorker who became a friend, that "this year he's going to be famous," meaning that his father would be ascending in '58. There may be no good time to become the offspring of a very famous father or mother, but *this* time, which Véra is trying hard to see as a corner-turning, with the mountain climbing and sportscar driving falling away, is especially delicate.

"Quiet day," Vladimir records for May 22, a Thursday. He spent it sorting more insects. They were his treasured snapshots: place and time and weather fixed. Before Véra became the sole keeper of the diary, before Hurricane Lolita hit in earnest, a beautiful interpolation: not the introduction of field notes or new fictional material, but the preservation of some old, a week's worth of his notes from '51 (June 24–July 1), made while he was intensely at work on *Lolita*. They are flavorful, these notes from that unique time: cost-of-gas figures, Russian words, pencil sketches, and phrases in English now to be found nearly unchanged in the novel. From this came that. The tone is amiable, sardonic, concerned with a "stinky river" behind a motor court and with an old farmer's "mummy's neck," and with a little boy seen " 'frogging' on a bike." It may be an accident that the empty page-a-day diary was not quite empty, that it contained these earlier jottings; they might have been torn out, but since they have not been they give a savor of days that must already have seemed legendary. Turn another page and you might find yourself on the road to Telluride with them, Véra at the wheel of the Olds, Vladimir beside her writing the note you're living. The floods and storms of Kansas are behind, they're in the real West now, the scenery on a gigantic scale, with the sun emerging with that special force it has after a rain.

ON ABOUT JULY 15, 1958, an advance copy of *Lolita* caught up with them in Waterton Lakes National Park, Alberta. They had seen a piece in the *New Republic* that had spoken of Nabokov in terms that they welcomed, terms of "true greatness." *Lolita* publication day was now only weeks off. Not in much of a hurry, but excited, they turned east. They stopped at Devils Tower National Monument, in northeastern Wyoming. Their cabin was across the road from the tower, which looked to Véra like a giant conical ice cream treat (in France called *plombières*) that "has just begun to melt at the base . . . purplish-chocolate-colored." When the weather was warm Vladimir collected leps.

"Sheridan [Wyoming] was engrossed in a big rodeo," Véra wrote. She hated seeing "poor cattle mistreated," but the local event was causing a stir: "We were almost driven off the road repeatedly and had to stop for cars passing other cars to get back in their lane—all of them . . . with horses in trailers." They saw "two trucks in collision—no one hurt but the vehicles; and, on the shoulder of the road, a cowboy, all decked out . . . dismally changing . . . a tire."

In early August they were in New York. Walter Minton, president of G.P. Putnam's Sons, the *Lolita* publisher, was throwing a press reception at the Harvard Club, and the author was the celebrity attraction. Minton was an "excellent publisher," Véra decided, someone who spent freely on "beautiful ads," and the book his house produced was itself beautiful, with a cover that the Nabokovs found tasteful (no image of the little girl). On August 18 Minton sent them a telegram:

EVERYBODY TALKING OF LOLITA ON PUBLICATION DAY YESTERDAYS REVIEWS MAGNIFICENT AND NEW YORK TIMES BLAST THIS MORNING PROVIDED NECESSARY FUEL TO FLAME 300 REORDERS THIS MORNING AND BOOK STORES REPORT EXCELLENT DEMAND CONGRATULATIONS.

Sales figures were immediately large. In the first four days, there were 6,777 reorders from retailers running out of copies, and by the end of September *Lolita* was number one on the *New York Times* bestseller list, where it remained for seven weeks.

At Minton's party Vladimir was "a tremendous success . . . amusing, brilliant and—thank God—did not say what he thinks of some famous contemporaries," Véra recorded. This party was a foretaste of gala events in Paris, London, and Rome the following year at which the author and his demurely glamorous, long-necked wife, with her snowy hair and *comme il faut* outfits (a black moiré dress and mink stole in Paris), graciously displayed themselves. The sales and *succès d'estime* of *Lolita* made Nabokov a new world celebrity. He had squared the circle, written a challenging work that was also an alluring sex book, still, at the time of its U.S. publication, under restriction in Britain and France. F. W. Dupee, a professor at Columbia and a freelance critic, called *Lolita* a "magnificently outrageous novel," also a "little masterpiece," also "a formidable addition to popular mythology." By mythology he meant that other stories had attached to the novel's story. The main one was the tale of the book's path to publication: how respectable New York houses had fled from it, how the brilliant author had had to send his manuscript to Paris, where a semi-pornographer had taken it on, and how the shunned work was now a "prodigy of the . . . business," "not only a novel but a phenomenon."

Those who now embraced *Lolita* included "all the brows—high, middle, and low," categories of reader not used to "celebrating together," Dupee wrote. The book had had "the luck to make its American appearance at just the right moment. The state of literary feeling . . . has been undergoing . . . a change here during the past year," and *Lolita* had "both profited by the change and helped to crystallise it."

Dupee was trying—more successfully than any other early comment-ator—to locate what was large in the little masterpiece. The author was an unlikely source for a change in national temper, Dupee thought: he was a foreigner, to begin with, serenely out of step with a postwar turn that Dupee half-deplored, a "gone native" movement that believed in local traditions and hoped to place morality at the center of American literary discourse. "Into this situation Nabokov failed to fit at all." Nor was his pre-*Lolita* reputation promising—"admirable but rather scattered" work that "seemed to belong to the . . . obsolescent category of avant-garde writing."

Dupee, a mordant person who knew how to enjoy himself, found a rich new taste in the book. "It has helped to make the fading smile of the Eisenhower Age give way to a terrible grin," he wrote, and this death's-head imagery might have been the best way he could find to suggest the wrenchingly disparate moods of the book, moods of "disgust and horror" but also of a weird, writhing mirth, darkly knowing, scathingly sophisticated. ("The book, they tend to say, is not pornography, having no four-letter words in it. And again Humbert Humbert can be heard to laugh.") Dupee had been waiting a long time to catch this new tone. *Lolita* was a book "too shocking for any great tradition to want to own," but *he* owned it; it answered something needful in him.

On September 13, a friend phoned the Nabokovs to congratulate them on what he had just read in the *Times*: that movie rights had been sold to Stanley Kubrick for $150,000. That was a phenomenal sum in '58. Along with royalties soon to begin flooding in, it was far more than Nabokov had earned from all his previous work as a professional writer. In the diary Véra noted, "V. supremely indifferent—occupied with a new story, and with the spreading of some 2000 butterflies." Probably he was not indifferent. The page-a-day preserves the mood of those weeks; Vladimir thought Véra's account was "important" to have, a kind of scientific field note, but it was *his* splashy success (and hers), hard-won after a long struggle, and it mattered to them. Inquiries from "movie companies and agents, letters from fans etc." kept coming, along with requests for interviews. All this "ought to have happened thirty years ago," Nabokov wrote his sister, adding, "I don't think I shall need to teach any more."

A team from *Life* came to Ithaca, led by staff writer Paul O'Neil and photographer Carl Mydans. Véra's account is amused but quietly thrilled—both Nabokovs knew the meaning of being portrayed in *Life*'s pages. "To think that three years ago," she wrote, "people like Covici, Laughlin, and . . . the Bishops strongly advised V. never to publish Lolita, because . . . 'all the churches, the women's clubs [would] crack down on you.' " Now a Mrs. Hagen from the local Presbyterian church had called to ask if Vladimir would address their women's group. Delicious irony! Yet the others had not been wrong: to have published four years before would have been to serve up another victim, probably, *Lolita* and its author sharing the fate of Wilson with *Memoirs of Hecate County*. The book's having gone first to France, where its louche publisher fought early censorship battles, had contributed to the cultural shift that F. W. Dupee praised. *Lolita* had birthed its own birthing.

They "could not believe our ears," Véra wrote when, on Sunday, December 7, they saw on *The Steve Allen Show* a skit about "new 'scientific' toys. Last item: doll-girl who can do 'everything, oh but everything.' . . . 'We shall send this doll to Mr. Nabokov.' We both heard it distinctly."

And on Dean Martin's show, the singer explained that he had gone to Vegas but had had nothing to do because "he did not gamble. So he sat in the lobby and read . . . children's books—*Polyanna*, *The Bobsie Twins*, *Lolita*."

Furthermore, "In his first show of the new year . . . Milton Berle opened with . . . 'First of all let me congratulate Lolita: she is 13 now.' " And Groucho Marx was heard to say, "I've put off reading *Lolita* for six years, till she's eighteen."

For his own first TV appearance, Nabokov went to Manhattan to be filmed for a Canadian show, hosted by CBC personality Pierre Berton and featuring scholar-critic Lionel Trilling, a fan of *Lolita*. Véra and Dmitri were in the studio. Dmitri felt proud of his father, and Véra thought that her husband "spoke beautifully." "Then the warning came: Stand by! . . . three minutes left . . . two . . . one . . ." The stage set suggests a writer's study, or a Vincent Price movie version of one, with a candelabra on a table, a sofa, statuary, books on shelves. The celebrity novelist has a rumpled look. At fifty-nine he has a thick, powerful neck and is mostly bald, but unwrinkled. Trilling, a slighter, younger man, looks older, troubled, brooding. He smokes throughout.

"On they were," Véra recorded, and her hero proves an "ideal guest" (so the producers said), magnanimous toward those willing to try his book while dismissive of "bigots and philistines." He retails stock Nabokovian ideas. He is not interested in producing emotions in his readers, nor in filling their heads with ideas. "I leave the field of ideas to Doctor Schweitzer and Doctor Zhivago," he says, *Doctor Zhivago*, recently published, being an irritant to Nabokov, who considered it trash and its publication in the West an obvious Soviet ploy. (Supposedly anti-Communist, it did not go far enough, the Nabokovs felt.) Instead of emotions, Vladimir says he wants readers to get "that little sob in the spine," the flash of aesthetic bliss, when reading his work, and the chat-show host cannot let this statement pass: he asks Trilling if he felt no emotions when he read the book, and Trilling says, "I found it a deeply moving book. . . . Mister Nabokov may not have meant to move hearts, but he moved mine."

Nabokov denies any satirical intent. He is not criticizing America, "holding up the public abuses to ridicule." Trilling replies, "But there *is* an underlying tone of satire through the book," and, "we can't trust a creative writer to say what he has done; he can say what he meant to do, and even then we don't have to believe him."

Both men are a bit sententious. This was the only filmed interview, as well as the last interview of any kind, for which Nabokov did not insist on the submission of all questions in advance, thus it provides as unscripted and *in vivo* an impression of the author as exists. Even so, he has a bunch of cards in his lap on which he has written phrases; when he can, he quotes himself.

Nabokov grins behind Trilling's back. He grins when the critic says that we can't trust writers to do what they say; there is at least the possibility that he is grinning also because he knows that much of the ower of his novel *is* due to a social critique, a deep and excoriating one, a critique that has caused "terrible grins" to appear on many American faces. A darkly dissident cultural skepticism comes into play with *Lolita*. The extent of it will become clear over the next decade and a half, and tonal similarities abound—in the movies, in productions like Hitchcock's *Psycho* (1961) and Kubrick's *Dr. Strangelove* (1964), and in literature and other cultural domains touched by the roiling intensity now associated with the term "the sixties." Alert readers pick something up. The suburban world of Ramsdale and Beardsley, Charlotte Haze's taste-free house, the forties roadside reality of motor courts and mindless miles racked up: Nabokov had done his homework, and for him to insist on an imaginary America, an America "just as fantastic as any inventor's," conjured in his workshop and not based on the observable world ("It was fun to breed her in my own laboratory," he says), came across as fussy and false.

He had looked around him and recognized a curious, half-asleep people—a perky populace with gloomy secrets, inhabiting a magnificent landscape that it tended to crap up, prone to stifling social norms best depicted via caustic comedy. Gunplay would arrive in the last act, as it did in so many of the nation's stories. Sex would be the springboard for all else—nonstandard, indeed perverted, sex, because the country in its youthful aspect was fresh and sexy but also strapped in with prohibitions. The author swore he had no reforming purpose, did not wish to cause any sort of "awakening," and in this he can be trusted: America for a writer of his kind was perfect as found.

Trilling maintains a dignified stillness. Nabokov twists, lunges, and half-reclines on the sofa, his ovoid head angling and swiveling. He grins again when Trilling, trying to explain what is "shocking" about the book ("a young girl, someone . . . usually preserved from the sexual attentions of men; a *very* young girl, of twelve as I recall"), seems to be fighting a grin of his own, and Nabokov casts a look at the moderator: "Is he not licking his lips, sir? Oh, I fear your distinguished critic has read my book in the wrong way, just a little!"

Peter Sellers's scrutiny of this documentary footage, as he prepared to play Clare Quilty in Kubrick's film—and his liberal quoting from it, in the three roles he played later in *Dr. Strangelove*—is hard to gainsay. Dr. Zempf, a school psychologist (Quilty in disguise), borrows Trilling's biting way with certain loaded words ("sex," "sexual"), and Trilling's way with a cigarette, reminiscent of Edward R. Murrow's, includes both the usual forefinger/middle-finger wedge and a much more peculiar (in the American context) thumb/forefinger grip, the smoking tip pointing upward. Sellers works brilliant changes on this when Dr. Strangelove, in the later movie, explains the Doomsday Machine. The pomposity of the whole encounter seems to have galvanized Sellers and his director: the two clubby men of letters talking about sex with a comely child, almost giggling despite themselves; Nabokov modestly admitting that, yes, he is an expert on clinical pedophilia and on butterflies, in addition to being a great writer; Trilling with his hollow-eyed stare, looking like a man who has just gotten bad news from his gastroenterologist.

Both men are also appealing. Trilling loses his lugubriousness when he talks about the novel, which has truly excited him: he *has* been touched by the girl's plight, by the tragic trajectory, by passages of sad tenderness. We suspect he even laughed at the wicked parts. And Nabokov connects, despite all his squirming. Even on this comical stage set, typecast as a condescending aesthete, he peers repeatedly from behind the mask, wanting to make contact with whoever may be out there. Shamelessly he plays the great man, but every now and then a beautiful, boyish smile breaks out on his big face—vulnerable, whole-hearted, it is the smile of someone never far from helpless laughter.

17.

A truly shocking incident (Véra seems to have been shocked, possibly because her own son was involved):

In New York on Tuesday, November 25, the day before the TV shoot, the Nabokovs had dinner with publisher Walter Minton at a restaurant on Third Avenue, Café Chambord, a well-known theatrical hangout. Minton's wife, Polly, came too. The Mintons were in a bad way. A "slithery-blithery onetime Latin Quarter showgirl" had become a "fast friend" of the publisher, and Mrs. Minton had learned of the affair only the previous week—via an article in *Time*. Polly was distraught, in pain. "She is a pretty girl," Véra wrote in the page-a-day diary, "frightened, bewildered," a wholesome mother of three. The couple had been happy till *Lolita* came along, Polly said, "for that was when Walter began to see a lot of people and get mixed up" in the tornado around the novel. It was even more baroque than that: Minton's lover was the person who had first brought *Lolita* to his attention (he had been unaware of its existence till June '57, despite the Paris edition) and was therefore owed a finder's fee, per Putnam's acquisitions policy.

That Polly would display her deep pain to "a perfect stranger" unnerved Véra, a much more reserved quantity. Then Dmitri showed up. He had been at the weekly meeting of his Army unit; the dining party walked around the corner for a look at his latest car, a '57 MG that even his mother admitted was "a little beauty." Polly Minton asked for a ride in it. Dmitri zoomed off with her, and Minton and the Nabokovs then took a cab to their hotel, where, as Véra noted in diary lines she later crossed through, "we three sat and waited and waited." Minton, another confessional American, had told them in the cab that in

N.Y.   1958-59

Dmitri and 1957 MGA

addition to his showgirl he had been carrying on with the writer of the *Time* article, a woman who had taken the opportunity to score off her rival in print, calling her a "superannuated . . . nymphet [with] a bubbly smile on her face." "Between his two little harlots," Véra wrote solemnly, "M[inton] ruined his family life." He spoke "quite openly" within the cabdriver's hearing, too. "Amazing Americans!" she concluded.

And still they waited. Maybe the joyriders had gotten in an accident. "Finally, they did come." The Mintons left, then "Dmitri, with a sly smile, informed us that they had driven straight to his home from the restaurant, put the car in the garage, then—he had to get something from his flat, Polly wanted to see his flat (after having seen his car) and so on. . ."

"And next day," Véra wrote, "Minton told V., 'I hear Dmitri gave Polly a good time last night.' " Slightly aghast, she concluded, "I wonder if this sort of thing is normal or typical of today's America? A bad novel by some O'Hara or Cozens suddenly come to life."

Clearly, the publicity tornado could carry people away. The excitement of being number one on the bestseller chart and having coinages from your book entering the language—*nymphet*, for instance—could have odd consequences. Edmund Wilson remarked on the strange "rampancy" of *Lolita*, which "evidently struck a deep chord in the great American breast." Its lurid aspect attracted readers and made many find it revelatory. America *was* lurid; its literature had long been a bearer of sensational news, particularly sensational sexual news. The bestselling novel of the American fifties, Grace Metalious's *Peyton Place* (1956)—a book that Nabokov amusingly claimed never to have heard of—was its steamy twin. Both found sexy secrets behind facades of tame normalcy; both featured a stepfather raping a daughter; both had a New Hampshire setting. There was also murder in both, and rampant lust. Part of the comedy of *Lolita* is that refined Continental Humbert finds himself in such a text, up to his neck in potboiler elements. Not everyone cared that the book was a *parody*.

The interviews, the constant trips to New York, new concerns about foreign editions and how to deal with so much sudden income made it wise, as well as attractive, to set down the burden of teaching. Nabokov requested a year's leave, and Cornell granted it, on condition that he find someone to take over his courses. On November 16, *Doctor Zhivago* became the number-one bestseller in the *Times*. Pasternak had been awarded the Nobel Prize in October, a spur to sales, and *Lolita* was just behind *Zhivago* on the list for the next few months. Another whopping payout came from the sale of paperback rights ($100,000) in mid-November, and Véra, trying to vet the complicated movie-sale contract and aware, in a general sense, of looming tax problems, spoke to law professors at Cornell and to the contracts specialist at Putnam's, and in early '59 she sought counsel at Paul, Weiss, Rifkind, Wharton & Garrison, in Manhattan. The Nabokovs were unnerved not only by an impending change in tax bracket. They had lived through two ruinous inflations, one after the Revolution and another in Weimar Berlin, and Vladimir, in the days just after the movie sale, requested that his publisher pay half his earnings in "government bonds or other safe stock" as an inflation hedge.

From inside the tornado they thought of Dmitri. The job of trans-lating *A Hero of Our Time* had not worked out as hoped; even so, when Nabokov had the ear of his publisher, in the fizzy days just before *Lolita* exploded, he brought up the idea of a translation of *Invitation to a Beheading*, stipulating that "the translator must be: 1) male, 2)

American-born or English. He must also have a sound and scholarly knowledge of Russian. I do not know anyone who would meet these requirements except my son—but he is unfortunately much too busy."

By January '59 Dmitri had become available, and his father signed an agreement whereby Dmitri collected an immediate advance. "I cannot tell you how delighted I am by this," Véra wrote her friend Elena Levin in Cambridge. Dmitri had not been well. He had had "permanent little ailments," Véra wrote in her diary; "he is so big and strong, and his health has been excellent before he entered the military service. Then he caught that cold, or flu, or virus or whatever it was and could not get rid of it." In fact, he had been ailing for a year. In '62 he was diagnosed with Reiter's syndrome, an inflammatory polyarthritis often seen in young men following a venereal infection. Véra thought he was overworked and approved when he gave up his office job—the only office job he would ever hold.

January 19, 1959, Nabokov taught his last class at Cornell, "to which some glamour was added," he told Minton, by "a reporter-photographer" who snapped pictures throughout. The attention from the world press was nonstop. In Manhattan in late February, the Nabokovs fielded calls from *Time*, *Life*, the *New York Times*, the London *Daily Mail* and *Daily Express*, and other journals, and Nabokov declined three TV appearances. Véra was writing up to fifteen letters per day for business.* Meetings and bouts with minor illnesses kept them in New York until April 18, and they were being lionized the whole time—Véra recalled this period as "wonderful" and recorded that hundreds of people showed up to honor them.

Before they took off for the West again, Nabokov settled some business that meant a great deal to him, placing *Eugene Onegin*, the central work of scholarship of his life, with the Bollingen Press of Princeton. Other elements of a writer's apotheosis rarely seen outside of writers' dreams now also attended him. The publisher of the upcoming British edition of *Lolita*, George Weidenfeld, met with the Nabokovs during their New York stay and made promises—almost all of which were eventually kept—to publish new or first English editions of *Bend Sinister*, *Invitation to a Beheading*, *Nikolai Gogol*, *Speak, Memory*, *Laughter in the*

---

* In a letter to Sylvia Berkman in early February '59, Véra said, "I meant to write you this much sooner but I am simply losing track of things because of the impossible pressure of work. Vladimir refuses to take the least interest in his own business matters, and I do not feel equipped to handle them properly. Besides, I am by no means a Sévigné, and writing ten to fifteen letters in one day leaves me limp."

Dark, and *The Real Life of Sebastian Knight*, along with either *The Gift* or *The Defense*. Weidenfeld faced a still uncertain censorship environment in England, and publishing worthy, nonpedophilic titles by Nabokov might burnish *Lolita*'s case, but it was his canny sense that his author would now carry all before him—that he was now, on the strength of his groundbreaking novel, one of those writers whose every word would attract readers for many years—that led him to be bold.

The excellent French translation of *Lolita*, from Gallimard, had been completed; Nabokov checked proofs while in New York. Dmitri's work on *Beheading* was also looking good. The annoyance of having to do their son's work for him would not be repeated, at least never on the scale of *A Hero of Our Time*; the fond hope of bringing him aboard the family ark, every Nabokov volume going back to *Mary* (1926) sharing a berth with its approved translation, seemed now likely of fulfillment. All this plus a long western vacation. They took a southerly route out of New York, wanting to get to warm weather as directly as possible. An early stop was Gatlinburg, Tennessee, gateway to Great Smoky Mountains National Park, which they had first seen in '41, on the epochal first trip west. "We drove slowly," Véra noted of this part of their journey, and the Tennessee highlands were "full of flowering dogwood and numberous . . . bushes and trees which colored the whole mountainsides."

THE NABOKOVS SAID a long farewell to America. They did not know it was farewell, or admit that it was; they were aware of a certain indelicacy in having scored big, only to turn their backs on the country that had refuged them, that, one might argue, had made Nabokov a world writer.* In the encounter between his cut-glass sensibility and the strange and multicolored American material had been shaped great books. *Pale Fire* was the last, half-American (conceived in the United States but mostly written abroad; American in settings before taking off for Kinbote's fantasyland); after that came *Ada*, the magnum opus, clever and relentless and high-handed, full of mechanistic mating in a Hugh Hefnerian dreamscape, full also of antic wordplay, reminiscent of

---

* In the fall of 1959 the Nabokovs traveled to Europe for the first time in two decades to attend celebrations for *Lolita*. Dmitri, meanwhile, was planning to move to Italy for further operatic training. He did move, and eventually his parents settled nearby—it was ever their wish to live near him.

Finnegans Wake, which Nabokov had once pronounced "a cold pudding of a book, a persistent snore in the next room."

Véra's "Amazing Americans!" suggests fondness, and that was a big part of her response to America, also of Vladimir's. But they were also appalled. The Dmitri project did not relent for years. In America it had always been challenging, with their son's large appetite for risky experience working against their reasonable desire to see him well placed, to see him make something of a good mind and advantages. Then with Vladimir's immense success, their arguments against buying this car or that, against running through money that wasn't his, were undermined—why *not* live a large, playful life?

Véra was also an early alarm-sounder about American turmoil. In May '58 she recorded, "Last night a howling mob of Cornell students converged on President Malott's house. When he came out to speak to them, they pelted him with eggs and rocks." The reason for the protest was "the projected prohibition of so-called 'apartment parties,' which may be unfair but cannot be refuted by mob violence," Véra warned sternly. "Professor Sale's youngest son, Kirk"—Kirkpatrick Sale, editor of the student paper and future author on the left—"who was to be graduated in June, [was] suspended as recognized 'whipper up' of the student crowds."

Véra's reaction can be ascribed to her long memory for Bolshevik street actions. Or she might have found youthful destruction repellent in its own right. Windows were broken in the Cornell president's house. Her strict anti-Communism led sometimes to odd ideas, for instance the conviction, shared with her husband, that Boris Pasternak was willingly serving Soviet masters; that the manuscript of *Zhivago* had been cleverly delivered into the hands of (no surprise here) a *Communist* publisher in Italy, Giangiacomo Feltrinelli; that Soviet denunciations of the novel were false, having "the object of increasing foreign sales," generating foreign exchange that "they would eventually pocket and spend on propaganda abroad," as Vladimir explained to an interviewer. "Any intelligent Russian would see . . . that the book is pro-Bolshevist and historically false, if only because it ignores the Liberal Revolution of spring, 1917," the takeover attempt by Nabokov's father's party.

By the late sixties, from Montreux, Véra's dislike of noisy students had hardened. She considered them fanatics, and by '72 she was proud to say, "We are all for Nixon, emphatically against McGovern whom we find an irresponsible demagogue who deliberately misleads his followers and is doing damage to America. . . . We are completely disgusted by

The NY Rev. of Books (the 'radical chic' medium)" because of its stance against the Vietnam War, which both Nabokovs supported.

Gone from America, they found America frightening. They took at face value young radicals' estimates of their power—the idea that they could make a revolution, for instance. In the seventies they became friendly with William F. Buckley, who gave them a subscription to his conservative *National Review,* which they read. Other sources led Véra to understand that America was on the verge of a race war, that you took your life in your hands to venture out on the streets of New York, that the wheels had come off the society. At the same time, they detested America bashing and defended U.S. foreign policy. In '66, when de Gaulle led France out of NATO, defying the United States, they canceled a French vacation near Mont Blanc. Insults to the American flag, by burning it or misquoting its image, enraged them.

Often they promised to return to see American friends, but those friends made pilgrimage to Montreux instead, obeying the rules about how to behave, how not to inconvenience. The Nabokovs returned in '62, to attend the premiere of Kubrick's film, and in '64 to support the release of the Bollingen *Onegin.* Those trips were fun but also hard work. At the 92nd Street Y in New York, on April 5, 1964, Nabokov recited poetry and prose in a stentorian voice, his playfully reproving tone and occasional King's Englishism—a-*gane* for again, re-*wawd* for reward—furthering a resemblance to the Romanian-born actor-producer John Houseman, especially his performance in Smith Barney ads. Nabokov's spoken English is subtle—capable of lampooning while also asserting superiority—and always intelligible. Some remnants of Russian pronunciation, and possibly his dentures, impose a slight impediment, but he turns this to advantage, affecting a sonorous, hortatory style that a native English speaker on such a stage could only have intended ironically.

Eight years later, he considered another return. McGraw-Hill was soon to release his collection of *ex cathedra* pieces, *Strong Opinions* (1973), and Nabokov, mulling a new multibook contract, dusted off the idea of *Speak On, Memory* once more. "I have already accumulated a number of notes, diaries, letters, etc.," he told McGraw-Hill, "but in order to describe my American years adequately I should need money to revisit several spots," among them the Grand Canyon and "other Western localities." One last gambol over the landscape, on a publisher's dime. His notes include part of a foreword, and he declares at the outset his annoyance at having been misidentified as a satirist of America: what he

248 / ROBERT ROPER

has written, he says, is in no way satire, although, one has to admit, the ways of Americans are peculiar. "An average émigré Russian . . . will not borrow your comb, walk barefoot on a hotel carpet, or plug up a public washbasin before use, as his American counterpart thinks nothing of doing." This tendency to misread him on America makes him "prodigiously anxious," he says—in the end, too anxious to write the book.

His insistence on not being labeled a satirist hangs on a technicality. He knew he wrote in a ridiculing way, but this was not true satire, because satire implies moral judgment and corrective measures, he felt. The Russian reformers of the nineteenth century had indeed had change in mind; in fact, they had devalued literature that did not serve reform. But Nabokov and the European modernists—and even some primitive Americans, going back at least to Poe—preferred not to look beyond the text, pointedly severing writing from its social reality. Edmund Wilson, who visited him in Montreux, would have recognized the stance; he might even have agreed with it. The text was sufficient, Wilson had often acknowledged, was incommensurable, if it chose to be, with the world. On the question of what mattered in literature, though, the two men remained in deep disagreement. Wilson campaigned for the "trashy" and politically dubious *Doctor Zhivago*. He published two long articles, one in *The New Yorker* and one in *Encounter*, representing it as "one of the great events in man's literary and moral history." Pasternak had "the courage of genius," Wilson thought. A poet whom even Nabokov had once respected, who had fallen into silence during the years of Soviet horror, had produced an epic novel that said no to the regime, that stood defiantly against the horror.

Moreover, it was a *modern* novel. "Certain critics . . . have completely missed the spirit and the shape of the book," Wilson argued. They had been misled by

> the English and American translations, which . . . have eliminated so much of the poetry and ignored the significant emphases. *Doctor Zhivago* is not at all old-fashioned: in spite of some echoes of the Tolstoyan tone in certain of the military scenes, there is no point in comparing it with *War and Peace*. It is a modern poetic novel by a writer who has read Proust, Joyce, and Faulkner, and who, like Virginia Woolf . . . has gone on from his predecessors to invent in this genre a variation of his own.

The book was a complicated, profound weave of symbols and parallels, Wilson maintained. It allegorized cleverly and in parts was "very much in the manner of Joyce. . . . Pasternak has been influenced by *Finnegans Wake*," Wilson found.

He knew how it annoyed his friend. As he was finishing his *New Yorker* piece, Wilson told a correspondent that he had been talking to Vladimir on the phone and that he was "behaving rather badly about Pasternak. I have talked to him . . . three times lately about other matters and he did nothing but rave about how awful *Zhivago* was. He wants to be the only Russian novelist in existence." Some impish urge—a desire to tweak Vladimir's nose—seems to have entered the process. Nabokov's habit was to run down other writers, and Wilson had long detested it. He "has just discovered that Stendhal is a complete fraud," he wrote to another friend, "and is about to break the news to his class. He has also read *Don Quixote* for the first time, and declares it is completely worthless."

Nabokov perverted the meanings of stories. He turned *The Death of Ivan Ilyich*, by Tolstoy, into something full of "cruel little ironies"— something by Nabokov, perhaps. There was a divergence in sensibility and also in views of the novel's likely future. Wilson wanted to recruit "this genre," what he took for modernism, to a tradition that on occasion had produced works of moral genius, acts of momentous truth-telling that also satisfied aesthetically. Nabokov wanted nothing like that, and in fact he had bet his career on the impossibility of it. Desperate to escape the smothering Russian Problem, he had enunciated over and over a *non serviam* that rejected the path of personal suffering, the bearing of witness from within the beast. He would not be a Pasternak or Mandelstam or, in the next generation, a Solzhenitsyn. As much as he revered and served the Russian heritage, he would never write the kind of book that Pasternak had, a religio-historical saga about, again, the Problem—humanist, generic, "inspiring."

He responded with fury to "Edmund's symbolico-social criticism and phoney erudition" about *Zhivago*. Never again must a blurb from Mr. Wilson be used to promote one of his books: so he instructed Walter Minton regarding the translated *Invitation to a Beheading*. He had Véra write Wilson,

> As you know by now, New Directions are bringing out a new edition of *The Real Life of Sebastian Knight*. You have been kind to this book in 1941, when it was first published, and for this reason New Directions have taken it upon themselves to ask your endorsement. . . . Vladimir deplores the publishers' practice of pestering

famous people. . . . He begs you to refuse. He has written New
Directions that he is against such solicitations.

In case Edmund did not feel the chill, she added, "The reason I am
writing this letter (and not V. himself) is that he wants it mailed
immediately, but, after having been writing for the last four days, he
feels absolutely exhausted."

The letter found Wilson in his upstate New York home. It was July of
'59, and he was indeed famous, enjoying a late prime. *The Scrolls from the
Dead Sea* (1955) had been a triumph, a *New York Times* bestseller for
thirty-three weeks, product of a typical Wilsonian effort, first the learning of a new language (Hebrew), then deep reporting for the *New
Yorker*, then the writing of two immensely popular articles and finally of
the book, a shapely, politically alert, elegantly expressed, scholarly
unraveling of a complicated topic. The topic becomes fascinating by
virtue of Wilson's telling. William Shawn, the *New Yorker* chief editor,
considered Wilson's expository style one of the half-dozen best in
the history of English. Soon he would produce another work of
complicated contemporary history, *Apologies to the Iroquois* (1960), based
on painstaking reportage à la *The American Jitters*, and two years later
he brought out the classic study of Civil War literature *Patriotic Gore*
(1962), his great work of American remembrance. In Nabokov's parlance,
Wilson, too, created worlds. He was not notably unfulfilled as a writer,
torn with envy. Roger Straus, a publisher who became a close friend,
said that Wilson was "not only the man I admired most but the man
who gave me the most pleasure to be with," and the core of that
pleasure was "the excitement of his enthusiasm for other writers present
and past." If envy explains Wilson's disrespect of *Lolita*, it was not a
quality others found in him.

The correspondence that had lasted twenty years, the source and sign
of their splendid friendship, now abated. They never wrote at length
thereafter, and though there are affectionate phrases in their brief notes,
Wilson's appreciation of *Doctor Zhivago* had finished something. The
great feud that erupted six years later, in the summer of '65, when
Wilson published an intemperate, funny, slapdash pan of *Eugene Onegin*
in the *New York Review of Books*, was prefigured in the *Zhivago* affair.
Nabokov's cruelty to other writers seems to have unhinged Wilson, and
his attack on his friend's translation is unapologetically an attack on its
author:

This production though in certain ways valuable, is something of a disappointment; and the reviewer, though a personal friend of Mr. Nabokov—for whom he feels a warm affection sometimes chilled by exasperation—and an admirer of much of his work, does not propose to mask his disappointment. Since Mr. Nabokov is in the habit of introducing any job of this kind . . . by an announcement that he is unique and incomparable and that everybody else . . . is an oaf and an ignoramus . . . usually with the implication that he is also . . . a ridiculous personality, Nabokov ought not to complain if the reviewer . . . does not hesitate to underline his weaknesses.

The year before, Nabokov, clearing brush for his *Onegin*, had scorched a prior version by a scholar at the University of North Carolina. Now Wilson offered his stark opinion on the matter:

Mr. Nabokov . . . took up a good deal of space in these pages to denounce [that book]. [His] article—which sounded like nothing so much as one of Marx's niggling and nagging attacks on someone who had had the temerity to write about economics and to hold different views from Marx's—dwelt especially on what he regarded as Professor Arndt's Germanisms and other infelicities. . . . Arndt had attempted the tour de force of translating the whole of *Onegin* into the original iambic tetrameter. . . . Nabokov decided that this could not be done with any real fidelity. . . . The results [of Nabokov's approach] have been more disastrous than those of Arndt's heroic effort. It has produced a bald and awkward language which has nothing in common with Pushkin.

Likening Nabokov to Marx: surely he goes too far. Nabokov's response and Wilson's response to the response and contributions by third parties played out over the next three years. Nabokov's main riposte has him rubbing his hands over how a "number of earnest simpletons consider Mr. Wilson to be an authority in my field. . . . I am not sure that the necessity to defend my work . . . would have been a sufficient incentive for me to discuss [his] article," but Wilson's mistakes are so awful as to be "a polemicist's dream come true, and one must be a poor sportsman to disdain what it offers."

Skewering those mistakes, Nabokov puts Wilson in his place: "a mixture of pompous aplomb and peevish ignorance" distinguishes his style, his use of English being "singularly imprecise and misleading." And then there's his Russian:

> A patient confidant of his long and hopeless infatuation with the Russian language and literature, I have invariably done my best to explain to him his monstrous mistakes of pronunciation, grammar, and interpretation. As late as 1957 . . . we both realised with amused dismay that, despite my frequent comments on Russian prosody, he still could not scan Russian verse. Upon being challenged to read *Evgeniy Onegin* aloud, he started to perform with great gusto, garbling every second word . . . with a lot of jaw-twisting haws and rather endearing little barks that . . . soon had us both in stitches.

Nabokov vents his "utter disgust" with "amoral" and "philistine" critics of his *Onegin*. Wilson is the representative enemy (he also discusses, with poisonous disdain, other offenders). Wilson fails on every score. Maybe most serious is his indulgence in "the old-fashioned, naïve, and musty method of human-interest criticism . . . that consists of removing the characters from an author's imaginary world" and examining "these displaced characters as if they were 'real people.' "

There is some glee, some good fun. Gouty, short Wilson comes into focus when Nabokov speaks of his "stubby pencil," but the overall tone is strained and bullying. He fails in the primary task of an essayist—even one defending his own work—which is to spark and sustain interest, and the litany of offenses goes on for eight thousand picky words, leaving an impression of Pushkin's poem as food for pedants. Nabokov's supple and vibrant translation, by miles the most faithful in English and more than sufficiently beautiful, despite his relaxation of rhyme and meter, is left out. He seems half-cowed by the comments of some reviewers and speaks of his "rather dry, rather dull work" on the poem, calling it "not ugly enough" and promising that "in future editions I plan to defowlerise it still more drastically . . . turn it entirely into utilitarian prose, with a still bumpier brand of English . . . in order to eliminate the last vestiges of bourgeois poesy." Even if he is only pretending humility, he is unlike himself in turning his pen against his own work. The essay is sorrowful, despite its high spirits; it is an act of destruction, of friendship murder—unavoidable, perhaps, given Wilson's attack, but woeful, ruinous, and strange.

IN EUROPE THE NABOKOVS often went afield in the warm months, collecting more alpine butterflies. They were comfortable in Switzerland, a land of mountains and tidiness, although sometimes they missed "our native West," as Nabokov put it in a letter. Dmitri lived nearby, and in the course of pursuing his operatic training in Italy, he became fluent in Italian and translated some of his father's works into that language. He owned fabulously valuable and rare sports cars that he raced. His fields of accomplishment were many and offer an alternate version, in a different key, of his prodigious father's: not poet/novelist/lepidopterist/ scholar/translator but translator/musician/climber/driver/sailor/lothario/ essayist, with an easy mastery of skiing and Ping-Pong, among other pastimes.

In 1980, three years after his father's death, Dmitri crashed a Ferrari 308 GTB on the road between Montreux and Lausanne, fracturing his spine at the second cervical vertebra and sustaining third-degree burns over much of his body. He was convinced his car had been sabotaged. As he revealed in an interview twenty years later, he had been working all along for the CIA: "I had two military ranks. . . . I was asked to be [an agent] and it was quite understandable from the ideological view-point. Everything was organized at a very high diplomatic level." In the sixties, Italy was "dangerously shifting to the left," and "I was to find support for the right-wing parties and understand their goals. It was as difficult as a game of chess." An American friend of more than forty years, intimate with his living situations and preoccupations, agrees that Dmitri worked "for the CIA or some security agency. He was part of the apparat that welcomed escapees and immigrants from Eastern Europe," debriefing them when they arrived in Italy. In the eighties, she met Dmitri's intelligence handler. She also met the Italians who ran a safe house where Dmitri dealt with escapees.

Dmitri never told his father of these activities. After his accident, following treatment in a burn center and rehab lasting more than a year, he emerged "with new priorities," determined to focus on "writing, both my father's and my own." He did not give up racing. He acquired "a faster Ferrari of a slightly darker blue." He was fond of speedboats, too, and competed in multiday races in the Mediterranean and the Caribbean, as part of a subculture of well-heeled enthusiasts, a cosmo-politan milieu in which he was welcomed because of his charismatic confidence, his languages, his name, his charm.

His father quickened to many things—to America, its norms and codes—by way of his young son. Humbert also reads America through the medium of a child. Both fathers are besotted; they love without limit. At the end of his last U.S. visit, in '64, having spoken at Harvard as well as at the 92nd Street Y, Nabokov wrote that the professor who introduced him in Cambridge "mentioned that the writer's son had climbed the walls within which his father was [now] lecturing"— referring to a stunt well known among members of the Harvard Mountaineering Club. "Your father embraces you, my dearest," Nabokov concludes this note to Dmitri. "I am writing standing up; that is why the handwriting is so *nabokiy* [lopsided]. . . . I love you. My dearest! Keep well!"

SOMETHING HAS GONE OUT of American writing with Nabokov's passing. Other novelists have come along, some of them identifiable as his heirs, borrowers of his approach, modernists and postmodernists and dark humorists (although the belief in the towering work of novelistic art that carries all before it has gone undercover, too overweening to be easily admitted). Readers of Nabokov-style books are not increasing in number the way video-game players are, and they may even be decreasing. At the same time, computer tools make it possible to search for literary borrowings in texts with remarkable ease. The traditional method, Nabokov's, relied on scholarship and intuition and many hours in libraries. His method of composing his artworks, which relied, to a great degree, on elaborating or parodying earlier work, may have a rebirth assisted by the new tools or others soon to be developed; more will no doubt follow of this masquerade.

Nabokov was an intimate writer. His reticences, his formal estrangements, his denial of interest in any reality beyond the text all need to be measured against that. *Maximum closeness*: not the closeness of ostentatious empathy but the closeness of one mind addressing another in the most thrilling terms. He speaks into the ear, sometimes dripping a little poison. He contrives to have a reader identify intimately with a protagonist or narrator, but even that is not enough; the reader receives secret handshakes from the author himself, behind a narrator's back. Kinbote, in *Pale Fire*, is the high-water mark of this development. The poet Shade's confessions in verse yield to the infinitely more self-revealing confessional of the mad, ever-burgeoning commentary, and meanwhile Nabokov and the reader exchange looks over Kinbote's shoulder: so sad, he is, but so much fun! Such a shameless liar!

The voice of Kinbote takes on the ease, the hauteur, the unmistakable self-pleasure of Nabokov writing in his "own" voice, the voice of, for instance, the commentary to *Eugene Onegin*:

> Pushkin's critical acumen is curiously absent in the extravagant praise he bestows . . . on Sainte-Beuve's derivative and mediocre *Vie, poésies et pensées de Joseph Delorme* (1829). He found therein unusual talent and considered that "never, in any language, has naked spleen expressed itself with such dry precision"—an epithet that is singularly inappropriate in regard to Sainte-Beuve's florid platitudes.

In a more typical note, focusing on a single word, he writes,

> languorous/ . . . This characteristic favorite [term] of Pushkin's and his school . . . is basically equivalent to all the varieties of "languish" typical of the French and English sentimental writers; but because of its resemblance to *tyomniy*, "dark," and owing to its Italianate fullness of sound, the Russian epithet surpasses in somber sonority its English counterpart and lacks the slight ridicule attached to the latter.

As if he has been reading the Bollingen *Onegin*, Kinbote writes,

> Good old Sylvia! She had in common with [Fleur, a fragile beauty sent to seduce the king] a vagueness of manner, a languor of demeanor which was partly natural and partly cultivated as a convenient alibi for when she was drunk, and in some wonderful way she managed to combine that indolence with volubility reminding one of a slow-speaking ventriloquist who is interrupted by his garrulous doll.

Kinbote is like Nabokov, finally, in pursuing intimacy so fiercely that the nature of truth is transformed. Scientific truth—positivist, evidentiary, truth like a pinned insect on your research bench—yields to the truth of the passionate *divo*, the truth of an intimate plaint so prodigal and diverting as to carry all before it. He *must* exist, this crazy king; he *does* exist, because his words make his madness real.

Nabokov's animadversions on reality—which does not concern him at all, and need not concern you, his reader—are incoherent. In the books of his American period, reality reigns: a verifiable American reality. It is a boldly truer reality that he communicates, so intimately and freely rendered as to be a little frightening; the reader of *Lolita* feels "its heat [applied] to the entire sensibility, including the sense of humor," giving rise to "horrid laughter." The book works because the America it shows convinces. First comes shock, a little distaste; then "the supreme laugh may be on [those who fail] to see how much of everyone's reality lurks in its fantastic shadow play." It has a sense of "the gag that life is," as F. W. Dupee memorably put it, writing in the startled first moment of the novel's American birth. Its images "are ghastly but recognizable," and Humbert's "horrid scrapes become our scrapes." The Haze-Humbert household is, undeniably, abnormal, yet it reflects "the painful comedy of family relations in general." Without this convincingness, *Lolita* would have been less effective—might by now have been forgotten.

IN THE MID-SIXTIES, from his Swiss aerie, Nabokov undertook an experiment with time, an experiment that he borrowed from the writer J. W. Dunne, who in 1927 published a treatise on dreams. Dunne's basic idea was that human minds make time seem to go in one direction: forward. In fact, time is not a river that flows but an ocean—the past, present, and future all mingled and all available, if we but learn how to separate them out. He had had dreams that occurred on "the wrong night," Dunne said, before and not after some sensational story in the papers. The most unnerving instance was a dream about an island exploding, with the loss of four thousand lives; a few days later came news reports of the eruption of Mount Pelée, on Martinique, on May 8, 1902, an event in which, according to first estimates, forty thousand people had died.

Dragooning Véra into his project, Nabokov recorded their dreams for three months, beginning in October '64. The first thing to note about his dream reports is that they belie his complaints of insomnia. He sleeps every night without fail; he may be sleeping less than he wants, or less deeply, but sleep he does. He dreams, too, and the reports pile up; he has so many dreams that he can make general observations, including that the "common features of my dreams" are

1) v. exact clock time awareness but hazy passing-of-time feeling
2) many perfect strangers—some in almost every dream
3) verbal details

4) fairly sustained, fairly clear, fairly logical (w/in special limits) cogitation
5) great difficulty in recalling a complete dream even in outline
6) recurrent topics & themes

He was working on the novel *Ada* meanwhile, one part of which expands on these observations and others. (The character Van Veen is a psychiatrist who has an interest in dreams.) Another part is a treatise that Van works on, called "The Texture of Time." Nabokov recorded an eerie dream about Edmund Wilson, whom he saw for the last time in the flesh in January '64, during Edmund's brief stay in Montreux:

> Am coming down steps of Lausanne-like railway station and meet Edmund. . . . He is about to catch a train. I tell him I'll go "upstairs" to see him off. He says: only Russians use "upstairs" in that sense. He walks briskly along the platform and I notice how fit he looks in a dark-grey suit. We lose each other in the crowd and the train glides away.

In another dream, Nabokov bursts into tears, crying the way he used to as a child of five. He does not explain the cause of his distress.

The dream reports are companionable. Like most adults Nabokov dreams of needing to accomplish an urgent task, being hurried and under pressure. Unlike most dreamers of such dreams, he usually succeeds at his task. He edits his reports, not wanting to burden the reader with details of his nightmares. (He reports only one at length: finding himself in a terrain full of wonderful butterflies but having no net.) Who is "the reader" for whom he organizes and selects what to report of his many dreams? He was writing, first, for himself, or for scholars who might one day look at his dream notes in an archive; for their benefit, he admits that he has certain recurring baleful dreams, "fatidic" dreams, dreams that tell of a terrible ultimate catastrophe, but in general he downplays the importance of bad dreams. He is a highly conscious, rational man, in his telling, someone who by dint of will remains levelheaded even in the funnyland of dreams.

The accounts are enjoyable. They are full of strangeness and movement, with a savoring of incongruities. Sometimes while asleep he thinks that he should be writing this down, and then he quickly awakens to do so. For those readers who will always miss him, who find the literary landscape wan and the voices thin without him, whose experience of the literature of the twentieth century is rich and unforgettable because of him, he seems to live again, the voice at the ear, the sense of the joke:

8 AM Oct. 16, 1964, Friday

Was dancing with Ve. Her open dress, oddly speckled and summery. A man kissed her in passing. I clutch him by the head and bang his face with such vicious force against the wall that he almost gets meat-hooked on some fixtures. . . . Detaches himself with face all bloody and stumbles away.

17 Oct. . . . 8:30 AM

Sitting at round table in the office of the director of a small provincial museum. He (. . . colorless administrator, neutral features, crewcut) is explaining something about the collections. I suddenly realize that all the while he was speaking I was absentmindedly eating exhibits on the table—bricks of crumbling stuff which I had apparently taken for some kind of dusty insipid pastry but which were actually samples of rare soils. . . . I am now wondering not so much about the effects upon me of those samples . . . but about the method of restoring them and what exactly they were—perhaps very precious. . . . The director is called to the telephone [and] I am now talking to his assistant.

One dream achieves, with a flourish worthy of the awake writer, something like J. W. Dunne's vision of past, future, and present all over-laid in one event:

Woke up early, decided to get this down though very sleepy. . . . I am lying on a couch and dictating to Ve. Apparently I have been dictating from written cards in my hand, but then I dictate in the act of composing. . . . It refers to a new, expanded The Gift. My young man F[yodor] is speaking of his destiny, *already accomplished*, and of his having vaguely but constantly realized that it was to be a great one. I am saying this slowly in [Russian]. . . . I am declaiming this . . . weighing every word, hesitating whether to use [one Russian word], wondering if [it] did not make the inward extending shadow too long and large. . . . Simultaneously, I am thinking rather smugly that nobody had ever rendered the name of nostalgia better than I and that I had subtly introduced . . . a certain secret strain: *before* actually anybody had left forever those avenues and fields, a sense of never-returning was . . . inscribed into them.

There are many more dreams. They are a last trove, written not for publication but—because it was his inconquerable instinct—to be savored by whoever might come along, who might be drawn to him thereby, who might find delight.

ACKNOWLEDGMENTS

Like anyone embarking on a book project, I was nervous as I found myself edging into this one. Great authors intimidate even as they attract, and Nabokov is immense: all of Western literature is in play with him, finds a conduit through him. He is the great python of art, having made bulging repasts of Russian literature, French literature, and English literature from Shakespeare forward; throwing in his own twentieth century, from the Silver Age poets of his youth to the post-modernism he largely brought into being, he becomes about the longest literary snake ever. I have enjoyed reading him since I was very young. The pleasure I take has a lot to do with time: not how he handles it as a theme, but how I experience it as I read him. His sentences happen at a pace that makes my brain happy, that intoxicates, and I find that I have "enough time" to read this or that passage without worrying, for once, about how many pages remain until I've finished yet another book. For me there is something unique with him, something very like the "enchantment" he often spoke of wanting his readers to feel.

He has been much studied, by professional scholars and by amateur appreciators. The devotion of these Nabokovians takes the form of conferences, websites, listservs, newsletters, societies organized in his name, numberless articles and books, and so forth. I myself am a Nabokovian—I say it proudly, while fully aware of its taint of fandom. Yet as a Nabokovian I am uncomfortable, mildly, with the tone of adoration. The promiscuous use of the word *genius*, for example, unsettles me. The great writer is reckoned a genius of the novel, of poetry, of entomology, of the short story; of college teaching to classes of three or four hundred, of the chess problem of the "solus rex" type; of the theater play, of the essay. All right, I will allow that he was a very talented fellow—an extremely talented fellow.*

---

* There is also the school of testy carping, of taking on the great man and knocking him down a peg or two. This is probably best exemplified by the writer Andrew Field, whose studies of Nabokov in the seventies and eighties seemed to want to prove that the critic

I am put in mind, however, of a concept first explained to me by the historian Judith Walkowitz: the concept of the bar mitzvah boy. The bar mitzvah boy is gifted at everything, he insists that you admire him, and if you don't believe he's wonderful and the best there is, you only have to ask his mother. The issue is not whether Nabokov achieved superb things of several kinds, but why, 115 years after his birth, distinguished scholars are still carrying water for him, arguing for his status as a polymathic genius. Why did Nabokov himself maneuver to be recognized as such? You would think that he would have grown up.

Worship leads to possessiveness, I've noticed, and what I most feared as I set out was that a network of scholars, all of whom knew each other well and many of whom knew Nabokov's work (especially the work in Russian) much, much better than I, would resent my uninvited intrusions. But as it happens, when I did get in touch with this or that Nabokov authority, he or she was unfailingly kind. I realized at some point that I needed to read everything that had been written about him. I sat in a comfortable chair for two years and ingested the biographical and critical literature. Much of it, to my pleasure, was witty, substantial, revelatory. In itself it was enjoyable to read—as literary commentary should be. The best of it took me back to my halcyon college days, when I read well-phrased ruminations by the likes of John Crowe Ransom, I. A. Richards, F. R. Leavis, Lionel Trilling, Allen Tate, Robert Penn Warren, Edmund Wilson—men I imagined as tweedy gents smoking pipes in rooms full of books, a fire in the grate, snow drifting down outside the mullioned window. I had gone to a small college where the philosopher Monroe Beardsley—co-author of the important New Critical pronunciamento "The Intentional Fallacy"—lectured, and though I had never made it into one of Beardsley's classes, his approach somehow rubbed off on all the young English professors on campus. They taught me to avoid a biographical approach, taught me to look for "structure" and "patterns of imagery" in texts whose purpose I was not to worry about, and the books of criticism they assigned us to read were, as I said, engaging in their own right.

The scholars who answered my occasional queries include Professor Brian Boyd, of the University of Auckland; Professor Eric Naiman, of

was just as smart as his subject. The current author hopes not to be Fieldian. He also hopes that his study will not be seen as a vulgar nationalist assault on the assertively multi-nationalist VN, claiming him for xenophobic America, tucking him deep into the American Lit folder and saying that that's the last word to be said about him. There are no last words.

the University of California, Berkeley; and Professor Emeritus Stephen J. Parker, of the University of Kansas. For an enjoyable lunch and discussion of some matters that had long puzzled me, though for him they were old hat, I wish to thank Professor John Burt Foster Jr., of George Mason University, whose *Nabokov's Art of Memory and European Modernism* is the single most suggestive work on Nabokov's cultural inheritance that I found. Professor Foster read the present book in manuscript and pointed out a number of embarrassing mistakes. The manuscript also benefited from—and the author took encouragement from—a close reading by Professor Galya Diment, of the University of Washington, whose own writing about Nabokov is full of quiet humor and strong feeling. Other readings came courtesy of the writer/ epidemiologist Andrew Moss, of San Francisco, and the novelist/ memoirist Rob Couteau, of New Paltz, New York.

Herb Gold, who knew Dmitri Nabokov as a tennis partner and who took over Vladimir's classes at Cornell, entertained me with stories of both men—very funny stories. Richard Buxbaum, hired to help with the drive to Utah one summer, gave me a feeling for what it had been like to be cooped up with the family in a moving vehicle for a few weeks: in a word, fascinating.

At the Berg Collection of the New York Public Library, the richest archive of Nabokov materials in the world, the staff were always welcoming, their ethos of tolerant professionalism making the Berg a joy to visit, even if the main reading room is sometimes a degree too cold. My uncertain questings found focus through the assistance of curator Isaac Gewirtz and librarians Becky Finer, Anne Garner, and Lyndsi Barnes. At the American Museum of Natural History, David Grimaldi, curator of the Division of Invertebrate Zoology, helped me understand the kind of lepidopterological literature Nabokov was likely to have read in the 1940s. (Taxonomic rather than theoretical: Nabokov was uninterested in, or at any rate uninformed about, breakthrough concepts in population genetics developed in the twenties that would come to undergird modern evolutionary thinking.) Suzanne Rab Green, also of the AMNH, gave me a colorful account of her discovery, with Dr. Grimaldi, of insect specimens Nabokov had collected in '41 and given to the museum, which had then languished in a closet for seventy years. Andrew Johnston, scientific assistant for lepidoptera, helped me search out other Nabokov gifts to the museum.

At the Museum of Comparative Zoology, at Harvard, Rod Eastwood was generous with his time, despite my being only the latest in a long line of fans curious to see where Nabokov had worked, what his bugs had looked like, which window his workbench sat under, etc. Also at Harvard, Peter McCarthy, the undergraduate president of the Harvard Mountaineering Club, answered questions about club tradition and led me down to the meeting room in Claverly Hall, with its old climbing gear lying about, its tattered climbing books, and its general air of a fraternity basement.

As I put together the story of the Nabokovs' flight from France in May 1940, I spent some days at the YIVO Institute for Jewish Research, in New York, where I was guided by Fruma Mohrer, chief archivist, and by archivists Gunnar Berg, Leo Greenbaum, and Roberta Elliott. Valery Bazarov, HIAS director of Family History and Location Services, gave me an understanding of that organization's actions early in World War II and of its role in getting the Nabokovs out. Tanya Chebotarev, of the Bakhmeteff Archive at Columbia University, guided my reading of Nabokov's Russian-language correspondence. Simon Belokowsky ably translated all documents from Russian, although the final wording in English is my responsibility. Olga Andreyev Carlisle, memoirist and clear-eyed participant in some of the monumental politico-literary dramas of the twentieth century, entertained and enlightened me during a discussion of Nabokov's grudges against the Soviets and against history itself. Sarah Funke Butler, of Glenn Horowitz, Bookseller, in New York, helped me track down N.'s personal copy of Edmund Wilson's *A Window on Russia*, with N.'s bemused marginal notations on Wilson's comments on N.'s career. Avery Rome, one of the sharpest editors I've ever encountered, heard me out and offered typically thoughtful advice at numerous points in my writing and research. Michael Doise, literary investigator in Rouen, France, discovered the cost of steamship tickets for the Nabokovs in 1940 on the French Line vessel *Champlain*. For my portrait of Dmitri Nabokov, I was fortunate to be able to interview the closest American friends of his young adulthood: Barbara Victor, Sandy Levine, and Brett Schlesinger, all of New York. Ivan and Peter Nabokov, Dmitri's cousins and the older two sons of Nicolas Nabokov, helped me understand some themes of the family's protean encounter with America. Their accounts of their lives and careers were extraordinary "speakings of memory."

At the Houghton Library, Harvard, the Beinecke Library, Yale, and the Library of Congress, I was benignly left alone by considerate and efficient staff who made me feel, as I always feel when I visit institutions like these, that I am deeply fortunate to be a citizen of an open society, one that has provided, so far, adequate resources for the preservation of the written past.

My astute wife, the historian Mary Ryan, held my hand, listened to me complain, argued with me, and seemed oddly confident that I would eventually find a way to write about Nabokov in America. I thank her and embrace her. Michael Carlisle, my redoubtable, ever-cheering agent, was a brick and a joy to have on my side, and Anton Mueller, my editor at Bloomsbury, and his colleague Rachel Mannheimer added insight and calming good counsel at various points. I wish also to thank personal friends who engaged with me in the sort of discussions that make projects like this one, with so many aspects and complications, feel doable. Robert Spertus and Paul Gruber, deep readers and men of learning who wear it lightly, were especially helpful, as was Peter Jelavich, the great scholar of modern Germany. For this writer, the most treasured friends are those before whom one finds oneself unable not to speak freely.

PHOTO CREDITS

Page 5: Little Cottonwood Canyon: Author's photograph.

Page 31: SS *Champlain*: photographer unknown. Credit: Heritage-Ships.

Page 45: Edmund Wilson: photographer unknown. Courtesy the Edmund Wilson Papers. Yale Collection of American Literature, Beinecke Rare Book and Manuscript Library, Yale University

Page 50: El Rey Court: Author's photograph.

Page 64: Bears and cars in Yosemite: Photographer unknown.

Page 81: Craigie Circle: Author's photograph.

Page 83: MCZ butterflies: Author's photograph.

Page 94: Alta Lodge: Unknown photographer. Courtesy Alan Engen and David Davenport.

Page 98: An approach to Lone Peak.

Page 120: Columbine Lodge stationery: Courtesy of the Bakhmeteff Archive of Russian & Eastern European Culture, Columbia University. Copyright The Estate of Vladimir Nabokov. Used by permission of The Wylie Agency, L.L.C.

Page 122: Longs Peak: By permission of Allen Matheson.

Page 123: Columbine Lodge cabin: Author's photograph.

Page 151: Tetons postcard: Unknown photographer. Courtesy the Edmund Wilson Papers. Yale Collection of American Literature, Beinecke Rare Book and Manuscript Library, Yale University.

Page 153: Leatherstocking Tales cover: Illustration by Carl Offterdinger.

Page 156: Disappointment Peak: Author's photograph.

Page 168: Telluride hillside: Author's photograph.

Page 182: Dmitri in his first MG TC: unknown photographer. Courtesy Roger Boylan, *Autosavant* Magazine, and Ariane Csonka.

Page 187: Corral Log Motel outside view: Author's photograph.

Page 189: Corral Log inside view: Author's photograph.

Page 230: Mt. Carmel cabin: Author's photograph.

Page 230: Mt. Carmel cabin, interior: Author's photograph.

Page 233: Nabokov at Plaza Motel: Carl Mydans for *Life* magazine.
  © Getty images.

Page 242: Dmitri beside '57 MG: unknown. Courtesy Roger Boylan,
  Autosavant Magazine, and Ariane Csonka.

Endpaper design: Katya Mezhibovskaya/Endpaper illustrations: Elnora
  Turner

BIBLIOGRAPHY

Abrams, M. H., ed. *The Norton Anthology of English Literature*, vol. 2, 4th ed. New York: W.W. Norton and Co., 1979.

Adkins, Lynn. "Jesse L. Nusbaum and the Painted Desert in San Diego." *Journal of San Diego History* 29, no. 2 (Spring 1983).

Agee, James. "The Great American Roadside." *Fortune* 10 (September 1934): 53–63, 172, 174, 177.

Ahuja, Nitin. "Nabokov's Case Against Natural Selection." *Tract*, 2012. http://www.hcs.harvard.edu/tract/nabokov.html.

Alden, Peter D. "H.M.C. Climbing Camp, 1953." *Harvard Mountaineering*, no. 12 (May 1955).

Alexander, Victoria N. "Nabokov, Teleology, and Insect Mimicry." *Nabokov Studies* 7 (2002–2003): 177–213.

Alexandrov, Vladimir E. "Nabokov and Bely." In Alexandrov, *Garland Companion*.

——. *Nabokov's Otherworld*. Princeton, N.J.: Princeton University Press, 1991.

Alexandrov, Vladimir E., ed. *The Garland Companion to Vladimir Nabokov*. New York: Garland, 1995.

Altschuler, Glenn, and Isaac Kramnick. " 'Red Cornell': Cornell in the Cold War," part 1. *Cornell Alumni Magazine*, July 2010.

Amis, Martin. "Divine Levity: The Reputation of Vladimir Nabokov Is High and Growing Higher and There Is Much More Work Still to Come." *Times Literary Supplement*, December 23 and 30, 2011, 3–5.

——. "The Sublime and the Ridiculous: Nabokov's Black Farces," in Quennell, *Vladimir Nabokov, His Life*.

——. *Visiting Mrs. Nabokov and Other Excursions*. New York: Vintage International, 1995.

Appel, Alfred, Jr. "The Road to Lolita, or the Americanization of an Émigré." *Journal of Modern Literature* 4 (1974): 3–31.

——. *Nabokov's Dark Cinema*. New York: Oxford University Press, 1974.

Appel, Alfred, Jr., ed. *The Annotated Lolita*. New York: McGraw-Hill, 1970.

Appel, Alfred, Jr., and Charles Newman, eds. *Nabokov: Criticism, Reminiscences, Translations, and Tributes*. London: Weidenfeld and Nicolson, 1971.

Bahr, Ehrhard. *Weimar on the Pacific: German Exile Culture in Los Angeles and the Crisis of Modernism*. Berkeley: University of California Press, 2007.

Baker, Nicholson. *U and I: A True Story*. New York: Vintage, 1992.

Banta, Martha. "Benjamin, Edgar, Humbert, and Jay." *Yale Review* 60 (Summer 1971): 532–49.

Barabtarlo, Gennady. "Nabokov in the Wilson Archive." *Cycnos* 10, no. 1(1993): 27–32.

Barth, Werner, M.D., and Kinim Segal, M.D. "Reactive Arthritis (Reiter's Syndrome)." *American Family Physician* 60, no. 2 (August 1, 1999): 499–503.

Belasco, Warren James. *Americans on the Road: From Autocamp to Motel, 1910–1945.* Cambridge, Mass.: MIT Press, 1979.

Benfey, Christopher. "Malcolm Cowley Was One of the Best Literary Tastemakers of the Twentieth Century. Why Were His Politics So Awful?" *The New Republic,* March 3, 2014.

Bentley, Eric. *The Brecht Memoir.* New York: PAJ Publications, 1985.

Berger, John. *The Success and Failure of Picasso.* New York: Pantheon, 1989.

Berkman, Sylvia. "Smothered Voices." *New York Times,* September 21, 1958.

Bishop, Morris. "Nabokov at Cornell." In Appel and Newman, *Nabokov: Criticism.*

Bloom, Harold, ed. *Herman Melville's "Moby-Dick."* New York: Chelsea House, 1986.

——. *Vladimir Nabokov.* New York: Chelsea House, 1987.

Booth, Wayne C. *The Rhetoric of Fiction.* Chicago: University of Chicago Press, 1983.

Borges, Jorge Luis. *Labyrinths.* New York: New Directions, 1964.

Boyd, Brian. "MSS." In Alexandrov, *Garland Companion.*

——. "Nabokov Lives On." *The American Scholar,* Spring 2010.

——. "The Psychologist." *The American Scholar,* Autumn 2011.

——. *Stalking Nabokov: Selected Essays.* New York: Columbia University Press, 2011.

——. *Vladimir Nabokov: The American Years.* Princeton, N.J.: Princeton University Press, 1991.

——. *Vladimir Nabokov: The Russian Years.* Princeton, N.J.: Princeton University Press, 1990.

Boyd, Brian, and Robert Michael Pyle, eds. *Nabokov's Butterflies: Unpublished and Uncollected Writings.* Boston: Beacon Press, 2000.

Boyd, Brian, Jeff Edmunds, Maria Malikova, and Leona Toker. "Nabokov Studies: Strategic Development of the Field and Scholarly Cooperation." In Leving, *Goalkeeper.*

Brodhead, Richard. "Trying All Things: An Introduction to *Moby-Dick*." In *New Essays on Moby-Dick,* edited by Richard Brodhead. New York: Cambridge University Press, 1986.

Bruss, Elizabeth. "Illusions of Reality and the Reality of Illusions." In Bloom, *Vladimir Nabokov.*

Buehrens, John. "Famous Consultant and Forgotten Minister." UUWorld. http://www.uuworld.org/2004/01/lookingback.html.

Carlisle, Olga Andreyev. *Under a New Sky: A Reunion with Russia.* New York: Ticknor & Fields, 1993.

Castiglia, Christopher. *Bound and Determined: Captivity, Culture-Crossing, and White Womanhood from Mary Rowlandson to Patty Hearst.* Chicago: University of Chicago Press, 1996.

Chiasson, Dan. "Go Poets." *New York Review of Books,* April 3, 2014.

Clinger, Mic, James H. Pickering, and Carey Stevanus. *Estes Park and Rocky Mountain National Park Then and Now.* Englewood, Colo.: Westcliffe, 2006.

Clippinger, David. "*Lolita* and 1950s American Culture." In Kuzmanovich and Diment, *Approaches to Teaching.*

Cohen, Michael P. *The Pathless Way*: *John Muir and American Wilderness*. Madison: University of Wisconsin Press, 1984.

Connolly, Julian W. *A Reader's Guide to Nabokov's "Lolita."* Boston: Academic Studies Press, 2009.

Connolly, Julian W., ed. *Nabokov and His Fiction*: *New Perspectives*. Cambridge, UK: University of Cambridge Press, 1999.

——. *The Cambridge Companion to Vladimir Nabokov*. New York: Cambridge University Press, 2005.

Corliss, Richard. *Lolita*. London: British Film Institute, 1994.

Corrsin, Stephen D. "Nabokov in America." *Columbia Literary Columns* 33, no. 2, (February 1984): 22–31.

Couteau, Rob. "Abandoning Hope to Discover Life: Commemorating the 51st Anniversary of the Grove Press Edition of Henry Miller's *Tropic of Cancer*, with a Special Tribute to Barney Rosset." *Rain Taxi Review*, August 2012. http://www.raintaxi.com/abandoning-hope-to-discover-life.

——. Review of *Kerouac Ascending: Memorabilia of the Decade of "On the Road,"* by Elbert Lenrow. *Evergreen Review*, Summer 2013.

Dabney, Lewis M. *Edmund Wilson*: *A Life in Literature*. Baltimore: Johns Hopkins University Press, 2007.

Davidson, James A. "Hitchcock/Nabokov: Some Thoughts on Alfred Hitchcock and Vladimir Nabokov." *Images*. http://www.imagesjournal.com/issue03/features/hitchnab1.htm and http://www.imagesjournal.com/issue03/features/hitchnab4.htm.

Davie, Donald. *The Poems of Dr. Zhivago*. New York: Barnes & Noble, 1965.

De Grazia, Edward. *Girls Lean Back Everywhere*: *The Law of Obscenity and the Assault on Genius*. New York: Random House, 1992.

Delbanco, Andrew. "American Literature: A Vanishing Subject?" *Daedalus* 135, no. 2 (Spring 2006): 22–37.

Davis, Dick. "Obituary: Janet Lewis." *The Independent*, December 15, 1998.

Diment, Galya. "A Tale of Two Lolitas: Mrs. Parker and the Butterfly Effect." *New York*, December 2, 2013.

——. "Two 1955 Lolitas: Vladimir Nabokov's and Dorothy Parker's." *Modernism/Modernity* 21, no. 2 (April 2014): 487–505.

——. *A Russian Jew of Bloomsbury*: *The Life and Times of Samuel Koteliansky*. Montreal: McGill–Queen's University Press, 2011.

——. *Pniniad*: *Vladimir Nabokov and Marc Szeftel*. Seattle: University of Washington Press, 1997.

Dirig, Robert. "Karner Blue, Sing Your Purple Song." *American Butterflies*, Spring 1997.

——. "Theme in Blue: Vladimir Nabokov's Endangered Butterfly." In Shapiro, *Nabokov at Cornell*.

Dolinin, Alexander. "What Happened to Sally Horner? A Real-Life Source of Nabokov's *Lolita*." *Times Literary Supplement*, September 9, 2005, 11–12.

Douglas, Ann. "Day into Noir." *Vanity Fair*, March 2007.

——. Introduction to *The Dharma Bums*. New York: Viking, 2008.

Dragunoiu, Dana. *Vladimir Nabokov and the Poetics of Liberalism*. Evanston, Ill.: Northwestern University Press, 2011.

Dunn, Susan. *1940: FDR, Wilkie, Lindbergh, Hitler—the Election amid the Storm*. New Haven, Conn.: Yale University Press, 2013.

Dupee, F. W. " 'Lolita' in America." *Encounter* XII, no. 2 (February 1959).

———. "Introduction to Selections from *Lolita*." *Anchor Review* 2 (1957): 1–3, 5–13.

Emerson, Ralph Waldo. *The Spiritual Emerson*. Edited by David M. Robinson. Boston: Beacon Press, 2003.

Epstein, Joseph. "Never Wise—But Oh, How Smart," *New York Times*, August 31, 1986, section 7, p. 3.

Espey, John. "Classics on Cassette: 'Speak, Memory.' *Los Angeles Times Book Review*, October 20, 1991, 8.

Faulkner, William. *Big Woods: The Hunting Stories*. New York: Vintage International, 1994.

Federal Writers' Project. *The WPA Guide to New York City: The Federal Writers' Project Guide to 1930s New York*. Introduction by William H. Whyte. New York: The New Press, 1992. First published 1939 by Random House.

Fermi, Laura. *Illustrious Immigrants: The Intellectual Migration from Europe, 1930–41*. Chicago: University of Chicago Press, 1968.

Field, Andrew. *Nabokov: His Life in Part*. New York: Viking Press, 1977.

———. *VN: The Life and Art of Vladimir Nabokov*. New York: Crown, 1986.

Flanner, Janet. "Goethe in Hollywood, Parts I and II." *New Yorker*, December 13 and 20, 1941.

Fleming, Donald, and Bernard Bailyn, eds. *The Intellectual Migration: Europe and America, 1930–1960*. Cambridge, Mass.: Belknap Press, 1969.

Fluck, Winfried. "Power Relations in the Novels of James: The 'Liberal' and the 'Radical' Version." In *Enacting History in Henry James: Narrative, Power, and Ethics*, edited by Gert Buelens. New York: Cambridge University Press, 1997.

Foster, John Burt, Jr. "*Bend Sinister*." In Alexandrov, *Garland Companion*.

———. "Nabokov and Modernism." In Connolly, *Cambridge Companion*.

———. *Nabokov's Art of Memory and European Modernism*. Princeton, N.J.: Princeton University Press, 1993.

Freeman, Elizabeth. "Honeymoon with a Stranger: Pedophiliac Picaresques from Poe to Nabokov." *American Literature* 70, no. 4 (December 1998).

Frosch, Thomas R. "Parody and Authenticity in *Lolita*." In Bloom, *Vladimir Nabokov*.

Gerke, Sarah Bohl. "Bright Angel Cabins." Arizona State University/Grand Canyon Association. http://grandcanyonhistory.clas.asu.edu/sites_southrim_brightangelcabins.html.

Gerschenkron, Alex. "A Manufactured Monument?" *Modern Philology* 63, no. 4 (May 1966): 336–347.

Gezari, Janet. "Chess and Chess Problems." In Alexandrov, *Garland Companion*.

Gibian, George, and Stephen Jan Parker, eds. *The Achievements of Vladimir Nabokov*. Ithaca, N.Y.: Cornell Center for International Studies, 1984.

Gilmore, Michael T. *Twentieth Century Interpretations of "Moby-Dick."* Englewood Cliffs, N.J.: Prentice-Hall, 1977.

Gogol, Nikolai. *Dead Souls*, trans. Constance Garnett. New York: Modern Library, 1926.

Goldberg, J. J. "Kishinev 1903: The Birth of a Century." *The Jewish Daily Forward*, April 4, 2003.

Goldman, Shalom. "Nabokov's Minyan: A Study in Philo-Semitism." *Modern Judaism* 25, no. 1 (2005): 1–22.

Goldstein, Richard. *Helluva Town: The Story of New York City During World War II*. New York: Free Press, 2010.

Green, Hannah. "Mister Nabokov." *The New Yorker*, February 4, 1977.

Grimaldi, David, and Michael S. Engel. *Evolution of the Insects*. New York: Cambridge University Press, 2005.

Grossman, Lev. "The Gay Nabokov." *Salon*, May 17, 2000.

Guerney, Bernard Guilbert. "Great Grotesque." *New Republic*, September 25, 1944.

Haegert, John. "Artist in Exile: The Americanization of Humbert Humbert." *ELH* 52, no. 3 (Fall 1985): 777–94.

Hagerty, Donald J. *The Life of Maynard Dixon*. Layton, Utah: Gibbs Smith, 2010.

Hall, Donald. "Ezra Pound Said Be a Publisher." *New York Times Book Review*, August 23, 1981, 13, 22–23.

Hamsun, Knut. *Pan*. New York: Penguin, 1998.

Hardwick, Elizabeth. "Master Class." *New York Times Book Review*, October 19, 1980, 1, 28.

Harris, Frank. *My Life*. New York: Frank Harris, 1925.

Haven, Cynthia. "The Lolita Question." *Stanford Magazine*, May/June 2006.

Heaney, Thomas M. "The Call of the Open Road: Automobile Travel and Vacations in American Popular Culture, 1935–1960." Doctoral dissertation, University of California, Irvine, 2000.

Heilbut, Anthony. *Exiled in Paradise: German Refugee Artists and Intellectuals in America, from the 1930s to the Present*. New York: Viking Press, 1983.

Hellman, Geoffrey T. "Black Tie and Cyanide Jar." *New Yorker*, August 21, 1948, 32–47.

Ireland, Corydon. "Harvard Goes to War." *Harvard Gazette*, November 10, 2011.

Isaac, Joel, and Duncan Bell, eds. *Uncertain Empire: American History and the Idea of the Cold War*. New York: Oxford University Press, 2012.

Jahoda, Marie. "The Migration of Psychoanalysis." In Fleming and Bailyn, *Intellectual Migration*.

Jakle, John A., Keith A. Sculle, and Jefferson S. Rogers. *The Motel in America*. Baltimore: Johns Hopkins University Press, 1996.

James, Clive. "The Poetry of Edmund Wilson." *The New Review* 4, no. 44 (November 1977), 37–44.

Johnson, D. Barton. "Nabokov's Golliwoggs: Lodi Reads English, 1899–1909." *Zembla*. www.libraries.psu.edu/nabokov/dbjg01.htm.

———. "Nabokov's House in Ashland." Vladimir Nabokov Forum, Listserv.UCSB. edu, n.d. https://listserv.ucsb.edu/lsv-cgi-bin/wa?A2=ind9910&L=NABOKV-L&P=R348&1.

———. "Strange Bedfellows: Ayn Rand and Vladimir Nabokov." *Journal of Ayn Rand Studies* 2, no. 1 (Fall 2000): 47–67.

———. "Vladimir Nabokov and Captain Mayne Reid." *Cycnos* 10, no. 1 (1992).

Johnson, D. Barton, and Sheila Golburgh Johnson. "Nabokov in Ashland, Oregon." Penn State University Libraries, n.d. http://www.libraries.psu.edu/nabokov/dbjas1.htm.

Johnson, Kurt, and Steve Coates. *Nabokov's Blues*: *The Scientific Odyssey of a Literary Genius*. Cambridge, Mass.: Zoland Books, 1999.

Jordy, William H. "The Aftermath of the Bauhaus in America: Gropius, Mies, and Breuer." In Fleming and Bailyn, *Intellectual Migration*.

Judge, Edward H. *Easter in Kishinev*: *Anatomy of a Pogrom*. New York: New York University Press, 1992.

Kakutani, Michiko. "The Lasting Power of Dr. King's Speech." *New York Times*, August 28, 2013, A1, A18.

Karl, Frederick R. *Franz Kafka, Representative Man*. New York: Ticknor & Fields, 1991.

Karlinsky, Simon. "Nabokov's Russian Games." In Roth, *Critical Essays*.

Karlinsky, Simon, ed. *Dear Bunny, Dear Volodya*: *The Nabokov-Wilson Letters, 1940–1971*, annotated and with introductory essay by Karlinsky. Berkeley: University of California Press, 2001.

Kelly, Aileen. "Getting Isaiah Berlin Wrong." *New York Review of Books*, June 20, 2013.

Kernan, Alvin. "Reading Zemblan: The Audience Disappears in *Pale Fire*." In Bloom, *Vladimir Nabokov*.

Kerouac, Jack. *On the Road*. New York: Penguin, 1976. First published 1957 by Viking Press.

——. *The Dharma Bums*. New York: Viking, 2008. First published 1958 by Viking Press.

Khrushcheva, Nina L. *Imagining Nabokov*: *Russia Between Art and Politics*. New Haven, Conn.: Yale Universisty Press, 2007.

Kopper, John M. "Correspondence." In Alexandrov, *Garland Companion*.

Kuzmanovich, Zoran. "Strong Points and Nerve Points: Nabokov's Life and Art." In Connolly, *Cambridge Companion*.

Kuzmanovich, Zoran, and Galya Diment, eds. *Approaches to Teaching Nabokov's "Lolita."* New York: Modern Language Association of America, 2008.

Larmour, David H.J., ed. *Discourse and Ideology in Nabokov's Prose*. New York: Routledge, 2002.

Laskin, David. "When Weimar Luminaries Went West Coast." *New York Times*, October 3, 2008.

Lawrence, D.H. *À Propos of "Lady Chatterley's Lover" and Other Essays*. London: Penguin, 1961.

——. *Studies in Classic American Literature*. Edited by Ezra Greenspan, Lindeth Vasey, and John Worthen. New York: Cambridge University Press, 2003. First published 1923 by Thomas Seltzer.

Leamer, Laurence. *Ascent*: *The Spiritual and Physical Quest of Willi Unsoeld*. New York: Simon & Schuster, 1982.

Levin, Harry. "Two *Romanisten* in America: Spitzer and Auerbach." In Fleming and Bailyn, *Intellectual Migration*.

Leving, Yuri. " 'The Book Is Dazzlingly Brilliant . . . But'—Two Early Internal Reviews of Nabokov's *The Gift*." In Leving, *Goalkeeper*.

——. "Selling Nabokov: An Interview with Nikki Smith." *Nabokov Online Journal* 7 (2013). http://www.nabokovonline.com.

Leving, Yuri, ed. *The Goalkeeper*: *The Nabokov Almanac*. Boston: Academic Studies Press, 2010.

Lilly, Mark. "Nabokov: *Homo Ludens*." In Quennell, *Vladimir Nabokov, His Life*.

Lock, Charles. "Transparent Things and Opaque Words." In *Nabokov's World, Vol. 1: The Shape of Nabokov's World*, edited by Jane Grayson, Arnold McMillin, and Priscilla Meyer. London: Palgrave, 2002.

Lodge, David. "Exiles in a Small World." *The Guardian*, May 7, 2004.

Maar, Michael. *Speak, Nabokov*. Translated by Ross Benjamin. New York: Verso, 2009.

Mahaffey, Vicki, and Cassandra Laity. "Modernist Theory and Criticism." *The Johns Hopkins Guide to Literary Theory & Criticism*, 2nd ed., edited by Michael Groden and Martin Kreiswirth. Baltimore: Johns Hopkins University Press, 2005.

Manolescu-Oancea, Monica. "Inventing and Naming America: Place and Place Names in Vladimir Nabokov's *Lolita*." *European Journal of American Studies* I (2009).

McCarthy, Mary. "F. W. Dupee, 1904–1979." *New York Review of Books*, March 8, 1979.

——. "On F. W. Dupee (1904–1979)." *New York Review of Books*, October 27, 1983.

McCrum, Robert. "The Final Twist in Nabokov's Untold Story." *The Observer*, October 24, 2009.

McGill, Meredith L. *American Literature and the Culture of Reprinting, 1834–1853*. Philadelphia: University of Pennsylvania Press, 2003.

McKinney, Jerome B., and Lawrence Cabot Howard. *Public Administration: Balancing Power and Accountability*. Westport, Conn.: Praeger, 1998.

Melville, Herman. *Moby-Dick, or The Whale*. Evanston, Ill.: Northwestern University Press, 2001. First published 1851 by Harper & Brothers.

Meyer, Priscilla. "Nabokov's Critics: A Review Article." *Modern Philology* 91, no. 3 (1994): 326–38.

Meyers, Jeffrey. *Edmund Wilson: A Biography*. Boston: Houghton Mifflin, 1995.

Miłosz, Czesław. *Emperor of the Earth: Modes of Eccentric Vision*. Berkeley: University of California Press, 1977.

Minchenok, Dmitry. "Dmitry Nabokov. Life Like Fiction," interview. Voice of Russia, February 28, 2012. Recorded in 2005. http://sputniknews.com/voiceofrussia/2012_02_28/67099376.

Mizruchi, Susan. "Lolita in History." *American Literature* 75, no. 3 (September 2003).

Moynahan, Julian. "Lolita and Related Memories." In Appel and Newman, *Nabokov: Criticism*.

——. *Vladimir Nabokov*. Minneapolis: University of Minnesota Press, 1971.

Myers, Steven Lee. "Time to Come Home, Zhivago," *New York Times*, February 12, 2006.

Nabokov, Dmitri. "A Few Things That Must Be Said on Behalf of Vladimir Nabokov." In Rivers and Nicol, *Nabokov's Fifth Arc*.

——. "Close Calls and Fulfilled Dreams: Selected Entries from a Private Journal." In *Our Private Lives*, edited by Daniel Halpern. Hopewell, N.J.: Ecco Press, 1998.

——. "On a Book Entitled *The Enchanter*." In V. Nabokov, *The Enchanter*, 97–127.

——. "On Returning to Ithaca." In Shapiro, *Nabokov at Cornell*, 277–84.

——. "On Revisiting Father's Room," *Encounter*, October 1979, 77–82.

——. *Russische Lieder*. Program notes and English verse translations by Vladimir Nabokov. MPS Records, Stereo 20 21988-7, 1974, 33⅓ rpm.

Nabokov, Dmitri, and Matthew J. Bruccoli, eds. *Vladimir Nabokov: Selected Letters, 1940–1977*. New York: Harcourt Brace Jovanovich, 1989.

Nabokov, Nicolas. *Bagazh*: *Memoirs of a Russian Cosmopolitan*. New York: Atheneum, 1975.

Nabokov, Peter. *A Forest of Time*: *American Indian Ways of History*. New York: Cambridge University Press, 2002.

Nabokov, Peter, and Lawrence L. Loendorf. *Restoring a Presence*: *American Indians and Yellowstone National Park*. Norman: University of Oklahoma Press, 2004.

Nabokov, V. D. *V. D. Nabokov and the Russian Provisional Government, 1917*. Edited by Virgil D. Medlin and Steven L. Parsons. Introduction by Robert P. Browder. New Haven, Conn.: Yale University Press, 1976.

Nabokov, Vladimir. "Inspiration." *The Saturday Review*, January 6, 1973, 30–32.

——. Introduction to *Bend Sinister*. New York: Time-Life Books, 1964.

——. "On a Book Entitled 'Lolita.' " In *Lolita*, 329–35.

——. "The Russian Professor." *The New Yorker*, June 13 and 20, 2011, 100–4.

——. *A Russian Beauty and Other Stories*. New York: McGraw-Hill, 1973.

——. *Ada or Ardor*. New York: Vintage International, 1990.

——. *Bend Sinister*. *Time* Reading Program Special Edition. New York: Time Inc., 1964.

——. *Conclusive Evidence*. New York: Harper & Brothers, 1951.

——. *Glory*. New York: Penguin, 1974.

——. *King, Queen, Knave*. New York: Vintage International, 1989.

——. *Laughter in the Dark*. New York: New Directions, 2006.

——. *Lectures on Russian Literature*. New York: Harcourt Brace Jovanovich, 1981.

——. *Letters to Véra*. Translated and edited by Olga Voronina and Brian Boyd. London: Penguin Classics, 2014.

——. *Lolita*. London: Everyman's Library, 1992.

——. *Nabokov's Dozen: Thirteen Stories*. New York: Penguin, 1971.

——. *Nikolai Gogol*. Corrected edition. New York: New Directions Paperbook, 1961.

——. *Pale Fire*. New York: Vintage International, 1989.

——. *Pnin*. New York: Vintage International, 1985.

——. *Poems and Problems*. New York: McGraw-Hill, 1970.

——. *Speak, Memory: An Autobiography Revisited*. New York: G.P. Putnam's Sons, 1966.

——. *Strong Opinions*. New York: McGraw-Hill, 1973.

——. *The Enchanter*. Translated by Dmitri Nabokov. New York: G.P. Putnam's Sons, 1986.

——. *The Eye*. New York: Phaedra, 1965.

——. *The Gift*. New York: Vintage International, 1991.

——. *The Original of Laura (Dying Is Fun)*. Edited by Dmitri Nabokov. New York: Alfred A. Knopf, 2008.

——. *The Real Life of Sebastian Knight*. New York: Penguin, 1964.

——. *The Stories of Vladimir Nabokov*. New York: Vintage International, 1997.

Nabokov, Vladimir, selector and translator. *Verses and Versions*: *Three Centuries of Russian Poetry*. Edited by Brian Boyd and Stanislav Shvabrin. New York: Harcourt, 2008.

Nachbar, Jack, ed. *Focus on the Western*. Englewood Cliffs, N.J.: Prentice-Hall, 1974.

Naiman, Eric. "Vladimir to Véra," *Times Literary Supplement*, October 29, 2014.

Nicol, Charles. "Politics." In Alexandrov, *Garland Companion*.

Norman, Will, and Duncan White, eds. *Transitional Nabokov*. New York: Peter Lang, 2009.

"Obituary: C. Bertrand Thompson (1882–1969)." *Academy of Management Journal* 12, no. 1 (March 1969): 66.

O'Brien, Michael. *John F. Kennedy: A Biography*. New York: Thomas Dunne Books/St. Martin's Press, 2005.

O'Connor, Brian. *Adorno*. New York: Routledge, 2013.

Oates, Joyce Carol. "A Personal View of Nabokov." *The Saturday Review*, January 6, 1973, 36–37.

Packer, George. "Don't Look Down: The New Depression Literature." *New Yorker*, April 29, 2013, 70–75.

Parker, Hershel. *Herman Melville: A Biography*, vol. 1. Baltimore: Johns Hopkins University Press, 1996.

Parker, Stephen Jan. "Library." In Alexandrov, *Garland Companion*.

——. "Nabokov Studies." In Shapiro, *Nabokov at Cornell*.

Parker, Stephen Jan, ed. *The Nabokovian*. Lawrence: University of Kansas Press, 1984–2013.

Pasternak, Boris. *Doctor Zhivago*. New York: Pantheon, 1958.

Pavlik, Robert. "In Harmony with the Landscape: Yosemite's Built Environment." *California History* 69, no. 2 (Summer 1990): 182–95.

Pellerdi, Marta. "Aesthetics and Sin: The Nymph and the Faun in Hawthorne's *The Marble Faun* and Nabokov's *Lolita*." In Leving, *Goalkeeper*.

Perret, Geoffrey. *Jack: A Life Like No Other*. New York: Random House, 2002.

Peterson, Dale E. "Nabokov's *Invitation*: Literature as Execution." In Bloom, *Vladimir Nabokov*.

Pickering, James H. *In the Vale of Elkanah: The Tahosa Valley World of Charles Edwin Hewes*. Estes Park, Colo.: Friends Press of the Estes Park Museum, 2007.

Pifer, Ellen. "Consciousness, Real Life, and Fairy-Tale Freedom: *King, Queen, Knave*." In Bloom, *Vladimir Nabokov*.

——. *Nabokov and the Novel*. Cambridge, Mass.: Harvard University Press, 1980.

——. "Reinventing Nabokov: Lyne and Kubrick Parse *Lolita*." In Shapiro, *Nabokov at Cornell*.

——. "The *Lolita* Phenomenon from Paris to Tehran." In Connolly, *Cambridge Companion*.

Pitzer, Andrea. *The Secret History of Vladimir Nabokov*. New York: Pegasus, 2013.

Pomeroy, Earl. *In Search of the Golden West: The Tourist in Western America*. Lincoln: University of Nebraska Press, 1990.

Prieto, José Manuel. "Reading Mandelstam on Stalin." *New York Review of Books*, June 10, 2010.

Proffer, Carl R. *The Widows of Russia and Other Writings*. Ann Arbor, Mich.: Ardis, 1987.

Proffer, Ellendea. "Nabokov's Russian Readers." In Appel and Newman, *Nabokov: Criticism*.

Proffer, Ellendea, ed. *Vladimir Nabokov: A Pictorial Biography*. Ann Arbor, Mich.: Ardis, 1991.

Pushkin, Aleksandr. *Eugene Onegin: A Novel in Verse*. Translated with commentary by Vladimir Nabokov. 4 vols. Princeton, N.J.: Princeton University Press, 1975. First published in English 1964 by Bollingen Foundation.

——. *Eugene Onegin: A Novel in Verse*. New translation in the *Onegin* stanza with an introduction and notes by Walter Arndt. New York: E.P. Dutton & Co., 1963.

——. *Eugene Onegin: A Novel in Verse*. Translated with an introduction and notes by Stanley Mitchell. New York: Penguin, 2008.

Pushkin, Alexander. *The Queen of Spades and Other Stories*. Translated with an introduction by Rosemary Edmonds. New York: Penguin, 2004.

Pyle, Robert Michael. "Between Climb and Cloud: Nabokov among the Lepidopterists." In Boyd and Pyle, *Nabokov's Butterflies*, 32–76.

Quennell, Peter. *The Pursuit of Happiness*. New York: Little, Brown, 1988.

Quennell, Peter, ed. *Vladimir Nabokov, His Life, His Work, His World: A Tribute*. London: Weidenfeld and Nicolson, 1979.

Remington, Charles. "Lepidoptera Studies." In Alexandrov, *Garland Companion*.

Remnick, David, ed., with Susan Choi. *Wonderful Town: New York Stories from "The New Yorker."* New York: Random House, 2000.

Rivers, J. E., and Charles Nicol, eds. *Nabokov's Fifth Arc: Nabokov and Others on His Life's Work*. Austin: University of Texas Press, 1982.

Robbins, Chandler S., Bertel Bruun, and Herbert S. Zim. *Birds of North America*. New York: Golden Press, 1966.

Roberts, David. "Pioneers of Mountain Exploration: The Harvard Five." In *Cloud Dancers: Portraits of North American Mountaineers*, edited by Jonathan Waterman. Golden, Colo.: AAC Press, 1993.

——. "The Hearse Traverse." In *Escape Routes: Further Adventure Writings of David Roberts*, 166–74. Seattle: The Mountaineers, 1997.

Roberts, Neil. "Greenspan, Vasey and Worthen: *D.H. Lawrence: Studies in Classic American Literature*." *E-rea*, February 2, 2004. http://erea.revues.org/461.

Ronen, Omry. "The Triple Anniversary of World Literature: Goethe, Pushkin, Nabokov." In Shapiro, *Nabokov at Cornell*.

Roper, Robert. "At Home in the High Country." Introduction to *Galen Rowell's Sierra Nevada*, by Galen Rowell. San Francisco: Sierra Club Books, 2010.

——. *Fatal Mountaineer: The High-Altitude Life and Death of Willi Unsoeld, American Himalayan Legend*. New York: St. Martin's Press, 2002.

——. *Now the Drum of War: Walt Whitman and His Brothers in the Civil War*. New York: Walker & Co., 2008.

Rorty, Richard. "The Barber of Kasbeam: Nabokov on Cruelty." In *Contingency, Irony, and Solidarity*. New York: Cambridge University Press, 1989.

Roth, Phyllis A. "The Psychology of the Double in *Pale Fire*." In Roth, *Critical Essays*.

Roth, Phyllis A., ed. *Critical Essays on Vladimir Nabokov*. Boston: G.K. Hall & Co., 1984.

Rumens, Carol. " 'Mont Blanc' by Percy Bysshe Shelley." *The Guardian*, March 11, 2013.

Salinger, J. D. *The Catcher in the Rye*. Boston: Little, Brown, 1951.

Salzberg, Joel, ed. *Critical Essays on Salinger's "The Catcher in the Rye."* Boston: G.K. Hall & Co., 1990.

Sanders, Ronald. *Shores of Refuge: A Hundred Years of Jewish Emigration*. New York: Holt, 1988.

Saunders, Frances Stonor. *The Cultural Cold War: The CIA and the World of Arts and Letters*. New York: New Press, 2013.

Sayre, Gordon M. "Abridging between Two Worlds: John Tanner as American Indian Autobiographer." *American Literary History* 11, no. 3 (Autumn 1999): 480–99.

Scammell, Michael. "The Servile Path: Translating Nabokov by Epistle." *Harper's Magazine*, May 2001, 52–60.

Schiff, Stacy. "The Genius and Mrs. Genius." *The New Yorker*, February 10, 1997.

——. *Véra (Mrs. Vladimir Nabokov)*. London: Picador, 1999.

Schlesinger, Brett. "A Journey Down the Tyrrhenian Sea: My Great Italian Sea Voyage of 1975." Privately printed, 2012.

Schulz, Kathryn. "Kathryn Schulz on Amity Gaige's Novel Schroder." *New York*, February 18, 2013.

Schwartz, Delmore. "The Writing of Edmund Wilson." *Accent*, Spring 1942, 177–86.

Shapiro, Gavriel, ed. *Nabokov at Cornell*. Ithaca, N.Y.: Cornell University Press, 2003.

Shklovsky, Victor. "Art as Technique." In *Russian Formalist Criticism: Four Essays*, translated with an introduction by Lee T. Lemon and Marion J. Reis. Lincoln: University of Nebraska Press, 2012.

Shloss, Carol. "*Speak, Memory*: The Aristocracy of Art." In Rivers and Nicol, *Nabokov's Fifth Arc*.

Shrayer, Maxim D. "Jewish Questions in Nabokov's Art and Life." In Connolly, *Nabokov and His Fiction*, 73–91.

——. "Saving Jewish-Russian Émigrés." *Revising Nabokov Revising: The Proceedings of the International Nabokov Conference*. Kyoto: Nabokov Society of Japan, 2010, 123–30.

Skidmore, Max J. "Restless Americans: The Significance of Movement in American History (With a Nod to F.J. Turner)." *Journal of American Culture* 34, no. 2 (June 2011): 161–74.

Slawenski, Kenneth. *J. D. Salinger: A Life*. New York: Random House, 2010.

Sniderman, Alisa. "Vladimir Nabokov, 'Houdini of History'?" *Los Angeles Review of Books*, March 17, 2013.

Socher, Abraham P. "Shades of Frost: A Hidden Source for Nabokov's Pale Fire." *Times Literary Supplement*, July 1, 2005.

Stallings, Don B., and J. R. Turner. "Four New Species of Megathymus." *Entomological News* LXVIII (1957): 4.

——. "New American Butterflies." *Canadian Entomologist* 7, no. 7–8 (August 1946): 134–37.

Steed, J. P., ed. *"The Catcher in the Rye": New Essays*. New York: Peter Lang, 2002.

Stegner, Page, ed. *Nabokov's Congeries*. New York: Viking, 1968.

Stegner, Wallace. *The American West as Living Space*. Ann Arbor, Mich.: University of Michigan Press, 1987.

Steinle, Pamela Hunt. *In Cold Fear: "The Catcher in the Rye," Censorship Controversies and Postwar American Character*. Columbus: Ohio State University Press, 2000.

Sternlieb, Lisa. "Vivian Darkbloom: Floral Border or Moral Order?" In Kuzmanovich and Diment, *Approaches to Teaching*.

Stone, Bruce. "Nabokov's Exoneration: The Genesis and Genius of *Lolita*." *Numero Cinq* IV, no. 5 (May 2013).

Stringer-Hye, Suellen. "An Interview with Dmitri Nabokov." In Leving, *Goalkeeper*.

Sturma, Michael. "Aliens and Indians: A Comparison of Abduction and Captivity Narratives." *Journal of Popular Culture* 36, no. 2 (Fall 2002): 318–34.

Sweeney, Susan Elizabeth. " 'By Some Sleight of *Land*': How Nabokov Rewrote America." In Connolly, *Cambridge Companion*.

——. "Sinistral Details: Nabokov, Wilson, and *Hamlet* in *Bend Sinister*." *Nabokov Studies* 1 (1994): 179–94.

"The Lolita Case." *Time*, November 17, 1958.

Theroux, Paul. "Damned Old Graham Greene." *New York Times*, October 17, 2004.

Tóibín, Colm. " 'Edmund Wilson': American Critic." *New York Times*, September 4, 2005.

Toker, Leona. " 'The Dead Are Good Mixers': Nabokov's Version of Individualism." In Quennell, *Vladimir Nabokov, His Life*.

——. "Nabokov and the Hawthorne Tradition." *Scripta Hierosolymitana* 32 (1987): 323–49.

——. "Nabokov's Worldview." In Connolly, *Cambridge Companion*.

Updike, John. "Grandmaster Nabokov." In *Assorted Prose*. New York: Knopf, 1965.

——. *Hugging the Shore*: *Essays and Criticism*. New York: Alfred A. Knopf, 1983.

——. *More Matter*: *Essays and Criticism*. New York: Alfred A. Knopf, 1999.

——. *Picked-up Pieces*. New York: Knopf, 1975.

Vaingurt, Julia. "Unfair Use: Parody, Plagiarism, and Other Suspicious Practices in and Around *Lolita*." *Nabokov Online Journal* 5 (2001). http://www.nabokovonline.com.

Vickers, Graham. *Chasing Lolita*: *How Popular Culture Corrupted Nabokov's Little Girl All Over Again*. Chicago: Chicago Review Press, 2008.

Watts, Richard, Jr. "Comic-Strip Dictator." *New Republic*, July 7, 1947, 26–27.

Weil, Irwin. "Odyssey of a Translator." In Appel and Newman, *Nabokov: Criticism*.

Weiner, Charles. "A New Site for the Seminar: The Refugees and American Physics in the 1930s." In Fleming and Bailyn, *Intellectual Migration*.

White, Edmund. "Nabokov's Passion." In Bloom, *Vladimir Nabokov*.

——. *City Boy: My Life in New York During the 1960s and '70s*. New York: Bloomsbury, 2009.

Wilford, Hugh. *The Mighty Wurlitzer: How the CIA Played America*. Cambridge, Mass.: Harvard University Press, 2008.

Wilson, Edmund. "Doctor Life and His Guardian Angel." *The New Yorker*, November 15, 1958.

——. "Legend and Symbol in 'Doctor Zhivago.' " *Encounter*, June 9, 1959, 5–16.

——. "T. S. Eliot and the Church of England." *New Republic*, April 24, 1929, 283–84.

——. *A Window on Russia*. New York: Farrar, Straus & Giroux, 1972.

——. *Axel's Castle: A Study in the Imaginative Literature of 1870–1930*. London: Flamingo, 1979.

——. *Letters on Literature and Politics, 1912–1972*. New York: Farrar, Straus & Giroux, 1977.

——. *Memoirs of Hecate County*. New York: David R. Godine, 1980. First published in 1946 by Doubleday.

——. *Red, Black, Blond, and Olive*: *Studies in Four Civilizations*. New York: Oxford University Press, 1956.

——. *The American Jitters*: *A Year of the Slump*. New York: Charles Scribner's Sons, 1932.

——. *The Shores of Light*. New York: Vintage Books, 1961.

Wilson, Rosalind Baker. *Near the Magician*: *A Memoir of My Father, Edmund Wilson*. New York: Grove Weidenfeld, 1989.

Winawer, Jonathan, et. al. "Russian Blues Reveal Effects of Language on Color Discriminations." *Proceedings of the National Academy of Sciences* 104, no. 19 (May 2007): 7780–85.

Wolff, Tatiana, ed. and trans. *Pushkin on Literature*. Introductory essay by John Bayley. London: Athlone Press, 1986.

Wood, Michael. "Lolita in an American Fiction Class." In Kuzmanovich and Diment, *Approaches to Teaching*.

——. *The Magician's Doubts*: *Nabokov and the Risks of Fiction*. London: Chatto & Windus, 1994.

Wyllie, Barbara. "Nabokov and Cinema." In Connolly, *Cambridge Companion*.

Yochelson, Bonnie. *Berenice Abbott*: *Changing New York*. New York: The New Press and the Museum of the City of New York, 1997.

Zimmer, Dieter. The website of Dieter E. Zimmer. http://dezimmer.net/index.htm.

Zimmer, Dieter, and Sabine Hartmann. " 'The Amazing Music of Truth': Nabokov's Sources for Godunov's Central Asian Travels in *The Gift*." *Nabokov Studies* 7 (2002/2003): 33–74.

Zverev, Alexei. "Nabokov, Updike, and American Literature." In Alexandrov, *Garland Companion*.

Zweig, Paul. *Walt Whitman*: *The Making of the Poet*. New York: Basic Books, 1984.

NOTES

All translations from Russian are by Simon Belokowsky.

The names of research archives and of works by Nabokov and others are abbreviated as follows:

Bagazh *Bagazh: Memoirs of a Russian Cosmopolitan*, Nicolas Nabokov
Bakh Bakhmeteff Archive, Columbia University
Beinecke Beinecke Rare Book and Manuscript Library, Yale University
Berg Berg Collection of English and American Literature, New York Public Library
Boyd 1 *Vladimir Nabokov: The Russian Years*, Brian Boyd
Boyd 2 *Vladimir Nabokov: The American Years*, Brian Boyd
BS Bend Sinister
CE Conclusive Evidence
"Close Calls" "Close Calls and Fulfilled Dreams: Selected Entries from a Private Journal," Dmitri Nabokov
DBDV Dear Bunny Dear Volodya: The Nabokov-Wilson Letters
D.N. Dmitri Nabokov
DS Dead Souls, Garnett translation
EO Eugene Onegin, Nabokov translation
GIFT The Gift
Houghton Houghton Library, Harvard University
Letters Letters on Literature and Politics, Edmund Wilson
LITD Laughter in the Dark
LOC Library of Congress
NB Nabokov's Butterflies
NG Nikolai Gogol
PF Pale Fire
Schiff *Véra*, Stacy Schiff
SL Vladimir Nabokov: Selected Letters
SM Speak, Memory
SO Strong Opinions
TRLSK The Real Life of Sebastian Knight

Introduction

1 *"from 12 to 18 miles"*: DBDV, 116.
1 *specimens "on both sides"*: NB, 436–7.

1   *"man without pants"*: Ibid., 52.

1   *"My tongue is like"*: *DBDV*, 123. Nabokov was remarkably unvain about his teeth. To friend Roman Grynberg he wrote on December 25, 1943, "The dentist with a crack tore out all my top teeth; I walked with a bare mouth for the rest of the month and then made efforts to get used to the wide and absolute erasure. Now I have gotten used and only sometimes notice that my conversational partner quietly wipes either his cheek or brow." Bakh.

2   *Had they been in France:* Pitzer, 173–74. Jews were first interned at Drancy in August '41. The Nabokovs' voyage to America was the last of the SS *Champlain;* upon its return to France the ship was sunk at anchor off the French coast by collision with an air-laid German mine. The dangers of embarkation at Saint-Nazaire, the port where the Nabokovs caught the *Champlain*, are suggested by the fate of the HMT *Lancastria*, a British Cunard liner commandeered by the UK government and sunk off Saint-Nazaire a month after the Nabokovs embarked, with the loss of more than four thousand: it was the greatest loss of life ever in the sinking of a British ship (more than the combined losses of the *Titanic* and the *Lusitania*).

2   *"wondrous"*: Bakh, Véra to A. Goldenweiser, July 26, 1941.

2   *"During our motor-car"*: *DBDV*, 52.

4   *Nabokov's prolific tramping: The Gift*, which tells of cramped émigré life in an inimical German city, finds ways to send out tendrils of mountain adoration even so. The hero imagines his late father, an explorer of Central Asia, in high-mountain surroundings whenever he wishes to suggest the explorer's contentment, in an environment not unlike that of north-central Utah, in fact, a realm of snowmelt and granite. As if in uncanny foresight of his upcoming American adventures, Nabokov wrote (in 1938; first English translation, 1963) of "genuine Crimean rarities . . . to be found not here . . . but much higher, in the mountains, among the rocks"; of being "always off in wild lands, often mountainous, often high desert"; of "the constant feeling that our days here are only pocket money, farthings clinking in the dark, and that somewhere is stocked the real wealth, from which life should know how to get dividends in the shape of dreams, tears of happiness, distant mountains." *Gift*, 128–29, 136, 164.

5   *"one-sided conversation"*: *NB*, 52–53.

6   *reader of Whitman: BS*, 83. N. entitles a fictitious book "When Lilacs Last" in a fictitious review chapter written for but not finally added to *Conclusive Evidence. SL*, 105.

10 *taught to read English . . . before he learned to read Russian: SM*, 79. On p. 80, N. speaks of being with Miss Clayton, his governess, learning basic English from a grammar book; on p. 87, he is again with her and is aged four.

Chapter One

11 *trying to put together:* Schiff, 73–78.

11 *"afraid of living"*: Bakh, May 24, 1936. N.'s productions—his novels and novellas, with which this book is centrally concerned—are:

In Russian: (1926) *Mashenka* (Машенька); English translation: *Mary* (1970)
(1928) *Korol, dama, valet* (Король, дама, валет); English translation: *King, Queen, Knave* (1968)

(1930) *Zashchita Luzhina* (Защита Лужина); English translation: *The Luzhin Defense* or *The Defense* (1964); also adapted to film, *The Luzhin Defence* (2000)

(1930) *Sogliadatay* (Соглядатай), novella; first publication as a book, 1938; English translation: *The Eye* (1965)

(1932) *Podvig* (Подвиг [Deed]); English translation: *Glory* (1971)

(1933) *Kamera obskura* (Камера обскура); English translations: *Camera Obscura* (1936) *Laughter in the Dark* (1938)

(1934) *Otchaianie* (Отчаяние); English translation: *Despair* (1937, 1965)

(1936) *Priglashenie na kazn'* (Приглашение на Казнь [Invitation to an Execution]); English translation: *Invitation to a Beheading* (1959)

(1938) *Dar* (Дар); English translation: *The Gift* (1963)

(1939) *Volshebnik* (Волшебник); unpublished; English translation: *The Enchanter* (1986)

In English:

(1941) *The Real Life of Sebastian Knight*

(1947) *Bend Sinister*

(1955) *Lolita*; self-translated into Russian (1965)

(1957) *Pnin*

(1962) *Pale Fire*

(1969) *Ada or Ardor: A Family Chronicle*

(1972) *Transparent Things*

(1973) *Strong Opinions*

(1974) *Look at the Harlequins!*

(mid-1970s) *The Original of Laura*; fragmentary, published posthumously (2009)

12   *wrote her once a day:* Schiff, 78.

12   *"My life, my love":* SL, 22–24.

13   *pack of lies:* Both Boyd and Schiff say that the affair began in February '37, but Michael Maar, in his book *Speak, Nabokov* (2009), says it began in early '36. His evidence is the short story "Spring in Fialta," written April '36 and containing an "erotically irresistible" female "angel of death" figure such as would show up in many later works by Nabokov. There is already a figure of this kind in his novel *Laughter in the Dark* (first serialized in 1932), and the hero of *The Eye* (1930) has an affair with an irresistible, conscienceless woman whose husband beats him up.

13   *to judge by a story:* Boyd 1, 577n48.

13   *The crisis:* By some accounts, the Nabokovs' marriage was almost the last Russian marriage under the old dispensation, whereby the wife serves the immortal genius husband. Véra, in this version, joins the exalted ranks of Sophia Tolstoy, Anna Dostoevsky, Nadezhda Mandelstam, and Natalya Solzhenitsyn. Schiff's *Véra* is, among other things, an attempt to wrestle with this tradition and with Véra's extraordinary lifelong devotion in light of contemporary feminism.

13   *"Berlin is very fine":* Schiff, 92n.

13   *second child:* Ibid., 76.

14   *not a marriage:* Ibid., 139–41.

14   *two other novels:* Boyd 1, 407.

14   *"loose, shapeless":* SL, 13, 15.

14   *less than fully confident:* Boyd 1, 420. Altagracia de Jannelli was N.'s agent beginning 1934.

15 *Mandelstam's famous:* Prieto, "Reading."

15 *given him a vision:* Espey, "Speak."

15 *"Far as the eye":* Headless Horseman, 25.

16 *"The landscape":* Ibid., 26.

17 *"Through the curtains":* Ibid.

17 *"The edition I had":* SM, 195–96. There are traces of Mayne Reid in *Ada, Lolita, Glory,* and *The Gift:* Johnson, "Nabokov and Reid." Czesław Miłosz says that to "explore Reid's influence in Russia and Poland would call for a special study," noting that "Chekhov and other writers take for granted the reader's familiarity with the scenery of Reid's novels." *Emperor of the Earth,* 154–55. In a prose transla- tion, with commentaries, that N. wrote for Edmund Wilson about his poem "To Prince S. M. Kachurin" (1947), he says, "I am asking you, is it not time to return to the theme of the (Indian) bow-string, to the enchantment of the chaparral (the birds are already there) of which we read in The Headless Horseman? Is it not time to go back to Matagorda Canyon (place in Texas mountains) and there fall asleep on the burning stones—with the skin of one's face prickly dry from the aquarelle paints (with which we used to daub our faces when we played Indians) and with a crow's feather in one's hair? (in other words, let me take the direct road to America straight from my boyhood and the Wild West novels I used to love)." Barabtarlo, "Nabokov in the Wilson Archive."

17 *"Please find enclosed":* LOC.

18 *"We feel that":* Ibid.

18 *"occupy themselves":* Boyd 1, 409. In somewhat the same spirit, Ernest Hemingway, born the same year as Nabokov, writes in *A Farewell to Arms,* "There were many words that you could not stand to hear and finally only the names of places had dignity. . . . Abstract words such as glory, honor, courage, or hallow were obscene beside the concrete names of villages, the numbers of roads, the names of rivers, the numbers of regiments and the dates."

18 *Jannelli, who recognized:* Schiff, 94. Jannelli's phone number was Washington Square 1–3131. *Catalog of Copyright Entries,* LOC. According to a *New York Times* obituary, she died June 11, 1945, at 17 E. Ninth St.
  "As a child": LITD, 142–43.

20 *Faulkner being:* N. did read *Light in August,* at Edmund Wilson's urging. *DBDV,* 239–40. "I detest these puffs of stale romanticism," he wrote Wilson, likening Faulkner to Victor Hugo, with his "horrible combination of starkness and hyper- bole. . . . The book you sent me is one of the tritest and most tedious examples of a trite and tedious genre. The plot and those extravagant 'deep' conversations affect me as bad movies do. . . . I imagine that this kind of thing (white trash, velvety Negroes, those bloodhounds out of *Uncle Tom's Cabin* . . .) may be necessary in a social sense, but it is not literature. . . . The book's pseudo-religious rhythm I simply cannot stand. . . . Has *la grace* descended upon Faulkner too? Maybe you are just pulling my leg when you advise me to read him, or impotent Henry James, or the Rev. Eliot?"

20 *"with attractive":* Boyd 2, 14.

20 *"No, the 'Mr.' ":* LOC.

20 *"make you happy":* Ibid.

21 *"never, never, never":* Schiff, 96–97. Jannelli sent *The Gift* to two Russian readers, who had been hired by publishers to report on the novel's suitability for the American market. Both praised the book but advised against acquiring it. LOC. Alexander I. Nazaroff, a critic who had written about Sirin before, called the book "dazzlingly brilliant" but noted, "In its general type, *The Gift* sharply differs from that which hitherto was the common run of Nabokoff's novels. No matter how Nabokoff has always been fond of . . . tricks and artifices of composition and style, [his earlier books] are 'normal' novels [with] a well-constructed and developed dramatic plot . . . or are built 'biographically' around one central character which holds the reader's interest. . . . Now, in contradiction to this, *The Gift* is not a realistic novel. . . . It is an ultra-sophisticated and modernist piece of introspective, almost 'non-subjective' writing which . . . may be likened to James Joyce's *Ulysses*." Nabokov was flattered but irritated by this report. He argued that "there is a lot more in my book both for the connoisseur and the lay reader" than Nazaroff saw. *SL*, 27. Nazaroff's mix of praise with cool market calculation went to the painful crux for Nabokov. Leving, 257. He was faced with the torturous choice between the Joycean way, resoundingly acclaimed by sophisticated critics, and something else, something unknown, a more commercially promising approach, perhaps, more "American" style. It would be twelve years before he hit upon a method that was even simpler in the structural sense than that of his supposedly "normal," well-plotted earlier books. He had broken ground with *The Gift* but had to come back, far back, to one of the most comprehensible and simplest story forms, the voyage account—an American terrestrial *Odyssey*.

21 *"quite understand":* SL, 28–29.

22 *American Mercury:* By 1937–38 both Mencken and Nathan had left the magazine, though they contributed occasional pieces.

Chapter Two

23 *nice secure lectureship:* N. told an interviewer, "A first-rate college library with a comfortable campus around it is a fine milieu for a writer." *SO*, 99.

23 *captured a Blue:* Boyd 1, 488; *NB*, 637–38. His find was not a new species, but a hybrid of others already known. *NB*, 74.

23 *poor as they had ever:* Schiff, 94.

23 *Vladimir had inherited:* Boyd 1, 121. Conversion from Dollar Times, http://www.dollartimes.com/inflation/inflation.php.

24 *Russian Literary Fund:* Boyd 1, 489.

24 *gleeful speeder:* "Sergei Rachmaninoff," IMDb.com, http://www.imdb.com/name/nm0006245/bio; "Sergei Rachmaninoff," *Wikipedia*, http://en.wikipedia.org/wiki/Sergei_Rachmaninoff.

24 *definite plan:* Schiff, 96, 394n.

24 *"the family's hold":* Ibid., 96.

24 *faring remarkably:* Bagazh, 195.

25 *"twelve languages":* FBI file.

25 *"always late":* Saunders, 12. In his FBI file, which runs to 120 pages, one of the citizens asked to comment on Nicolas's political coloration makes an understandable

mistake, describing him as "anti-Socialist, and . . . his father held a high position in Russian circles prior to the Russian Revolution in 1917. His father was killed by the Bolsheviks." This is Vladimir's father, not Nicolas's (although V. D. Nabokov was killed not by Bolsheviks, either, but by fanatical rightists); Nicolas's father was still alive in '48, when the FBI conducted its investigation, and the informant, a Cornell history professor, casually recast Nicolas as the son of V. D. Nabokov because Nicolas himself had nearly done the same. In one of his early turnings toward the most famous personage in any room, Nicolas attached himself to V. D. Nabokov, sitting at his feet and through him taking on a rich infusion of cultural and historical savoir faire. V. D., distinguished legal scholar, one of the principals of the Constitutional Democratic (Kadet) Party in the Russian Duma, a party that contended strenuously with the Bolsheviks during the momentous events of 1917; V. D., editor-publisher of *Rech'* (Speech), the Kadet paper, an enemy of Russian absolutism in all its forms, son of an historically very, very high-up man himself (Dmitri Nikolaevich Nabokov, minister of justice under two tsars)—this same V. D. Nabokov was, as we learn in *Speak, Memory*, a refined aesthete as well as a politician, a sophisticated reader of modern literatures, a connoisseur of the plastic arts, and, unlike Vladimir, a music lover.

"On Sunday mornings we would take the Berlin subway," Nicolas writes in *Bagazh*, his colorful if not always reliable memoir, headed for "the general rehearsals of the Berlin Philharmonic Orchestra." This was shortly after the expulsion from Russia; V. D. had experienced "all the horrors . . . all the abominations of the Bolshevik orgy," and the collapse of his political fortunes and the loss of his personal fortune as well. Uncle and nephew were "the rare Nabokovs who truly loved music," and when they arrived at the hall where the orchestra practiced—next door to a smaller hall where would be staged, on the evening of March 28, 1922, the political meeting at which V. D. would be murdered—they stood together under a light in the back; V. D. always brought along a pocket score, and they followed the music together.

"The Nabokov flat in Berlin," Nicolas tells us, was "a center of émigré cultural life." Both V. D. and wife Elena Ivanovna had "brilliant minds, quick wits," and the "stimulating ambience of their home was for me a Russian haven and the intellectual catalyst I badly needed." In V. D.'s rooms the nephew encountered Konstantin Stanislavsky, co-founder of the Moscow Art Theatre and theorist of performance, as well as Olga Leonardovna Knipper-Chekhov, widow of the playwright and an actress destined to find success under the Soviets, as she had found it under the *ancien régime*. It may be pressing things to say that Nicolas encountered in his uncle and aunt's salon the model for a life of physical and spiritual proximity to talent, to influence, and honed there his own personal presentation, whereby he gained acceptance within an entire galaxy of twentieth-century cultural circles; in any case, the concertgoing and the study of scores represented "the first truly useful and lasting part of my musical education," and his adoration of his uncle was complete.

25 *well-known publisher father:* V. D. Nabokov published his son in *Rul'* and also published his nephew in its pages, naming him music critic. *Bagazh*, 107.

25 *"find it refreshing":* SO, 292.

26 *"extraordinary openness"*: *Bagazh*, 188.

26 *Mark Aldanov:* Boyd 1, 511; Boyd 2, 22.

26 his English subpar: Field, *Life in Part*, 195.

26 *two courses:* Boyd 2, 22.

27 *"nom de plume":* LOC.

27 *"Please allow me":* Bakh (translation: Belokowsky and author).

28 *largely on a loan:* Schiff, 103.

28 *follow him:* Ibid., 157.

28 *"fifty dead ... ruined":* V. D. Nabokov, "The Kishinev Bloodbath," Hoover Institution.

29 *next twenty years:* Judge, 13.

29 *"regime of oppression":* V. D. Nabokov, "Bloodbath."

29 *expressed his nonchalance: V.D. Nabokov and the Russian Provisional*, 3.

29 *"no courts for them":* V. D., Nabokov, "Bloodbath."

29 *a forecast:* "The historian Rufus Learsi once wrote that the 1903 Kishinev pogrom must be seen as 'a dress rehearsal' for the far bloodier wave of anti-Semitic violence two years later, following the 1905 revolution, which left some 3,000 Jews dead. But that violence was only a rehearsal for the genocidal fury of the 1918 Russian civil war, in which Ukrainian militias under Simon Petlura massacred as many as 200,000 Jews. And that, of course, was just a dress rehearsal for the Holocaust." Goldberg, "Kishinev 1903."

29 *Mendel Beilis:* V.D.N. also acted as unofficial legal counsel for the accused. Boyd 1, 104.

29 *Hessen:* Boyd 1, 206.

30 *"like many":* Ibid., 521; Boyd 2, 11.

30 *"assisting non-Jews":* Schiff, 105.

30 *"Jewish rescue organization":* Ibid.

30 *only half fare:* HIAS did not normally pay for passage of immigrants. R. Sanders, *Shores of Refuge*, 275.

30 *"splendid ship's funnel":* SM, 309–10.

31 *"We were given":* Field, *Life and Art*, 226. That there was an upgrade is not in dispute. Whether this was the work of a French officer or of a Jewish friend probably does not matter much in the fullness of time, but a source that Schiff cites for her account—a letter Véra wrote in 1958—says only, "We had a 1st-class cabin, but this was owed to an enviable [cabin] assignment. We had paid for third class," which leaves the identity of the upgrader unspecified. Bakh, Véra to A. Goldenweiser. Routinely, HIAS put a representative on board on the day of embarkation; problems of many kinds arose in the last hours. Perhaps Frumkin saw a chance to make the trip to America even more memorable for the Nabokovs; perhaps things had been planned this way, as a surprise.

Frumkin also, before the day of embarkation, took Nabokov around Paris to some wealthy Jewish families, soliciting donations, accompanied also by Mark Aldanov; in this way, Nabokov at last was able to put together the cost of his half-fare tickets. Boyd 1, 522.

Véra may have mistaken Frumkin's man for a French ship's officer. However, that seems unlikely. In matters of Jewish identity and survival, she was not prone to misperception. She was proudly, deeply, insistently Jewish; she had fallen out with an older sister over the sister's conversion to Catholicism, and in Berlin, as the Nazis came to power, and later in America, as the Nabokovs ran into homegrown anti-Semitism here and there, she let the world know that she was Jewish—she would not let the world *not* know. Boyd 1, 403; Boyd 2, 363.

31 *"Your letter":* Berg.

32 *had been a bestseller:* Boyd 2, 365.

32 *classic writer's idyl:* Ibid., 407–8. Though N. is credited as the screenwriter of Kubrick's *Lolita*, Kubrick wrote another version and mostly shot from that. N. was fond of the film, calling it "absolutely first-rate," singling out the actors for "the highest praise" and declaring the killing of Quilty a "masterpiece." While acknowledging that "I had nothing to do with the actual production," he insisted he had had a role that was more than nominal: "All I did was write the screenplay, a preponderating portion of which was used by Kubrick." *SO*, 21. At other times, he was not so sure about the size of his contribution; see "Vladimir Nabokov's Script for Stanley Kubrick's *Lolita*," Open Culture, http://www.openculture.com/2014/06/vladimir-nabokovs-script-for-stanley-kubricks-lolita.html.

32 *"ghastly":* Boyd 1, 486.

32 *disputed the chicken:* Schiff, 104.

32 *matter of being desperate:* N. implored an organization that assisted émigrés to help secure his family's passage to New York; the woman he spoke to remembered his frank "panic," his "wild fear at the prospect of war," which made upon her an unpleasant impression. Field, *Life and Art*, 197, 393.

Chapter Three

33 *Natalia had signed an affidavit:* Interview with Ivan Nabokov, April 25, 2013. Serge Koussevitzky's name was also on the emigration documents, according to Ivan. Mikhail Karpovich also "stood surety" for N. Boyd 2, 14.

33 *Madison . . . West Eighty-seventh:* Véra's notes, Berg. Natalia secured a scholarship to the nearby Walt Whitman School for Dmitri, who entered first grade in fall '40 and was soon promoted to second grade, despite having no English to begin with.

33 *"the first part of it excellent":* New York Times, May 1, 1940, 1.

33 *"Flanders pocket":* New York Times, May 28, 1940, 1.

33 *"heavy tidings":* New York Times, May 29, 1940, 1.

33 *morning was cloudy:* New York Times, May 28, 1940, 1. The page one weather notice reads, "Mostly cloudy, with scattered showers and little change in temperatures today and tomorrow." An article on the 1940 season of the New York World's Fair noted that it had been "hounded by rain and unfavorable weather" for over two weeks: Ibid., 25. thirty thousand: Goldstein, *Helluva Town*, 92. The time period of the thirty thousand arrivals from France is summer '40 to spring '41.

34 *Lévi-Strauss:* Ibid., 97.

34 *Léger:* Ibid., 100.

34 *lilac tinge:* Boyd 2, 11.

34 *synesthete:* SM, 34–35.

34 *"I simply loved":* NB, 120; Boyd 1, 259.

34 *influenced the direction:* Boyd, "Nabokov, Literature, Lepidoptera," in NB, 24–25.

34 *Comstock was:* Zimmer, http://www.d-e-zimmer.de/eGuide/Biographies.htm.

35 *this was a method:* NB, 41.

35 *Andrey Avinoff:* Hellman, *New Yorker,* August 21, 1948, 32–47; Boyd 2, 16. Avinoff's *New Yorker* profile notes that "He became an American citizen a few years after settling down here [in 1917]; he had begun to feel at home in this country rather quickly, partly because many American butterflies, such as the red admiral, the mourning cloak, the painted lady, and certain varieties of cabbages, skippers, yellow swallowtails, and fritillaries, have identical counterparts in Russia."

35 *Avinoff was another devotee:* Hellman, 36; "Andrey Avinoff," *Wikipedia,* http://en.wikipedia.org/wiki/Andrey_Avinoff.

35 *"I have hunted":* SM, 125–26.

36 *"Frankly":* SO, 46–47.

36 *"untrammeled, rich":* Lolita, 335.

36 *"should not ignore":* SO, 40.

36 *"extensive and elaborate":* SM, 135.

37 *drawn to the newer ones:* SM, 122.

37 *"Spring was in full tilt":* Hamsun, *Pan,* 19–20.

37 *"Sphinx moths":* Ibid., 32–33.

38 *"it was many years":* SM, 127.

38 *"On the other side":* Ibid., 138.

39 *"soaking, ice-cold":* Ibid., 121.

39 *"wound he cannot":* Boyd 1, 8.

39 *"Already it was warmer":* Faulkner, "The Bear," 57.

39 *"gained absolute control":* SM, 123.

39 *"landscape lives twice":* SO, 40.

40 *scene out of:* Schiff, 109. N. said of Turgenev that he wrote a "weak blond prose." DBDV, 59.

40 *put him in touch:* Nicolas Nabokov to Edmund Wilson, August 1941, Beinecke.

41 *"My cousin Nicholas":* DBDV, 33.

41 *those for whom he acted:* Meyers, 248–50.

41 *his favorite:* Ibid., 166.

41 *"That was awfully sweet":* Nicolas Nabokov to Edmund Wilson, February 8, 1944, Beinecke.

42 *"It occurred to me":* Nicolas Nabokov to Edmund Wilson, December 7, 1947.

42 *"I hope (so much)":* Nicolas Nabokov to Edmund Wilson, December 1950.

42 *"The seven years":* LOC. The review never appeared in the *New Republic.* DBDV, 46.

43 *"in the hope":* Pitzer, 169.

43 *noted in a letter:* Meyers, 223.

44 *"There are today":* Wilson, "An Appeal to Progressives," *New Republic,* January 14, 1931.

44 *"a rending":* Wilson, *Shores of Light,* 496, 498.

44 *his reportage:* Packer, *New Yorker,* April 29, 1913, 70.

44 *reported his earnings:* Dabney, 173–74.

44 *"kept telling us":* Wilson, *Shores*, 499.

44 *"more and more impressed":* Ibid.

46 *"dingy":* Wilson, *Red, Black, Blond, and Olive*, 167.

46 *"prairies and wild rivers":* Dabney, 206.

Chapter Four

47 *"one hundred lectures":* SO, 5.

47 *his 1922 translation:* Boyd 2, 25; *SO*, 286–87.

47 *"a purring success":* DBDV, 47; Boyd 2, 26.

48 *from all the migrations:* Véra, 115.

48 *sciatica:* Ibid., 113.

48 *system of numbered:* Skidmore, *Restless Americans*, 9.

48 *3,600 Jews:*
http://www.holocaustresearchproject.org/nazioccupation/frenchjews.html.

48 *"For almost 25":* DBDV, 53.

48 *called it Pon'ka:* Zimmer, http://www.d-e-zimmer.de/HTML/whereabouts.htm.
The Nabokovs called Dorothy "Dasha." Véra's Diary 1958–59, Berg.

48 *Nabokov compiled:* LOC.

49 *Nabokovs stayed:* Boyd 2, 140; interview with Richard Buxbaum, August 14, 2013.

49 *located near rail stations:* Belasco, 46.

49 *motor courts common:* Jakle, 45; Belasco, 138.

49 *two staff scientists:* Interview with David Grimaldi, January 5, 2013; Suzanne Rab Green, e-mail to author, May 22, 2013.

50 *close reader: Lolita* describes two periods of extended travel by car, and for his travels in fictional 1947–48 Humbert Humbert relies extensively on the three-volume AAA *Travel Guide*, in particular the "Western" volume. Humbert calls it "the Tour Book of the Automobile Association" and uses it to find accommodations and as a source of roadside diversions to amuse a young girl. *Lolita*, 153, 162, 163, 164, 166. Through continuous use the *Travel Guide* becomes "an atrociously crippled tour book" without a cover, "almost a symbol of my torn and tattered past," Humbert says. See also Zimmer, http://www.d-e-zimmer.de/LolitaUSA/Trip1.htm.

51 *"During our":* DBDV, 52.

51 *"Beyond the tilled":* Lolita, 161.

52 *too much staring blue:* Dirig, p. 6 of 7.

52 *paint Dmitri's face:* Schiff, 120.

52 *"No, I am . . . houses by the road":* Berg.

52 *"odd attachment":* Ibid.

53 *"am driving off":* DBDV, 51.

53 *"celebrated American dentist":* Boyd 1, 84.

53 *wettest year:* "Texas Annual Rainfall," Texas Weather, http://web2.airmail.net/danb1/annualrainfall.htm.

53 *took specimens:* Green, e-mail to author.

53 *"lovely":* Berg.

53 *huddled in the car:* Boyd 1, 29.

53 *slushy mule track:* N. to Comstock, February 20, 1942, Berg.

53 *working for the Atchison:* Colter's direct employer was the Fred Harvey Company.

53 *Colter's mix:* Gerke, "Bright Angel Cabins"; "Bright Angel Lodge," *Wikipedia*, http://en.wikipedia.org/wiki/Bright_Angel_Lodge.

54 *rustic style:* "National Park Service Rustic," *Wikipedia*, http://en.wikipedia.org/wiki/National_Park_Service_rustic.

54 *Hopi House:* "Hopi House,"*Wikipedia*, http://en.wikipedia.org/wiki/Hopi_House. N.'s travels in the West and Southwest did not provoke in him a marked interest in Native Americans. Unlike D. H. Lawrence, to take an example of another foreign writer who also traveled west, N. did not sense a "crisis of consciousness" in civilized modern man, a severing from primordial "blood knowledge." For N., nothing was wrong with modern man in the aggregate—nothing that had not always been wrong—and besides, little of use could be said about man in the aggregate. Specific individuals might be cruel, evil, sociopathic—it had ever been thus. There is no historical irony in Nabokov.

54 *among his captures:* N. to Comstock, February 20, 1942, Berg; Boyd 2, 28–29.

54 *consummation long wished:* SM, 136. The specimen was not of a new species but of a subspecies of an insect that had not formerly been known to range north of Mexico. The subspecies is now called *Cyllopsis pertepida dorothea*: NB, 9.

54 *"I found it":* N., "On Discovering a Butterfly," *New Yorker*, May 15, 1943, 26.

54 *further stops:* Green, e-mail to author, January 7, 2013.

Chapter Five

55 *pseudo-pueblos:* Adkins. Southwest Indian dwellings graced the St. Louis World's Fair (1904), the Panama-Pacific International Exposition (1915), the Chicago World's Fair (1933–34), and the Golden Gate International Exposition (1939–40).

55 *"Ivestigate and you will":* Agee, "Roadside," 174.

55 *"A good cave":* Ibid.

56 *Humbert, seeking distractions: Lolita*, 160.

56 *"slow suffusion": Lolita*, 161.

56 *butterflies at his feet:* N. to Dobuzhinski, July 25, 1941, Bakh.

56 *comfortable deck chair:* DBDV, 52.

56 *swimsuit:* Boyd 2, 33.

56 *cactus-green Buick:* Perret, 87.

57 *"girls are quite attractive":* O'Brien, 114. JFK's book developed out of his undergraduate thesis at Harvard. Two professional writers, both associates of his father, helped turn the thesis into a marketable book, but the student paper already presents a sophisticated argument about the disadvantages of democracies at times of impending war, and as the son of a notoriously isolationist father, who made impolitic and defeatist statements to reporters ("If you can find out why the British are standing up against the Nazis you're a better man than I am"), young Kennedy wished to assert a different position while remaining a loyal son. O'Brien, 103–9. The debate over intervention dominated the season of N.'s arrival in the States; it

intensified with Dunkirk and the defeat of France (Paris taken June 14, 1940) and persisted until nearly the end of '41.

57 *fury of effort:* Boyd 2, 29.

57 *a froth:* Ibid.; Field, *Life and Art*, 209.

57 *"I assign myself":* Bakh. Pushkin had called translations "the post-horses of civilization." Boyd 2, 32.

58 *Laughlin offered:* Boyd 2, 33. The advance paid was $150. Laughlin acquired *Sebastian Knight* on the recommendation of hired reader Delmore Schwartz. Schwartz was also an astute appreciator of Wilson's prose; see "The Writing of Edmund Wilson," *Accent* 2 (Spring 1942): 177–86.

58 *limpid and a bit cool:* Boyd 2, 33, paraphrasing a letter from N. to Aldanov, July 20, 1941.

58 *"I have a fear":* DBDV, 49.

58 *sitting in:* Schiff, 116n. He also gave a few lectures to the campus at large.

58 *"prime object of a playwright":* Boyd 2, 30.

58 *as a speaker, charismatic:* Ibid., 32. One student recalled, "He shared with us his creative activity and experience. Never was there richer fare in any course taught on a college campus, but it was as impossible to reduce to notes as to convert a Rolls-Royce into tin cans with a tack hammer."

58 *became friends:* Schiff, 117. The Nabokovs especially enjoyed socializing with Yvor Winters and his wife, Janet Lewis, Yvor being the well-known poet and critic and Janet the extraordinary poet and novelist. Boyd 1, 33. Janet Lewis was N.'s exact contemporary (1899–1998) and author of *The Indians in the Woods* and *The Wife of Martin Guerre*, among other titles. *Martin Guerre* was published the year of N.'s residence at Stanford. Its radiant lucidity and casually worn moral weight, qualities intrinsic to its clever working of a mysterious plot, make it one of the distinguished twentieth-century novels and one of the few fine American novels of the day to have escaped Wilson's ken, Nabokov's also. (Another, of the same order, was Henry Roth's *Call It Sleep*.) See Dick Davis, "Obituary: Janet Lewis," *Independent*, December 15, 1998, http://www.independent.co.uk/arts-entertainment/obituary-janet-lewis-1191516.html.

58 *"tall, narrow man":* Haven, "Lolita Question," *Stanford* magazine.

59 *"Ah, if only":* Gift, 186.

59 *stark prototype:* The American movie comedy *Dirty Rotten Scoundrels* (1988), directed by Frank Oz and starring Michael Caine and Steve Martin, is another example, perhaps on a lesser level of attainment, of a creative project coming into sharper focus, finding its definitive style, in a second attempt, the first being Ralph Levy's adequate but unsurprising *Bedtime Story* (1964), with David Niven and Marlon Brando playing the Caine and Martin parts. Two of the three writers of *Scoundrels* were also writers of *Bedtime*. The female lead in the remake, played by Glenne Headly, has been given a richer part, but the real discovery is in the confident, excited, absurdist performances of Caine and Martin, who act rather than impersonate themselves as celebrities.

60 *centrally about this matter:* Amis, "Levity," 5.

60 *"participate in orgies":* Field, *Life and Art*, 210–11. California natives may scratch their heads at the suggestion of the rural San Francisco Peninsula of the Depression

years, a place of struggling truck farms and nut orchards, as a site for Sadeian outrages on a weekly basis.

60 *"a long infection":* Haven.

61 *"with a shrug":* TRLSK, 14.

61 *died in the Neuengamme:* Pitzer, 306, 310.

62 *"mortal quest for another's":* Boyd 1, 499.

62 *most severe modernist:* Foster, ix–xii. Modernism shows first, clearly, with *Invitation to a Beheading*, published two years before the writing of *Sebastian Knight*. Foster demonstrates—in the most thoughtful and comprehensive study of N.'s literary inheritances—that N. was decisively on the Gallic side of things, temperamentally attuned to Proust and Bergson (his ideas on time, on memory, on art) and allergic to the Anglo-American modernism of Pound and Eliot, with its devaluation of specific character and promotion of a "mythical method." N. was opposed to depth psychologies, to all one-size theories of sexuality and the unconscious. His foundational gift was for the quiddity of things. From Proust he borrowed, excitedly elaborated, the mixing of fictional and autobiographical elements, and also the approach that begins in involuntary memory and proceeds to a purposeful unearthing of the past. The characteristic flow of Proust's prose, with currents of narrative suddenly onrushing to a conclusion that stuns, finds correspondences in Nabokov. N. continually rewrote himself (through translations and new editions), and his recapture via memory of the homeland he lost resembles Joyce's recall of Dublin. He was shaped as a writer also by the "modernism of underdevelopment," the Russian responses to contact with the destabilizing West; the Petersburg tradition of Pushkin, Gogol, Dostoevsky, Bely, and Mandelstam was his lifeblood. The intertextual gestures in his works are an honoring of, an endless playing with, these myriad literary inheritances.

63 *a California vacation:* Boyd 2, 33.

63 *family seemed fine:* Schiff, 118. Many of the Nabokovs' friends and relations were trapped in Europe, destined to die there or escape only with great difficulty. From the $150 advance for *Sebastian Knight*, they sent $50 to Anna Feigin, Véra's cousin, who was marooned in southern France. Schiff, 117.

63 *much enjoyed:* Schiff, 115.

63 *"beauty spots":* Berg.

63 *Bertrand, almost old enough:* Schiff, 313.

63 *character out of an American novel:* John Buehrens, "Famous Consultant and Forgotten Minister," UUWorld, January 2001, www.uuworld.org/2004/01/lookingback.html; McKinney, 149–51. Thompson in some ways followed a path pioneered by W. E. B. Du Bois, who earned a Harvard B.A. (as Thompson did) before undertaking graduate studies that took him to Berlin. Thompson lived and worked in Berlin for a time, like Du Bois. Thompson's turn to business might have been influenced by Booker T. Washington's gospel of black entrepreneurship. Thompson apprenticed himself to Frederick Winslow Taylor and became a lecturer at the Harvard Business School. He is frequently credited with having invented the occupation of international business consultant.

65 *In 1917, Thompson published:* McKinney, 149.

65 *driving an aged Studebaker:* Schiff, 313.

65 *studying biochemistry:* He had earlier studied it at Harvard.

65 *new '41 Studebaker:* Schiff, photograph following 210; the photo shows a 1941 Studebaker Commander. See John's Old Car and Truck Pictures, http://oldcarandtruckpictures.com/Studebaker/1941_Studebaker_Commader_4_DoorSedan-jan20.jpg. The Studebaker Co. sold a model between 1927 and '37 that was called the Dictator, ostensibly because Studebaker models "dictated the standard" that all other automobiles followed; there might have been a nod intended to the contemporary political meaning of *dictator,* too—other Studebaker models had the names President, Commander, and Champion.

65 *by his ninth decade:* Buehrens, "Famous Consultant"; "Obituary," *Academy of Management Journal,* 66.

65 *Muir being in some ways:* Roper, "High Country," 9.

65 *designed the Yosemite Museum:* "Yosemite Museum," Yosemite National Park, National Park Service, http://www.nps.gov/yose/historyculture/yosemite-museum.htm.

65 *stepped on a sleeping bear:* Boyd 2, 33.

66 *like the motor camps:* *Yosemite National Park Guidebook,* National Park Service, 1940. The guidebook for '41 has many more photos but has stopped quoting exact prices for lodging.

66 *made day trips:* *Yosemite National Park Guidebook,* National Park Service, 1941.

67 *when the Nabokovs came:* Pavlik, 187.

67 *September is blissful:* "Temperatures & Precipitation," Yosemite National Park, National Park Service, http://www.nps.gov/yose/planyourvisit/climate.htm.

67 *drove them back:* Boyd 2, 33–34.

67 *Russian speakers have been shown:* Winawer.

67 *"how wonderful was":* Bakh.

67 *a restless people:* Skidmore.

67 *the kind of traveler:* Berg.

68 *to own a cabin:* SO, 28.

68 *"little bit of desert":* DBDV, 52.

Chapter Six

69 *arrived by train:* Schiff, 118.

69 *established in an apartment:* Ibid., 119.

69 *"just rolled back":* DBDV, 53. The house was built in 1934. "19 Appleby Rd, Wellesley, MA 02482," Zillow, http://www.zillow.com/homedetails/19-Appleby-Rd-Wellesley-MA–02482/56617394_zpid.

69 *"I got that Guggenheim":* DBDV, 106–7.

70 *to say that Nabokov:* Boyd 2, 61; Meyers, 159.

70 *"a big spaseebo":* DBDV, 44–45.

70 *"I am leaving":* Ibid., 42.

70 *"In doing future":* Ibid., 34.

71 *"All Americans are":* Boyd 2, 21.

71 *Wilson's stewardship:* A writer of N.'s energy and ambition was unlikely to remain unpublished in America. But Wilson's mentorship made a difference—a difference in the potential size and scope of the career. Publication in obscure journals, no Guggenheims at dire moments, no real earnings from writing, no introductions to

the likes of Katharine White, J. Laughlin, Edward Weeks, William Shawn: this conceivable alternate career history might have affected not only which books N. was able to publish but the audacity of those he was able to conceive.

71 *"Nabokov was introduced":* Boyd 2, 21.

71 *"My English novel":* DBDV, 52.

71 *"I don't want to mention":* Ibid., 50.

72 *"Could you god-father":* Ibid., 51.

72 *"I get aboard my boat":* Ibid., 166.

72 *close to Fitzgerald since:* Meyer, 259. Wilson deeply grieved his lost friends. He served Fitzgerald superbly as posthumous editor and wrote a profound elegy of Rosenfeld. Wilson, *Classics and Commercials*, 503–519.

72 *"You are one of":* DBDV, 237.

73 *other male friends:* N. to Dobuzhinsky, Grynberg, and Karpovich, in Bakh.

73 *"I hope you":* DBDV, 105.

73 *"if I keep talking":* Ibid., 50.

73 *"an absolute ball":* Boyd 2, 26.

73 *"my closest":* Field, *VN*, 57.

73 *"without the impetus . . . forsake":* LOC.

74 *"I am expected to participate . . . mimetic phenomena":* DBDV, 54.

74 *Shortly after Pearl:* Schiff, 120.

74 *by spring of '43:* DBDV, 105; Schiff, 125.

74 *only after she had left:* Boyd 2, 42–43. While the Wellesley College president was finding Nabokov not quite desirable, members of the Italian, Spanish, German, and French departments found him entirely captivating and wrote to the dean asking that he be retained, and members of the English department organized a petition drive on his behalf.

74 *community-wide addresses:* Boyd 2, 41.

75 *"little white-bearded":* Boyd 1, 34.

75 *"Have you noticed":* DBDV, 54. In '58, on a summer trip that took them to Glacier National Park, near the Montana-Alberta border, Vladimir and Véra read *War and Peace* to each other while sitting out days of bad weather in a cabin. Nabokov later told an interviewer that they gave up because the book now struck them as childish and old-fashioned: Boyd 2, 362.

75 *match the passage of time:* Ibid., 41.

76 *"not go into the mill":* Hall, 13.

76 *"none of this":* Laughlin, "Taking a Chance on Books: What I Learned at the Ezuversity," National Book Awards acceptance speech, 1992, National Book Foundation, http://www.nationalbook.org/nbaacceptspeech_jlaughlin.html#. VEoygOe6XdA.

76 *the independent:* Hall, 13.

76 *poorly translated:* Boyd 2, 45.

76 *"dry shit":* SL, 41.

76 *"Russian literature was purblind":* NG, 86.

77 *"The big overgrown":* DS, Garnett, 158–59.

77 *"An extensive . . . dark bird":* N., *Lectures on Russian Literature*, 25.

78 *"Strands of hop":* NG, 87–88.

78 *"tendrils faintly stirring":* DS, Garnett, 159.

79 *was the focus of a question:* Boyd 1, 194.

80 *"I ride my balloon-tired":* D.N., "Close Calls," 303–4.

80 *"wonderful thing will happen":* Ibid., 304.

81 *"I sit on the lawny grounds":* Ibid., 304–5.

81 *"dingy":* N., "Introduction," *BS*, xi.

81 *under old lady:* Ibid.

81 *looking trim:* SL, 58. A suit with a red jockey cap might have provoked some amusement among Dmitri's American schoolmates. Véra, in a letter to friend Elena Levin, also spoke of looking out at the world from that window on Craigie Circle. Houghton.

81 *he informs Elena:* SL, 58.

81 *gone to weeds:* Ibid.

81 *transformation of Harvard:* Ireland. So transformed was Harvard that by 1944 graduating seniors numbered nineteen, the fewest since 1753. Harvard's turn toward war research led to the development of the Mark I "Automatic Sequence Controlled Calculator," a protocomputer used for Manhattan Project calculations, and to the development of Harvard's first cyclotron, crucial aspects of sonar, fiberglass, napalm, chaff (strips of aluminum foil used to dupe enemy radar), blood plasma derivatives, synthesized quinine, antimalarial drugs, and new treatments for burns and shock. Twenty-seven thousand Harvard students, faculty, staff, and alumni served during the war; 697 died.

82 *"My museum":* SL, 58–59.

82 *fourteen-hour days:* DBDV, 145; Schiff, 128.

82 *"already in the blue darkness":* SL, 59.

82 *"Funny—to know Russian":* DBDV, 72.

83 *"book is progressing slowly":* Ibid., 75.

84 *"I envy so bitterly":* Ibid., 100.

84 *"urge to write":* Schiff, 128n.

84 *Isaiah Berlin:* Kelly, 51. Berlin's conversation was with Vera Weizmann, Chaim Weizmann's wife.

84 *sixty dollars a month:* Schiff, 129.

84 *"scene is unpleasant":* NG, 2.

85 *The book develops:* Ibid., 36–37.

85 *"strange; it is only your":* NG, 140.

86 *"amusing to think":* DBDV, 76.

86 *first scientific papers:* N. had previously published two other entomological papers in America. *NB*, 238–43. In Europe he had also published earlier papers: Remington, 279, 283n9.

86 *"am taking advantage":* N. to Comstock, February 20, 1942, Berg.

86 *English was thereafter:* SO, 5.

87 *"A broad cinereous":* NB, 254. By sending this article (and other science writings) to Wilson, N. might have overtaxed the professional literary man, who read some of N.'s later literary productions hastily, almost casually, perhaps out of habit. N.'s science writing was often quite charming as well as precise.

87 *developed a system:* Boyd 2, 67–68.

87 *his butterfly prose:* SM, 134, 136.

Chapter Seven

88 *"married a genius"*: Boyd 2, 46.

88 *he set off in October:* Schiff, 123.

88 *"creepily silent melancholic"*: N., "Russian Professor," 104.

89 *"Arrived here, on"*: Ibid.

89 *"After lunch"*: Ibid., 102.

89 *or Whitman's when:* Roper, *Drum*, 37–38.

90 *"since at the numerous stations"*: N., "Russian Professor," 100.

90 *makings of another book:* Ibid., 100, 102–3.

90 *weirdly foliaged:* This was the Okefenokee Swamp. Boyd 2, 51.

90 *shows himself as a bumbler, too:* N., "Russian Professor," 104.

90 *iconic African Americans:* Ibid., 103. N. memorably sketched Du Bois in a letter to Wilson: "Celebrated Negro scholar and organizer. 70 years old, but looks 50. Dusky face, grizzled goatee, nice wrinkles, big ears,—prodigiously like a White Russian General in mufti played sympathetically by Emil Jannings. Piebald hands. Brilliant talker, with an old-world touch. Tres gentilhomme. Smokes special Turkish cigarettes. Charming and distinguished. . . . Told me that when he went to England he was listed as 'Colonel' on the Channel boat, because his name bore the addition 'Col.' on his passport." *DBDV*, 97.

90 *racial segregation: SO*, 48.

90 *"and the prosperity"*: N., "Russian Professor," 102.

91 *"I need not tell you"*: *DBDV*, 2; Boyd 2, 644.

91 *"cost me more trouble"*: *SL*, 45.

92 *"art-speech"*: Lawrence, 13.

92 *"which belongs"*: Ibid.

92 *Lawrence's book cost him: Classic American* took Lawrence seven years to write, longer than any of his other works except *Women in Love*. The essays changed a great deal over time; at first they were cautious and sober, but in the end they achieved a tone "notoriously flippant, opinionated, disrespectful and informal," not unlike the tone of *Nikolai Gogol*. Neil Roberts, "Studies in Classic."

92 *"There is a new feeling"*: Lawrence, 14.

93 *Style is what makes meaning:* Lawrence's two chapters on Melville in *Classic American* contributed substantially to the rediscovery of Melville in the twenties. Delbanco, 24. N. performed a similar unearthing with *Nikolai Gogol*. Lawrence wrote an essay, "À Propos of 'Lady Chatterley's Lover,'" after the 1928 publication of his famous novel; it might have suggested to N. the postscript he wrote, "On a Book Entitled 'Lolita,'" in '56, although the two essays are otherwise quite different.

93 *gotten his Guggenheim:* Boyd 2, 61. The grant was for the writing of a novel. *Bend Sinister* at this point bore the working title "The Person from Porlock," that person being the untimely visitor who supposedly interrupted Coleridge while he was transcribing *Kubla Khan*, which had come to him entire in a dream and which, as a result, remained unfinished.

93 *"near a place which"*: *DBDV*, 111.

93 *"going to tell me"*: Ibid.

93 *tumbling canyon:* The canyon, commonly called Little Cottonwood Canyon, is popular among rock climbers. The local cliffs contributed giant blocks of quartz monzonite to the construction of the Salt Lake Temple of the LDS Church. "Little Cottonwood Canyon," *Wikipedia*, http://en.wikipedia.org/wiki/Little_Cottonwood_Canyon.

93 *"a propensity. . . . butterflies are to me":* SL, 58–59.

93 *"vain, quick-tempered":* Ibid., 59.

94 *The waywardness:* Berg.

94 *"anxious to take a course":* N. to Jakobson, January 28, 1952, Berg.

95 *"landlord and the poet":* DBDV, 116.

95 *"Well . . . read further":* NG, 151–52.

96 *especially keen disregard:* N.'s savaging of other writers is so consistent a feature of his literary discourse that it probably served many purposes, professional as well as psychological. It may be that the Russian literary milieu rejoiced in such vituperation, but other writers of the emigration were more temperate. Speaking of Mark Aldanov, N. wrote, "I am sorry that you discussed my poem with friend Aldanov who for twenty years has been eyeing my literature with a kind of suspicious awe under the impression that my chief business was to demolish brother-writers. . . . Aldanov regards literature as a sort of enormous Pen Club or Masonic Lodge binding talented and *talentlos* writers alike to a smug contract of mutual good-will . . . assistance and favorable reviews." *DBDV*, 137.

    N. did not mellow with age. His denunciations became more performative—N. playing himself—but their effect was to define worthwhile writing as excludingly as had the social-reform critics he denounced in *The Gift*. There is a plant of the American Southwest that N. knew well, called creosote bush, that is long-lived and that creates a dead zone around itself, outcompeting all other species by the efficiency of its root system and by producing chemicals that poison them.

96 *Faulkner he dismissed:* DBDV, 236–37. "I am appalled by your approach to Faulkner," he wrote Wilson. "It is incredible that you should take him seriously . . . that you should be so fascinated by his message (whatever it is) as to condone his artistic mediocrity."

96 *"As to Hemingway":* SO, 80.

97 *influenced American film:* Among American movies of the past twenty-five years, *Pulp Fiction* and *No Country for Old Men*, for instance.

97 *"liked very much Mary's":* DBDV, 117n3.

97 *read, and lustily hated:* Ibid., 116, 117n4.

97 *"a he-man":* Ibid., 116.

97 *"Twenty years ago":* Ibid.

97 *probably McTeague:* Ibid., 117n6.

97 *marks of desolation:* NG, 151.

97 *"delicate sunset was framed":* NG, 151.

98 *known as pugs:* NB, 12.

98 *"wrote every day":* Time morgue file, Berg.

98 *with a pen:* DBDV, 115. "He went to the bathrm, took a cold shower . . . and tingling with mental eagerness and feeling comfortable and clean in pyjamas and dressing gown, let his fountain pen suck in its fill." *BS*, 170.

98   *weather kept them indoors:* Schiff, 127.

98   *"a draggle-eared black":* NG, 153.

98   *"I climb easily":* DBDV, 115–16.

98   *Lone Peak the most arduous:* "Lone Peak," SummitPost.org, http://www. summitpost.org/lone-peak/151267.

98   *"white shorts and sneakers":* Time morgue file, Berg.

98   *"incredibly steep . . . sheer wall":* "Lone Peak 11,253'," Climb-Utah.org, http:// climb-utah.com/WM/lonepeak.htm.

98   *"lost his footing":* Time morgue file, Berg.

99   *"footing and began to slide":* Hall, "Ezra Pound Said."

99   *sent a squad car out:* Schiff, 127.

99   *"trudged and climbed some 600":* DBDV, 117.

100   *"living in wild eagle country":* Bakh, August 6, 1943; NB, 289–90.

100   *"In the meantime":* DBDV, 294–95.

100   *Unsoeld was hired:* Leamer, 50–51. The next fall, Unsoeld began graduate theology studies at Oberlin.

101   *well-regarded doctoral thesis:* Roper, *Fatal Mountaineer*, 47. Like Unsoeld, N. read Bergson carefully and held him in esteem.

Chapter Eight

102   *sharp decompression:* DBDV, 294.

102   *"work on the Blues":* Ibid., 126.

102   *"milk shakes and banana":* Bagazh, 188.

103   *"poignantly authentic":* Ibid., 191.

103   *"Not only their tunes":* Ibid., 190.

103   *"has had a serious":* DBDV, 132.

104   *collaborate on "a book":* Ibid., 121.

104   *"You may find them":* Ibid., 118.

104   *"I am returning":* Ibid., 119. On November 23, 1943, N. wrote, "It is wonderful that anybody could write about Russian letters as you do."

104   *superb journalism:* Wilson also read Prince Mirsky on Pushkin. DBDV, 74, 79.

104   *gestures of respect:* Only with Wilson did N. seriously consider co-writing a book. DBDV, 121–22.

104   *"So I am still looking":* Ibid., 76.

104   *"If I had the leisure":* Ibid., 78.

105   *"the whole book":* Ibid., 120. Nabokov and Wilson did in the end author a book together, the posthumous *The Nabokov-Wilson Letters* (1979), later expanded to become *Dear Bunny, Dear Volodya* (2001). In '66, N. told an interviewer, "The only time I ever collaborated with any writer was when I translated with Edmund Wilson Pushkin's 'Mozart and Salieri' for the *New Republic*." SO, 99.

105   *"An obscure paper":* DBDV, 132, 142.

105   *"Are you writing":* DBDV, 112.

105   *"eager to see . . . excellent":* Ibid., 138.

106   *written two years later:* BS, introduction, xi; Boyd 2, 91.

106   *"programmatic refusal":* Boyd 2, 106.

106 *"There at the door"*: BS, 22.

107 *"The main theme"*: Ibid., xiv.

107 *A secondary character:* Ember is the translator of Krug's *The Philosophy of Sin*, which makes Krug successful in America—"banned in four states and a best seller in the rest." *BS*, 26.

107 *Wilson's failure:* Sweeney, "Sinistral Details." The McCarthy novel was *The Company She Keeps*.

107 *Wilson, when the book:* In '52, when N. worked a reference to Wilson into a story published in the *New Yorker*, Wilson wrote, "I'm sorry you told me that there was something about me in [the story 'Lance'], because I have to make it a rule never to read anything in which I am mentioned, for fear it will influence my judgment." *DBDV*, 303.

107 *"I had had some doubts"*: Ibid., 209–10.

107 *"For you, a dictator"*: Ibid., 210.

107 *"dull thud"*: N., "Introduction," *BS*, xii.

107 *"I think, too"*: Ibid.

107 *reminded him of Thomas:* DBDV, 210.

109 *"She was standing"*: BS, 145.

109 *"slammed the door"*: Ibid., 158. The play, the lap, and a daughter taken sexually predict *Lolita*, 61–64 and passim.

109 *"Good night"*: BS, 174.

109 *"lost his wife"*: Ibid., 174–5.

110 *"He opened"*: Ibid., 175.

110 *"You know too little"*: Ibid., 176–77. Cf. *Lolita*, 71.

110 *American slang:* BS, 143, 160.

111 *" 'Sure,' said Mac"*: Ibid., 180.

111 *"a steak for five"*: Ibid., 178.

111 *"He saw David"*: Ibid., 168.

112 *"It is rather"*: Hardwick, 20.

112 *fully take command:* In April '47, he wrote two friends, the Marinel sisters, "As for Russian prose, I seem to have completely lost the knack.": *SL*, 74.

112 *"I have not had"*: DBDV, 215.

112 *wonderful, enchanting books:* Updike, 191–92, 202. "To my taste his American novels are his best," Updike wrote. "In America his almost impossible style encountered . . . a subject as impossible as itself. . . . He rediscovered our monstrosity . . . the eerie arboreal suburbs, the grand emptinesses, the . . . junk of roadside America . . . the wistful citizens of a violent society desperately oversold . . . on love." About *Speak, Memory* Updike observed, "Nabokov has never written English better than in these reminiscences; never since has he written so sweetly." *Ada* did not find favor with the American-born novelist: "I confess to a prejudice: fiction is earthbound. . . . His vision and flair are themselves so supermundane that to apply them to a fairyland is to put icing on icing. There is nothing in the landscapes of *Ada* to rank with the Russian scenery of *Speak, Memory* or the trans-American hegira of Lolita and Humbert Humbert.

112 *the chorus of praise:* DBDV, 230.

112 *"Mother take you and me"*: Lolita, 47.

113 *"As I lay":* Ibid., 56.

113 *"Oh, my Lolita":* Ibid., 33.

113 *"School was taught":* SM, 180.

114 *"I see very clearly":* Ibid., 53–54.

114 *"rather dejected":* DBDV, 142.

114 *plan to return west:* Ibid.

114 *"hooligans":* DBDV, 146.

114 *cleanest lake:* The Inn on Newfound Lake, home page, http://www.newfoundlake
.com/main.html.

114 *"filthy":* Schiff 134.

114 *a story about anti-Semitism:* Boyd 2, 107.

114 *other versions of the story:* Schiff, 134; Appel, *Annotated*, 424.

114 *he went to a hospital:* DBDV, 194.

114 *"There are lots of wonderful":* Ibid., 188. N. also referred to "impotent me" in a letter
on May 25. Ibid., 192. Wilson's *Memoirs of Hecate County* sold sixty thousand copies
in its first year of publication. It then became the subject of an obscenity prosecution and was put under ban. The cost to Wilson in lost royalties was severe. The
novel was not republished until '59, when *Lolita*'s difficult but legally less troubled
march to market signaled a promising change in the atmosphere. Wilson's reversals
were not lost on N. But *Hecate County*'s tantalizing early success showed the potential of an artfully written novel that was sex-centered to excite readers. Wilson
considered *Hecate County* his best book. De Grazia, 209–10.

115 *smell of fried clams:* Schiff, 134; *NB*, 397. N. had many pleasurable experiences
collecting east of the Mississippi, but on the whole he preferred the West, for its
less domesticated, grander, more mountainous landscapes. To a Russian friend,
Roman Grynberg, he wrote, "Boring is the spring in Boston with its recalcitrantly
green trees and yellow monotonous forsythias in garden plots. Oh, the porous
snow in spring." January 8, 1944, Bakh.

115 *"I had to invent America":* SO, 26. N. spoke often of inventing places, inventing
worlds, and this provocative locution, with its Promethean echoes, was in line
with the modernist upending of naturalism. But in a less provocative sense, N. was
underscoring his performance of a task shouldered by all novelists—all storytellers,
for that matter: the investing of a locale with sufficient color and drama to interest
and excite readers, leading to a feeling of familiarity and comprehension, as if now
the place can be seen as it really is. That an observable reality may not exactly match
the lineaments of a fictionalized ground does not much bother most readers; make-
believe is allowed, in service to other truths. Faulkner's comment, in a *Paris Review*
interview of 1956, about realizing with *Sartoris* that "my own little postage stamp
of native soil was worth writing about," and his witty signing of the hand-drawn
map that he appended to *Absalom! Absalom!*—naming himself "Sole Owner &
Proprietor" of fictional Yoknapatawpha County—were gestures not unlike
Nabokov's. See "Sketch Map of the Nabokov Lands in the St. Petersburg Region,"
with N.'s trademark freehand butterfly. *SM*, 17.

116 *"pale porpoise":* DBDV, 308.

116 *conversant with:* Sweeney, "Sinistral," 65.

116 *"Keep it Kold":* N., "The Refrigerator Awakes," *New Yorker*, June 6, 1942, 20.

116 *"sharp-sightedness":* N., *Poems and Problems*, 145.

116 *represent his American surroundings:* Flanner, "Goethe," part I, 34, and part II, 28, 30, 35. Mann did ponder a Hollywood novel but finally did not write it. "Whether the German exiles liked Los Angeles depended on whether they liked nature." Bahr, quoted in Laskin. Mann often walked his poodle, Niko, in Palisades Park, Santa Monica, before lunch.

116 *Ayn Rand:* Johnson, "Bedfellows."

117 *"I am also old":* N., *Stories*, 584.

117 *"marvelous picnics":* Kopper, "Correspondence," 60–61.

Chapter Nine

118 *Wilson sent him:* DBDV, 229n1.

118 *Of a wealthy family . . . beyond control:* Ibid. Simon Karlinsky, editor of *DBDV*, in his thorough account of this episode, displays the careful and suggestive scholarship that everywhere distinguishes his volume.

118 *"Many thanks":* Ibid., 230.

119 *his entomology friends:* Berg, letters of Harry Clench.

119 *Remington wrote him:* Berg. N. hoped to answer "critical unsolved problems in butterfly classification." Remington, "Lepidoptera Studies," 278.

119 *Schmoll:* "Hazel Schmoll," Colorado Women's Hall of Fame, http://www .cogreatwomen.org/index.php/item/162-hazel-schmoll.

119 *advance of $2,000:* DBDV, 200.

119 *book–talk fee:* Boyd 2, 116.

119 *had been reading entomological:* N. read and wrote French, English, Russian, German, and Latin.

119 *"Taken by Haberhauer":* Berg.

120 *"jam of logs":* Ibid. The account originally appeared in *National Geographic*, June 1944: 672.

    "the summer of 1834": Berg.

121 *"N. Colo.":* Ibid. "Ecology" appears in a letter to Wilson of November 21, 1948. *DBDV*, 241. "Ecological" appears in that letter and also in lepidopteral notes from '44. *NB*, 307.

121 *"On a hot August":* NB, 403.

121 *"is forced open oysterwise":* Ibid., 322.

121 *"It may well be":* Ibid., 422.

122 *"I had done no collecting":* Ibid., 126.

123 *"can be defined as a Polyommatus":* Berg.

123 *center of a coterie:* N.'s entomological friends read him carefully. Cyril dos Passos, of the AMNH, said about N.'s "Notes on the Morphology of the Genus *Lycaeides*," "It is a most interesting paper and I certainly enjoyed reading it. . . . The article cannot be mastered at one reading and I have promised myself the pleasure of giving it further study." Berg. Dos Passos also wrote N., on May 31, 1949, "You have doubtless read Munroe's paper in The Lepidopterists' News . . . on the genus concept in RHOPALOCERA, in which he holds up Warren, Grey, yourself, and myself as horrible examples of splitters and returns to the old outworn ideas. . . .

Warren and I have been having some correspondence on the subject and feel that Munroe should be taken down a peg or two. It is our opinion that you are the person to do this": *NB*, 447.

123 *boarded at Columbine Lodge:* AAA *Guide*, 38.

123 *during his stay:* "As many as four lepidopterists have visited me here to pay their respects and take me to distant collecting grounds." *DBDV*, 219.

123 *Tolland Bog:* Remington was conducting research at the University of Colorado's Science Lodge, near Schmoll's ranch. *NB*, 49–50.

124 *feet-on-the-boggy-ground:* Garland Companion, 277–78.

124 *"We have a most comfortable":* *DBDV*, 218.

124 *lodge was within a half-mile:* Pickering, 15. The Longs Peak Inn was built by the nature writer Enos Mills. Pyle, 50.

124 *"to the Tahosa Valley":* Pickering, 7. The Nabokovs ate in the communal dining hall and might have had electricity and indoor plumbing in their cabin. Author's visit, September 15, 2012.

124 *with beaver dams:* Pickering, 18.

124 *kinnikinnick gave way:* Ibid; author's visit.

124 *Véra enjoyed:* Schiff, 143. Novelist Edmund White, working for *The Saturday Review* in the early seventies, oversaw a cover story on the occasion of the publication of N.'s *Transparent Things*. White, "How Did One Edit Nabokov?" *City Boy* (New York: Bloomsbury USA, 2009).

125 *Don Stallings:* Berg.

125 *"Some new":* Psyche 49 (September–December 1942).

125 *"There will not be any fee":* Berg.

125 *"a flock of unnamed races":* Berg, letter of May 13, 1943.

125 *tutored by Nabokov:* Berg, letter of February 12, 1947.

125 *ran the idea by:* Berg, letter of May 26, 1943.

125 *"This giant race":* Stallings and Turner, "New American." Stallings was still relying on genitalic identification ten years later. Stallings and Turner, "Four New Species," 4. N. coined several terms of genitalic morphology, among them *humerulus, alula, bullula, mentum, rostellum, sagum,* and *surculus. NB*, 498.

126 *"You will find":* Berg, letter of March 21, 1944.

126 *"my ideas run along":* Berg, letter of November 12, 1943.

126 *"Also received":* Berg, letter of February 13, 1946.

126 *teach him the names:* Berg, letter of March 21, 1944.

126 *"Did some dissecting":* Berg, letter of April 14, 1944.

126 *"Uncle Sam":* Berg, letter of November 12, 1943.

126 *"D-Day":* Berg, letter of July 8, 1944. N. registered for the draft on February 16, 1942, soon after Pearl Harbor. In the Registrar's Report on Vladimir Nabokoff (Serial Number 726, Order Number 10207) he is described as five feet eleven and a half inches tall, one hundred seventy pounds, of ruddy complexion, with an appendix scar. National Archives, National Personnel Records Center.

126 *dated from this time:* N. claimed to have done some writing of *Lolita* in '47, but he also wrote Wilson on January 16, 1952, that at Harvard for the semester "I shall have some timespace for certain pleasurable labors that I contemplate—a novel (in English) that I have been palpating in my mind for a couple of years." *DBDV*, 298.

126 *Humbert drives immediately:* Lolita, 283.

127 *a promising site:* DBDV, 294. N. told Wilson that Telluride had "awful roads, but then—endless charm, an old-fashioned, absolutely touristless mining town full of most helpful, charming people—and when you hike from there, which is 9000', to 10000', with the town and its tin roofs and self-conscious poplars lying toylike at the flat bottom of a cul-de-sac valley . . . all you hear are the voices of children playing." Ibid.

127 *"absence of her voice":* Lolita, 326. N. might have seen the name Telluride at the MCZ when reading of the capture of a type specimen in 1902 by a man named Weeks at "Telluride, San Miguel Mts., S.W. Colorado, alt. 10,000 to 12,000 ft." NB, 425. But N. never mentions Weeks or Telluride in his first two main papers about the genus *Lycaeides*, "The Nearctic Forms of *Lycaeides* Hüb[ner]" and "Notes on the Morphology of the Genus *Lycaeides*." Stallings's talk of interesting captures he made there during summer of '47 might have ignited N.'s desire to go.

127 *"most delightful":* Berg.

127 *"collect my way":* Boyd 2, 121; *"Erebia Magdalena,"* Butterflies and Moths of North America, http://www.butterfliesandmoths.org/species/Erebia-magdalena.

127 *"forget your face":* Berg, letter of January 8, 1948.

128 *"sending you":* Berg, letter of February 23, 1948.

128 *years:* Boyd 2, 116. N. remained an active collector for the rest of his life, but not a lab worker or theorist.

128 *still the boy:* N. to sister Elena, August 30, 1950, NB, 465.

128 *eventually to appear:* DBDV, 219. The Nabokovs' long stay at Columbine Lodge was possible only because of the sale of "Portrait of My Uncle" and another story to *The New Yorker*. On July 24, 1947, he had written Wilson, "I am rather in a fix at the moment (as always in summer)." Ibid., 217.

128 *blue of summer:* SM, 119.

128 *of Longs Peak:* Ibid., 138–39. N.'s butterflies are biologically true but also totemic, like Hemingway's trout of "Big Two-Hearted River" and the Irati River in *The Sun Also Rises*.

128 *superimpose one part:* Ibid., 139.

129 *a lost country:* NB, 323.

130 *vivid memories:* SO, 22.

130 *way with slang:* Schiff, 140.

130 *Brecht, for instance:* Bentley, 17. Brecht was famously derisive of Americans. But "there was an 'on the other hand' . . . to his anti-Americanism. If the Americans . . . were hopeless, they were also not so hopeless. . . . They were human, and he liked some of their habits so much he affected them: not shaking hands upon being introduced, for example, or saying 'so what?,' an expression that did not exist in German until Brecht first said, 'so was?'" Ibid.

130 *Henry Koster:* "Henry Koster," IMDb.com, http://www.imdb.com/name/nm0467396/bio.

130 *"how well he had known me":* NB, 46.

130 *"uninhibited":* Ibid., 45.

130 *Moby-Dick:* Ibid. There are appropriations from Melville in BS, which N. was working on at this time.

130 *native habitats:* Boyd 2, 82.

130 *about the trouble:* Ibid.

131 *"a strange wave":* DBDV, 146.

131 *"complete collapse":* Ibid., 148.

131 *"hot music":* Ibid., 149.

Chapter Ten

132 *"rather startling":* Bishop, "Nabokov at Cornell," 234.

132 *talked up:* DBDV, 225.

132 *leery of hiring:* Boyd 2, 123.

132 *grant was tapped:* Diment, *Pniniad*, 30–1.

133 *Widening Stain:* Tom and Edith Schantz, "Morris Bishop," August 2007, Rue Morgan Press, http://www.ruemorguepress.com/authors/bishop.html.

133 *"pretty worthless":* SL, 83; Schiff, 153.

133 *"a strong appeal":* Ibid., 82.

133 *Harvard failed:* Boyd 2, 303. N. had vexed relations with the Harvard structuralist Roman Jakobson, who blackballed his appointment to a position at the university in '57. Ibid., 698n50. Their cooperation on a three-man translation (plus annotations) of *The Song of Igor's Campaign* (the third man was Cornell historian Marc Szeftel) came to naught, and N. wrote Jakobson a letter in '57 that said, in part, "I have come to the conclusion that I cannot collaborate with you. . . . Frankly, I am unable to stomach your little trips to totalitarian countries." (Jakobson had traveled to the USSR.) Berg. Before the contretemps surrounding the Harvard appointment, N. had said of his collaborator's work, "Jakobson's studies [are] especially brilliant." DBDV, 241.

133 *struggle was over:* Boyd 2, 129. Wilson frankly admired what N. had done: to have arrived as a penniless immigrant and within a decade to have become a professor at a distinguished university, with an exciting literary career in a new language. Wilson might have found a place for himself in the academy, but he demurred; the "whole thing . . . is unnatural, embarrassing, disgusting" for a writer, he felt, and at a time of financial difficulty he still "decided to try to hang on with journalism and publishers' advances." *Letters*, 401. He was playing in a different league financially from N., on a salary from the *New Yorker* that, at the time of the writing of *Hecate County*, was $10,000 plus $3,000 for expenses. (N. was paid $5,000 a year by Cornell.) Ibid., 404; de Grazia, 211–12; Schiff, 152n. N. began angling for better-paying jobs as soon as he arrived at Cornell, and he constantly asked for advances against his salary. Schiff, 153.

134 *Never shall I forget:* PF, 19–20.

134 *Windows, as well known:* Ibid., 87–88.

135 *Most faculty:* Appel and Newman, 236.

135 *a professor's trim house:* Boyd 2, 219.

135 *services to her husband:* Véra was more and more called upon to handle N.'s swelling business, personal, and literary correspondence, including the authorship of thousands of letters under his signature: Schiff and Boyd, passim.

135 *attention-getting part:* Schiff, 151.

135 *"cocoon of love"*: Shapiro, 282.

135 *home for a winter vacation:* Gibian and Parker, 159.

136 *Each of the houses:* Shapiro, 281–82.

136 *Evenings passed:* Shapiro, 282.

136 *same age:* Dmitri was born May 10, 1934; Lolita's birthday was January 1, 1935. *Lolita*, 69.

136 *"very very grateful"*: Berg; Boyd 2, 129.

136 *"I was not always"*: Shapiro, 282.

136 *"vulgar cad"*: Berg.

136 *about a third:* Schiff, 152n.

136 *lived on the perilous border:* D.N., "Close Calls," 305–6.

137 *"phoney"*: *Lolita*, 202.

137 *"adjustment"*: Ibid.,187.

137 *"is obsessed"*: Ibid., 207.

137 *"low-Mexican"*: Ibid., 209. Urinals had special foul meaning for N. In his notes for "Speak On, Memory," he wrote, "In an age when literature is supposed to come from one's favorite public urinal . . . my formal prose [can please] only the mature reader of yesterday." Berg.

137 *sexual hijinks:* D.N., "Close Calls," 306 and passim.

137 *"regime"*: *Lolita*, 197.

137 *"rapist"*: Ibid., 198.

137 *on the right track:* At his parents' urging, Dmitri applied to Harvard Law School and was accepted, but he never matriculated.

137 *"little limp Lo!"*: *Lolita*, 168.

138 *"Ladies and gentlemen"*: Ibid., 93.

Chapter Eleven

139 *"the four D's"*: *Lolita*, 187.

139 *"gleeful pleasure"*: *SO*, 47.

139 *his best novel:* Ibid. N. insisted that *Lolita* was intensely pleasurable for him to contemplate in retrospect. "On a Book Entitled," 333–34; *SO*, 47.

141 *Sex in Nabokov:* There were many more-graphic writers, Henry Miller and D. H. Lawrence being the most noted.

141 *violet-clad girl:* *Enchanter*, 27.

141 *"scrap"*: Ibid., 16.

141 *"not pleased"*: Ibid., 12.

141 *"a beautiful piece"*: Ibid., 16.

141 *off-putting:* The beginning recalls the difficult *Invitation to a Beheading* and looks forward to *Bend Sinister*, rather than to the reader-inviting *Speak, Memory, Lolita,* and *Pnin*.

141 *"thin, dry-lipped"*: *Enchanter*, 25.

142 *its simplicity:* *Enchanter* plays changes on "Little Red Riding Hood," while *Lolita* plays with/refers to some sixty other works.

142 *"But what struck"*: *Hecate County*, 250–1.

142 *"I remember"*: *Hecate County*, quoted in de Grazia, 214.

143 *forbidden terms:*   Dabney, 326. Wilson mentions Miller occasionally in his correspondence: *Letters*, 537, 663. That N. also read Miller, or hastily sampled him, can be deduced from his comment to his sister that "Miller is talentless obscenity." *NB*, 464.

143 *an American take:*   de Grazia, 239. Edel edited Wilson's journals of four decades (twenties through fifties).

143 *"avalanche of erotic":*   Edel, *The Twenties*, quoted in de Grazia, 239. John Updike was a percipient admirer of Wilson's erotic writing and named "The Princess with the Golden Hair," the central story in *Hecate County*, "my first and to this day most vivid glimpse of sex through the window of fiction." Updike, *Hugging*, 196.

143 *"subordinate clause":*   *Enchanter*, 29.

143 *"Already his gaze":*   Ibid., 88–89.

144 *"All my previous books":*   *SL*, 96.

144 *"Now let's sit down":*   *Enchanter*, 45.

144 *"Please, try":*   Ibid., 52–53.

145 *"immobilized fraction":*   *Lolita*, 46.

145 *"soot-black lashes":*   Ibid.

145 *"plaid shirt":*   Ibid., 43.

145 *"knew I could kiss":*   Ibid., 51.

146 *"first cloth coat":*   Ibid., 198–99.

146 *"perversions":*   Ibid., 3.

146 *" 'aphrodisiac' ":*   Ibid., 4.

146 *"great work of art":*   Ibid., 5. In a private journal, in '58, Véra wrote, "I wish, though, somebody would notice the tender description of the child's helplessness, her pathetic dependence on monstrous HH, and her heartrending courage all along. . . . They all miss the fact that . . . Lolita, is essentially good . . . or she would not have straightened out after being crushed so terribly and found a decent life with poor Dick." Berg. N. wrote a similar self-review of *Speak, Memory* that in the end he decided not to place in the published book, but which appeared twenty years after his death in the *New Yorker. NB*, 456–58. Though in "On a Book Entitled" N. says, "I am neither a reader nor a writer of didactic fiction and, despite John Ray's assertion, Lolita has no moral in tow," in '56 he wrote Wilson, "When you do read LOLITA, please mark that it is a highly moral affair." *DBDV*, 331.

147 *"some interesting":*   *Lolita*, 11.

147 *indites one:*   N. mentions John Cleland's *Fanny Hill: Memoirs of a Woman of Pleasure* in "On a Book Entitled," and from Wilson he received a copy of *Histoire d'O*, which the two men chuckled over like naughty schoolboys, according to Véra.

147 *"the one of perfect liberty":*   Harris, vi.

147 *"Next moment":*   *Lolita*, 61.

147 *"state of excitement":*   Ibid., 61.

148 *"Talking fast":*   Ibid., 62.

148 *"plane of being":*   Ibid., 63.

148 *"in the pungent":*   Ibid., 63.

148 *"I was a radiant":*   Ibid., 63–64.

148 *"it's nothing":*   Ibid., 64.

149 *"a euphoria":*   Ibid.

149 *composition:* Berg, notes for "Speak On, Memory"; Boyd 2, 226.

149 *"Once or twice":* Lolita, 330.

149 *real attempts:* Schiff, 166–67, for 1948; Boyd 2, 170, for 1950.

149 *"are keeping":* Schiff, 167.

149 *cards he composed on:* Boyd 2, 169. The method of composing on index cards was borrowed from his lepidopteral work, where he routinely made notations on four-by-six-inch cards. Normally he destroyed early manuscript versions of his works, but in '58 the Library of Congress began offering tax concessions in return for donations of his papers, and thereafter he saved his manuscripts. Boyd 2, 367.

149 *"interruptions":* Lolita, 330.

150 *"some forty years":* Ibid.

150 *"optimistic":* "The Female of *Lycaeides argyrognomon sublivens*," NB, 481. "Sky island" is a term that originated in the early forties and was brought into currency over the next twenty-five years. "Sky Island," *Wikipedia*, http://en.wikipedia.org/wiki/Sky_island.

150 *brought from Europe:* Berg. It was brought unwittingly. N. thought his sole copy had been destroyed, but in '59, according to a letter he wrote to publisher Walter Minton, he found it again, and in '86 it appeared in a translation by Dmitri. Berg. This account is thrown into doubt, however, by a letter Wilson wrote on November 30, 1954, giving his response to *Lolita*, which he had just read in manuscript: "Now about your novel: I like it less than anything else of yours I have read. The short story that it grew out of was interesting, but I don't think the subject can stand this very extended treatment." *DBDV*, 320. Unless there is a story by N. that scholars have somehow overlooked, the short one Wilson refers to is likely to be *The Enchanter* or part of it.

151 *Wilson was a new recruit:* Wilson was already explicit in what he wrote in his journals but not yet in his fiction.

151 *"trying to be an American":* Lolita, 333.

152 *"little money":* SL, 122.

152 *To reach:* "I am sick of having my books muffled up in silence," he wrote Wilson in June '51. *DBDV*, 292.

152 *"in the matter of":* DBDV, 289. Twain, like N., resisted those who sought morals or ideas in his novels; see his "NOTICE" after the title page of *The Adventures of Huckleberry Finn*. N. knew well who Twain was and where he had come from; in Hannibal, Missouri, he observed "the brown and the blue struggling for ascendancy in the Mississippi." Berg, journal for '51.

152 *first American bestseller:* Castiglia, *Bound and Determined*, 1.

152 *thirty editions:* Sturma, "Aliens and Indians," 318.

152 *seven hundred:* Ibid.

152 *"enthusiastic review":* Sayre, "Abridging," 488.

152 *"artlessness":* Wolff, 411.

152 *"moose":* Ibid., 422.

153 *reached its height:* DBDV, 311. N. rejoiced in his work at the Widener Library at Harvard, tracking down every literary allusion in *Eugene Onegin*.

153 *Pushkin had done:* Wolff, 410–11. Pushkin considered Chateaubriand's and James Fenimore Cooper's novels about America "brilliant works." Ibid., 411. Mayne Reid counted among his entranced readers Frank Harris and Theodore Roosevelt.

154 *what tale to tell:* N.'s model for the theme of an intensely jealous man and a sweet cheat who is a deceptive captive is most likely Proust. Field, *VN*, 328–29.

154 *found him smart:* Boyd 2, 141. N. spent time particularly with Ransom, and they made several live radio broadcasts together while in Salt Lake. Field, *Life in Part*, 272.

154 *Buxbaum:* Interview with Richard Buxbaum, August 14, 2013. At the time of the interview, Buxbaum was the Jackson H. Ralston Professor of International Law (emeritus) at the University of California, Berkeley.

154 *resembling the route:* Zimmer, http://dezimmer.net/LolitaUSA/Trip2.htm.

154 *"ah, that first whiff":* Lolita, 222.

154 *nonfictional travelers:* Interview with Buxbaum. Buxbaum noticed the separate beds because his own parents slept in one.

155 *"We wish you":* Lolita, 223.

155 *"a woman's hair":* Ibid.

155 *"commercial fashion":* Ibid. Such big motels were appearing—a few, though they were not yet the fashion.

155 *"beautiful bones":* Interview with Buxbaum.

155 *conferred with Klots:* NB, 447.

155 *"meet ten bears":* Boyd 2, 142. Klots was the future author of *Field Guide to the Butterflies of North America, East of the Great Plains.*

155 *South of the Tetons:* Berg, "Notes for a second volume (twenty years in America) of Speak, Memory."

155 *an adventure:* Boyd 2, 142. The author, aged sixty-six, in a perhaps ill-advised attempt to understand that adventure, undertook the trek to the base of Disappointment Peak, which gains three thousand feet in five miles. The weather became stormy. His solo climb of the rocks ended with the arrival of purple clouds and lightning. Half an hour later, after an undignified retreat, he found himself bathed in warm sunlight, the sky beautifully clear; he did not return to the rocks, but enjoyed a day of cautious hiking in the heart of the Tetons, legendary summits all around.

156 *"lost many pounds":* DBDV, 254.

156 *"soft-bosomed":* Ibid.

156 *go where they wanted:* the Nabokovs became American citizens in '45.

156 *"amazing white Impala":* Schiff, 268. A '54 Buick Special bought new cost between $2,200 and $3,163. Theirs was a two-door sedan, the smallest model. The Special was Buick's bestselling car. "1954 Buick Special—Classic Car Price Guide," Hagerty, http://www.hagerty.com/price-guide/1954-Buick-Special.

156 *is a staging:* Steve Coates, "His Father's Siren, Still Singing," *New York Times*, May 4, 2008, http://www.nytimes.com/2008/05/04/weekinreview/04nabokov.html.

Chapter Twelve

157 *researches were extensive:* Humbert Humbert on occasion reports what must have been N.'s own research experience—for example, that he never figured out Humbert's legal status vis-à-vis his stepdaughter, although he consulted "many books on marriage, rape, adoption and so on." *Lolita*, 181–82. In the Library of

Congress are ninety-four four-by-six cards with research notes for *Lolita*. N. reminds himself to look up certain words in a dictionary or thesaurus—not all his immense vocabulary, as some have feared, was immediately available to him.

157 *enema tip:* LOC.

157 *girlish slang:* LOC; Boyd 2, 211. N.'s slang collection informs *Lolita*'s "furious harangues" when she uses such expressions as "swell chance," "I'd be a sap," "Stinker," and "I despise you." *Lolita*, 181.

157 *scene with Miss Pratt:* Boyd 2, 211.

157 *"hawk-faced" to "blue-green eyes":* Dolinin, 11.

158 *"detention home":* *Lolita*, 159.

158 *"impaired the morals":* Ibid.

158 *journal for '51:* Berg. Also known as the page-a-day diary.

159 *"paradox of pictorial":* *Lolita*, 160–61.

159 *"line of spaced trees":* Ibid., 161. The passage continues, "and a passing glimpse of some mummy-necked farmer." A diary note for June 30 reads, "farmer with a mumy's [*sic*] neck, furrowed and tanned . . . grim El Greco horizon." Berg.

159 *arrives at existence:* N. was in this sense antipositivist or Kantian.

159 *"I myself learned":* *Lolita*, 160. This process parallels one of learning to see Lolita with loving eyes, not only via a sexually devouring gaze.

160 *"a series of wiggles":* Ibid., 162. See, regarding Humbert's travels and for many other matters Nabokov-related, Dieter Zimmer's indispensable website, at http://dezimmer.net/index.htm.

160 *"sobs in the night":* Ibid., 186.

160 *"when we sat reading":* Ibid., 184.

160 *"trains would cry":* Ibid., 154.

161 *"dreadful giant Christmas trees":* Ibid., 162. The trees echo a diary entry for June 28, 1951, "yesternight highbrow trucks like dreadful huge Christmas trees in the darkness." Berg. These notes from the '51 western trip went directly into *Lolita* so often that it raises the question: Did N. save this notebook so that scholars of the future could learn from it something of his compositional process; or was it saved because it happened to have many unwritten-upon pages, on which Véra, in '58, could jot an account of the events surrounding the American publication of *Lolita*? See chapters 15 and 16 of this book.

161 *"mysterious outlines":* *Lolita*, 162.

161 *"smooth amiable roads":* Ibid., 160.

161 *"and the desert":* Ibid., 162.

162 *a con man:* N.'s use of *Who's Who in the Limelight* (p. 33) to announce early in his book the avatars and connections of Clare Quilty closely echoes Black Guinea's early list (chapter 3) of the disguises of the con man in Melville's *The Confidence Man*. Appel, *Annotated*, 351n5.

162 *"Although everybody should know":* *Lolita*, 332.

162 *"We came to know":* Ibid., 153–54.

162 *"Chateaubriandesque":* N. considered Chateaubriand the first European writer to describe the American natural scene well; the Frenchman came to America in 1791 and wrote novels such as *Les Natchez, Atala*, and *René*.

162 *"sewerish smell":* This derives from a page-a-day diary entry, Berg.

162 *"various types . . . the females"*: Ibid., 154.

162 *"We came to know . . . tense thumbs"*: Ibid., 168.

163 *"to whom ads were dedicated"*: Ibid., 156.

163 *"I was not really"*: Ibid.

163 *the novel's allusions:* this list is only partial. N. parodies himself in the sense that Humbert's self-serving autobiography is a travesty of N.'s scrupulous *Speak, Memory*. Humbert's confessions also evoke those of Jean-Jacques Rousseau. "There is the same sense of childhood lost and the same paranoid suspicions emerging as the work progresses. Nabokov simply gives another turn to the screw of Rousseau's attempt to justify himself and disarm his tormentors by means of absolute and sensational sincerity." Bruss, 29.

163 *the Romantic confessional novel:* Appel, liii.

164 *"a parody . . . with real suffering"*: Ibid., liv.

164 *"involving the reader"*: Ibid., lx.

164 *just amusing enough:* For many readers, he is amusing enough, but for others an absolute rejection of child sexual abuse as a legitimate theme makes *Lolita* objectionable. It will probably always be so.

164 *made by Alfred Hitchcock:* The affinities between some of Hitchcock's works and some of N.'s are many, if superficial: motels (the ones in *Lolita* and the one in *Psycho*); doppelgängers (Hermann and Felix in *Despair*, Guy and Bruno in *Strangers on a Train*); national parks (*Lolita* and *North by Northwest*); mental health workers who explain all (John Ray in *Lolita*'s foreword and the psychiatrist who limns Norman Bates's character at the end of *Psycho*); author cameos (virtually every Nabokov novel, beginning with *King, Queen, Knave*, and all the American-made Hitchcock films, beginning with *Rebecca*). The two auteurs had an appreciation for each other, and they exchanged phone calls and letters in '64, in hopes of finding a film project to work on together. After seeing *The Trouble with Harry*, N. commented, "His humor noir is akin to my humor noir, if that's what it should be called." Davidson, 4. Both were born in 1899, both emigrated to the United States as war broke out, each arriving after career attainments abroad. Hitchcock asked N. to work on the screenplay for *Frenzy*, but he was unavailable. "The primary affinity is in the similar relationship that Hitchcock and Nabokov established with their audience . . . a relationship of playfulness, obtuseness, self-allusiveness and parody": Ibid., 10.

164 *so concerned for order:* Other authors of the postwar moment mocked a sanitized America, prominent among them Miller and Kerouac. Kerouac's work of the forties and fifties would seem definingly un-Nabokovian, but *The Dharma Bums*— even more than *On the Road*, with its Humbertian wanderings all over the map— stubbornly lays hold of Nabokovian materials and approaches. Kerouac began bumming west, looking for America, looking for something, in July '47; N. was in Colorado that summer, and Humbert and Lolita begin their travels at the same time, mid-August '47. Both *Dharma* and *Lolita* are works of deep subjectivity, but both batten on precise reports of locales, specific American locales, and Ray, the scruffy Buddhism-intoxicated hero of *Dharma*, has ecstatic reponses to high-mountain areas (Matterhorn Peak, the Skagit Country) he traverses on foot, just as did the lepidopterophile Nabokov. *Lolita* and *Dharma* end in illuminations of love.

Their respective protagonists are importers of alien ideologies—Buddhism in Ray's case and Euro hyper-aestheticism in Humbert's. Nabokov's delightful conflation of Longs Peak, Colorado, with locales he remembers from his Russian boyhood has an eerily exact echo in *Dharma*, mountain-climbing Ray being "happiest when he has a sense that he already knows this wilderness, when he feels 'something inexpressibly broken in my heart as though I'd lived before and walked this trail.'" Douglas, xxiii. Ray and Humbert are terrified of cops, and society at large unnerves them. But both love, even adore, certain people, and Ray coming off the mountain is thrilled to "begin to smell people again." Ibid., xxii. "The true story of postwar America in all its speed, tomfoolery, and sorrowfulness," according to Kerouac, "could only be told as interior monologue and confession." Ibid., x. N., who wrote his first-person masterworks in America, might have said amen to that.

Chapter Thirteen

166 *"mania"*: *Lolita*, 253.

166 *"After all, gentlemen"*: Ibid.

166 *"around 1950 I"*: Ibid., 184.

167 *"abominable nausea"*: Ibid., 325.

167 *"I went to Telluride"*: DBDV, 294. The mountains are not mainly granitic; the geology of the mountains around Telluride is complex, and though there is some granite, volcanic breccia is more common. The "self-conscious poplars" are probably balsam poplars, a.k.a. black cottonwood, deciduous broadleafed trees that grow on wet ground from six thousand feet in elevation to the tree line.

168 *"heroic wife"*: Ibid. This capture was probably the most significant of N.'s years in North America. He had described the butterfly, *Lycaeides argyrognomon sublivens*, on the basis of nine male specimens found at the MCZ; the males had been taken near Telluride in 1902. *NB*, 425, 480–81. On a steep, brushy slope above his Telluride motel in '51, N. "had the pleasure of discovering the unusual-looking female." Ibid., 481. The insect is now known as *Lycaeides idas sublivens* Nabokov. Ibid., 754.

168 *"Small grasshoppers spurted"*: *Lolita*, 325–26.

168 *"A very light cloud was opening its arms"*: One of the reasons N. is beloved of some readers is that he finds words for perceptions many people have had or, when they read him, suddenly feel they have. The fact that he has had the same perceptions— noticing two cloud patches moving at different rates of speed, one catching up with the other—draws him close.

169 *"divinely enigmatic"*: *Lolita*, 326.

169 *"Every natural fact"*: Emerson, 34.

169 *signs of unusual talent*: Dmitri became Massachusetts and all–New England high school debating champion at the Holderness School, Plymouth, New Hampshire. D.N., "Close Calls," 306.

170 *compromised innocence*: In this regard, *Lolita* has affinities with *The Scarlet Letter*, *Uncle Tom's Cabin*, *The Adventures of Huckleberry Finn*, *The Turn of the Screw*, "Bartleby the Scrivener," *Billy Budd*, *Moby-Dick*, and *The Sea Wolf*, among others.

170 *"Dmitri has set his heart"*: Houghton, letter of May 3, 1950.

170 *"always a pleasure"*: Houghton, letter of May 8, 1950. Ivan is Nicolas's eldest son.

170 *"in complete honesty"*: Bakh, letter of November 2, 1951. In spring '51, N. borrowed $1,000 from Grynberg. Boyd 2, 199.

170 *last short story:* Boyd 2, 206.

171 *could not understand it:* Boyd 2, 208. Ross died December 6, 1951, aged fifty-nine. The story appeared in the magazine on February 2, 1952.

171 *impoverished:* Schiff, 152n.

171 *feeling especially broke:* In September '51, he wrote Wilson, "at present I am in quite awful circumstances, despite a thousand dollars I borrowed from Roman in spring." *DBDV*, 295.

171 *other positions:* Schiff, 153.

171 *"long since":* Bakh. He wrote Wilson, "*The New Yorker* has bought in all 12 of the 15 [chapters] submitted to them. One piece was in the *Partisan*." *DBDV*, 262.

171 *"mumble back":* *DBDV*, 273. N.'s teeth were extracted by "Dr Favre, a Boston dentist." Berg, note for "Speak On, Memory."

171 *"doctor says":* *DBDV*, 294.

171 *poor sleep:* N. complained of lifelong insomnia, but to judge by the accounts of his dreams he began keeping in his sixties, he slept every night for at least a few hours. Berg.

171 *"letters from private individuals":* *DBDV*, 292.

171 *Salinger:* Boyd 2, 608.

172 *men entranced by younger girls:* The situation occurs in "Slight Rebellion Off Madison" (December 1946), "A Perfect Day for Bananafish" (January 1948), "A Girl I Knew" (February 1948), "I'm Crazy" (December 1948), "For Esmé—with Love and Squalor" (April 1950), and *The Catcher in the Rye* (1951).

172 *slang:* Salinger, passim; e.g., "phony," "crumby," "that killed me," "I got a bang out of that." "The Catcher in the Rye," *Wikipedia*, http://en.wikipedia.org/wiki/The_Catcher_in_the_Rye.

172 *Both authors venture:* N. ventures but scrupulously avoids profanity; Salinger employs profanity on occasion.

172 *first refusal deal:* Boyd 2, 73, for N.; Slawenski, 166, for Salinger.

172 *off and on for years:* Salinger worked for more than ten years on his novel, considering that Holden Caulfield appeared in "Slight Rebellion Off Madison," sold to *The New Yorker* in Nov. '41 (though not published till after the war). "Catcher," *Wikipedia*. N. worked for five years on *Lolita*, although he could be said to have developed the theme beginning in the late thirties, for a total of fifteen years.

172 *"pretty little ears":* Salinger, 88. "Roller-skate skinny" might have been borrowed from *The Enchanter*.

173 *"very emotional, for a child":* Ibid., 89.

173 *"She was laying there":* Ibid., 206–7.

173 *"one of her old nightgowns":* Lolita, 135–36.

173 *"had for object":* Ibid., 136.

174 *write about St. Mark's:* Berg, note of February 18, 1951; Boyd 2, 122, 685n40.

174 *This work, with scholarly:* SL, 130.

174 *they sublet a house:* Schiff, 172. N. wrote Wilson, "We have a very charming, ramshackle house, with lots of bibelots and a good bibliotheque, rented unto us by a charming lesbian lady, May Sarton." *DBDV*, 303.

174 *she was upset:* Schiff, 173.

174 *at nine or ten: EO,* vol. 2, 328.

174 *a supreme work of art:* Pushkin was second only to Shakespeare in N.'s poetic pantheon.

174 *"at heart a pedant": DBDV,* 262.

174 *"two months in Cambridge":* Ibid., 311.

175 *"weary negligence":* Shakesepeare, *King Lear,* act 1, scene 3. Goneril is speaking of the attitude her minions should show her father. Pushkin was reading Byron as he composed *Eugene Onegin* and other concurrent poems. Mitchell, xxvii–xxxi. In his exile to Kishinev (of the infamous pogrom eighty years later), Pushkin befriended a family that introduced him to Byron's verse. Ibid., xxvii.

174 *" 'Tis now, I know, within your will": EO,* vol. 1, 165. The tone is not unlike that of Charlotte Haze in her landlady's letter to Humbert. This quotation and all others are from N.'s translation of the poem.

175 *"him does the snake": EO,* vol. 1, 115.

176 *"without avail":* Ibid., 114.

176 *shade of red:* Ibid., vol. 3, 181–83.

176 *less than one hundred:* Ibid., vol. 2, 209. N. is counting backward from the time of the completion of *Onegin,* 1831. The Russian language had been standardized for the first time only in the eighteenth century. Mitchell, xi. The borrowing from other literatures came via French translations.

175 *"Pétri":* Ibid., vol. 2, 5–10.

176 *"tipping a flippant tale": EO,* vol. 2, 5–6. On the first page of his commentaries (vol. 2, 5), N. in effect footnotes a footnote; about the epigraph, he asserts that it is almost certainly fictitious, but "for those who like to look for the [living] models of fictional characters," take a look at some lines (vol. 1, p. 115, stanza 46), which, to be understood, must be read along with his comments in vol. 2, pp. 173–74. We are already in the sort of mad chase, involving fingers holding places in multiple locations, that begins the novel *Pale Fire,* which he conceived in the same years dedicated to his long labors on *Onegin.*

177 *"Why did you visit us": EO,* vol. 1, 165. In his comments on these lines, N. says his italicizing of the word *Why* was "influenced by a wonderful record (played for me one day in Talcottville by Edmund Wilson) of Tarasova's recitation of Tatiana's letter." Ibid., vol. 2, 391.

177 *"No, to nobody":* Ibid., vol. 1, 166.

177 *She is replicating:* Ibid., vol. 2, 391–92.

177 *"the dashes":* Ibid., vol. 1, 261.

177 *"And by degrees":* Ibid., vol. 1, 262.

178 *"At this point":* Ibid., vol. 3, 85. When discussing Pushkin, N. believes in a straightforward way in evidence and reality. Cf. *The Real Life of Sebastian Knight,* where a reader/investigator can never quite know an author/brother.

178 *"with soft-melting gaze":* Ibid., vol. 1, 259.

178 *inspired by:* This painting was displayed at the British ambassador's residence in Athens. "Lord Byron," *Wikipedia,* http://en.wikipedia.org/wiki/Lord_Byron. The statuette could also be of Napoleon. Other translations of *Onegin,* e.g. those by Charles Johnson and Walter Arndt, say definitively that it is Napoleon. N. is silent

on the matter; he might have noticed that Napoleon is almost universally shown not "with arms crosswise compressed," as Pushkin has it, but with one arm bent at the elbow and the hand disappearing in a tunic. The Phillips painting shows Byron with arms crosswise.

179 *like émigré scholars of the day:* In an interview in '51, N. confessed that he did not read young American novelists very often but that he was "a great reader . . . of the critics." Harvey Breit, "Talk with Mr. Nabokov," *New York Times*, February 18, 1951, http://www.nytimes.com/books/97/03/02/lifetimes/nab-v-talk.html.

179 *"This is a confession":* *Lolita*, 71. Charlotte's "but what would it matter" resembles Tatiana's "who knows" (both appearing in parentheses).

179 *Nabokov the scholar traces:* EO, vol. 3, 98–100. Eugene when he travels carries with him copies of *René, Adolphe*, and Charles Maturin's *Melmoth the Wanderer* (the name Melmoth is borrowed for an automobile in *Lolita*).

179 *"His is a checkered nature":* Ibid., 100–1.

180 *something in the novel to ripen . . . refreshed himself:* Boyd 2, 225, 310.

180 *wrote nothing:* DBDV, 308.

180 *"By the age of 14":* SO, 46.

181 *a kind of trial run:* Brodhead, 13.

181 *"compel a man":* Parker, 768.

181 *"looking for":* N., letter to the editor, *New York Review of Books*, October 7, 1971.

181 *"sardine":* Boyd 2, 502.

181 *"Pierre Point":* Lolita, 34.

181 *syllabus:* Boyd 2, 200.

181 *he had already worked up:* Harvard made him add *Don Quixote*.

181 *precursors:* Appel, lviii; Borges, 201.

182 *anxiety about the world:* Brodhead, 5.

182 *"I wonder":* Moby-Dick, 511.

182 *"Sir, I mistrust it":* Ibid., 521; author's versing.

183 *parodies:* For example, the Quilty-Humbert duality in *Lolita*, a kind of extended parody of the double theme à la Dostoevsky.

183 *Boyd shows:* Boyd 2, 246–47.

184 *"Greek-like simplicity":* Gilmore, 109.

184 *there* is *a child:* Pip is not, strictly speaking, a cabin boy, though he lives with Ahab in his cabin and might have served him as one. He was a ship's hand who normally performed as a shipkeeper—one who stayed aboard when the harpoonists ventured out in whaleboats.

184 *"Thou touchest":* Moby-Dick, 522.

184 *three blacks:* The other two are Daggoo, an African harpooner, and Fleece the cook.

184 *"velvet shark-skin":* Ibid.

185 *"Unless it can be proven":* Lolita, 300.

Chapter Fourteen

186 *"Wyoming, 1952":* NB, 489–94.

186 *Gathered around a central space:* author's visit, September 2012. The establishment was still in business as the Corral Motel but about to undergo a renovation. The

log cabins of the American West closely resemble log dwellings common in western Russia at the time of N.'s boyhood.

186 *"In early August"*: NB, 493.

186 *"palpating"*: DBDV, 298.

186 *begun writing:* Ibid.

186 *wrote little:* Ibid., 308.

187 *"spent almost two weeks"*: Ibid., 262.

187 *annoying duties: DBDV,* 300. N. wrote Wilson, "I am sick of teaching," but he also reported on the fun of working up *Mansfield Park* and *Bleak House* for lectures, saying, "I think I had more fun than my class." Ibid., 282.

187 *"tempestuously"*: Ibid., 298.

187 *"focus briefly"*: D.N., "Close Calls," 306.

187 *"the following order"*: SL, 122. N. also said of his son that he had "a magnificent brain." Ibid., 138.

188 *"partner for tennis"*: "Close Calls," 307.

188 *associated with ascents:* Roberts, "Hearse Traverse," "Harvard Five."

188 *climbers went to:* Harvard Mountaineering Archive.

188 *did not climb on a rope with:* Interview with Peter McCarthy, HMC president, May 14, 2012.

188 *published an article: American Alpine Journal* no. 28 (1954): 196–200.

188 *first ascent of Gibraltar:* Alden, 30, 33. The year of Dmitri's first ascents, '53, was the year of Art Gilkey's death on K2 and of the British first ascent of Mount Everest.

188 *"an elderly Packard"*: "Close Calls," 309.

188 *"doubt if we shall ever"*: Ibid.; *SL,* 139.

188 *climbers died: Harvard Mountaineering* no. 12, May 1955; "Close Calls," 311.

188 *"his third car"*: SL, 138.

188 *often worried:* Dmitri's climbing passion slackened in '55, when he took two falls in the Canadian Rockies. He decided to quit before killing himself. Boyd 2, 268.

188 *Ashland:* The well-known Shakespeare Festival dates from modest beginings in 1935.

188 *"no greater pleasure"*: DBDV, 308.

188 *modest wooden houses:* Theirs, at 163 Mead Street, belonged to a professor at Southern Oregon College of Education. It was perched on a steep street, and it burned down in September '99: Johnson, Nabokv-L.

189 *"more or less . . . coily thing"*: SL, 140.

189 *Véra hand-carried:* Schiff, 199. The Nabokovs feared sending it through the mails because the Comstock Act made it a crime to distribute obscenity that way. Ibid., 204. Schiff also shows that White held off reading *Lolita* for another three years, until March '57; one reason was that she disliked having to conceal the manuscript from her colleague William Shawn. A detailed account of the shenanigans, showing White to have been ardent about getting an early look (before she then became reluctant), is to be found in Diment, "Two Lolitas."

189 *more shockable:* Schiff, 199.

190 *to friend Wilson:* DBDV, 314.

190 *on the sixth:* Berg, notes for "Speak On, Memory."

190 *"sensuous . . . this fiasco"*: DBDV, 317.

190 *tormenting:* Was N. suffering and unhappy while writing *Lolita*? According to what he told his *New Yorker* editor, possibly. But a contemporaneous letter to his sister says, "I am fairly fat . . . everything is going wonderfully well." *SL*, 139. He was joyful when he had the time to work on what he wanted.

190 *as his own agent:* Véra did all secretary work and much strategizing.

190 *Epstein esteemed:* Schiff, 205–6.

190 *a better chance:* For Laughlin, see *SL*, 152; for Covici, see Schiff, 201. Joyce had had to publish *Ulysses* first in France.

190 *willing to part:* Schiff, 201; *SL*, 147.

190 *brought convictions:* de Grazia, 7–9. *The Little Review* daringly published episode 13, "Nausicaa."

191 *rose garden:* Rose imagery abounds in the novel, perhaps appropriately for a novel written partly in Ashland. This includes reference to Lolita's intimate "brown rose."

191 *paperback from Grove:* de Grazia, 338, 370. The legal publication of *Lolita* in America in '58 led to the republication of *Hecate County* the next year. Schiff, 236.

191 *theme of sex with children:* Incest was a theme in Mary Shelley's long-suppressed *Mathilda* and in *The Heptameron*, by Marguerite de Navarre. Dostoevsky treated pedophila in *Crime and Punishment* and in a chapter of *The Devils*, "At Tikhon's," not published until 1922.

191 *a novel for readers:* Schiff, 236.

191 *sold extremely well:* The novel sold 100,000 copies in its first three weeks of release; it was the first novel since *Gone with the Wind* (1936) to do so. Schiff, 232.

192 *best work:* DBDV, 317.

192 *"character entirely new":* SL, 178.

192 *"one of the few words":* Lolita, 330.

192 *"exhilarating":* Ibid., 333.

192 *high spirits:* All of N.'s books, written wherever and whenever, evince a measure of gleeful verve.

193 *"Indian paupers":* SL, 150. Dmitri had better memories, recalling "an adobe house in Taos . . . rented from a pair of opera-loving gentlemen. Its painful quaintness was . . . compensated by . . . a WWII Jeep in which I chauffered Father on lepidopterological hunts, and the first recording I had ever heard of Verdi's *Requiem*," which became his favorite piece of music. "Close Calls," 315.

193 *notorious widow:* Schiff, 203.

193 *on his own:* Ibid.

193 *"what agony it was":* SL, 149.

193 *"poor Pnin":* SL, 143.

193 *market wisdom:* Boyd 2, 256–57.

193 *unusual focus on things Russian:* Diment, *Pniniad*, 45, says *The New Yorker* had an "unusual amount of Russian material" in '53. It was the year of Stalin's death and of Beria's arrest.

193 *thought bubble:* Pnin, 60–61.

193 *"no other work":* Maar, 80.

194 *"very amusing and quite brilliant":* DBDV, 304.

194 *campus novel:* Before McCarthy's, there were C. P. Snow's *The Masters*, Willa Cather's *The Professor's House*, and Dorothy Sayers' *Gaudy Night*.

194 *"sheer sympathy"*: Pnin, 35. The "Egg and We" nods, perhaps, to the popular memoir *The Egg and I* (1945), by Betty MacDonald, the basis of a film under the same name (1947).

194 *"Although forbidden"*: Ibid., 40.

194 *"Whereas the degree"*: Ibid., 11.

194 *"Well, to make"*: Ibid., 33–34.

195 *Based partly on:* Diment, *Pniniad*. Szeftel came to Cornell in '45, and he was on the hiring committee that brought N. to the university. He was delighted to have another Russian aboard, and one, like him, with a Jewish wife. Ibid., 31. Despite these commonalities, Szeftel never could establish an intimacy. Another Cornell professor, Robert M. Adams, said, "Many had a sense that Nabokov did not have any desire for real friendships, that Véra was . . . all that he needed, and that even the Bishops, who were the Nabokovs' most frequent companions . . . were in no way their intimate friends." Ibid., 35. Szeftel's comical English and professorial oddities inform the portrait of Timofey Pnin in the novel. Szeftel was more successful than his representation and was hired by the University of Washington in '61. Ibid., 56.

195 *"I must warn"*: Pnin, 34.

195 *"mourning for an intimate part"*: Ibid., 39.

195 *boarding school:* Ibid., 93–96.

195 *"now a secret"*: Ibid., 8.

195 loves *his hero:* To a potential publisher N. described *Pnin* as a figure of "great moral courage, a pure man . . . a staunch friend, serenely wise, faithful to a single love [who] never descends from a high plane of life characterized by authenticity and integrity." Boyd 2, 292–93.

196 *VN knew Pnin:* VN's account of their past is fluent but not to be trusted; Pnin disagrees with it at several points. *Pnin*, 179–80.

196 *telling him:* Ibid., 84.

196 *"I intended"*: SL, 150.

196 *"All of a sudden"*: Pnin, 146; "Pnin Gives a Party," *New Yorker*, November 12, 1955, 47.

196 *"The good doctor"*: Pnin, 155; "Pnin Gives a Party," 50.

196 *fight over everything:* Boyd 2, 270. In March '55, he wrote White, "I have cheerfully agreed to accept some thirty minor alterations" in a segment of the novel that was being called "Pnin's Day," but other changes he found insupportable: they "would affect the inner core of the piece which is built on a whole series of inner organic transitions; it would be agony even to contemplate replacing" them. SL, 156–57.

196 *"well-padded"*: Pnin, 155–56.

197 *"singularly delightful"*: Ibid., 144.

197 *spruce trees and old elms:* Ibid.

197 *"suburban"*: Ibid.

197 *"dark rock wall"*: Ibid., 164.

197 *"At last"*: Ibid. N. never acquired property in America. This might have been his ideal: a secluded modest house (not too hard to heat), among fields and forest, with a cliff nearby and lepping possible. "Pheasants visited the weedy ground between the garage and the cliff," we are told; those iconic American shrubs, lilacs, "crowded

in sapless ranks along one wall of the house," and a great tree cast "Indian-summer shadows" on the porch steps. Ibid., 145.

197 *"old brown loafers"*: Pnin, 156.

197 *"a detailed diary"*: Ibid., 157.

198 *"blundered from chair to chair"*: Ibid., 163.

198 *"During the eight"*: Ibid., 62. The scene looks toward the Ray Carver story "Why Don't You Dance?"

198 *designed to charm*: Boyd 2, 271–87. Boyd's discussion of *Pnin* is superb, supplying an ample gloss, a great service to readers of this oft-perplexing author. His biography provides a gloss for every book.

198 *"large bowl"*: Pnin, 153.

199 *"perfectly divine"*: Ibid., 157.

199 *living words*: With an entire scene, N. here achieves an effect usually obtained only with single phrases of brilliance and intense seeingness.

199 *"beautiful bowl was intact"*: Ibid., 172–73.

199 *"is inviting"*: Ibid., 169.

199 *he was offended*: SL, 179. "I do not write sketches," he told Pascal Covici.

199 *"central axis"*: Maar, 77.

199 *Mira Belochkin*: Boyd 2, 282.

200 *remarkable sales*: Ibid., 307.

200 *"highly satisfying"*: Pnin, 69.

200 *"walked down the gloomy stairs"*: Ibid., 70.

200 *"started to lose his sight"*: Ibid., 70–71.

201 *"We can't know more"*: SL, 178.

201 *good at schematics*: N. was a first-rate composer of chess problems, though not a first-rate chess player. Gezari, 44–54.

201 *Nabokov knew this*: In his letter to Oskar Pollak of November 8, 1903, Kafka wrote, "I think we ought to read only the kind of books that wound and stab us. If the book we are reading doesn't wake us up with a blow on the head, what are we reading it for? . . . We need the books that affect us like a disaster, that grieve us deeply, like the death of someone we loved more than ourselves. . . . A book must be the axe for the frozen sea inside us." Karl, 98.

201 *"Elena loved"*: DBDV, 316.

201 *"you may at last have made contact"*: Ibid., 343.

201 *"I like it less"*: Ibid., 320. Wilson implies that he has read an earlier treatment of the pedophilia theme; this may mean that he had been shown *The Enchanter* or part of it. See note "brought from Europe," p. 308.

202 *"Bunny, I liked very much"*: DBDV, 322. N. refers to Wilson's article "Eretz Yisrael," in *The New Yorker*, December 4, 1954. "The Scrolls from the Dead Sea," a different article, appeared six months later.

202 *came to feel, erroneously*: Wilson did read the whole manuscript, as he was careful to assert in his original draft of the letter. Beinecke.

202 *"sold my LOLITA"*: DBDV, 325.

202 *"depresses me"*: Ibid., 330.

202 *"read his complete works"*: Ibid., 306.

202 *promising an* étude: Ibid., 318.

203 *"The heroes":* Wilson, *Window*, 232.

203 *"Nabokov has gone on record":* Ibid.

203 *"sado-masochism":* Ibid., 237.

203 *"aggrieved and indignant":* Ibid., 230–31.

203 *"humiliate":* Ibid., 237. There is surely, as Wilson felt, something like schaden-freude in N.'s reports of the sufferings of some of his characters. Those reports are wickedly funny. But there is also a quality of authorial nonseparation from such sufferings. N. wrote about his own pratfalls, too. His writings do not evince what is usually thought of as authorial compassion, but there is often an "in it with you" quality to his presentation of his characters at their most shamed and helpless.

203 *"The sadist, here":* Ibid.

203 *invades his text:* As Pushkin does in *Eugene Onegin*, asserting a friendship with his fictional protagonist.

203–04 *"the warm rose-red silk":* Pnin, 134. The cardiac event has even more the charac-ter of an anxiety attack. Interview with Professor Tristan Davies, Johns Hopkins University, November 13, 2013. The cardiac aspect of the fit, whatever it is, may be a remnant of N.'s first plan for the book, in which Pnin did indeed die.

204 *the foulness:* See Pitzer, passim.

204 *"gentle heart":* Pnin, 135.

204 *"a great number of deaths":* Ibid.

204 *Anne Frank figure: The Diary of a Young Girl*, published in English in '52, became a smash bestseller the year before N. began *Pnin*. Readers encountering Mira in the novel might well have been reminded of Anne. But Anne in her diary has many shadings of temperament; the world is what makes her emblematic of Jewish female victimhood—that was not her own intention. The squirrels in *Pnin* are emissaries of Mira in heaven, sent to help Pnin. Ibid., 136. N., who often devised plots via parody and the construction of intertextualities, was relatively without such models when he set about creating Pnin's story. Thrown on his own resources, he encountered difficulties. He was unable to enlarge the narrative. Finally, he "discarded many vistas . . . eliminating everything that was not strictly justified in the light of art." *SL*, 178.

Chapter Fifteen

205 *blown up far too high:* The writer Edward Dahlberg said about Wilson, "He never ceased to show me kindnesses . . . and [was] quite ready to help a writer provided that he felt that he was superior to him." Meyers, 448–49. Lillian Hellman noted Wilson's gallantry toward women, but with an uppity man, as she explained to book reviewer Joseph Epstein, who then paraphrased her comments, "he would have to knock you down intellectually by demonstrating that he knew more about your subject than you did, had read key books you hadn't in languages you didn't know, and otherwise establish himself as the brightest guy on the block." Ibid., 449; Epstein, "Never Wise—But Oh, How Smart," *New York Times*, August 31, 1986, section 7, 3.

205 *books he liked:* Karlinsky, *DBDV*, 24.

205 *did not take extensive notes:* Beinecke. Such notes are conspicuous by their absence at the large Wilson archive at Yale.

205 *"Is there any chance":* DBDV, 312.

205 *"I have been aiming":* Ibid., 312.

206 *"dealt with the roots":* Ibid., 25. Karlinsky was born in Harbin, China, and emigrated to Los Angeles in the late thirties. "In Memoriam," University of California, http://senate.universityofcalifornia.edu/inmemoriam/simonkarlinsky.html.

206 *"You aren't good at this":* DBDV, 210. Wilson's advice to N. mirrors his advice to Malcolm Cowley, who remained Stalinist too long, and who needed to move on before he humiliated himself. Christopher Benfey, "Malcolm Cowley Was One of the Best Literary Tastemakers of the Twentieth Century. Why Were His Politics So Awful?" *New Republic,* February 28, 2014, http://www.newrepublic.com/article/116499/long-voyage-selected-letters-malcolm-cowley-reviewed.

206 *writer of aesthetic trifles:* Gift, 255. The author read Chernyshevsky's novel *What Is To Be Done?* in translation in college, an experience of staggering boredom.

206 *"When in the mornings":* Ibid., 333.

207 *"Fyodor climbed aboard":* Ibid., 163.

207 *"A truck went by":* Ibid., 362.

207 *it does present itself:* The argument about Chernyshevsky and his thought is not confined to one section of the book; N.'s criticism of novels of ideas and the social conditions of "the post-war generation" is there from the start, from chapter 1.

207 *"You have no idea":* Ibid., 210.

208 *An art of narcissism:* N. was "a man who disdained to let moral questions suffocate his fiction." Kopper, 64. He felt acutely a need to escape from the operatic charnel house of Russian history. He, for one, was not going to undergo his historical suffering and then ostentatiously wear it, as others had. As a result, he can appear trivial next to Solzhenitsyn, Pasternak, Akhmatova—the gallery of those who stayed and suffered and barely survived.

208 *one of the three best:* Boyd 2, 293.

208 *"the filthiest book":* John Gordon, "Current Events," *Sunday Express* (London), January 29, 1956, 6; Schiff, 212–13.
   not been mentioned: Boyd 2, 293.
   "I am extremely irritated": DBDV, 331.

208 *"all offensive books":* Graham Greene, "The John Gordon Society," *The Spectator* (London), February 10, 1956, 182.

208 *society actually met:* Boyd 2, 295.

208 *"shocks because it is great art":* Harvey Breit, "In and Out of Books," *New York Times Book Review,* March 11, 1956, 8. The source of some of the sentiments quoted by Breit was Harry Levin, and N. thanked him for his kind words in a letter that November: "I shall always remember your kindness to her [*Lolita*] on the Harvey Breit episode." Houghton.

209 *"foul little flurry":* DBDV, 331.

209 *Gallimard . . . Nouvelle Revue:* Boyd 2, 295.

209 *publishers now contacted:* Schiff, 213.

209 *Longy School:* Nadia Boulanger was at the school from 1938 to 1945; she taught composition to Aaron Copland, Quincy Jones, and John Cage, among others.

209 *"My first MG"*:   D.M., "Close Calls," 311. Dmitri's father, when a student at Cambridge in 1920, similarly failed to produce in a timely fashion a translation that his father had arranged for him to do. Boyd 1, 178.

209 *nervously supporting his hopes:*   Véra to Berkman, June–July 1955, Berg. "The Longy School gave Dmitri all sorts of tests," Véra wrote. "They find him very good and full of excellent promise and strongly recommend that he study voice and music. I am quite reconciled to the idea that this will be an experimental year."

209 *"very wonderful"*: SL, 155.

209 *would supervise:* Ibid., 156.

209 *"I have a piece"*: Berg, July 1, 1955.

210 *"The contract (if passed)"*: Ibid.

210 *"Your father"*: Berg, December 5, 1962.

210 *"expects"*: Berg, July 1, 1955.

210 *"Also, please review"*: Berg, June 8, 1956.

210 *"love for moving things"*: Berg, Véra's notes on Dmitri, 1950.

211 *hard to bear:* Boyd 2, 83.

211 *"She is one of our"*: Berg, March 10, 1955.

211 *put her name forward:* Berg, October 10, 1956. In his letter to Henry Allen Moe of the Guggenheim Foundation, recommending her, N. also puts himself forward, asking for a third grant, this one to complete studies of "lepidopterous fauna of the Rocky Mts." SL, 189. The Foundation turned him down.

211 *get behind it:* Berg, February 2, 1959.

211 *worshipful:* Berg, November 14, 1955.

211 *"installments are superlative"*: Ibid.

211 *some of the same friends:* Berg, Véra letter of February 2, 1959.

211 *"all the way South"*: Berg, August 10, 1959. She stayed at hotels, not motels, because cheap hotels were clustered around bus stations. The "filthiest" she found was in Butte, Montana.

212 *explorations by writers:* Heany, 127–93. Other notable books in this vein are *Travels with Charley* (1962), by John Steinbeck, and *Going Away: A Report, a Memoir* (1962), by Clancy Sigal.

212 *"What I . . . learn"*: Berg, November 14, 1955.

212 *problematic as a model:* Berkman's story "Blackberry Wilderness," in the book of the same name (1959), is nominally Nabokovian in being about an artist. In tone it suggests a fable by Hawthorne. N. himself seems to appear on pp. 149–50. *Blackberry Wilderness* (Garden City, N.J.: Doubleday, 1959).

212 *"I've been delighted"*: Berg, January 16, 1958. Berkman reviewed N.'s story collection *Nabokov's Dozen* for the *New York Times*, September 21, 1958. She notes that the author often focuses on small people crushed by history and that he gets many, many tonal "hues" in each story. "One may observe of Mr. Nabokov's mind that he perceives experience not in the tone of a single shade (black or white) but as a spectrum." N. asked her to take over his classes at Cornell in spring '59, but she could not, as she was on her way to Stanford on a writing fellowship.

212 *"specific detail"*: DBDV, 331.

213 *"characters had a kite of meaning"*: Ibid., 321. McCarthy seems unironic in her use of the term "haziness." In '62, she reviewed *Pale Fire* in discerning and awestruck terms in the *New Republic*.

214 *"somehow Mind is involved"*: *PF*, 227. The speaker is Kinbote.

214 *metaphysical speculation*: Henry James's ghost stories posit the existence of lowly spirits but seem agnostic about a higher spiritual realm. Twain deals with ghosts humorously and stays out of churches. Emersonians no longer, they are not in search of "spiritual facts"—indeed, the concept has become oxymoronic.

214 *not unknowable*: Fluck, 24.

214 *two chapters of a never-to-be-completed novel*: N., *Russian Beauty*, introduction to "Ultima Thule," 147.

215 *something more*: Berg.

215 *"Hurricane Lolita"*: The term appears in Véra and Vladimir's page-a-day notebook, Berg, but is also to be found in the poem "Pale Fire," line 680, commentary on p. 243.

215 *"sophisticated spiritualism"*: Boyd 2, 306.

215 *"insular kingdom"*: Ibid. N. predicts, in '57, that in a few years a "President Kennedy" will be involved with the king's search for sanctuary.

215 *"to Colorado"*: Ibid., 306–7. Kinbote, after the events of the novel, goes to a western state and holes up in a motor court, à la the Nabokovs; it's in a town called Cedarn, "in Utana, on the Idoming border." *PF*, 182.

215 *novel's central conceit*: Kinbote may be someone else, but for purposes of narrative simplicity he will here be called Kinbote. N. later wrote, "I wonder if any readers will notice the following details: 1) that the nasty commentator is not an ex-King and not even Dr. Kinbote, but Prof. Vseslav Botkin, a Russian and a madman 2) that he really knows almost nothing about ornithology, entomology and botany 3) that he commits suicide before completing his Index." Berg, notebook for 1962. This raises the issue of a book escaping its author's intent. N. held in high regard the poem ("Pale Fire") he composed for the book. Schiff, 277–78. But Kinbote at times seems not so impressed. *PF*, 263, 286, 296–97.

215 *"the most perfect novel"*: Boyd 2, 425.

215 *"Two pages into"*: Ibid., 425–26.

216 *novels of which Nabokov was aware*: Boyd 2, 398.

216 *The humbling*: Considering where his books always sold the most, and where he said he found wonderful readers, N. was addressing an American readership. Therefore, it is the American reader who is being humbled.

216 *"Although these notes"*: *PF*, 28.

216 *"wise in such cases"*: Ibid., 28.

216 *"brilliant achievement"*: Boyd 2, 439.

216 *"few better things to offer"*: Ibid., 440.

216 *other writers*: Kernan, 102–4.

217 *"my name / Was"*: *PF*, 48.

217 *"Maud Shade was eighty"*: Ibid., 40. Light verse is a case of "the form happily driving the expression." Chiasson, 63.

217 *"When I'd just turned eleven"*: *PF*, 38.

217 *like Wordsworth's*: The poet referred to "The Prelude" as "the poem on the growth of my own mind." *Norton Anthology*, 230.

218 *he told an interviewer:* SO, 18.
218 *"abstract bric-a-brac":* PF, 67. *Pale Fire* also includes sincere-sounding comments from Kinbote on prejudice, on how blacks and Jews ought to be referred to. Ibid., 216–18.
218 *"democracy of ghosts":* Pnin, 136.
218 *"cradle rocks":* SM, 19.
218 *"colossal efforts":* Ibid., 20; Alexandrov, 23–24.
218 *"everything that happens":* SM, 218.
218 *"taps his knee":* Ibid.
219 *seems present in:* Alexandrov, 187.
219 *"plexed artistry":* PF, 63.
219 *"Existence, or":* Ibid., 69.
219 *"There was a time":* Ibid., 39.
220 *"may not be a beauty":* Ibid., 44.
220 *"no use, no use":* Ibid.
220 *"still the demons":* Ibid., 44–45.
220 *"Are we quite sure":* Ibid., 49.
221 *"ruby ring":* Ibid., 49–50.
221 *contrapuntal movement:* Kinbote, in his commentary to lines about the parents watching TV as the daughter drowns, observes that "the synchronization device has been already worked to death by Flaubert and Joyce." Ibid., 196.
221 *Charles Xavier Vseslav:* Ibid., 306.
221 *"distant northern land":* Ibid., 315.
221 *"Oh, I did not expect":* Ibid., 296–97.
222 *"I was the shadow of the waxwing":* Ibid., 33. Probably this is a cedar waxwing; the more colorful Bohemian waxwing is a bird more of the American Northwest and western Canada. *Birds of North America,* 240–41. Waxwings are eerily perfect, as if made not of feathers but of some seamless stuff.
222 *"All colors made me":* Ibid., 34.
222 *"How fully I felt nature":* Ibid., 36.
222 *"And from the inside, too":* Ibid., 33.
223 *"no desire to twist":* Ibid., 86.
223 *"I turned to go":* Ibid., 23.
223 *"We shall now go back":* Ibid., 123, 125. N.'s use of kingship in *Pale Fire* miscalculates American readers slightly—kings are for us only to be deposed, are conclusively anachronistic—but he might have been writing already for a world readership, not an American one.
223 *"Well did I know":* Ibid., 97–98.
223 *"One day I happened":* Ibid., 24.
224 *"His laconic":* Ibid., 20–21.
224 *"Dear Jesus": Ibid., 93.*
224 *"a very loud amusement park":* Ibid., 13, 15.
224 *he chooses Popian prosody:* This is not really odd, since Shade is a Pope scholar. He may be, like other writers, so captured by his own learning as to be unable to choose otherwise. Boyd 2, 443–44.
224 *wisdom in its own failure:* Kernan, 124–25.

225 *"desponder"*: Ibid., *173*.

225 *"frozen mud"*: Ibid., *258*.

225 *"moments of volatility"*: Ibid., 173.

225 *"admiration for him"*: Ibid., 27.

225 *"an organic miracle"*: Ibid.

225 *"Clink-clank, came the horseshoe"*: Ibid., *289*.

225 *"Solemnly I weighed"*: Ibid. Kinbote is awed but perfectly willing to twist the meaning of the manuscript and invent his own lines.

225 *"enchantment and"*: Ibid., 246. N. describes the landing zone as a "hay-feverish" field with "rank-flowering weeds." They are probably ragweed. "Up to half of all cases of pollen-related allergic rhinitis in North America are caused by ragweeds," and the yellow flowers are indeed rank. "Ragweed," *Wikipedia*, http://en.wikipe-dia.org/wiki/Ragweed.

226 *"phantom companion"*: Ibid., 233. The author experienced this delusion descending from Mount Humphreys, Sierra Nevada, 1987.

226 *such a friend:* Another friendship in the poem is between Shade and local farmer Paul Hentzner, who "knows the names of things." Ibid., 185.

226 *mountain-minded:* Ibid., 62. "I love great mountains," says Shade on p. 52.

226 *"How serene . . . first full cowbell . . . lacy resistance . . . Mr. Campbell . . . mountain mead . . . strip naked"*: Ibid., 119, 140, 139, 139, 140, 142. The puzzling exhaustive-ness of this account expresses, perhaps, N.'s Shade-like love of great mountains and Dmitri's ardent attraction to them also. Mountaineers often tell long and exhaust-ive stories.

226 *"pinhead light"*: Ibid., 140.

226 *"dark Vanessa"*: Kinbote refers to the insect, *Vanessa atalanta*, as a "memento mori," and one that has been fluttering throughout the book settles on Shade's sleeve just before he is shot to death. Ibid., 290. Most likely the famous photo of Walt Whitman with butterfly—fake butterfly—on finger had nothing to do with this.

226 *"I came among these hills"*: *Norton Anthology*, 156.

226 *a beautiful passage: PF*, 57, lines 662–64.

226 *repetition of similar lines:* Ibid., 143, 239.

226 *a fantastic gloss that takes off:* Boyd argues that Shade wrote all of *Pale Fire*, includ-ing the commentary presented as the work of Kinbote. Boyd 2, 443–56. The present author rejects Boyd's reasonable thesis as reductive.

227 *"I am capable"*: Ibid., 289. The drive to arrive at an inarguable solution to a book like *Pale Fire* is understandable, but unresolved mysteries, messy half solutions, also attract. There is an argument to be made from laziness. N. told an interviewer that "reality is an infinite succession of steps, levels of perception, false bottoms, and hence . . . unattainable. You can know more and more . . . but you can never know everything . . . it's hopeless." In another context, he recommended that "we have the humility and the hard sense to recognize that the real world always escapes us." Bloom, 99. Kinbote, despite his claim to be incapable of writing verse, may be the author of persuasively Shadeian lines. "We all are, in a sense, poets," he tells Eberthella Hurley, a local faculty wife. *PF*, 238. He also adduces many variant lines to Shade's poem, and in the novel's tendentious index he seems to admit to having written several: "the Zemblan King's escape (*K*'s contribution, 8 lines), *70*;

the Edda (*K*'s contribution, 1 line), *79*; Luna's dead cocoon, *90–93*; children finding a secret passage (*K*'s contribution, 4 lines), *130*." *PF*, 314.

227 *transcendental verses:* Kernan, 104–5. Shade is "in that surprising American way of Emerson and Thoreau . . . a mystic and a visionary, irreligious but persuaded that beyond this seen world there is another unseen, that life here is but a step on the way to a transcendental beyond." Ibid.

227 *"Gradually I regained":* PF, 297.

227 *"large, sluggish man":* Ibid., 286. N. might have felt sluggish following ten years of archival work on *Eugene Onegin*. The description is actually of Conmal, Duke of Aros, the first, crude translator of Shakespeare into Zemblan. Ibid., 306.

228 *disagrees with Shade's skepticism:* Ibid., 224–27.

228 *"in an elevated state":* Ibid., 258.

228 *"all at once":* Ibid., 259.

Chapter Sixteen

229 *"thick batch of U.S. roadmaps": Laura,* introduction.

229 *"violins but trombones":* Field, *Life in Part,* 32. N. speaks of a throb in "Inspiration." *SO,* 310.

231 *ex-San Francisco bohemian:* Hagerty, *Life of Maynard Dixon,* passim.

231 *Dixon's widow:* Edith Dale to Véra, February 9, 1956, in Boyd 2, 698n30. Dixon's previous wife was the photographer Dorothea Lange.

231 *drive to the southeast: SL,* 186. Nabokov was very fond of his "beautiful little cottage." Ibid. To Wilson he described the "Pink, terra-cotta and lilac" crags nearby that formed a "sympathetic background to the Caucasus of Lermontov"—he was finishing Dmitri's translation of *A Hero of Our Time,* with Véra's help. *DBDV,* 333.

231 *famously empty:* U.S. Census, 1950. http://en.wikipedia.org/wiki/1950_United_ States_Census#State_rankings.

232 *poet's death in a duel: EO,* vol. 3, 43–51. N.'s explanation of the Lenski-Onegin duel in the poem and of the famous duel on January 27, 1837, in which Pushkin was shot by Georges d'Anthès has a tone of grave simplicity hardly to be found anywhere else in the Nabokov canon.

232 *splendid mind and literary sense:* Leving, 3. Nikki Smith, literary agent and representative, with Peter Skolnik, of the Nabokov estate from 1987 to 2008, says that Véra operated as N.'s "agent-of-origin" from the early days, from about 1930 on. An agent of origin parcels out an author's work to publishers and to subagents, Altagracia de Jannelli being one of the subagents. Leving, 4.

232 *"The air was keen":* Pnin, 190, 191.

232 *eight thousand miles:* Boyd 2, 363.

232 *quick sketch of everything:* Berg, page-a-day.

233 *they denominate periods:* Berg.

233 *"Ford-Keyser" . . . '38 Buick:* D.N., "Close Calls," 307, 310. Dmitri called the Buick "stately."

233 *Dmitri the madcap:* Berg. Dmitri's job was as a translator at International House, Columbia University, according to Dmitri's friend Sandy Levine. Dmitri "met a lot of girls that way." Interview with Sandy Levine, June 3, 2012. According to Boyd,

the job was at the *Current Digest of the Soviet Press*, presumably as a translator. Boyd 2, 362. Dmitri's apartment was at 636 West End Avenue, no. 8; phone, Lyceum 5–0516.

233 *reserve unit that met:* Interviews with Sandy Levine and with Brett Schlesinger, November 27, 2012. The reserve meetings in New York City were at 529 West Forty-seventh Street.

234 *Song of Igor's:* Diment, *Pniniad*, 40. In Sept. '58 N. was polishing his translation, in May '59 Véra was typing it, and in '60 it was published.

234 *"he's going to be famous":* Interview with Schlesinger.

235 *preservation of some old:* Berg.

235 *sun emerging:* Berg, page-a-day.

235 *advance copy:* Ibid. The diary indicates that the copy caught up with them in Waterton Lakes National Park, Alberta. Boyd 2, 363, says it was delivered in Babb, Montana. Schiff, 228, guesses Glacier National Park.

235 *"true greatness":* Berg. The *New Republic* editorial was in an issue that also included a vicious pan of *Lolita.*

235 *"begun to melt":* Berg, page-a-day.

235 *"engrossed in a big rodeo":* Ibid. Véra's account seems to inform (of course it does not) the rodeo in a small Nevada town in John Huston's *The Misfits* (1961).

235 *"excellent publisher":* Ibid. Earlier the Nabokovs thought Minton a bumbler. Boyd 2, 364; Schiff, 229.

236 *"EVERYBODY TALKING":* SL, 257. *Times* reviewer Orville Prescott was shocked: "To describe such a perversion with the pervert's enthusiasm without being disgusting is impossible. If Mr. Nabokov tried to do so he failed." "Books of the Times," *New York Times*, October 18, 1958.

236 *6,777 reorders:* SL, 258.

236 *Times bestseller list:* Schiff, 230. *Lolita* was number 1 from September 28 till November 9, 1958. From November 16 till March 8, 1959, it was number 2 behind *Doctor Zhivago*. It fell to number 3, behind *Zhivago* and Leon Uris's *Exodus*, on March 8. Hawes Publications, http://www.hawes.com/1958/1958.htm and http://www.hawes.com/1959/1959.htm.

236 *black moiré:* Schiff, 255.

236 *under restriction:* There were no such restrictions in the United States. N. was proud of his country of citizenship for never banning it. "America is the most mature country in the world now in this respect," he told the *New Haven Register.* Boyd 2, 367. In France, following publication of the Olympia Press edition in 1955, the state imposed a ban, only to lift it in January 1958. Boyd 2, 364. The ban was in response to a request by the British government; copies of *Lolita* had been making their way across the Channel. de Grazia, 260. In May 1958, a new ban was instituted in France, under which sales to those under eighteen were forbidden, as were bookshop displays. Boyd 2, 364. A British edition of *Lolita* became possible only with passage of the liberalizing Obscene Publications Act of 1959. de Grazia, 266.

236 *"magnificently outrageous":* Dupee, " 'Lolita' in America," 30.

236 *"prodigy":* Ibid.

236 *"all the brows":* Ibid., 35.

236 *"the luck":* Ibid.

237 *a postwar turn:* Ibid., 31.

237 *"Into this situation":* Ibid., 30, 31.

237 *mordant person:* McCarthy, "F.W. Dupee"; McCarthy, "On F. W. Dupee."

237 *"the fading smile":* Dupee, 35.

237 *"Humbert can be heard":* Ibid.

237 *"too shocking":* Ibid., 31. Dupee welcomed *Lolita* as the first sign of what would become the 1960s turn. He enjoyed seeing American normalcy subjected to humorously disrespectful analysis. In his introduction to a long, expurgated selection from *Lolita* in *The Anchor Review*, he wrote, "The book's general effect is profoundly mischievous. . . . The images of life that *Lolita* gives back are ghastly but recognizable." Dupee quoted poet John Hollander as saying that the novel "flames with a tremendous perversity of an unexpected kind," yet had "no clinical, sociological or mythic seriousness." Dupee disagreed about the lack of seriousness. He tried to show how Humbert's situations were "our" situations in fifties America. "The supreme laugh may be on the reviewers for failing to see how much of everyone's reality lurks in its fantastic shadow play." In an article in *Encounter*, Dupee said that Nabokov sounded "most like a know-nothing native writer" when, in his afterword to *Lolita*, he denied the reality of his American portrait.

237 *just read in the* Times: Schiff, 232.

237 *phenomenal sum:* $150,000 in '58 equaled about $1.2 million dollars in 2014. DaveManuel.com, http://www.davemanuel.com/inflation-calculator.php.

237 *Véra's account was "important":* Berg. The word *important* appears in N.'s hand on a graph-paper-lined three-by-five card inside the page-a-day diary. The note reads, "My diary notes, summer 1951, while writing 'Lo' and, more important, Véra's diary kept during the first months following the publication of 'Lo' in America."

237 *Inquiries:* Berg, page-a-day.

237 *"ought to have happened":* SL, 259.

237 *team from* Life: Boyd 2, 366.

238 *The book's having first gone to France:* In the prolonged process, *Lolita* had time to gather encomiums from Greene and other respected figures. *Lolita's* unprosecuted publication in the United States cleared the way not only for a reissue of *Memoirs of Hecate County* but also for the successful defense and first legal publication of *Lady Chatterley* in the UK. Schiff, 236.

238 *"could not believe":* Berg.

238 *Dean Martin's show:* Ibid.

238 *"Milton Berle . . . Groucho Marx":* Boyd 2, 374.

238 *first TV appearance:* Berg.

238 *obvious Soviet ploy:* Boyd 2, 372. Published just days after *Lolita*, *Doctor Zhivago* supplanted it at the head of the *Times* bestseller list, and the books would be 1 and 2 into the new year. What N. had against Dr. Schweitzer was his work with Bertrand Russell on SANE, his do-gooding, his windy theology.

239 *he asks Trilling:* "Vladimir Nabokov Discusses 'Lolita' Part 1 of 2," YouTube video, posted by JiffySpook's Channel, March 13, 2008, http://www.youtube.com/watch?v=Ldpj_5JNF0A.

239 *"there is an underlying tone":* Ibid.

239 *he quotes himself:* Dieter Zimmer, "Vladimir Nabokov: The Interviews," http://www.d-e-zimmer.de/HTML/NABinterviews.htm. One hundred twenty-five interviews are known, fifteen or so from the *Lolita* publication period.

240 *half-reclines on the sofa:* See *DBDV*, 300n1, for N.'s affinity for sofas and couches. He says, "I like to eat and drink in a recumbent position (preferably on a couch) and in silence."

240 *"a young girl, someone":* "Vladimir Nabokov Discusses 'Lolita' Part 2 of 2," YouTube video, posted by JiffySpook's Channel, March 13, 2008, http://www.youtube.com/watch?v=0-wcB4RPasE.

240 *hard to gainsay:* Ibid., especially minutes 1:33 and 1:45.

240 *when Dr. Strangelove:* "Dr. Strangelove and the Bomb," YouTube video, posted by vilixiliv, November 6, 2010, http://www.youtube.com/watch?v=-mUCLHzWiJo.

240 *beautiful, boyish smile:* His smile recalls that of the actor Montgomery Clift after his car accident.

Chapter Seventeen

241 *Café Chambord:* The restaurant was at 803 Third Avenue, between Forty-ninth and Fiftieth. It was a hangout of theatrical folk, Orson Welles, Joseph Cotten, and Margaret Sullavan among them.

241 *Minton's wife:* Also present were a couple named Thaller; he was the "second in command" at Putnam's, Véra believed. Berg, page-a-day.

241 *Latin Quarter showgirl:* "Books: The *Lolita* Case," *Time*, November 17, 1958.

241 *"for that was when Walter":* Berg, page-a-day.

241 *even more baroque:* The finder's fee was $20,000. Schiff, 237n. The fee was equal to 10 percent of the author's royalties for the first year of publication plus 10 percent of the publisher's share of subsidiary rights for two years. Ibid., 236n.

241 *'57 MG:* Berg, page-a-day.

242 *"superannuated":* *Time*, "The *Lolita* Case."

242–43 *"I wonder if this sort of thing":* Berg.

243 *nymphet:* This coinage was mentioned during N.'s TV interview with Trilling.

243 *"rampancy":* *DBDV*, 363.

243 *Peyton Place:* Schiff, 229.

243 *New Hampshire:* Ramsdale and Beardsley in the novel seem to be fictionalized New Hampshire locations.

243 *on condition that he find someone:* He asked Berkman, who was unavailable, then hired novelist Herb Gold, who had been recommended by a former colleague at Wellesley. Boyd 2, 376.

243 *Nobel Prize:* Pasternak was forced to decline the prize. Ibid., 372.

243 *$100,000:* Ibid., 374.

243 *law professors:* Berg, page-a-day, November 16, 1958.

243 *Paul, Weiss:* Schiff, 247.

243 *"government bonds":* *SL*, 262.

243 *"the translator must be":* Ibid., 258.

244 *his father signed:* Ibid., 276. Dmitri went to work on the translation in late '58 and brought home a first installment on Christmas to show his father, who liked

it and urged Dmitri to give up his New York job to concentrate on translating. Boyd 2, 377.

244 *"how delighted":* Houghton, letter of February 12, 1959.

244 *"Then he caught that cold":* Berg.

244 *venereal infection:* Barth and Segal, 1. N. wrote Dmitri a letter on January 16, 1961, that included this: "I have interrupted my literary labors to compose this instructive little jingle: In Italy, for his own good / A wolf must wear a Riding Hood. / Please, bear this in mind." *SL*, 324.

244 *only office job:* Interview with Brett Schlesinger, November 27, 2012.

244 *last class at Cornell: SL*, 276.

244 *attention from the world press:* Schiff, 246; Boyd 2, 380. N. also declined invitations from David Susskind and Mike Wallace: Berg.

244 *fifteen letters:* Berg.

244 *people showed up:* Schiff, 247.

244 *made promises:* Boyd 2, 381. Weidenfeld was half of the new firm of Weidenfeld and Nicolson, his partner being Nigel Nicolson, son of Harold Nicolson and Vita Sackville-West. Boyd 2, 378.

245 *checked proofs:* Boyd 2, 381.

245 *likely of fulfillment:* Dmitri quickly learned Italian, in pursuit of his operatic studies, and he made translations of his father's works into that language, too.

245 *"full of flowering":* Berg, page-a-day.

246 *cold pudding: SO*, 71. He also wrote *Transparent Things* (1972) and *Look at the Harlequins!* (1974).

246 *"Last night a howling mob":* Berg, page-a-day. Sale was reinstated in time to graduate the next month. Sale's friend and sometime roommate Richard Fariña wrote of the incident in his novel *Been Down So Long It Looks Like Up to Me* (1966). Sale's wife, Faith Sale, became an editor at G.P. Putnam's Sons. *The Enchanter* (1986) was one of the books she edited for Putnam's. Berg.

246 *windows were broken:* Berg, page-a-day.

246 *a* Communist *publisher:* Boyd 2, 372; *SO*, 205.

246 *"ignores the Liberal Revolution": SO*, 206. The Nabokovs also believed progressive education to be a "Communist plot to destroy the American educational system." Houghton, Véra to Elena Levin, August 19, 1969.

246 *"We are all for Nixon":* Houghton, Véra to Elena Levin, July 27, 1972. In March '68, Véra wrote Alison Bishop, "Nothing could be worse than this war, but we honestly do not see what the President . . . can do about it. Leave the country and the entire Far East to the Communists? . . . This is a life and death struggle against Communism, not just a little war somewhere." Berg.

247 *conservative* National Review: Berg, N.'s notes to Field, February 20 and March 10, 1973. Jack Kerouac was also a reader of *National Review.*

247 *America was on the verge:* Schiff, 338.

247 *de Gaulle led France:* Schiff, 335.

247 *American flag:* Ibid., 338.

247 *actor-producer John Houseman:* Born Jacques Haussmann in 1904, of an Alsatian Jewish father and a Welsh-Irish mother; educated at Clifton College, Bristol, England, which made special accommodations to welcome

Jewish boys. "John Houseman," *Wikipedia*, http://en.wikipedia.org/wiki/John_Houseman.

247 *remnants of Russian pronunciation:* See "75 at 75: Brian Boyd on Vladimir Nabokov," recorded April 5, 1964, posted July 18, 2013, http://92yondemand.org/75-at-75-brian-boyd-on-vladimir-nabokov.

247 *"I have already accumulated":* SL, 508. The documents N. refers to were stored in Ithaca and brought to Montreux in '69 so that biographer Field could look at them.

248 *"An average émigré":* Berg, notes for a second vol. of *Speak, Memory*.

248 *even some primitive Americans:* Zweig, 225; McGill, 173–74.

248 *dubious Doctor Zhivago:* SL, 264. N. called it, in a letter to Dwight Macdonald, "that trashy, melodramatic, false and inept book, which neither landscaping nor politics can save from my wastepaper basket."

248 *two long articles:* Wilson, "Doctor Life and His Guardian Angel," *New Yorker*, November 15, 1958, 213–38, and "Legend and Symbol in 'Doctor Zhivago,'" *Encounter*, June 9, 1959, 5–15.

248 *epic novel that said no:* In January '59, on stationery of the Congrès pour la Liberté de la Culture, a CIA-funded arts organization of which he was secretary-general, Nicolas Nabokov wrote, "my Polish friends who publish what is generally agreed to be the only good Polish magazine in existence, would very much like to have your and the NEW YORKER's permission to print a Polish translation of your NEW YORKER article on Pasternak. . . . The name of the magazine is KULTURA. It is printed [in Paris] and clandestinely read by all the Polish intelligentsia in Poland." Beinecke.

248 *"the English and American translations":* Wilson, "Legend and Symbol." *Doctor Zhivago* bears a distant resemblance to *Pale Fire*, being about a poet yearning for a conclusive illumination and containing substantial amounts of that fictional poet's verse.

248–49 *"very much in the manner":* Ibid.

249 *"behaving rather badly":* Schiff, 243–44.

249 *"Stendhal is a complete fraud":* Wilson, *Letters*, 578.

249 *"cruel little ironies":* Ibid.

249 *rejected the path:* Pitzer, 17.

249 *"symbolico-social":* SL, 293.

249 *"As you know by now":* DBDV, 362.

250 *thirty-three weeks:* Hawes Publications, http://www.hawes.com/1956/1956.htm.

250 *two immensely popular articles:* "On First Reading Genesis," May 15, 1954, and "The Scrolls from the Dead Sea," May 14, 1955. "On First Reading Genesis" was reprinted in thousands of copies.

250 *Wilson's expository style:* Dabney, 351.

250 *Apologies:* Peter Nabokov, second son of Nicolas, was a student at Columbia, with an interest in American Indians and anthrolopogy. He met Wilson at a party given by Nicolas in January '61 and wrote him, after *Apologies* was published, asking for advice about a career that would combine fieldwork with authorship. Peter pursued such a career with marked success. Beinecke.

250 *"the man who gave me the most pleasure":* Dabney, 353.

250 *never wrote at length:* A careful student of the correspondence has observed that the two men missed like ships in the night, were silent in response to signals of affection

from each other. Kopper, 58. N. was especially reserved when responding. Both men might have been embarrassed by their feelings. Nabokov, while missing some of Wilson's cues, was often truly warm and embracing. Wilson came to feel that there was something of the arrogant rich man in Nabokov, a bully streak. Their letters came to be full of apologies for missed opportunities to meet in person.

251 *"This production though in certain ways valuable":* Wilson, "Strange Case," *New York Review of Books,* July 15, 1965.

251 *"Nabokov . . . took up a good deal of space":* Ibid. Arndt, in a letter responding to N.'s mauling, was gentlemanly yet noted "the fine sparkle of pure venom behind the sacerdotal . . . solicitude for textural integrity." Beinecke. Arndt shared the Bollingen Translation Prize for his *Onegin* in '62.

251 *"number of earnest simpletons":* SO, 247.

252 *"A patient confidant":* Ibid., 82.

252 *"utter disgust":* Ibid., 80.

252 *"musty method of human-interest":* Ibid., 88. N. might have been aware of Susan Sontag's "Against Interpretation" essay of '64. Sontag introduced him at his reading at the 92 Street Y that year.

252 *"stubby pencil":* Ibid.

252 *"rather dry, rather dull":* Ibid., 81.

252 *The essay is sorrowful:* The Wilson papers at Yale have much more material on Pasternak than on Nabokov: thirteen folders vs. two, some of the thirteen packed to bursting. The notes Wilson did write evince distaste: "hatred of the middle class" in *Despair* and *Camera Obscura,* "sordid bourgeois horror of post-war Germany," "morbid and murderous undercurrent, much as you [find] in German films of the period," "the taint of a touch of merde, sexual perversity, petty and pricking sadism," "a certain amount of old-fashioned Petersburg foppery and fantasy." He tries to get at the heart of N. by careful titration of a sample of his story materials, especially in the Berlin period. In a psychoanalytical way, he seems to feel, this will reveal N.'s hidden essence—that he is cruel, sadistic, likes a touch of filth, etc. The truth of a psychoanalytical approach is taken for granted. Wilson is anxious not to be duped, and he is troubled by what he sees as N.'s nastiness toward his characters. The notes were written at the end of Wilson's life, and for whatever reasons, N.'s works did not open a door in him, provoke in him a release of Wilsonian sensitivity and wisdom. Of *Pale Fire* he said, "I read it with amusement, but it seems to me rather silly." Bakh, letter to Grynberg, May 20, 1962.

253 *"our native West":* DBDV, 357, March 30, 1958.

253 *fabulously valuable and rare sports cars:* Roger Boylan, "Dmitri Nabokov, Car Guy," Autosavant, November 2009, http://www.autosavant.com/2009/11/24/dmitri-nabokov-car-guy; Boylan, "Dmitri Nabokov, Car Guy: Take Two" Autosavant, 2010, http://www.autosavant.com/2010/04/15/dmitri-nabokov-car-guy-take-two.

253 *Ping-Pong:* D.N., "Close Calls," 320.

253 *working all along for the CIA:* Dmitry Minchenok, http://sputniknews.com/voiceofrussia//2012_02_28/67099376/.

253 *"dangerously shifting to the left":* Ibid.

253 *An American friend:* Interview with Barbara Victor, May 30, 2012. The author filed Freedom of Information Act requests with the CIA, among other agencies, and his

appeal of the CIA's unforthcoming responses resulted in a declaration by the Agency Release Panel that, "with respect to records that would reveal a classified connection between the subject of your request and the CIA, if any, the ARP determined that, in accordance with Section 3.6 (a) of Executive Order 13526, the CIA can neither confirm nor deny the existence or nonexistence of records responsive to your request." CIA letter to author, August 28, 2013, Reference: F–2013–00275.

253 *never told his father:* Minchenok.

253 *"with new priorities":* "Close Calls," 320.

253 *"a faster Ferrari":* Ibid.

253 *multiday races in the Mediterranean:* Schlesinger, "Journey Down the Tyrrhenian."

254 *"My dearest!":* SL, 353. Dmitri was sometimes called "Lolito" in the Italian press. He appeared in a movie and lent his name and Milan apartment to a casting competition for a young actress to play Lolita. "My father [happened] upon a magazine photo of the bevy of 'finalists' surrounding me on my oversized, satin-covered bed," Dmitri wrote, and cabled the command, "STOP LOLITA PUBLICITY IMMEDIATELY." "Close Calls," 313. In *Ada*, the character Van Veen is a lanky playboy seducer; there is a suggestion of his singing lieder, as Dmitri did on *Russische Lieder*, an LP produced in Vienna in '74. *Ada* seems dated in part, with milieus vaguely out of *Playboy* magazine; *Lolita* does not seem dated.

254 *secret handshakes from the author:* Booth, 300–9.

255 *"Pushkin's critical acumen":* EO, vol. 2, 154.

255 *"languorous":* Ibid., 382.

255 *"Good old Sylvia!":* PF, 248.

255 *the books of his American period:* There is also a persuasive, verifiable Russian reality in *Speak, Memory*.

256 *"its heat . . . the painful comedy of family relations in general":* Dupee, "Introduction."

256 *an experiment:* Berg. N. read *An Experiment with Time* but also consulted Gerald Whitrow's *The Natural Philosophy of Time.* Boyd 2, 487.

256 *most unnerving instance:* There is no real evidence of Dunne's precognition provided in his book; readers are convinced, rather, by his clubby gentleman's tone of probity. N. borrowed from Dunne his perspicacity in reporting fugitive mental states.

256 *"common features of my dreams":* Berg. N. also wrote a personal dream typology.

256 *"Am coming down steps":* Berg, dream recorded December 4, 1964. In '67, N. recorded another dream of Wilson: "Odd dream: somebody on the stairs behind me takes me by the elbows. E.W. Jocular reconciliation." Boyd 2, 499.

257 *Nabokov bursts into tears:* Berg, notes for "Speak On, Memory."

257 *remains levelheaded:* N. censors sex, too, recording in this vein only "Several dreams one of them keenly erotic, replay (for perhaps the five hundredth time) with perfect freshness a fugue of my early youth." Berg, dream of October 14, 1964, 8:30 AM. And on December 13: "Interesting erotic dream. Blood on a sheat." Berg.

INDEX

Note: page numbers in italics refer to images. Those followed by n refer to notes, with note number for endnotes.

A NOTE ON THE AUTHOR

Robert Roper has won awards for his fiction and nonfiction alike. His previous works of nonfiction include *Now the Drum of War*, a biography of Walt Whitman and his brothers in the Civil War, and *Fatal Mountaineer*, a biography of American climber-philosopher Willi Unsoeld, which won the 2002 Boardman Tasker Prize from the British Alpine Club. His works of fiction include *Cuervo Tales*, a *New York Times* Notable Book, and, most recently, *The Savage Professor*, a novel. He has won prizes or grants from the NEA, the Ingram Merrill Foundation, the Joseph Henry Jackson competition, and the Royal Geographical Society of London. His journalism appears in the *New York Times*, the *Los Angeles Times*, *American Scholar*, *Outside*, and other publications. He lives in California.

1 GRAND CANYON, SOUTH RIM, AZ In 1941, on the family's first western trip, Nabokov caught specimens of what he believed to be a new species of butterfly

2 OAK CREEK CANYON, AZ A favored collecting and vacation spot, spring-summer 1959

3 PALO ALTO, CA Nabokov taught summer school at Stanford in 1941

4 ESTES PARK, CO The nearest sizable town to Columbine Lodge, where the Nabokovs spent summer 1947

5 LONGS PEAK, CO Dmitri, aged thirteen, climbed the 14,259' peak; Nabokov collected below the rocky summit, in the vicinity of Peacock Pool

6 ROLLINSVILLE, CO Summer 1947, Nabokov collected here (in the nearby Tolland Bog) in the company of lepidopterist Charles Remington

7 TELLURIDE, CO The town is the inspiration for a memorable scene in *Lolita*. On a mountain slope above the town, Nabokov also caught the female of a butterfly he had long sought, *Lycaeides argyrognomon sublivens*

8 GLACIER NATIONAL PARK, MT The Nabokovs stayed nearby and collected, when weather permitted, summer of 1958

9 WEST YELLOWSTONE, MT Summer 1941, the Nabokovs passed through West Yellowstone on their way to the Duck Ranch outside of Yellowstone National Park

10 TAOS, NM Here the Nabokovs stayed, summer of 1954, in a cabin ten miles north of town

11 ASHLAND, OR Vladimir and Vera stayed in a rented home in Ashland while Dmitri climbed and worked construction elsewhere in the West

12 ALTA, UT Site of Alta Lodge (in Little Cottonwood Canyon) the resort part-owned by publisher James Laughlin, where the Nabokovs spent the summer of 1943

13 LONE PEAK, UT Nabokov and Laughlin climbed this formidable mountain

14 MT. CARMEL, UT The Nabokovs stayed in a cabin here, summer 1956. The cabin was close to excellent areas of collection that included Zion National Park, Bryce Canyon, and the North Rim of the Grand Canyon

15 AFTON, WY A small Mormon town along the Salt River, one of the Nabokovs' favorite spots. It was close to excellent butterfly hunting grounds along creeks draining a mountain range

16 DUBOIS, WY The Nabokovs stayed at the Rock Butte Court in Dubois, summer 1952; Nabokov collected along the windy Wind River in view of the Absaroka and Wind River mountain ranges

17 JACKSON, WY The Nabokovs stayed near Jackson in 1949, '51, and '53. Dmitri climbed prolifically in Grand Teton National Park north of Jackson

18 RIVERSIDE, WY The senior Nabokovs stayed here summer 1952 in a log ranch house. Dmitri worked as a lifeguard at a pool in the nearby town of Saratoga. Nabokov collected along and in the vicinity of the Continental Divide

WASHINGTON

COLUMBIA RIVER

OREGON

⑪ Ashland

NABOKOV IN

CALIFORNIA

③ Palo Alto